GOD'S GOVERNMENT BEGUN

RELIGION IN NORTH AMERICA

CATHERINE L. ALBANESE AND STEPHEN J. STEIN

EDITORS

GOD'S GOVERNMENT BEGUN

THE SOCIETY FOR UNIVERSAL INQUIRY AND REFORM, 1842–1846

THOMAS D. HAMM

INDIANA UNIVERSITY PRESS

BLOOMINGTON AND INDIANAPOLIS

The paper used in this publication meets the minimum
requirements of American National Standard for Information
Sciences—Permanence of Paper for Printed Library Materials,
ANSI Z39.48-1984.
Manufactured in the United States of America

Library of Congress Cataloging-in-Publication Data

Hamm, Thomas D.
God's government begun : the Society for Universal Inquiry and
Reform, 1842–1846 / Thomas D. Hamm.
p.   cm.
Includes bibliographical references (p.   ) and index.
ISBN 0-253-32903-5 (cloth : acid-free paper)
1. Society for Universal Inquiry and Reform—History.
2. Collective settlements—United States—History.   3. Utopias—
United States—History.   I. Society for Universal Inquiry and
Reform.   II. Title.
HX656.S55H35   1995
335′.9771765—dc20
94-49162
1 2 3 4 5   00 99 98 97 96 95

❖   IN MEMORY OF   ❖
WILLARD HEISS
(1921–1988)

CONTENTS

❖
_____

FOREWORD

IN THIS VOLUME Thomas D. Hamm has written the account of record on the Society for Universal Inquiry and Reform. Founded in Oakland, Ohio, in 1842, by a coalition of Hicksite Quakers and New England evangelicals, the society gave rise over the next several years to eight communities populated by several hundred men and women intent on establishing the "Government of God." Within a short time these experiments in communal living failed, but the desire to be free of human government based on coercion and to replace it with the force of moral suasion has not passed completely from the American scene. Remnants of that ideal of nonresistance still drive visionaries today.

In the mid-nineteenth century reform was in the air. Individuals and groups sought to mobilize the forces of society and government on behalf of one cause or another—for example, abolition, temperance, pacifism, and women's rights—in an effort to reshape and improve their world. Historians have documented many aspects of this reform impulse in the United States. By contrast, relatively little attention has been shown to the relationship between nonresistance and the establishment of utopian communities. The radical reformers who spearheaded the effort to make concrete this ideology in communitarian experiments are the focus of Hamm's study.

Because members of the Society for Universal Inquiry and Reform are far less well-known than contemporaries such as William Lloyd Garrison, the Grimke sisters, and Adin Ballou, Hamm has been forced to focus on their leaders, using private manuscript collections and elusive references in the reform press of the 1840s. From these sources he has reconstructed an account of the principals involved, their background prior to joining together, early attempts to establish a national organization, subsequent unsuccessful efforts to form lasting alternative communities, and the fate of the leading reformers who took part in the society. Hamm's work illumines a little-known aspect of reform history in America and provides an absorbing narrative.

More importantly, Hamm integrates this particular ultraist endeavor into the larger picture of nineteenth-century religious and social history. He demonstrates how the antislavery movement in America fostered the drive for universal reform. He points out significant links to leading radical reformers in Great Britain. Likewise, through his careful biographical research, he shows how earlier splits within the ranks of Quakerism, including that between the Hicksite and the Orthodox factions, played out in political and social terms. (Hamm is the author of a previously published, prize-winning manuscript on nineteenth-century conflicts within Quakerism.) Finally, he situates the story of the communal efforts of these radical reformers within the larger context of the communitarian movement in nineteenth-century America.

Few issues escaped the attention of the members of the Society for Universal Inquiry and Reform. They adopted new and radical views of government, religion, education, and the social order. But at the heart of all their views was the principle of noncoercion. They shared the desire to remake human society with other advocates for reform in their day, including persons committed to the ideas of the French socialist and reformer Charles Fourier and those of the Scottish industrialist and reformer Robert Owen. Many members of the society had already previously rejected clerical authority, the claims of religious orthodoxy, and traditional forms of schooling. In their place, some turned to free-thinking, others to ideas sharply critical of the conventions of the day. In their communitarian efforts they attempted to institutionalize alternatives to private property, patriarchal marriage, and human government. Underlying much of this effort was a near-millennial vision of the future.

But the realities of life in community wreaked havoc on the eight experimental communes. With the largest and most well-known located in Skaneateles, New York, the majority were situated in Indiana and Ohio. In each location, reformers made strenuous efforts to recast the structures of life, but in every case, conflict over leadership and responsibility, financial difficulties, and internal tensions quickly brought dissolution. By the end of 1846 all eight communities had failed.

It is a mistake, however, to write off the Society for Universal Inquiry and Reform as inconsequential. On the contrary, Hamm makes clear that the experiences of these radical reformers influenced their subsequent choices and activities, both religious and social. Many of the universal reformers joined the most radical wing of the Quakers, the Congregational Friends. Others became very active in the cause of women's rights in the Midwest. And still others—perhaps most of the participants—were drawn toward the spiritualist movement in the 1850s. In other words, for a good number of nineteenth-century religious and social radicals, time spent in movements such as the Society for Universal Inquiry and Reform, even when those experiments failed, proved a shaping and reinforcing influence on their subsequent commitments. This society, preoccupied with the ideology of nonresistance, was but one attempt by these reformers to structure their religious and social dissent.

Catherine L. Albanese
Stephen J. Stein
Series Editors

❖

―――――――――――――――

ACKNOWLEDGMENTS

THIS BOOK BEGAN almost half a century ago, when Willard Heiss became fascinated by an account of the Union Home Community, founded in 1844 in his native Randolph County, Indiana. Willard's occupation was selling furniture at the L. S. Ayres Department Store in Indianapolis, but his avocations were history and genealogy. In the back of his mind was a plan to write about Union Home, its founder, Hiram Mendenhall, and the broad communitarian movement of which they were a part. And so he began to collect information from any available source, spending his lunch hours in the Indiana State Library and corresponding with historians and librarians all over the United States. On almost any vacation, he would find a reason for a side trip to some courthouse or library where he thought that he might be able to find some bit of information.

As Willard pursued his research, he frequently encountered the name of John O. Wattles, an itinerant lecturer and reformer. In 1950 he set out to find some of Wattles's family. He discovered that his youngest child, Theano Wattles Case, had died the year before at 96, but that a relative, Deborah Smith of San Diego, had inherited her papers. Willard opened an amiable correspondence with her that resulted, in 1952, in Smith giving him a trunk of John O. Wattles's manuscripts.

Ironically, however, even as he gained possession of the Wattles manuscripts, Willard turned to another project that would occupy him for two decades, editing, under the sponsorship of the Indiana Historical Society, abstracts of Indiana Quaker records. On the basis of this and other genealogical work, he achieved a national reputation in his later years as a genealogist. He published only one work, an article on Hiram Mendenhall and Union Home, as a result of all of his research. He never completely forgot about Wattles, however. When I met Willard in 1981, one of the first things he did was to show me his crate of Wattles papers. And when I began teaching at Indiana University-

Purdue University, Indianapolis, in 1985, Willard now nearing retirement as Indianapolis's city archivist, suggested that we take up the project together. For the next three years he happily searched the reform press for the 1830s and 1840s. Meanwhile, Willard had also discovered another equally valuable collection of papers, those of Valentine Nicholson, a coadjutor of Wattles and Mendenhall, in the hands of a descendant.

Willard died in August 1988. My debt to him is great. Although I did all of the manuscript research myself, and recombed the reform press as well, again and again I have depended on information that in the 1950s Willard combed from sources long vanished or people long dead now. My debt to his wife, Virginia, is as great. For five years, she entrusted me with the Wattles papers and periodically let me ransack Willard's study for some item I thought might still be there. This is a different work, more narrowly focused on the period 1842–46 than Willard envisioned, but I hope that it is one of which he would approve.

Second only to the Heisses in generosity has been Theodore L. Steele of Indianapolis. He entrusted me with the papers of his great-grandfather Valentine Nicholson, and was extremely gracious in answering every question, no matter how unlikely, that I put to him about his extraordinary family.

Numerous others have aided me along the way. My old teacher, Lewis Perry, now of Vanderbilt University, first encouraged my interests in abolition and radical reform, encouraged me to take up this project, and carefully read a draft of the manuscript. Robert M. Taylor, Jr., of the Indiana Historical Society spent many a lunchtime and afternoon pondering Universal Reform and communitarianism with Willard and me, and also read the manuscript. My colleague at Earlham College, Carol Hunter, gave up precious sabbatical time to read and comment on the final draft. Thomas D. S. Bassett of Burlington, Vermont, tracked down several obscure items for me in New England, including some critical information on John A. Collins. Roland Baumann of Oberlin College searched his collection for anything that had to do with the Wattleses. Elaine Nelson of the Lilly Library at Earlham College was wonderful in obtaining some of the most peculiar items through interlibrary loan. The Indiana Historical Society provided critical support for travel and research, and a grant from the Professional Development Fund at Earlham made it possible for me to do some important research in New York. A sabbatical funded by a grant to Earlham from the Joyce Foundation provided time for writing.

Finally, I owe a constant debt to my wife, Mary Louise Reynolds. She undertook to transcribe many of the Wattles and Nicholson manuscripts, typed most of the drafts, and has been my gentlest and most supportive reader and critic.

INTRODUCTION
Evangelicalism, Antislavery, Hicksite Quakerism, Communitarianism, and Reform

IN 1881 AN elderly gentleman who wandered from friends to relatives in Indiana and Ohio began, at the urging of his daughter, to compose an autobiography. Valentine Nicholson, at seventy-two, had no way of knowing that he still had nearly a quarter century of life ahead of him. His had been an eventful life, as his autobiography makes clear. The whole gamut of antebellum reform causes—antislavery, temperance, come-outer religion, diet and health reform, equality for blacks and women, spiritualism, and communitarianism—is found within its pages. The very act of memory, however, was dangerous; later the brother-in-law with whom Valentine sometimes lived was writing to Valentine's daughter that her father was almost mad; the memories of the 1840s had brought back for him so many blasted hopes and unfulfilled dreams that even to recall them seemed an exercise in self-destruction. At the heart of Valentine Nicholson's torment were the years from 1842 to 1845, when certain favored souls from the backwoods of Indiana and Ohio to the Burned-Over District of New York seemed to be on the verge of breaking through to new and higher visions of human life and destiny, and some were quite sure that the millennium was about to dawn over the hills of Harveysburg and Oakland, Ohio.[1]

The group of which Valentine Nicholson had been an integral part, and that sought to make this millennial vision reality, was the Society for Universal Inquiry and Reform, organized in Clinton County, Ohio, in 1842 by an alliance of Hicksite Quakers and New England Garrisonian abolitionists committed to the reconstruction of American society according to the principles of nonresistance and the Government of God. Its members, fortunately for historians, proved themselves not only ambitious but also articulate, and seeing their own communal arrangements as the prototype of the new order of human society that was destined to sweep the earth.

To carry out this vision, Universal Reformers had founded eight socialistic communities by 1846. Three were in Ohio, four in Indiana, one at Skaneateles, New York. None lasted longer than four years, some less than a year. In them, residents attempted to construct a new order for society. To usher in the Government of God, they would abolish all private landholding. They would replace a competitive, capitalist economy with one based on cooperation. They would make technology an instrument of liberation, rather than of oppression and suffering for workers. They would sweep away "sectism and priestcraft," replacing them with a pure, uncorrupted Christianity. New ways of education would raise up a generation fit for a world being made anew. Women would achieve equality, freed from domestic drudgery and male tyranny, and would find freedom to seek their own fulfillment. And through diet and health reform, humans would become fit to live in such a world.

The Universal Reformers sought to bring into their communities "the choice spirits of the age," both in Europe and in America. During their few years of association, they reached out to some of the leading reformers of their time. Associated with them were such luminaries as William Lloyd Garrison, Frederick Douglass, Lucretia Mott, Abby Kelley, Lydia Maria Child, and Robert Owen. But the role of these well-known figures was relatively minor. Universal Inquiry and Reform was largely the creation of men and women who had been on the margins of the leadership of the antislavery movement, like John A. Collins or Orson S. Murray or John O. Wattles, or even beyond the margins in the backwoods of Ohio and Indiana, like Valentine Nicholson, Abraham Brooke, and Hiram Mendenhall. The indebtedness of the Universal Reformers to the larger reform movement is clear. But the story of Universal Inquiry and Reform is one of the most rural, isolated adherents of reform, in places like Oakland, Ohio, or Randolph County, Indiana, taking abolition and nonresistance to their most radical, ultraist extremes, seeking to usher in the Government of God.

Central to understanding this enterprise is knowledge of the twists and turns of the antislavery movement in the 1830s. Those who embraced Universal Inquiry and Reform came out of its most radical or "ultraist" wing, those who were not content simply to advocate the immediate abolition of slavery (in itself extraordinarily radical), but who proudly called themselves "ultraists," and envisioned a new American, and a new world, society, in which want, evil, and, above all, the use of coercive force would disappear.

There had been organized antislavery activities in the United States since the

Revolutionary period. Most were the work of groups that sometimes viewed slavery as undesirable or inconvenient, sometimes as utterly evil. Their membership was made up disproportionately of Quakers, who had by the 1780s come to view slavery as unacceptable for Christians. These groups advocated emancipation on the model of the northern states after the revolution: providing for a period of "preparation," or freeing all those born after a certain future date. It was not unusual for such schemes to be tied to plans for removing freed slaves from the United States. Such schemes for "colonization" had numerous advocates, including prominent public figures like James Madison and Henry Clay. David Brion Davis has aptly summarized the views of these gradualists: "Frequently they seemed to think of slavery as a kind of unfortunate weed or fungus that had spread through the Lord's garden in a moment of divine inattention." Reformers, like "expert horticulturalists, imagined they could gradually kill the blight without injuring the plants."[2]

By 1830, however, antislavery had taken a new turn toward "immediatism," which had no patience with gradualism. As Davis puts it, immediate abolition was marked by "a personal commitment to make no compromise with sin." Abolitionists recognized slaveholding as a sin and, as believing Christians, saw it as incumbent on themselves to press slaveholders to cease their sinning.[3]

The roots of this change are complex. It was in part a tactical response to the political realities of the time. By 1830 there had been half a century of gradualism, with limited success. Even moderate efforts brought ferocious responses from defenders of slavery. A new attack seemed to be appropriate. Since moderation had failed, many reformers found a more strident, less compromising stand in order.[4]

Religion also moved such reformers toward immediatism. With a few notable exceptions (such as the Quakers), abolitionists were committed to evangelical Protestantism. At the heart of antebellum evangelicalism was conversion, or the immediate experience of salvation, in which the believer was, through grace, justified in the sight of God and saved from hell. Its vehicle was revivalism, which by the 1820s was touching the lives of thousands.[5]

By the 1820s, however, evangelicalism was moving in a new direction, with an emphasis on sanctification or perfection. The chief proponent of this "new measure" was the upstate New York minister Charles G. Finney, aptly labeled the "father of modern revivalism." Finney taught that it was the duty of every converted Christian to go on to a second experience subsequent to conversion—sanctification or perfection, in which the desire to sin would be purged away by the fiery baptism of the Holy Ghost. Those who knew such an experience would, as James B. Stewart described it, "perform acts of benevolence, expand the boundaries of Christ's kingdom, and recognize a personal responsibility to improve society." Thus they were drawn to works of reform and benevolence—temperance, education, Sunday schools, missions—as editors, teachers, and ministers.[6]

Considerable scholarship has been devoted to identifying the characteristics of these young reformers—religious, economic, social. There is broad agreement on certain scores—they tended to be of New England origins, were intensely religious, were fiercely competitive, and, in many cases, were in rebellion against the institutions around them that appeared to countenance or compromise with sin.[7]

Bound up with all of these were the reformers' millennial expectations. Since the middle of the eighteenth century, many evangelicals had seen America as having a special place in the divine plan for the ages. They were convinced that works of evangelism, benevolence, and reform were part of the process that would usher in the millennium, the thousand-year reign of Christ that the Book of Revelation foretold. Thus reform was more than just a way of ridding the world of some specific evil. It was part of God's plan to rid the world of all evil.[8]

Reformers with such views looking at the United States in 1830, however, did not see the millennium as imminent. Instead, they would have seen sin advancing on all fronts, unsurprising in a nation presided over first by the Unitarian John Quincy Adams and then by a profane, unbelieving, dissolute, adulterous gambler, Andrew Jackson. Some explanation had to be found for the persistence of such affronts to the divine order. And that was slavery.[9]

So it was that a variety of young reformers became committed to advocating the immediate abolition of slavery. Of these the Boston editor William Lloyd Garrison became the best known through his journal, the *Liberator,* which began publishing in 1831. By 1833 there were enough adherents to form the American Anti-Slavery Society. Members came largely from New England and from its cultural outposts—the Burned-Over District of New York, the Western Reserve of Ohio, Michigan, and northern Illinois.[10]

The American Anti-Slavery Society attacked slavery through "moral suasion." It explicitly disavowed the use of force or violence as incompatible with its high Christian calling. Instead, it depended on appeals to conscience, through books, pamphlets, journals, letters, and petitions. To forward the message abolitionists formed hundreds of local antislavery societies. Nonviolence, however, often found itself countered with violent opposition. Abolitionists were extraordinarily unpopular, not only in the slave states, where antislavery publications were banned from the mails and ferocious laws targeted those who challenged the "peculiar institution." (The Georgia state legislature actually offered a reward for William Lloyd Garrison's head.) In the North, too, there were mobs and attacks on antislavery lecturers; egging them was considered good sport in many communities. Opponents denounced abolitionists as advocates of miscegenation, disunion, and infidelity; they drew withering fire from almost all points on the political spectrum. Even so, the number of adherents and the number of antislavery societies increased steadily between 1835 and 1837.[11]

Even as the number of abolitionists increased, however, signs of stress appeared in the movement, and Garrison was their focal point. As James B. Stewart has written, Garrison seemed "to act as a magnet of fanaticism, drawing to the cause all manner and mode of eccentricity." Three particular areas of conflict emerged: religion, the roles of women, and nonresistance.[12]

Virtually all abolitionists were pious folk, and virtually all agreed that on this issue the churches left much to be desired. The great national denominations—Methodists, Presbyterians, Baptists—allowed members to own slaves. Their official positions on abolition ranged from lukewarm to hostile. Abolitionists usually had no reservations about blasting "proslavery" clergy and church members. By 1837, however, some, with Garrison at their head, were disturbing more religiously orthodox abolitionists with the ferocity of their attacks on the churches and by their questioning of certain traditional beliefs and practices, such as Sabbath observance.[13]

Another source of unease, especially for some abolitionist clergy, was the role of women in the antislavery movement. Women had long been active in moral reform and benevolent associations, but these were groups that consisted solely of women. In the early days of the movement, abolitionist women had followed this model by organizing female antislavery societies. In 1837, however, gender became an issue when two South Carolina-born abolitionists, Sarah and Angelina Grimke, embarked on a lecture tour of New England. Their original intention was to address only groups of women, but they attracted so much attention and interest that men began to attend as well. This quickly brought attacks from Congregational ministers, who in a pastoral letter proclaimed that women's place was to be instructed by men, not to instruct them. Abolitionists found themselves divided. For some the actions of the Grimkes were highly improper. More were probably sympathetic, or at least not condemnatory, but they also were far from agreeing about the implications of the Grimkes' actions. Some, led by Garrison, insisted on making the defense of woman's rights part of the antislavery crusade. Indeed, by 1840, a number of abolitionist women had come, through consideration of black slavery, to see what they called "the slavery of sex," how American society also oppressed women. Other abolitionists, while sympathetic to woman's rights, feared that agitating the cause would detract from and be detrimental to abolition. More immediately, abolitionists had to decide whether women could take part in the affairs of the American Anti-Slavery Society.[14]

A final issue that emerged late in the 1830s was nonresistance, and, closely related to it, politics. By 1838 abolitionists such as Garrison and Henry C. Wright had come to believe, in the words of Lewis Perry, that "slavery, government, and violence were . . . identical in principle." In their minds, slavery was evil because it was the epitome of coercive power, and coercive power was evil because its employment was contrary to the commands of Christ that his followers should "resist not evil," and "do good to them that persecute you." Since human governments were based on coercive force, true Christians had to eschew them.[15]

This position led critics to label nonresistants as "no-government men," or anarchists. In fact the nonresistants did believe in government—the Government of God. They believed that if the mechanisms of coercive human government were swept away, then God's Government—and the millennium—could begin. Theirs was a profoundly ordered view—it was in contemporary society that they saw disorder and anarchy, inevitable, they thought, because humans were opposing the will of God, and setting their own wills in its place.[16]

There was not complete agreement among nonresistants about all of the implications of the Government of God. Some raised questions about participation in *any* organization that employed *any* form of coercion—a church or reform society, for example. And nonresistance involved serious questions about the rights of slaves to resist slavery.[17]

All nonresistants agreed, however, that no consistent Christian could participate in affairs of government, since to do so was to involve oneself in sin. Thus a consistent nonresistant would not vote or be entangled in any way in affairs of party. This assured conflict when other abolitionists, led by James G. Birney and Gamaliel Bailey in Ohio and the Tappan brothers, Lewis and Arthur, in New York began to move toward political action through the formation of an abolitionist party, the Liberty party, for the 1840 election.[18]

This tangle of radical views on religion, woman's rights, and government had by the late 1830s come to polarize abolitionists. Those favorable to all three were usually known as Garrisonians, since it was to Garrison that they looked for leadership and in the *Liberator* that they expressed their views. It was from this wing of the abolitionist movement that the advocates of Universal Inquiry and Reform emerged. But not all were evangelicals—many, in fact, came out of a religious world largely concerned with combatting the inroads of evangelicalism. They were Hicksite Quakers.

Quakers, of course, are almost immediately identified in both the popular and the scholarly mind with good works, philanthropy, and reform. And that identification is in the main accurate. Quakers in antebellum America were disproportionately represented in the ranks of almost any group committed to reform and moral uplift, particularly groups concerned with blacks, Indians, and women.[19]

The lives of Quakers in the first half of the nineteenth century were anything but peaceful, however. They knew strife and division, and that strife and division had considerable impact on the Friends who embraced Universal Inquiry and Reform.

Central to the lives of Quakers in this period was the "Great Separation" of 1827–28, which divided Friends into Orthodox and Hicksite factions. The Orthodox were, generally, those Friends whose view of the authority of the Bible, the divinity of Christ, and the Atonement was closer to that of non-Quaker evangelicals. Many were involved with evangelicals in reform and benevolent work. There is also some evidence that they were more successful in adjusting to the economic changes that the nation passed through in the 1820s.[20]

The Hicksites were more diverse. Larry Ingle has argued convincingly that they saw themselves engaged in a work of reformation. The encroachment of outside, worldly forces—wealth, prosperity, and most of all, association with evangelicals—had brought doctrinal innovations that set at naught traditional Quaker views of the primacy of the Inner Light. (The Orthodox, of course, claimed that *they* were the traditionalists, and that the Hicksites had run off into deism and infidelity.) The lightning rod for conflict was the Long Island minister Elias Hicks, the most visible and articulate advocate of "reformation." He was an inspired and favored Friend in the eyes of the reformers, but the incarnation of error for the Orthodox. The Hicksites, however, came to their positions by different paths. Some certainly were liberals who were groping toward positions that resembled unitarianism. Others were more concerned with questions of power and authority than theology. The strongholds of the Orthodox were the "select" meetings of ministers and elders, which Hicksites saw as overreaching their proper limits. Still other Hicksites were primitivists, country Friends who saw in the wealth and non-Quaker ties of the Orthodox unacceptable and dangerous compromises with "the world."[21]

When the two groups did separate in 1827 and 1828, their distribution was uneven. Save for Nantucket and parts of Vermont, there were no Hicksites in New England. In New York, New Jersey, Pennsylvania, Delaware, and Maryland, Hicksites made up the overwhelming majority of Friends. To the south, save for some pockets in northern Virginia, there were only Orthodox. In the West, among Friends in Ohio and Indiana, the distribution was also uneven. In Ohio Yearly Meeting, which took in Quakers in western Pennsylvania and eastern Ohio, somewhere between a third and half were with the Hicksites. In Indiana Yearly Meeting to the west, there were about twelve thousand Orthodox and three thousand Hicksites. Most of the Hicksites there were in western Ohio, especially in Warren and Clinton counties.[22]

Unfortunately, the history of the Hicksites after the separation is almost completely unexplored. We do know that outwardly they remained almost identical to the Orthodox, using the same regulations or Discipline, preserving all of the peculiarities of traditional Quakerism, retaining identical organizational structures.

Yet there were critical differences. While both Orthodox and Hicksite Friends took part in the abolitionist movement in the 1830s, a dichotomy is clear—Orthodox Friends were drawn to the more conservative varieties of abolition that focused on political action (John Greenleaf Whittier being the best-known example), while Hicksite abolitionists were generally sympathetic to Garrisonian positions.[23]

Universal Inquiry and Reform was in large part a product of this Quaker world, as much as it was of evangelicalism. It began in the intellectual explorations of Hicksite Friends in southwestern Ohio. Four of its eight communities were in the midst of Hicksite settlements. Probably a majority of those who committed themselves to its brand of reform were Hicksite Friends. The movement exemplified certain strains of thought that Hicksite Friends had first shown in the 1820s. As noted above, some Hicksites were incipient liberals, at odds not only with their Orthodox opponents within the Society of Friends but with the dominant evangelical culture of the United States. Skepticism about religious orthodoxy would be prominent among Universal Reformers. So would a sense of isolation, of being at odds with the larger society, alone in an unkind world. Many Hicksites had also challenged authority within their society, which they saw not only as assuming unwarranted power, but as oppressing individual conscience. This resistance to received knowledge, and insistence on the primacy of individual conscience and inward leadings, would also distinguish the Universal Reformers. Finally, many Hicksites had shown themselves to be skeptical about and uncomfortable with the "Market Revolution" through which the United States was passing between 1800 and 1850. Indeed, "Hicksism" was most attractive, at least in the Philadelphia area, to those who were failing to make this transition successfully. Our knowledge of the economic circumstances of the Universal Reformers is limited, but they would be outspoken in their challenge to a market, competitive economy.[24]

Evangelical Reformers were in many ways unlikely partners for Hicksite Quakers, even when they shared a commitment to reform causes. Hicksites, as has been seen, were for varied reasons skeptical about evangelical doctrines on a number of counts. Evangelicals, in turn, were usually quite fearful of heterodoxy. While it might be possible to compromise such differences in uneasy alliances, one would not expect the results to make for close ties or harmony.[25]

Yet Universal Inquiry and Reform did bring together Hicksite Quakers and evangelicals, and, in all of the tensions and conflicts that later developed, this difference in background was seldom a line of cleavage. The reason appears to be, at least in part, that both were moving toward a common religious vision, what Catherine L. Albanese has called "nature religion." Albanese argues that such a religious vision has been characterized by urges toward mastery, innocence, permanence, and purity, features that adherents, especially in the nineteenth century, found in "nature" or the "natural order," vague ideas that they left undefined.[26]

As will be seen, the advocates of Universal Inquiry and Reform embraced all of these ideas. They saw Universal Reform as a way to reestablish peace and harmony in a world that had gone awry. "Natural Law" would be the statutes of the Government of God. This would allow all humans to find their proper places and would eliminate disorderly competition and strife. It would sweep away unneeded, oppressive structures and institutions. Most of all, it would end impurity and corruption through health and diet reform, education, and the withering away of competitive capitalism and "sectism." This new religious vision, challenging virtually all other faiths, would be central to everything that the Universal Reformers did.

The solution to the problems of the world that the Society for Universal Inquiry and Reform ultimately embraced was communitarianism—a series of utopian (a word that they seldom applied to themselves) communities that would serve as a model of reform and Christian society for the nation and the world. In this they were hardly unique. The 1840s probably saw the greatest outpouring of communitarian enthusiasm of any decade in American history before the 1960s. There were numerous alternatives—Fourierist, Owenite, Mormon, Shaker, Perfectionist. Some, like the Shakers and Mormons, were founded on sectarian faith. The Fourierists and the Owenites were militantly secular, and were in fact usually identified in the public mind with religious skepticism. Some focused on a charismatic or prophetic leader, like the Mormon heretic James Strang in Wisconsin or the Perfectionist John Humphrey Noyes in Putney, Vermont, and in the Oneida Community in New York.[27]

Historians have been aware of the interest of abolitionists in communities. The most studied has been Hopedale, the community at Milford, Massachusetts that the gentle Universalist minister and nonresistant Adin Ballou founded in 1841. Hopedale was a place that its inhabitants hoped would demonstrate to the world the efficacy of the principles of nonresistance. It survived, in various incarnations, until the 1870s. But, with the exception of the community at Skaneateles, New York, that John A. Collins organized and led, none of the communities based on nonresistance that emerged from the agitation for Universal Inquiry and Reform has been the subject of scholarly study, and even those who have studied Skaneateles have not seen it as part of a larger movement.[28]

This is unfortunate, since close analysis of the Society for Universal Inquiry and Reform has the potential to teach us much about the nature and dynamics of antebellum communitarianism. Historians of community have posed a variety of questions about ideology, membership, gender roles, economics, leadership, and dissolution. The experience of the advocates of Universal Reform will add to our knowledge of all of these. Through the letters that residents sent to the reform press, the reminiscences of participants, and, in some cases, the papers left from the lawsuits that followed breakdown, we can deal with many of these questions. They include the religious vision that underlay the communities, their forms of worship, doctrine, and religious authority. We will look at the backgrounds of those who came into the communities, particularly their religious backgrounds. We will take up the communities' views of the duties and roles of women, how they differed from, or were consistent with, those of the larger society. We will examine how the communities tried to survive economically, how they organized work and commerce, while at the same time challenging the established economic order. We will consider who emerged as leaders in these communities, if leaders did emerge, and what the basis for leadership would be. Finally, we will weigh why these communities failed, the comparative importance of economics, leadership, interpersonal conflict, and ideology.[29]

In the introduction to his definitive study of abolitionism and nonresistance, Lewis Perry summed up the progression of those who committed themselves to Universal Inquiry and Reform. "Besides attacking slavery, violence, institutional religion, and human government," Perry writes, abolitionists "occasionally tried to establish new, noncoercive styles in human relationships. This quest led them to new departures in religion, community life, marriage, spiritualism, and even political parties." The activities of the Society for Universal Inquiry and Reform, although short-lived, were among the most ambitious and wide-ranging of all to come out of the nonresistance movement. In eight communities, they attempted to begin a society that would live according to God's plans for humanity, that would have no laws but his. Ultimately they failed, but their attempt tells us much about nonresistance, abolition, and radical reform in the 1830s and 1840s, especially in the Old Northwest.[30]

GOD'S GOVERNMENT BEGUN

❖ 1 ❖

THE EVANGELICAL ROOTS OF
UNIVERSAL REFORM

Although the Society for Universal Inquiry and Reform came to be in Ohio, and found most of its followers among Hicksite Quakers, its intellectual roots were largely in the Northeast, especially in New England. It grew out of evangelical Protestantism, yearnings for holiness, agitation for immediate abolition, and commitment to nonresistance and the Government of God. It was in large part the product of the evangelical reform impulse and Garrisonian abolition.

Three New England evangelicals were at the heart of this effort. Two were ministers—one Baptist, one Congregationalist—and the third was an aspiring missionary who gave up the prospect of work among the heathen abroad for the more urgent needs of the United States. All three came from modest backgrounds, not completing their education until well into their twenties. All came from families of piety and religious devotion, and all had committed themselves to lives of soul saving and freeing the world from sin. In this they were like thousands of other young reformers in the 1820s and 1830s.

Yet each of the three had had a critical experience that brought him to advocate the most extreme varieties of radical reform. For John O. Wattles, it was contemplation of the evils of society while tutoring on an estate near Cincinnati. For John A. Collins, it was a trip to England that ended not only in the failure of his mission and the disappointment of his compatriots in the United States, but also in a horrifying realization of what economic change and industrialization could do to his own country. For Orson S. Murray, it was the recognition that the church in which he had been reared and was ordained was, like every other institution, dedicated to serving its own narrow interests rather than the cause of humanity.

By 1842, their experiences had brought all three men to a common commitment to begin the transformation of the world. Their duty, as they saw it, was to work for the coming of the Government of God.

John O. Wattles, ca. 1845.
In author's possession.

John O. Wattles

At the heart of this group, indeed, the link that married liberal Quakerism to New England Come-Outerism, was a Yankee of impeccable Connecticut lineage. His name was John Otis Wattles.

Although John O. Wattles wrote voluminously on family relations and the proper upbringing of children, he left little about his own early life. The first Wattles had come to New England in 1652. John O.'s grandfather, Daniel Wattles, had served in the militia during the Revolution. Like so many other New Englanders, after 1800 he and his wife moved into western New York. There is no evidence that his grandson ever knew him. Nor did John O. ever comment about his grandmother, Ann Otis Wattles, although she lived until he was 28 and died gruesomely. Stricken with blindness, at age 80 she wandered too near a fireplace and her dress took fire. One of their sons, James O. Wattles, was a successful lawyer who in 1824 joined Robert Owen's New Harmony Community. But there is no evidence of contact between him and his nephew.[1]

It was the other grandfather whose life seemed to strike some of the themes that would engage John O. Wattles. Peleg Thomas, born in 1736, had come of age in the unsettled Connecticut of the First Great Awakening. He was a man noted for his piety and honesty, and he was a rough poet of sorts. When his grandson experienced conversion in 1830, Peleg addressed a piece to him, the only item connected with his forebears that John O. apparently preserved:

> How preshus was the morn
> I wish it long to stay
> That did at first my fears alarme
> And taught my soul to pray
> To Christ my only hope—
> My soul I now resign
> And not travile with delight
> For I can call him mine—
> Yet oft with hope and fear
> I view my last abode
> How shall I stand in judgment there
> before an holy God—
> But yet I love the way
> That leads to Zions Hill
> O let me never go astray
> Or loose the Joys I feal
> Now may the love of Christ
> Increas to make me wise
> That I might run the Christian rase
> till death Shall close my eyes[2]

Erastus Wattles and Sarah Thomas, John O.'s parents, were married in Goshen, Connecticut, in 1802. Erastus made musical instruments and supplemented his income by playing them, a precarious existence at best. He was of sufficient social standing to be commissioned a captain in the militia during the War of 1812. After the war, as John O. told friends in Ohio many years later, Erastus disintegrated into alcoholism. He apparently was not greatly loved by his family, or so it appears—his son's references to him were as a drunkard, and after he died in 1839 his children, including those in comfortable circumstances, were content to let him lie in an unmarked grave beside the Thomases in the burying ground in Goshen.[3]

Sarah Thomas Wattles was of hardier stuff. John O. wrote of her with fondness, and when, after her husband's death, she went to live with her oldest daughter, who was married to a Yale graduate with a successful business in Newark, he always visited her. But of her influence on him he recorded nothing.[4]

Erastus and Sarah had five children between 1803 and 1813. The second son,

Augustus, would have a career that paralleled that of his brother, but with significant differences, in Augustus's case always in the direction of orthodoxy. The youngest daughter, Eliza, died in 1832 at the age of 19. There is reason to think that John was especially fond of this sister, the closest to him in age. All of his life he carried with him her scrapbook and the poem by grandfather Peleg that described her happy evangelical death.[5]

John O. Wattles was born in Goshen July 22, 1809. As noted previously, he wrote little about his early life. Bertram Wyatt-Brown's characterization of the origins of abolitionists, however, fits what we know: "a common upbringing under strict, orthodox evangelical parents; a conversion experience of rich personal meaning; a sense of special destiny, the product of compulsive application to study; a post-parental subjection to pious, admired superiors and elder friends who stirred religious ambitions; and finally a common decision to seek a risk-taking course for the sake of God and personal fulfillment." If we substitute for "strict, orthodox, evangelical parents" a pious, evangelical mother and grandfather, and add in a striking exemplar of the ill effects of sin in his father, we have the first twenty years of Wattles's life.[6]

Despite his family's slender resources, John was able to spend several years at the Goshen Academy. There is some reason to think that he may have considered taking up surveying—his earliest surviving notebooks are surveyor's problems. In 1833 he was teaching school in Tioga County, Pennsylvania, one of the northern tier counties that was settled largely by New Englanders.[7]

Wattles grew up attending the Congregational church in Goshen, and in 1830 he experienced conversion. This, of course, was the great turning point of the life of any evangelical—the gnawing sense of sin, the seeking after grace, the ecstatic moment in which he knew that God had forgiven his sins, that he was in a state of grace and acceptance with the Lord, and that should he die that day, that night he would have a room in one of heaven's many mansions.[8]

Many years later, Esther Wattles, his widow, recorded that after finding God John had determined on a career as a missionary. In this he was hardly unique: dozens of other New England men and women were looking overseas in the 1830s, feeling charged to bring the Gospel to perishing heathen souls. To do so acceptably, however, required ministerial standing, and that in turn required a classical education.[9]

Fortunately for John, there was a natural course to pursue. His older brother Augustus had for some time been a student in the Oneida Institute in Whitestown, New York. Founded as a manual labor school in 1827 by George W. Gale, an associate of the most influential of evangelical revivalists, Charles G. Finney, it grew rapidly—in 1830 it turned away 500 would-be students. Those enrolled worked for their room and board in wagon, carpenter's and blacksmith's shops. The labor was not, however, simply a primitive financial aid plan. It was considered desirable both for health and to avoid developing dangerous pride. The school took a new turn in August 1832 when Beriah Green arrived as the new president. An open advocate of abolition, Green called for Oneida's students to become "an abolitionist phalanx, young reformers who would identify with human weal and woe in every way." By 1834, Oneida was "every hour becoming more an abolitionist school."[10]

It was in this atmosphere charged with evangelical fervor that John arrived as a student in June 1833. The new student recorded ambiguously that "it is somewhat different than I expected. I am happily disappointed." Brother Augustus was still there, and he acted as one of his mentors. For two and a half years John remained pursuing the classical education that would fit him for his chosen career.[11]

Some of Wattles's notes on his reading and on the lectures he heard while at Oneida have survived. It is impossible to say, of course, what mirrors simple dutiful note taking and what reflects Wattles's own feelings and experience. Much of it reflected the theology of Reformed evangelicalism: Original Sin, the Atonement, Election. He dwelt much on judgment. All of these were beliefs that within a decade he would discard. But other ideas that surface would be prominent in his thinking. In an essay entitled "Holy Living," Wattles set out a series of rules for daily life. Holiness, of course, was central to the vision of Oneida's founders, and Wattles's regulations were probably not different from those of the other students.[12]

Still, feelings of inadequacy tormented the young man. He questioned his studies. Why should he be observing "mathematical demonstrations" when Satan had "broke loose unnumbered millions of demons of darkness"? Spiritual uncertainty also plagued him. He recorded that the faculty were kind—"My good teachers feel so much for me—pray so earnestly." But his sinful nature oppressed him. He contemplated the last judgment—"a sin-hating God . . . surrounded by such glorious beings who have never sinned or greaved him." "But I am so wicked he can't help noticing me a guilty rebel—perhaps he will say depart ye cursed into everlasting fire. . . . I shall have nothing to say my sentence is just—all heaven approves—Alleluia they say—when the smoke arises from my torment."[13]

His responsibilities teaching in a Sabbath School near Whitestown reinforced his fears. He and another student "found a place where they were hungering and thirsting for the bread and waters of life." He feared, however, that he would "lead them wrong point them in the way to heaven but lead them in the way to hell." Wattles found his heart too hard to feel the concern appropriate to so important a work, "like the northern lights on mountains of ice." He prayed for strength: "Oh help me to fast and pray till I can sound the trumpet of alarm and save them from the eternal hell." But he had a sense of barely hanging on himself. "Merciful God another week has run away and I am yet out of hell."[14]

John remained at Oneida until early in 1836. He made inquiries about attending Oberlin, but once again brother Augustus determined his new direction. In the fall of 1833 Augustus had gone to Cincinnati to enroll in Lane Seminary. Lane was intended as a model manual labor institution for the West as well as a stronghold of evangelical orthodoxy in the Mississippi Valley. To that end, Lyman Beecher, the veteran of many a battle for the faith once delivered unto the saints and the author of a widely read *Plea for the West,* which saw the future of the United States to be determined in the Mississippi Valley in a struggle with barbarism and popery, had come to Lane as its head. The students, however, had organized an antislavery society, much to the dismay of the trustees, who shared the general suspicion of abolitionism. Some students even went so far as to open schools for blacks in Cincinnati, a radical move in a city that was periodically wracked by riotous assaults on the African American quarters of the city. Augustus and Marius Robinson had early in 1834 actually given up their studies in the seminary to devote all of their time to running a school for blacks. It was the beginning of a long career by Augustus working with the black communities of Ohio and Indiana.[15]

John apparently spent about two years aiding his brother. He was impressed by what he found among the free black settlements of Darke County, Ohio, and Randolph County, Indiana—the hard work, the homely prosperity, the desire for schools and churches. There was also the darker side, as he found himself in the midst of an attack by a white mob on brother Augustus's school in Cincinnati: "The howling of the rowdies around the church . . . with the rattling of the window shutters and the whistling of the winter winds through the vacant panes and the cracks of the door, the rattle of the stones against the house, while the little ones within would gather up close to the teacher, and huddle closer together, trembling with fear and knowing not what to do, whether to stay and await the fire of the assailants, or run out and have the curses of the drunken mob."[16]

There was little money to be made in such endeavors, however worthy, so early in 1838 John found still another position, this one as a tutor in the family of James C. Ludlow at Ludlow Station, outside Cincinnati. Ludlow was a man after John's heart. One of the leading abolitionists in Cincinnati, he was a past president of the Ohio Anti-Slavery Society, a supporter of the Lane Seminary abolitionists, and a financial backer of the Cincinnati *Philanthropist*, which was the leading abolitionist journal of the Ohio Valley. A few other families of similar sentiments lived around the Ludlows, whose views may be inferred from an account of their July 4 celebration in 1838. There were the usual bands, speeches, and banquets—Wattles read a poem—but instead of martial displays, those present toasted "A Congress of Nations," "A Supreme Court of the World," "The Triumph of Intellect over Brute Force," and "The Morning Star of Universal Peace." In the vicinity was also "The Hall of Free Discussion," which James C. Ludlow had erected in 1832 "in the interest of religion, literature, and education."[17]

While at Ludlow Station, Wattles had continued to broaden his reform interests. The Ludlows and their neighbors, the Cloppers, were firm abolitionists, and, as their Fourth of July celebration implies, were also attracted to nonresistance. This became one of his new interests. In December 1838 the *Philanthropist* advertised that he was selling the "Declaration of Sentiments Adopted by the Peace Convention Held in Boston," suitable for framing.[18]

Such an existence was too quiet for a reformer who was becoming increasingly impressed by the urgency of the task to which he and like-minded enthusiasts had set themselves. In October 1838 he had formed his students into an association for reading and "Mental Improvement." In the preamble to the constitution, he wrote that the goal of the group was to discover the intellectual and moral laws by which God governed the universe, so that through obedience to them greater good might flow into the world. Wattles's mood was postmillennial—while "mankind generally expects that there will be signs in the sun and in the moon or the stars," such an outlook was like that of the Pharisees, "sensual and grovelling minded." The Kingdom would come when "the principles of men" became "the light of God's Truth."[19]

So in 1839, Wattles left Ohio to return to New England, seeking some "wider sphere to usefulness." He apparently hoped to obtain a school at Plymouth, Massachusetts, but was disappointed in that expectation. But another opportunity presented itself. The schism in the American Anti-Slavery Society had left the radical wing at a considerable disadvantage west of the Appalachians. The Ohio Anti-Slavery Society was desperately trying to avoid involvement in the schism, but Gamaliel Bailey, the editor of the *Philanthropist* and the most influential abolitionist in the Old Northwest, sympathized with political abolition. Wattles was familiar with the area, and so he was appointed to an agency.[20]

Wattles's work in Ohio, however, was short-lived; it is not clear that he ever took it up. By the summer of 1840 he was back in New England, lecturing on nonresistance. He received no pay, but did earn the gratitude of Henry C. Wright, the New England Non-Resistance Society's chief agent, and the approval of the *Pennsylvania Freeman,* which labeled him "our faithful and laborious friend." Wattles spent the summer and autumn of 1840 in Massachusetts; in December he was in Boston for an antisabbatarian convention. He spoke almost daily, in churches when the authorities would permit, in schoolhouses or groves when they would not. New Year's Day 1841 found him in Vermont, where he "lectured almost unremittingly on the various subjects that relate to the reformation of the world." He was encouraged by "the progress of truth in this part of the country."[21]

Thus Wattles moved from a single-minded concern with the salvation of souls to a broader vision of reform. By 1842, he had left behind the Calvinist orthodoxy he had embraced at Oneida Institute, but had put in its place a vision of a world remade according to God's designs. He was not alone in that vision, and by 1842 was finding others to share it.

John A. Collins

Of the founders of the Society for Universal Inquiry and Reform, probably the most important was John Anderson Collins. Certainly he had been the best-known and most widely traveled, for a time, at least, on the edges of the inner circle of Boston abolitionists that included William Lloyd Garrison and Wendell Phillips. From 1837 to 1842 he was intimately involved in the intricate machinations of antislavery politics, and through his life passed the best-known abolitionists of the day—Garrison, Frederick Douglass, Abby Kelley, Edmund Quincy, the Weston sisters. That makes it all the more frustrating that we know so little about his early life. Collins emerged from obscurity into prominence late in the 1830s, and within a decade had returned to obscurity.

Collins was born in Manchester, Vermont, in October 1810. We know only that his father was dead by the time John came of age, and that his mother was still living in 1835. Given his subsequent career, it seems likely that his parents were similar to those of Wattles and Murray—evangelical Congregationalists who reared their son in an atmosphere of faith. They may have been in more

John A. Collins, n.d. From Wendell Phillips Garrison and Francis Jackson
Garrison, *William Lloyd Garrison, 1805–1879*, vol. III.

affluent circumstances. Collins attended the Burr Academy in Manchester and was able to enter Middlebury College in 1835.[22]

In 1839 a friend wrote of Collins that he "had been almost everything in the course of his life." He may have lived in Massachusetts for a time—he married Adaline Burgess in Dedham in 1834. He apparently took some interest in reform. In college he had joined in a solemn vow with his classmates to wage unrelenting war on false religion and to expose corruption wherever he encountered it. He was also, at least until 1837, an adherent of the Whig party.[23]

Collins spent only a year at Middlebury, entering Andover Theological Seminary in 1836. He remained there three years. His move to Andover says much about his religious outlook. Founded in 1808 by orthodox Congregationalists who feared the Unitarian tendencies of Harvard, by the 1830s it had become the "West Point of Orthodoxy." As Sydney E. Ahlstrom has written: "Andover almost immediately became a major rallying point for Orthodoxy. Its faculty was brilliant and aggressive, its student body large and enthusiastic. In a few years its influence was being felt all across the country and far-flung mission fields abroad." Collins was almost certainly preparing for the Congregational clergy.[24]

Collins never embarked on that career. Instead, he became an abolitionist. Again, we have no indication of how this came about—Collins left no record. Certainly he would have had little encouragement from the Andover faculty. Abolitionist organizers made several attempts to enlist Andover students as a group, like those at Oneida and Lane. They made some notable converts, such as Jonathan Blanchard, the founder of Knox College, and Parker Pillsbury, a stalwart of the Garrisonian cause. But Andover's faculty, while professing abhorrence of slavery, convinced the overwhelming majority of students that their first responsibility was to complete their education before embarking on other endeavors. Collins, however, broke with his teachers to embrace abolition. Once converted, he identified himself with the Garrisonian faction to which he rendered in December 1838 what Garrison perceived as a great service.[25]

In 1837, a group of Massachusetts clergy had embarked on a campaign to seize control of the abolitionist movement in the state by issuing the first in a series of "Clerical Appeals." Led by Nathaniel Colver, a Baptist minister, and Charles T. Torrey, a Congregationalist, the ministers had appealed to the Massachusetts Anti-Slavery Society to cease its "hasty, unsparing, almost ferocious denunciation" of the churches. Later manifestos condemned Garrisonian support for unorthodox social reform causes, such as nonresistance and woman's rights. The motivation of these conservatives was complex. Some were un-doubtedly offended by abolition generally and wanted to use the unpopularity of certain Garrisonian views as a handy club to wield against it. But others, like Colver and Torrey, were old abolitionists who feared that Garrisonian excesses were driving away church members who otherwise would have been attracted to the movement. And, as fervent evangelicals, they were genuinely horrified by what they saw as the heterodoxies of the Garrisonians.[26]

The Massachusetts Anti-Slavery Society was to hold its annual meeting in January 1839. At that meeting, the conservatives, led by Torrey, hoped to take control of the organization by depriving women of the right to participate in its business meetings. A friend of Collins saw a letter from Torrey to another minister at Andover, telling of his plans. Collins somehow got word to Garri-son of the "conspiracy." It failed, and Collins's warning may have made a dif-ference. When the meeting was held, Garrison had arranged for the convention to be attended by large numbers of his warmest supporters, and the result was that the conservatives were pushed back on all fronts. Defeated, they split off to form a new, conservative organization, the Massachusetts Abolition Society, which embraced political abolition and soon began publishing its own paper.[27]

Whether or not Collins's warning was critical, it brought him into the Gar-risonian ranks, and Collins began to win the confidence of what Lawrence Friedman has called the "Boston Clique," the inner group centered around Garrison. It also gave him an alternative to remaining at Andover. After Collins had played an important role in a victory for Garrison at the expense of his clerical opponents, the atmosphere of the seminary was doubtless chilly. Col-lins left without taking a degree. And in 1839 and 1840 he fully justified the confidence of his new associates. Early in 1839 Amos A. Phelps, the Massachu-setts Anti-Slavery Society's general agent, resigned to cast his lot with the con-servatives. Collins took his place, and filled the position ably. "His executive power was remarkable," Oliver Johnson, one of his compatriots, wrote years later. "He did much to infuse courage into our broken ranks, to overcome op-position, to collect funds, and devise and execute large plans of antislavery la-bor." Collins at that time was, according to Johnson, "a man of tremendous energy, nothing could stagnate in his presence. He could set a score of agents in the field, and plan and execute a campaign on the largest scale." Soon Collins had moved his family to Boston, and was engaged in a daunting task, raising ten thousand dollars to fulfill a pledge made to the American Anti-Slavery So-ciety by its Massachusetts auxiliary. By the end of the year Collins had suc-ceeded. He did so through unrelenting efforts on the lecture circuit across the state. He came to hold other offices, serving as secretary and as a counselor of the Massachusetts society. He also became involved in the New England Non-Resistance Society, taking views on some matters, like refusing to serve in the militia, that were in advance of most nonresistants. His success was all the more impressive in view of his personal circumstances. In the summer of 1839 one of his new friends in Boston reported to her sister that Collins had "had numberless troubles, his wife and children not being very well, and he not having much money to get along with." That spring, he attended his first meeting of the American Anti-Slavery Society in New York, where he faithfully sustained Garrison's positions.[28]

The year 1840 was to prove one of trial for Collins; by the end of it, his prospects, seemingly so bright at the end of 1839, were in eclipse. He had continued his work as general agent to the satisfaction of all involved, and remained a successful fundraiser for the cause; when he left the Massachusetts group in 1843, it acclaimed him as the man who had raised more money for abolition than any other. Perhaps his greatest coup had come in the spring. All sides recognized that the 1840 annual meeting of the American Anti-Slavery Society would be critical. The national organization was moribund by 1840, and its conservative leaders wanted to dissolve it, leaving antislavery activity to the healthier state societies and the Liberty party. Garrison, however, saw the proposed course as an unthinkable victory for slavery. He feared, moreover, that conservatives would attempt to use the meeting to repeal the rule allowing women to vote, then use their new majority for an attack on nonresistance. Since there was no limit on the number of delegates, Garrison was apprehensive that the conservative group in New York would pack the meeting with local sympathizers. He could counter by making sure that an unusually large Massachusetts delegation made up of his supporters, was present.[29]

At this point Collins rendered his service. The problem with Garrison's plan was money—the cost of transporting the men and women to New York, and boarding them once they were there. Collins proposed the solution—to send the company to Providence via the railroad, then send them to New York on a chartered steamer. Once in New York City, they could board for 25 cents a day in the homes of black sympathizers. On May 11, the group left Boston in a festive mood, so many that a second train had to be added. In Providence, Garrison watched approvingly as Collins marched the troops on board, checking off each name. "There never has been such a mass of '*ultraism*' afloat," he exalted, "since the first victim was stolen from the fire-smitten and blood-red soil of Africa."[30]

The convention attracted nearly a thousand delegates, almost three times the number who had attended the year before. Garrison prevailed on all of the issues, after which the conservative minority withdrew to organize the American and Foreign Anti-Slavery Society. It was doubtless the high point of the year for Collins.[31]

In July 1840, Collins's wife died, followed very shortly by one of his children. We know nothing else of her. Collins was away from Boston, suggesting that death was sudden and unexpected.[32]

There is reason to think that this family tragedy took a toll on Collins, sending him into one of those strange physical and mental declines that struck other abolitionists down. On the other hand, it did not bring his organizing to a halt. In late summer he was trying to rouse enthusiasm for the abolition cause by arranging mass meetings in Springfield and Worcester. It was a discouraging, daunting project. Everywhere he went he found formerly faithful abolitionists swept up in the excitement of the politics of 1840. Men and women who had "eschewed sectarianism" and "lost their caste in the circle in which they moved" because of their commitment to abolition were now declaring that "they would sooner forego their abolitionism than their party." They were "Politically intoxicated," he wrote to Garrison. "The enthusiasm of Bank and Sub-treasury, Harrison and Reform, has taken entire possession of them." He also was a member of the committee that issued the call for the Chardon Street Convention in November in Boston, convened to consider the propriety of Sabbath observance and the relation of church and ministry to slavery, and "universal reform." It turned out to be the *ne ultra plus* of radical abolition and reform, in the words of John L. Thomas, "that singular conference of reformers and cranks which met for three days in November . . . without reaching any conclusions or passing a single resolution."[33]

Collins, however, was not present. A month earlier he had sailed for England and the critical experience of his career as a reformer.

When the Garrisonians took control of the American Anti-Slavery Society in the spring of 1840, they quickly discovered that its treasury was empty. Its only assets—the money-losing journal the *Emancipator* and a stock of pamphlets turned over to Henry B. Stanton in lieu of his salary, leaving him to ponder how he could use them to help make his marriage to Elizabeth Cady possible—had been transferred to safe conservative hands. With the conservatives had also gone Arthur and Lewis Tappan, the major financial backers of the organization. Now saddled with the costs of supporting both the Massachusetts and the American societies, the radicals' need for money was desperate. So in the early autumn the decision was made to send Collins, who had proved his prowess as a fundraiser, to Great Britain to try to replenish the empty coffers of Garrisonianism. On October 1 he sailed for Liverpool on the *Britannia*.[34]

There was less than solid support for Collins's mission. Charles C. Burleigh, for example, thought that the trip was a mistake, although whether that was a reflection on Collins or pessimism about his prospects for success is unclear. Garrison also watched the departure of his best agent with misgivings and considerable reluctance. The leaders did not advertise Collins's purpose, although they did not try to conceal it. His official credentials referred only casually to his status now as general agent of the American Anti-Slavery Society, emphasizing instead the deleterious effects of the death of his wife and child and his own health problems. Collins was being sent abroad because he was "almost wholly disabled from sustaining the responsibilities of his agency" in the hope that travel would help him "recruit his shattered constitution." In letters to sympathizers in England, however, Garrison made it clear that the financial situation of the American Anti-Slavery Society was critical, and that much depended on the success of Collins's efforts.[35]

Once in England, however, Collins found himself beset by a variety of difficulties. Conservative abolitionists in the United States, led by the Rev. Nathaniel Colver, whose plans Collins had helped to frustrate the previous year, wrote to friends in England to warn them that Collins had left "under suspicious circumstances." The *Massachusetts Abolitionist*, under the editorship of Colver's coadjutor Charles T. Torrey, accused Collins of "knavery" and "barefaced forgery," not to mention having embezzled three hundred dollars he had raised in Hatfield. Torrey wrote that sympathy for Mrs. Collins had moved those aware of these facts to withhold them from the public, but now the time had come for "his loathsome history [to] be brought more fully into view." "When such a man is needed as a tool, there's something rotten in the State of the Society that needs him," Torrey wrote.[36]

These charges may have had some impact, but the very fact of Collins's association with Garrison was doubtless telling in itself. The leaders of the English antislavery movement tended to be deeply evangelical in their religious views, and they were horrified by the accounts they received of Garrisonian infidelity. Colver further instructed them with extracts from some of the more radical of the speeches at the Chardon Street convention. When he arrived, Collins found that Charles Stuart, a veteran British abolitionist who had been an important figure in the early days of the American movement, was already spreading poison, charging that the American Anti-Slavery Society was a "woman's rights intrusion society," wholly dedicated to "overthrowing civil government and all law and order, the holy sabbath, a paid ministry and . . . the order and . . . harmony of society." Frustrated, Collins asked the British and Foreign Anti-Slavery Society in December for a donation of two thousand pounds. Three weeks later, the reply came that the group had not that much to spare for any group, but certainly not for the American Anti-Slavery Society, which had "alienated their confidence."[37]

Under the best of circumstances, without the baggage of Garrison's reputation, Collins would have had a difficult time. The resources of British abolitionists had been strained by staging the World's Anti-Slavery Convention that summer, and sympathizers had also just been subjected to the appeals of a delegation from Oberlin College. Even those sympathetic to Garrison warned that Collins was coming into what promised to be a barren field.[38]

These good reasons, however, were little comfort to Collins, stuck in a boardinghouse in Southwark, sharing quarters with an ailing Charles L. Remond, the black abolitionist who had been in England for some time, and with whose plight he had little sympathy. Remond, in turn, found Collins's absorption in abolitionist politics, as opposed to abolition, irksome. Only two contributors were found, and by the beginning of the new year Collins was thoroughly disgusted by his experiences: "I would as soon go among the Southern Slave holders to solicit aid, as among the abolitionists of Great Britain," he wrote to his friend Henry G. Chapman. They were bound up in sectarianism, he stormed, afraid of upsetting any established institutions.[39]

Collins, despite the failure of his fundraising activities, did have an impact. In February he ventured into Scotland. His visit served as a catalyst for a division among Scots abolitionists, between those sympathetic to Garrison and those who opposed him. In Glasgow, he was present as, after complex maneuvers, radicals sympathetic to woman's rights took control of the Glasgow Emancipation Society. Glasgow conservatives split off, contemptuously referring to their opponents as converts to "Yankeeism." Collins also encouraged female radicals to found a new group sympathetic to Garrisonian views. From Scotland, Collins went on to Ireland. Behind him he left a British antislavery movement that, once united, was now badly split, with groups in Scotland and Ireland seceding from the London-based British and Foreign Anti-Slavery Society. These schisms had deep roots, involving political and religious differences that had existed long before Collins ever thought of visiting England.

But Collins was the catalyst, forcing British abolitionists to choose between competing forces in America.[40]

There is little evidence that Collins was completely conscious of just what he had accomplished. His main concern was his utter failure to raise money—by the time he finally sailed for home on July 4, 1841, he had to borrow funds from Wendell Phillips, who sailed with him, to pay for his passage. The greatest impact of the visit on Collins was the widening of his reform vision. He was convinced that in England he had seen a glimpse of the future of American society, one that horrified him.[41]

While in England, Collins had made contact with a variety of reformers besides abolitionists. He had several visits with the utopian socialist and religious skeptic Robert Owen, an association that did not contribute to his good reputation among the more pious of the British antislavery forces. He also attended meetings of the Chartists—"the noble band," he called them, who sought far-reaching changes in British society, including universal male suffrage, improved working conditions, and the abolition of child labor. These ties apparently moved Collins to cast a critical eye on what was happening around him.[42]

What Collins saw in England in 1841 appalled him as much as slavery. Slavery, he wrote, involved "such high handed villainy," such "abominable outrages," that no one could doubt its evil. But England, over two hundred years, by "a series of the most cunning subtle and crafty movements" had subjected its poor "to the same thing in effect without the appearance of slavery." Indeed, it was worse than slavery, Collins concluded: "America is better for a colored man, degraded as he is, than England is for a poor man," he wrote to the *Pennsylvania Freeman*. The great masses of English men and women were ill fed, ill housed, ill clothed, despite providing the labor that had made their land the richest in the world. "With all their toil and pain, starvation surrounds them," he wrote to his new friend, the radical English Quaker Elizabeth Pease. "On account of their poverty, their families are thrust into some small and filthy corner of a hole." But the effects on the upper classes were just as bad, if less apparent. "When God's laws are violated a penalty must be paid," he concluded. "Dissolute, overbearing sensual and aristocratic habits check the growth of the moral and paralyses [*sic*] the physical energies of this class."[43]

For Collins, the source of this evil was obvious; it had arisen from a "system of exchange, by which one class of men can secure the fruits of the poor labourer without returning him an equivalent." The rich were devoting "all *their* wits time and strength to devise ways to and means to filch . . . from the operatives which will appear honest and fair" the fruits of their labors. The workers, deprived of all opportunity for "mental or moral reflection" were little better than beasts of burden. With the minds of the poor dulled, and those of the rich stultified, it was not surprising that Great Britain was eaten up with sin. The entire social system had to be changed.[44]

Collins's absence had caused his friends in America some anxiety. Garrison bemoaned his failure to report regularly on his activities, being forced to depend on English friends for news of Collins's arrival in England. Nevertheless, there is no evidence that the Bostonians regarded Collins's trip as a failure. When he arrived in Boston on July 17, with Phillips, black citizens marked the occasion with a "collation" in the Chardon Street Chapel in which Collins was hailed as the man who "saved the cause" in 1840, and Garrison, Phillips, the Chapmans, and Samuel J. May traded witticisms.[45]

By August Collins was back in the field. Garrison wrote that his return, along with Phillips, "infuses new life into the general mass." From July to December he traveled 3,500 miles, delivered more than ninety lectures in sixty towns, and attended four state and sixteen county conventions. Probably the most fateful of these was on Nantucket in August 1841, when Collins, Garrison, and Edmund Quincy heard Frederick Douglass, introduced as a fugitive lately from the South, deliver his first public address. Overwhelmed by Douglass's power, Collins immediately enlisted him as a lecturer, and they spent much of the rest of the year traveling together, often battling segregated railroads and ships. Collins wrote admiringly of Douglass's powers as an orator, and urged that other black agents be employed. By the end of the year, Collins was outwardly optimistic. "I have seen but little to dishearten, but, on the contrary, much, *very much* to strengthen and encourage us." True, he had encountered the "pestiferous atmosphere" of the "new organization" and the Liberty party, but the defection of such pseudo-abolitionists was no loss: "Better that our ranks be sifted, and reduced to the number of Gideon's army, than have our principles . . . or our measures . . . reduced and suited to the prejudices of public taste."[46]

In 1842 Collins kept up this frenetic pace of travel and organizing. In May he enthusiastically embraced a plan to raise fifty thousand dollars for the operations of the national organization. In the summer he hurriedly put together *The Anti-Slavery Picknick,* a collection of "Speeches, Poems, Dialogues, and Songs" for use at the celebrations that he hoped abolitionists would use to mark the anniversary of the abolition of slavery in the British West Indies. In June

Collins fell ill with an attack of "bilious colic," lying delirious for days. Apparently this left him in poor health for a considerable time, although it did not prevent his second marriage, to Eunice Messenger of Dedham, in October. It was not until November that he went back to speaking, joining Garrison in western New York. Garrison worried that Collins's "constitution seems to be greatly impaired."[47]

The most fateful action, however, had come in May, when he made his first trip west to attend the annual meeting of the Ohio Anti-Slavery Society. That meeting was to be critical, for it brought together Collins with Wattles and the Hicksite Quakers Abraham Brooke and Valentine Nicholson, in a meeting that would lead to Universal Inquiry and Reform.

Orson S. Murray

Of all of the men who took up the cause of "Humanity" in the winter of 1842–43, probably the most thoroughly radical and iconoclastic was Orson S. Murray. Like Wattles and Collins, he was a New Englander who found in the West the allies who were to help him realize his visions. But even before he came to know Valentine Nicholson or Dr. Brooke, Murray had approached the outer edges of reform; he was already "the leading light of ultraism in Vermont," as one historian described him. It says much about the real dedication of these reformers to free debate and toleration of diversity that Murray found a home among them.[48]

Murray was a Vermonter, born in Orwell, October 23, 1806. His father, Jonathan Murray, had come from Guilford, Connecticut, a few years earlier with his own parents, and in Orwell had married Rosalinda Bascom. Orson was the oldest of their eleven children.[49]

Unlike Wattles and Collins, Murray had limited opportunities for formal education His parents were poor, with a farm that afforded them only a meager income. Thus anything beyond a common school education was out of the question, although his parents encouraged his interest in books. As he approached adulthood, Murray supported himself and supplemented his family's income by teaching and working on the farms of neighbors.[50]

Murray, by his own account, grew up in a strict religious atmosphere. His parents were originally Congregationalists, but during his childhood became converts to the Free Will Baptists. Murray himself was baptized at the age of fifteen, although he backslid and did not consider himself thoroughly converted until he was twenty-three. By his late teens, he had become convinced

ORSON S. MURRAY.

Orson S. Murray in old age. In author's possession.

that he had a call to the Baptist ministry. Baptists required no formal theological preparation for licensing, but Murray was determined to have the classical education that the other ministers of his neighborhood possessed. Far older than most of the rest of the students, he studied at the Shoreham and Castleton academies. He persevered even after becoming a husband and father, and finally completed his course about 1832.[51]

In 1828 Murray married Catherine Maria Higgins, also of Orwell. Of her we know little; she does not seem to have shared in her husband's public career, although with nine children her opportunities, even had she been disposed to pursue them, must have been extremely limited.[52]

Murray's interest in reform began early. By the time he was seventeen, according to his own account, he became convinced that rum drinking, then apparently prevalent and widely accepted in Orwell, was wrong. His claim was that he came to feel thus before he had read any temperance literature or even knew of any temperance movement. Once temperance societies did become widespread in the state, Murray, again by his own account, became the first in his community to embrace total abstinence. He was convinced, he told friends, after watching a prominent Congregationalist minister, an agent for the Vermont Temperance Society, become tipsy drinking wine at a wedding celebration. The parallels with the early life of William Lloyd Garrison—the poverty, the limited education, the early interest in temperance—are striking. From temperance he moved to embrace the cause of anti-Masonry, which flourished in Vermont.[53]

In 1832 Murray reached the first critical turning point of his life: his discovery of Garrison's *Liberator,* and his reading of Garrison's *Thoughts on African Colonization.* Colonization had a number of supporters in Vermont. Founded in 1816, the American Colonization Society advocated linking emancipation with the forced expatriation of the freed blacks. The society's members varied in motivation. Some were true humanitarians who were convinced that an end to slavery would come only when the freed slaves were moved out of the United States, since the white majority could not conceive of a sizable free black population in the United States, the inevitable result of emancipation. Other colonizationists, who shared the racist assumptions of the overwhelming majority of white Americans, wanted to rid the United States of *all* blacks.[54]

This Garrison challenged directly as unchristian. God had made all people of one blood, he argued, and not only slavery, but the systematic degradation of free blacks, was a denial of the spirit of the Gospel. It was as reasonable for blacks to expel whites from America as for whites to send away blacks. "To make such a separation, we have no authority," he concluded. It was also a denial of the principles on which the United States supposedly had been founded. "They do not wish us to admit them to an equality," Garrison wrote to a brother-in-law, "they tell us we must always be hostile to the free people of color, while they remain in this country. If this be so, then we had better burn our bibles, and our Declaration of Independence and candidly acknowledge ourselves to be incorrigible tyrants and heathens."[55]

This reading made Murray an abolitionist. By the summer of 1833, he was ready for radical measures, accepting a commission as an agent for the New England Anti-Slavery Society to work in Vermont. "We must go to the *ne ultra plus* if we bring the people half way. To go but half way ourselves will not start them," he wrote to fellow abolitionist Amos A. Phelps. He encouraged Phelps, who was also involved in the New England Anti-Slavery Society, to greater zeal. Slavery was "a 'sin,'—a 'crime,'—atrocious, flagrant, damnable. Go on, my Brother, and make the people feel it."[56]

Murray's work as an agent was successful; one student of Vermont history says bluntly: "He forced the people of Vermont to consider the question of immediate emancipation of slavery." He flooded the Vermont press with letters that attacked colonization and supported abolition. Some thought that he was more diplomatic and moderate than other abolitionists, but others refused to print his articles, accusing him of being "intemperate." He undertook an ambitious lecturing and organizing tour as well. In Bennington, a mass meeting agreed to ban him from the town. In Middlebury, students from the college showered his meeting with corn. Still he was successful in organizing twenty local antislavery societies.[57]

In December, Murray lived up to his principles by attending the meeting that organized the American Anti-Slavery Society. It was a diverse assembly that reflected the abolitionist constituency—three of those present were black; four were women; a third were Quakers. Those who controlled the meeting were, however, much like Murray. In the words of James Brewer Stewart, they were "talented and aggressive white men who combined religious zeal with aspirations as editors, businessmen, clerics, and philanthropists." And they echoed Murray's views of the sinfulness of slavery, sin "unequalled by any other on the face of the earth."[58]

The question remained about what role Murray would play. He still hoped for a career as a minister, and he was finally licensed to preach in 1837. But to settle down as a pastor in some comfortable New England town when the horror of slavery still lay on the land was unthinkable. As John Greenleaf Whittier remembered forty years later, Murray was "a man terribly in earnest, with a zeal that bordered on fanaticism." Murray pondered publishing an abolitionist newspaper in Vermont, but finally decided that he was too young and inexperienced. He was willing, however, to continue the equally challenging and infinitely more dangerous work—organizer of local antislavery societies. In 1834 he took the lead in the organization of the Vermont Anti-Slavery Society, the first state organization founded after the formation of the American Anti-Slavery Society, and was appointed its secretary and agent. He then undertook the hard life of an agent, trying to rouse enthusiasm against slavery and bring new members into the local societies that were becoming the backbone of the movement.[59]

As an organizer, Murray had to depend largely on the power of his voice to persuade. It was not something that came easily to Murray. His son wrote many years later that "his words were perhaps more effective for their logic than for his oratory; for his reasoning, his analysis, his criticism, rather than for the polished persuasiveness of manner which some may have." Nevertheless he persevered. For example, he embarked late in 1834 on a four-week tour that resulted in the organization of several new local societies. In at least four towns, however, mobs prevented him from speaking, mobs that he accused colonizationists and the *Middlebury Free Press* of stirring up. In Windsor, for instance, when he tried to hold a meeting in the courthouse, opponents shouted him down: "Stamping, whooping, and yelling exceeded anything, and everything I had ever heard or could have imagined," he wrote. But he also had successes. Among his converts was Col. Jonathan P. Miller of Montpelier, a romantic figure who early in the 1820s had gone to Greece to fight against the Turks. He had come, he told Murray at the conclusion of a lecture, to raise a mob against him, but instead had become convinced of the truth of abolitionist positions. A member of the state legislature, he offered to introduce any resolutions or legislation that Murray drew up. Subsequently Murray kept Miller and the legislature busy with resolutions to memorialize Congress for the abolition of the interstate slave trade and the slave trade and slavery in the District of Columbia.[60]

For ten years, Murray had prepared for the pulpit. Yet, in 1835, he decided against becoming a pastor and instead purchased the controlling interest in the state Baptist newspaper, the *Vermont Telegraph*. It had been in existence for seven years, with a succession of editors. It would be tempting to think that Murray's outspoken abolitionist views had made him unacceptable to any Baptist church in the state. Yet there were other abolitionists in Baptist pulpits. The *Telegraph*, moreover, was under the control of the state convention, with its stock owned by a number of individuals. But Murray had won sufficient trust to persuade enough of them to sell their stock to him. The understanding apparently was that Murray would preserve the journal's character as a denominational organ. But as the main owner and editor, Murray could do whatever he chose, and he chose to make the *Telegraph* a different sort of publication.[61]

A few years later, Murray wrote that his intention on taking over the *Telegraph* was "to make the paper serve better the cause of freedom and reform."

He certainly did that. He denounced slavery, opposed aristocracy, and "discovered various forms of corruption in the churches, as well as out of them." He made attacks on slavery the focal point of his editorials. He also committed the *Telegraph* to the firm support of William Lloyd Garrison in his struggle with the more conservative elements of the American Anti-Slavery Society. Garrison's opponents, he fumed, were putting forth far more energy for the destruction of Garrison than they ever aimed at slavery. In the first number he edited, Murray enumerated the goals of the *Telegraph* under its new management: "I will make the *Telegraph* speak as much truth; expose as much error; rebuke as much sin; do as much good; and save as many souls as possible." The evangelical note of uncompromising war on sin was prominent. American cities, he warned, were "filling up with the very sins which destroyed Sodom and Gomorrah," and he was determined to sound the alarm. "Every man, woman and child through the country must be marshaled and drilled into one vast, solid, mighty moral phalanx, that shall come down upon the seats of Satan with overwhelming power," he warned in another biting editorial. "There is no time to be lost. The heavens already gather blackness. The tempests of divine wrath are ready to be poured down. The subjects are already ripening for destruction." [62]

Meanwhile, Murray was beginning to explore other areas of reform. Temperance was, of course, relatively uncontroversial, but by 1837 he was beginning to move toward nonresistance, a new vision of the nature of government, or, more, properly, nongovernment. With other abolitionists, he saw the mission of antislavery as simple obedience to the will of God. To follow that will to its perfect accomplishment, Christians had to renounce the use of coercive force in all situations. Instead, they must rely on moral suasion. As we have seen, "moral suasion" had been the stock tactic of abolition in the early days of the American Anti-Slavery Society, but by the middle of the decade some abolitionists, led by Garrison, undertook to carry this philosophy to its logical end. Any government that employed violence, or even the threat of violence, had to be renounced by real Christians. [63]

By 1837, Murray was moving in that direction. Articles about peace became a regular feature of the *Telegraph*, and in the summer of 1837 Murray became deeply involved in plans for the organization of a state peace society in Vermont. Garrison watched the project with considerable interest, and sent Murray a long letter of advice and instruction before the convention in Middlebury. His advice, for one who was painted as an inflexible, unthinking fanatic, was extraordinarily realistic. "Do not hope, should you organize a society on right principles, to see it popular in its infancy," he wrote. Antislavery and temperance were comparatively easy—it was easy to arouse sympathies for suffering slaves, easy to make others see the self-interest in abstaining from the poisons of alcohol. "To be a Peace man, in the true acceptation of that term, is to be forever powerless (physically), against injury, insult, and assault—to trust solely to the living God for protection," he told Murray. But the "*peace* man" was one made "perfect in love," who was "always willing to be delivered to death for Jesus' sake," who "when smitten on one cheek," would "turn the other." Such were not to be found in the American Peace Society, which condoned defensive war. Instead, the peace men must renounce all use of force. Guided by these principles, Murray became the guiding figure of the nonresistance movement in Vermont.[64]

The convention in Middlebury, however, proved to be a disappointment to Murray. When it opened, he was chosen its secretary, but immediately it set off in just the direction that Garrison had warned against. Its resolutions deploring war between nations as unchristian, and the pledge of all present to work for its extirpation, were welcome. Its adoption of a constitution that made it an auxiliary of the American Peace Society was not.[65]

Murray and Rowland T. Robinson, a Hicksite Quaker from Ferrisburgh, led the minority in opposition. Their objection was not so much to what the meeting had done, other than its affiliating with the temporizing American Peace Society. But they were disturbed by what the convention failed to include in its constitution and resolutions. Quite simply, it had compromised with sin. It admitted warfare to be unchristian, yet it countenanced the use of violence by government in a variety of situations, at least implicitly. And that was more than Murray and his compatriots could bear. "The minority discard the doctrine that the standard of truth should be raised by degrees, gradually, against popular views," Murray wrote in a long critique of the meeting. "They would elevate the standard at once, believing that the whole truth is better, and will be more effective, than half of it." He had little hope for the success of the organization, and afterwards usually ignored it in the columns of the *Telegraph*. This split was to prove fatal to the fledgling group; by the end of 1838 it was dead.[66]

Instead, Murray cast his lot with Garrison and other abolitionists who tried to move the peace reform more in the nonresistant direction. The climax came with the formation of the New England Non-Resistance Society in Boston in September 1838. In its declaration of sentiments, which Murray reprinted approvingly in the *Telegraph,* the convention renounced allegiance to all human governments; they would neither support nor oppose them. "We recognize but one King and lawgiver, one Judge and Ruler of mankind. We are bound by the laws of a kingdom which is out of the world, the subjects of which are forbidden to fight." That kingdom was the world and embraced all people. Thus the participants renounced not only war, but all preparations for war; all armaments; all monuments of war; all celebrations of it. They would not bear arms nor hold any military office. But they went beyond that—they could not hold office or vote, since all governments on earth sanctioned violence. They voluntarily renounced all claims of protection from human governments, thus giving indubitable evidence of their commitment. But while visionary, they were hopelessly realistic. They wrote that the world they envisioned would not come to be until "the kingdom of this world will have become the kingdoms of our Lord and of his CHRIST, and he shall reign forever."[67]

Murray was not in Boston for the convention, much to his regret, but he observed its proceedings admiringly from Brandon, and committed the *Telegraph* to the cause. "On the right settlement of this question every thing is depending to happiness on earth," Murray wrote in his commentary on the convention. For the editor, the situation was simple—just as abolition simply required ceasing the sin of slaveholding, the truth of nonresistance required only that all obey the commands of King Jesus: "Put up thy sword—put on 'pureness, knowledge, long suffering, kindness, the Holy Ghost, love unfeigned, the word of truth, the power of God, the armor of righteousness.'" As for the charge that nonresistance would be the end of all government, Murray responded that nonresistants simply followed the American tradition of placing obedience to God over obedience to human law. "The Peaceman believes that all laws and governments which assume the right of man to take the life of his fellow, do violence to the laws of Christ's kingdom, just as the religious-liberty-man believes in regard to the laws uniting church and state," he concluded. "The remedy for two is one—christian protestation and remonstrance, and in the mean time patiently suffering the wrong until these with the help of the Lord work deliverance."[68]

Such a direction was not one that readers of a denominational periodical would have expected, even in New England in the 1830s. Murray was almost alone among religious editors in accepting and promoting nonresistance. After 1838, the character of the *Telegraph* changed. The amount of space devoted to reform—education, temperance, and abolition—had always been relatively large, although there were the usual reprints of sermons, essays on religious subjects, and reports of successful revivals. But the attention given to revivals diminished as Murray added new departments on peace, health reform, and woman's rights. In 1840, in his sixth year of publication, Murray listed his goals: "the purification of the earth from sin and its defilements, and the general diffusion of truth and holiness—the destruction of the power of the adversary, and the salvation of his victims—the overthrow and extermination of the kingdom of darkness, and the establishment of the universal reign of King Immanuel—these are the objects to which my feeble powers are devoted, and I have enlisted during the war." Striking is what Murray does not include on his lists—revivals, conversions, winning souls to Christ. There was an overwhelming millenarian emphasis—the emphasis on the overthrow of evil and the ushering in of the Government of God. More and more Murray was thinking in terms of universal rather than individual redemption.[69]

Not all Vermont Baptists looked with equanimity on their editor's course. By 1840, many, individually and as churches and associations, were sending protests to Murray. Some charged vaguely that the *Telegraph* had become a "divisive influence"; others complained that while they sympathized with the causes that Murray was advocating, the journal no longer served the interests of the denomination. Murray attempted to rally his supporters by reminding them that preaching against sin was always unpopular in "the depraved world." But by 1842 Murray was running a regular notice to postmasters that he would not pay the postage on copies of the *Telegraph* returned to him. Early in 1843 there was an attempt to sell him out for debts.[70]

His growing estrangement from most Vermont Baptists, however, did not turn Murray from his course. Throughout the 1830s, he wrote later, he had been convinced that the church was the "pillar and ground" of truth, and that while it might, in certain respects, need reform and cleansing, it would endure. Murray was sure that he was advancing that through "free discussion and faithful utterance of truth." In 1837 the Baptist state convention set up a committee on slavery with Murray as a member. He saw a hopeful sign in the autumn of 1839, when Baptist preachers and laymen held a Vermont Baptist Anti-Slavery Convention in Brandon. Their resolutions were radical enough even for him, with the group adopting a "no fellowship with slaveholders" stand. A year later, Murray served as secretary of the National Baptist Anti-Slavery Convention in New York City. The national American Baptist Convention, sensitive to its large Southern constituency, condemned these efforts, much to Murray's disgust. In the fall of 1841, Murray called another meeting in Waterbury to condemn the course of the national group, which demanded the expulsion of all slaveholders from the church. The state convention saw this as too radical. It took the final steps of revoking Murray's license as a minister, repudiating the *Telegraph,* and establishing a rival journal. In the fall of 1842, the Addison County Baptist Association voted to censure him and his church suspended him. Faced with a choice between loyalty to a sect and apparent truth, Murray had chosen what he thought to be truth.[71]

As the clamor against him and the *Telegraph* grew, Murray fortified himself with the consolation that his was the course of righteousness. "It has not been so much my object to please my fellow beings where they are, as to get them where they ought to be," he wrote, "not so much to know what they call for, as to find out what they are in need of, and to proffer it to them." And that would continue to be his course. Opposition, he was convinced, emanated only from corruption, from "the wrath and spite of devoted sectarians and mercenary politicians," who had "alarmed the fearful, and disquieted all who wished to be let alone in their present chosen condition." And so Murray foreswore not only politics, which he had given up with the cause of peace five years earlier, but also religion, which in Murray's mind had become sectarianism. Truth demanded it. Murray became a Free Thinker, or, as many put it, an infidel.[72]

There are many uncertainties about Murray's progress. Years later, Orson's son ascribed it to his study of "cause and effects" and his interest in science. Never did Murray openly renounce Christianity or religion in the pages of the *Telegraph*—his targets always were sectarianism and "creedism." Publicly, he dismissed "the cry of infidelity." "I heed it not," he wrote in an editorial. "It has been raised against every true and faithful Christian who has lived in the midst of a wicked and adulterous generation." But in no denomination, no matter how liberal, did Murray find freedom from them.[73]

Murray's new religious vision did not explicitly dismiss all religion, or all churches, or all clergy. He admitted that many ministers were good, amiable men, often on the right side of great moral questions. But they were "*theologians, religionists,* when they should be *Christians, philanthropists.*" No one could be true to "sectism and theology," and to truth. "The things are as perfect antagonisms as selfishness and benevolence." They were at odds because all sectarians shared a commitment to "fixed principles in theology." They expressed them in creeds, and creeds were evil because they prevented human progress. A creed, Murray wrote, "looks back, instead of looking forward—downward, and not upward, outward, and not inward. It leads to men, instead of leading to God. It serves the party—not the community." A creed bound generations to follow; it obligated a man to believe the same things at seventy that he had believed at twenty. And Murray apparently was troubled by the problem that had troubled another Vermonter, Joseph Smith, a decade earlier— the variety of competing claims of the hundreds of creeds and sects. Had there been only one creed, there was at least the chance that it might be a fair statement of truth. But the variety meant that believers spent their time disputing with each other instead of working at the true business of religion—exposing errors and raising the standard of morality.[74]

Still, Murray claimed that he was a "professing Christian." "Christianity is a simple, plain, indivisible, indisputable doctrine. LOVE TO GOD AND LOVE TO MAN is the whole of it," he wrote. But that was not what the sects proclaimed. And he would not be bound by the standards of any sect, or by any man-made creed. He would subject the Bible "to criticism and examination in pronouncing upon its accuracies and its inaccuracies, its truths and its errors." He considered it "sound morality and true philosophy," but "the Bible was written and compiled by fallible man, and . . . from beginning to end it gives abundant evidence of such origin." But this was a religious vision that put him at odds with all but the Garrisonian wing of the abolitionist movement.[75]

At the same time that he pondered religion, Murray was also contemplating social relations. Church and state were corrupt, mutually corrupt, reinforcing each other in corruption. What Murray found most disturbing was "the *false estimate* of things prevalent, by which *manual labor* is made *disreputable,* and exemption from it *honorable.*" Whether this hurt the working or leisure classes more, Murray was uncertain, but he was sure that this was "one of the most pernicious delusions that ever came over the minds of human beings." The former overexerted their physical strength and lost almost all opportunities for exercise that allowed for their highest development of mind. If all labor were divided equally for all classes, Murray estimated, no one would have to work more than five or six hours a day. That would leave everyone ten to twelve hours a day for "intellectual, moral, and religious improvement." But "modern religion" was doing nothing to right this situation. It did not make man more humane or more honest; it did not convert him from grinding the face of the poor—from deceiving and defrauding his neighbor—from covering up deception and fraud—from "trading in slaves and souls of men . . . from any sin, from the least to the greatest, provided it be tolerated by the community." Even in this Murray found the truth of the course he had taken, for, Murray concluded, "nothing is more unpopular than the advocacy of humanity and holiness."[76]

From one thing Murray could take comfort. Despite all of his opponents, there were some kindred souls who were coming to realize the same truths that he had found. Oliver Johnson, a leading Garrisonian, pronounced him "the fire-tried Murray, . . . the Clarkson of Vermont," and the New England Non-Resistance Society praised him. Henry C. Wright wrote that Murray was doing more good than all the sects, churches and ministers in Vermont. He kept up his lectures and debates in the towns and villages of Vermont, and, if "sectarians" were canceling subscriptions, and he was shut out of churches, other enlightened men and women were noticing the *Telegraph* and contributing to its columns, and, on occasion, to its receipts. In its January 8, 1843, issue, Murray noted a convention of such people, one that had gathered the previous month in Oakland, Ohio, to discuss questions of social development. Although he thought the deliberations of John A. Collins, John O. Wattles, Valentine Nicholson, Abraham Brooke, and their compatriots deficient in a few aspects, he pronounced their movement the most comprehensive and promising taking place. And within two years he would be casting his lot with them in Ohio.[77]

Thus it was that by 1842 Wattles, Collins, and Murray had committed themselves to radical reform, to a transformation of the world that would have as its basis the Government of God. They had come to such conclusions by different courses—while they were acquainted, there is nothing to indicate extensive interaction among them. They came to their commitments, however, from remarkably similar backgrounds. None was defending a threatened social status; for all three a career in the clergy was a step upward from the subsistence farming or near poverty that they had known in childhood. All shared a fervent evangelical faith. All saw a world sick with sin, threatened by a wrathful God, and filled with nominal Christians who wanted to ignore or compromise with evil. All had embraced various reforms—education, Sabbath schools, temperance, abolition—as means of making war on sin. By 1840, all had become convinced their duty as Christians was to repudiate all forms of coercive force and to anticipate and make ready the way for the coming of the Government of God.

Wattles, Collins, and Murray were not alone in this, of course, but they were moving beyond other nonresistants in their exploration of the implications of nonresistance and the meaning of the Government of God. Collins in particular saw violations of the divine plan not only in slavery and "sectism" but also in competitive capitalism. Murray was extending his repudiation of coercive force to the point of renouncing even religion. And while Wattles's thinking is less clear, subsequent events suggest that he, too, was coming to see a complete reorganization of society as necessary and imminent.

Such pondering was not limited to a small group of New Englanders, however. To the west, by 1842, other abolitionists, these Hicksite Quakers, were coming to very similar conclusions. Their encounter with Wattles, Collins, and Murray would lead all of them in radical new directions, ultimately to communitarianism and a vision of beginning God's Government.

THE HICKSITE QUAKER ROOTS OF
UNIVERSAL REFORM

ORSON S. MURRAY was a man who had little love for organized religion, but there was a soft spot in his heart for Hicksite Quakers. While far from perfect, he wrote in 1844, they were more capable of "breaking their religious chains, and traveling on to religious liberty, than . . . any other sect in my acquaintance."[1]

Murray had become acquainted with Hicksite Friends in abolition and other reform enterprises; not surprisingly, as Hicksites were prominent in "ultraist" causes in the 1830s and 1840s. They supported the Garrisonian wing of the antislavery movement. They provided much of the backing for the nonresistance movement outside New England. They were the source of a disproportionate number of early woman's rights advocates. And they made up much of the Society for Universal Inquiry and Reform.

Three Hicksite Friends were at the heart of this movement. The youngest, Valentine Nicholson, was a farmer first drawn to communitarianism by his acquaintance with the Shakers. An encounter with a strange, blind clairvoyant who claimed fantastic powers and foretold a happy life for Nicholson that would be lived in community confirmed his commitment to reform. Abraham Brooke was a physician who had by 1842 become the leading Garrisonian abolitionist in Ohio. He came to communitarianism as the culmination of an unrelenting search for moral purity that led him to repudiate almost every institution, starting with church and state. Hiram Mendenhall was a landowner and aspiring inventor with hopes of both wealth and political prominence in the Whig party. The depression of the late 1830s undermined his prosperity, and his political standing crumbled when he tried to face down Henry Clay before an audience of ten thousand Whigs. Thereafter he sought rewards, not in competition for money and office, but in radical reform, cooperation, and communitarianism.

Although these three men came to Universal Reform by different paths (there is nothing to indicate that Mendenhall knew Brooke or Nicholson before

1842), there were certain common threads of experience among them. All had come to maturity amongst the reforming zeal of the Hicksite Quakers of the 1820s, who saw themselves restoring the primitive purity of the Society of Friends; all three illustrate the strains within Hicksite Quakerism that would be prominent in Universal Reform. Nicholson was the incipient liberal, reading Tom Paine to the horror of his elders and exploring clairvoyance. Brooke was the questioner of authority, first civil (and as will be seen in chapter three), then religious. Mendenhall was one of the victims of the emerging market economy. At first successful in it, by 1842 he had reason to be skeptical about its promise.

There were other common threads of experience as well. All had begun their careers as reformers with a commitment to abolition. All had known isolation from like-minded folk for at least part of their lives. All encountered other reformers or reform works at critical points in their lives, but in most respects all three were self-made reformers. They painfully worked out commitments to abolition and kindred reforms in the backwoods of Ohio and Indiana with relatively little contact with others. And they did not stop with abolition. Led by abolition to a commitment to the Government of God, they were willing to follow the logic of their commitment to almost any extreme.

Valentine Nicholson

If our knowledge of the early lives of John O. Wattles and John A. Collins is at best reconstructed from bits and pieces of what others said and remembered about them, our sources for the life of Valentine Nicholson offer a striking contrast. Nicholson lived to the age of almost ninety-five, and he spent much of the last quarter century of his life attempting to reconstruct his first four decades, trying to understand, and to explain to an uncertain audience, what drew him toward communitarianism, and what attracted him to it even after the Civil War.

Nicholson's background differed in fundamental ways from that of the New Englanders Wattles, Murray, and Collins. He was born in Clinton County, Ohio, May 27, 1809, the son of Daniel and Elizabeth (Pegg) Nicholson. The Nicholsons were an English Quaker family who had come to Pennsylvania in William Penn's time, but had subsequently fallen away from Quakerism before migrating into the North Carolina backcountry. The Peggs were originally from the Eastern Shore of Maryland, where they had joined a peculiar little sect, the Nicholites. They were followers of Joseph Nichols, whose teachings, including opposition to slavery, were similar to Quakerism in many respects. In the 1770s, Valentine Pegg, Elizabeth's father, had moved south with a number of other Nicholites to Guilford County, North Carolina, where most of them joined the Society of Friends. After Daniel Nicholson and Elizabeth Pegg married, they followed a mass migration of Quakers out of North Carolina into Ohio and Indiana. They settled in the northwestern corner of Clinton County, Ohio, on a little stream called Turkey Run. In 1812 the Nicholsons joined the Society of Friends, becoming members of the Caesars Creek Monthly Meeting, which took in Quakers in parts of Greene, Clinton, and Warren counties.[2]

Nicholson's life was probably similar to that of any other boy growing up in the Ohio backwoods in the 1810s and 1820s. He remembered playing games, clearing land, and attending Quaker meetings for worship in the meetinghouse at Caesars Creek and at Chester near Wilmington. One experience, however, set the young Valentine apart from most of his contemporaries. His mother's brothers, Nathan and Caleb Pegg, had moved from North Carolina to Ohio and had become converts to Shakerism. They lived in Union Village near Lebanon. Although the Shakers were the targets of considerable hostility from others in the area, the Nicholsons frequently visited Nathan and Caleb, and Valentine was impressed by what he saw. "Their singing and marching and dancing always made a deep and serious sort of impression on my mind," he remembered many years later. "I was interested always in their preaching and was satisfied in my own mind that they had more correct opinions in some respects than any other professing Christian denominations with which I was then acquainted." At Union, he met some of the leaders of the group, particularly Richard McNemar, who had been a leading New Light Presbyterian minister in Kentucky and Ohio early in the century before he caused a minor sensation by converting to Shakerism.[3]

Valentine, by his own memory, was unusual in other ways. Unlike most boys his age, hunting repelled him. He recalled his first sight of a skinned animal when he was, he claimed, less than two: "It was repulsive and shocking to my young mind to see the bloody and bruised animals." He was also precocious, unusually drawn to books. One cousin, he remembered, told his mother: "Aunt, you will never raize [sic] this child, he's too smart to live." His formal education, was, however, limited to a few years in a Quaker "monthly meeting" school. He was self-educated in the truest sense.[4]

In 1827 young Valentine's world was shaken by the Hicksite separation among Friends. Waynesville, a few miles west of the Nicholson farm, was a center of Hicksite strength, as was Center a few miles to the east. At both

Valentine and Jane Nicholson, ca. 1850. Original in possession of
Theodore L. Steele, Indianapolis.

places young Nicholson heard leading Hicksite ministers—Thomas Wetherald,
Priscilla Hunt Cadwallader, Elias Hicks himself—preach. Valentine never left
an account of why he chose to cast his lot with the Hicksites, recording simply
that he was more in sympathy with them than with the Orthodox. Family connections were against it. His Pegg relatives—uncle John Pegg and aunts Lydia
Cook in Indiana and Mary Mendenhall back in North Carolina—were pillars of Orthodoxy. His only sister Bathsheba, married to Caleb Harvey, also
remained with the Orthodox. But in this, Valentine may have led his parents, since they did not request membership in the newly organized Hicksite
monthly meeting until two years after the separation.[5]

In 1830 Valentine married Jane Finley Wales. She was three years his elder,
and like Valentine came from a North Carolina Quaker family. She was born
in Iredell County, North Carolina, February 1, 1806, and came north to Ohio
with her parents, Isaac and Ruth (Welch) Wales, in 1815. The Waleses were a
close-knit group. Jane's sisters Nancy, married to Henry T. Butterworth, and
Caroline, who had married Milton Macy, and her brother Thomas M. Wales,
all stayed in Warren County, Ohio, and would remain an important, and largely
disapproving, influence in the lives of the Nicholsons.[6]

In 1835 Valentine and Jane, with two young daughters, moved far to the north and west, where they bought a farm on the prairie land of LaPorte County, Indiana. A little group of Hicksite Friends, mainly from Wayne County, Indiana, had settled in the area. The Nicholsons found the prairies beautiful, but the Indians still in the neighborhood and the wolves terrified Jane. LaPorte County did not become a center for Friends, and so in 1837 the Nicholsons went back to Warren County. They bought the old farm on Turkey Run from Valentine's parents, who had moved to Indiana. It was a struggle. The Nicholsons had sold the LaPorte County farm on credit, and in the hard times that began in 1837 the buyer had trouble keeping up the payments. Valentine had to make more than one trip back to try to come to terms. In 1838 they sold the Turkey Run farm and moved to Greene County, Ohio, just to the north. They remained there three years, before returning to live comfortably in Harveysburg in Warren County near Jane's mother.[7]

The trips between Ohio and LaPorte were to have at least two important consequences, at least in Valentine's mind. The first was to introduce him to reform; the second was to convince him that he was destined to live to see a new order of society.

There is a strain that can almost be described as mystical running through Nicholson's autobiographical writings, related probably at least in part to his later interest in spiritualism. Nicholson himself saw three such experiences as critical. The first of these took place while he still lived at LaPorte. Mowing marsh hay while standing in shallow water with a broiling sun brought on "a very severe spell of sickness." As he lay, apparently delirious, he found himself pondering "the strugle [sic] for wealth and fame," the necessity of storing minds with "useful knowledge," and the "injurious custom of monopolizing the land by those who had money." From his sickbed he began to exhort those around him, who told him that he was "out of his head." But he remained sure that he had, in the throes of sickness, come to some special insight.[8]

The second was the result of a chance encounter on a trip back to LaPorte. North of Logansport, he stopped for the night at a country tavern. The landlord and his wife were, in Valentine's words, "intelligent and kind people" with a number of books in their sitting room, among them Thomas Paine's *The Age of Reason*. Valentine had often heard "Tom Paine" and "the awful book called 'The Age of Reason' . . . referred to in sermons" and had heard Paine described as "one of the most dangerous and wicked men," and one "whose writings were dangerous books to read." Seeing it before him, he looked "into it just to see how bad it was," and was pleasantly surprised to find that he could agree with most of its sentiments, save its "harsh and sarcastic remarks concerning Jesus of Nazareth." He begged the loan of it from the landlord, who agreed, happy "to find a man who dared to honestly read and judge of the merits of the book." Returning home, he sent for all of Paine's published works, and encouraged several of his friends and family to follow suit. He thus found himself stirring considerable controversy. As he remembered in one case, "Uncle Ben Butterworth was greatly pleased and wanted to hear more of the sentiments and opinions of the author. Aunt Juda was frightened and wanted the book burned up." To this experience, he traced back the beginnings of his doubts about all religious orthodoxies.[9]

The last experience came in the winter of 1842–43. He had made another trip to LaPorte and was on his way home on a cold winter evening when he stopped at a hotel in Eaton, Ohio. Going into the barroom "as where the men were expected to spend the evening was in those days called" he looked at the various posters and advertisements that plastered the walls and saw one headed "The Science of Phrenology." It said that a blind man then in Eaton would prepare phrenological charts and would tell fortunes, telling about lost friends and relatives, and if and when they would ever meet again; and would find lost or stolen goods and identify the thieves. The landlord assured Nicholson that many of his neighbors had visited the strange man and had returned "perfectly thunderstruck declaring that he can do all he promises to do." That night Nicholson was troubled. As a Friend, he was bound by the exactions of the Discipline, which made it an offense to visit or encourage anyone who pretended to "any secret mode of telling things." Valentine as a boy had heard of such things, but had been taught that they were done through "conjuring" and the "black art." But, finally, he convinced himself that he "had the natural right, and not only the right, but . . . [the] duty to gain all the knowledge I could reasonably acquire if my motive was to use such knowledge for human welfare." And so he resolved to go.[10]

The next day, after breakfast, he headed for the Eagle Hotel, where he met a portly well-dressed man, his black hair and beard streaked with gray. "The moment I came near him," Nicholson remembered, "I felt a peaceful quiet and tranquil glow of happiness, trust, confidence, and repose, the same sort of interior feeling that I remember to have often felt in religious meeting when an excellent sermon was being delivered by some of our most eminent ministers. All fear and all doubt as to whether he was a good or a wicked man vanished away." The phrenologist, Dr. June, then gave Valentine an astonishing demonstration of his powers by first describing his personal appearance, then telling him of a number of events in Valentine's past life that Nicholson was sure could not have been known to anyone in Eaton—how he had spent his life, where he had lived, even the buildings on each of his farms. Then he foretold Valentine's future. He would live to old age; he had enjoyed life because he was "naturally cheerful, hopeful, and social in your nature and have kept your concince [sic] mostly clear." June went on to the heart of his predictions: "I see you come into acquaintance with a few others where there is mutual confidence and trust in the honesty and integrity of each other. I see you and two or three others go a long distance and draw writings for a large tract of land. And upon that land I see the most beautiful village spring up. I just love to look at it. The architectural finish of the houses is so verry [sic] beautiful, and the streets and gardens and shrubbery and groves all are so well arranged that there is not yet any thing on earth to equal the beauty of this village and you are directly interested in all this I know this will come true."[11]

Here the blind phrenologist paused and warned Valentine that the time would come when he would have to choose between two courses. He could follow the advice that June gave him, which would spare him considerable "loss and suffering," or he could choose to follow his own counsel and pass through trial and hardship, although the outcome would ultimately be happy. June left the choice to Valentine. And here, despite his confidence in the doctor, Nicholson decided not to ask for his advice. "If I should find myself following the advice of man whom the multitude would call a wizard in the place of following my own best judgement, it seemed to me I should lose a portion of my own self respect," he remembered years later. "In those days I was cheerful and buoyant in spirits, with a good deal of 'power of endurance,' and had met with disappointments, and thought I knew what it was to endure suffering for conscience sake." So he decided to "risk taking the experience." The doctor replied that ultimately all would be well, but "you will see the time when you will wish you had let me save you from the loss and suffering you are destined to pass through."[12]

Before the two men parted, Dr. June offered one other proof of his abilities. At no time in their conversation had Valentine identified himself, his occupation, or his reasons for traveling. Now the doctor told him that he would read to the incredulous Valentine the next two letters he would receive, neither of which had yet been written. One, June said, would be a check from a man who was buying a farm from him, made possible by the unexpected good fortune of the purchaser. The other would impress him more deeply—it would tell of the death of Valentine's sister's child.[13]

When he arrived home, Valentine found two friends, the equally zealous reformer, Dr. Abraham Brooke, and Barkley Gilbert, visiting with his wife. He told them of his experiences, and they responded with incredulity, ridiculing him for his gullibility and for "advocating so many silly, nonsensical and imposible [sic] things." So firmly convinced of June's abilities was Valentine, however, that he responded to his friends with a proposition. If the next two letters he received were not in every particular as June had described them, Valentine promised that he would "consent that you appoint a guardian for me and I promise I will never go from home or spend another dollar of my own money without the consent of my appointed guardian." But if he was right, then, as Valentine put it, "all I require of you will be to believe his other predictions . . . likely to prove true. And in that case you are to come to me for council [sic] about what books and papers you had better procure and read." All of them agreed. A few weeks later, Valentine arrived home from an antislavery meeting in Lebanon to find his wife, Dr. Brooke, and Gilbert in a state of consternation. The two letters had arrived, exactly in every detail as Dr. June had predicted.[14]

There is no evidence that any of the three lived up to their agreement—certainly Dr. Brooke and Valentine parted company on a number of points, and there is abundant evidence that Jane Nicholson did not defer to her husband even to the extent one would expect of a nineteenth-century wife, let alone one who had agreed that her husband possessed certain insights into the future. But for him it was a critical experience. As he wrote years later, "it will be easy to perceive, how the exact and perfect fulfilling of the prediction touching those two letters might have the effect to stimulate my hope and strengthen my faith and increase my zeal in the direction of Socil [sic] Reform or Cooperative, or Community life." In his view, the strange blind clairvoyant had "revealed the most astonishing evidence concerning possibilities and capabilities of the human mind." It was now clear to him that there were men and women who "had gained higher attainments in experience, in knowledge, and in ability to explain the mysterious portions of Nature's laws, than some of the rest had acquired the capacity to do." Earlier many of his friends, even his associates in antislavery activities, had ridiculed him for his interest in phrenology, mesmerism, and communitarianism. But now he had been given proof that it was possible to go beyond the normal limits of the human mind. For Nicholson, his life would be not so much effort as waiting—waiting for the men and women to appear who would possess the knowledge to take society into a new order, waiting for the proper time and circumstances for the fulfillment of Dr. June's vision.[15]

Valentine later saw Dr. June's prophecies as the turning point of his life, and they undoubtedly strengthened his commitment to reform. But it was an acceleration of a course on which he had already embarked. By his own account, he had been interested in "the reforms of our times" since "early childhood." In the 1830s, as organized antislavery activities auxiliary to the American Anti-Slavery Society began in Ohio, Valentine gave it his support. Indeed, his interest went back to the 1820s, when he had become a subscriber to Benjamin Lundy's *Genius of Universal Emancipation.* He also aided fugitive slaves who passed through Warren and Clinton counties on occasion. He remembered his first experience as a "conductor." About 1831, coming home from an election in Wilmington, he fell in with a black man, trudging along the road, a small bundle in his hand, who eyed him "verry [*sic*] earnestly." When Valentine asked where he was going, the black man answered, "to Canada," and confessed that he was a runaway slave. Somewhat surprised, Nicholson asked "if he told people generally whom he met on the road." "O, no Sir. I don't tell anybody." He went on to say that he trusted Nicholson because of the Quaker coat he wore, "and we know the Quakers are our friends." Valentine took him to other Quakers who helped him on his way to Canada.[16]

In all of his introspections, there are some maddening omissions. One of them is what drew Valentine Nicholson toward the Garrisonian wing of the antislavery movement. Writing about his memories of antislavery lecturers, Nicholson implies that the divisions in the East were not relevant to him and his compatriots. Nicholson recorded that one of the abolitionists he admired most was Arnold Buffum, who was a firm adherent of the "new society," allied with James G. Birney, Gamaliel Bailey and other political abolitionists. When he first met John O. Wattles, Wattles was staying with Jesse Harvey, another " 'new society' abolitionist, in Harveysburg. Indeed, he thought that some Garrisonians needed to lose their "tusks and claws." Nicholson, however, was attracted to many of the same things that distinguished Garrisonian abolitionists: woman's rights, nonresistance, religious "come-outerism." But what drew Nicholson toward them is still shadowy. It would be easy to say that his regard for these movements was the product of his Quakerism, and doubtless there was some relationship. But it would be an oversimplification to say that Nicholson was drawn to these causes because he was a Quaker. As we will see, many Quakers, while opposed to slavery, had reservations about abolition. Quakers did accept the equality of women within the Society of Friends, at least to an extent far beyond that of any other religious denomination, and Hicksite Quaker women would in the 1840s take a leading role in the nascent woman's rights movement. But they were exceptional; most Quaker women did not become feminists before the Civil War, and there was nothing inherent in Quakerism that automatically translated the equality of men and women as ministers into civil and social equality. As for nonresistance, it was different from traditional Quaker pacifism in a number of important ways. Probably most notably, Quaker pacifism had been, in its simplest, most basic form, a refusal to bear arms or to perform actions that had the effect of supporting war—drilling with the militia, selling supplies, paying taxes that were levied directly for war or in lieu of military service. But up to Nicholson's day, few Friends challenged the desirability of government or the likelihood that non-Quaker governments might have to resort to the use of force under certain circumstances. Nonresistance went far beyond that.[17]

So Valentine Nicholson and Jane Nicholson waited. And their lives were to be touched by the arrival in Clinton County of Friends from the East who brought a wider vision, the Brookes.

Dr. Abraham Brooke

In the background of all of these men, and in the background of Garrisonian abolition and radical reform generally in the West, is a shadowy figure, Dr. Abraham Brooke. To some at the time, he was the essence of the communitarian impulse, his life the incarnation of all radical reform. To others, he was an absurdity, a bundle of oddities and eccentricities who was a living caricature of the impossible consequences of the theories and doctrines he had embraced. Unfortunately, although Brooke was, in the words of the most careful student of Garrisonian abolition in the West, Douglas Gamble, its "leading figure," we know far less about him than his importance makes desirable. Unlike Nicholson, he left no autobiography; unlike Collins and Wattles, his papers and writings do not illuminate all of the aspects of his life. Instead, we have a handful of letters to other abolitionists, some articles written for reform journals, the comments of his enemies, and the memories of a few of his compatriots. Nonetheless, the effort to make sense of these is vital, since Brooke, in the minds of every one of his contemporaries, sympathetic and hostile, was central to these activities.[18]

Abraham was born in the Quaker community of Sandy Spring, Montgomery County, Maryland, in 1806, the son of Samuel and Sarah (Gerrigues) Brooke. The family was a prominent one; among Abraham's not distant relatives was Roger Brooke Taney, the Chief Justice of the United States Supreme

Court. The Brookes had been Roman Catholics and large slaveholders, but when James Brooke, Abraham's great-grandfather, married a Quaker, he embraced her faith. Abraham's grandmother, Mary Matthews Brooke, was a prominent Quaker minister. His mother's family the Gerrigueses, were Huguenots who had become Friends in Philadelphia in the eighteenth century.[19]

Of Brooke's early life we know nothing. There was a Quaker school of some note at Sandy Spring, so it seems likely that he attended it, but of even that we cannot be certain. A county history says that he attended lectures and graduated from a medical college in Baltimore. When the Hicksite separation took place among the Quakers in 1828, the Friends of Baltimore Yearly Meeting, of which Sandy Spring was a part, overwhelmingly sided with the Hicksite party. The Brooke family were among the majority. In 1829, Abraham married Elizabeth Lukens, a member of a large and prominent Quaker family. Two years later, Abraham and his brother William Brooke moved west and settled in Marlborough Township, Stark County, Ohio, a little north of the city of Alliance. By 1836, he and Elizabeth had become the parents of three children, Harriet, Henry, and Caroline Elizabeth, the first of whom died before the age of five.[20]

Once in Marlborough, Brooke found modest prosperity and the apparent respect of his neighbors. He bought farm land, perhaps as an investment, perhaps to supplement his earnings from his medical practice. He also won appointment as Marlborough's postmaster. This was somewhat surprising, since Brooke, like most Quakers, was a Whig in his political views. By 1833 Andrew Jackson had become the incarnation of everything nearly all Friends, Orthodox or Hicksite, found objectionable—a slave-owning, profane, military chieftain, of uncertain religious views.[21]

The turning point of Brooke's life came in 1836, with the arrival in Marlborough of Sereno W. Streeter, an agent of the American Anti-Slavery Society. Streeter was fresh from a successful organizing tour in Medina County, Ohio, in which he had faced down infidels and mobs. He was one of the shock troops of the early abolitionist cause—a convert of Charles G. Finney from the Burned-Over District of New York, a classmate of Augustus Wattles at Oneida, one of the "Lane Rebels," and a Presbyterian minister with close ties to Oberlin College. Streeter had come to Stark County, as he reported to Theodore Weld, to "stir up the abolitionists, see how the land lay, get our friends to turn out to the meeting of the County Society which was already appointed."[22]

Streeter was accustomed to opposition—"tar and feathers," "wooden horses," and "rails," as he put it, and when he came to Marlborough to give antislavery lectures, among those who attended with an entirely skeptical attitude was Abraham Brooke. We can only guess at what motivated Brooke's antiabolitionism—perhaps a liberal Quaker antipathy to a zealously evangelical Presbyterian, perhaps politics, perhaps a commitment to the older Quaker vision of gradual emancipation. For whatever reason, Brooke came to Streeter's first lecture with a set of notes in his pocket with which he intended to demolish the abolitionist's arguments. Instead, by the end of Streeter's course of four addresses, an antislavery society had been formed in Marlborough; Abraham Brooke was its secretary; and Streeter had made the Brooke home his headquarters. Once committed, Brooke was fully committed. He corresponded with the treasurer at Oberlin about sending his wife's half-brother and sister, Joseph and Susan Lukens, there as students, to advance their education and to remove Joseph from the proximity of evil companions. And in April Brooke was present at the meeting of the Ohio State Anti-Slavery Society.[23]

Brooke apparently led many of his family into abolition. The families of Abraham and William had been joined in Marlborough in 1832 by their parents, Samuel and Sarah Brooke, sisters Mary and Margaret, and brother Edward. Edward was also to be an active abolitionist, although there is no evidence that he shared all of his brother's other interests.[24]

Late in the 1830s, the Brooke family uprooted itself and moved across the state to Clinton County, buying farms near the crossroads town of Oakland in the northwest corner of the county. Abraham and Elizabeth went in 1837, with the rest of the family, save for Edward, following in 1839. Again, we have no indication of what drew them to Oakland, and ultimately the family all returned to Marlborough. But those years in Clinton County were to be critical.[25]

Abraham Brooke bought fifty-five acres on the road from Wilmington to Waynesville. Almost immediately he and his wife made their mark on local antislavery activities. They led in organizing a Chester Township Anti-Slavery Society in the late summer of 1839. They pondered the implications of using slave produce. They became involved in a spectacular slave rescue case. And they led the split of Garrisonian abolitionists from the larger abolitionist movement in Ohio.[26]

After his move to Oakland, Brooke continued to play an active role in the affairs of the Ohio Anti-Slavery Society. In the late 1830s, the pressures that were creating tensions among abolitionists in the East also began to affect the Ohio group. Brooke identified himself with the Garrisonian group, as did many other Hicksite Quaker abolitionists in Ohio, on issues such as nonresistance, woman's rights, and relations with the established denominations. The

Clinton County Anti-Slavery Society, and several of its local affiliates, however, were by no means united on that score. They included Orthodox Friends who saw Garrisonianism as synonymous with infidelity, and others, who, for whatever reason, took a more conservative view of the most effective antislavery strategy. In the late summer of 1839 Charles C. Burleigh, a New Englander with close ties to Garrison, toured Ohio giving lectures. One of his stops was Oakland, where he presided over the formation of a new local antislavery society affiliated with the American Anti-Slavery Society. The Brooke family were members of the new group, which began its career by passing resolutions that expressed their "entire approbation" of the "firm and uncompromising stand" that Garrison had "taken in opposing a pro-slavery clergy; 'dumb dogs' that will not bark." Significantly, and in contrast to most other antislavery societies, which separated men and women, the new group at Oakland was "mixed," including men and women on equal terms.[27]

Brooke was by this time pondering the economic implications of slavery and antislavery. This made him an early advocate of the Free Produce movement, one of the logical outgrowths of antislavery. In August 1838 he penned a piece for the *Philanthropist* in Cincinnati. The Discipline of Friends, he pointed out, required them to bear a testimony against "prize goods" as a logical consequence of their testimony against war—just as Friends could not take part in wars, so they could not use or traffic in goods or merchandise that had been seized as a result of war. Brooke argued that abolitionists should be equally scrupulous in avoiding the use of the products of slavery. "What difference can there be in my holding [slaves] here, did the law permit it, to cultivate my wheat and corn, or to pay an agent there to drive them, to the task of raising my sugar and cotton?" he asked. Yet Brooke was not completely certain himself of the logic of his position. "I wish some correspondent in the Philanthropist would resolve these doubts of mine," he wrote, "for I find that abstinence from these products is somewhat inconvenient, yet with my present feeling am constrained to submit to this inconvenience." This note of moral uncertainty was one that would seldom recur again in Abraham Brooke's life. Rather the dominant chord would be the one on which he closed his exhortation. "Doubtless, if as a body we should refuse to use or to vend the produce of slave-labor, we should thereby produce a strong impression on the ranks of slavery," he concluded, "but our main purpose should be to purify ourselves individually from all participation in this horrible sin." By 1841, he would have no doubts. "To have a conscience void of offence is my reason for advocating and practicing total abstinence," he wrote to the editor of a new periodical, the *Free Labor Advocate.*

This would be the center of Brooke's life: a crusade for absolute purity, a quest to disassociate himself from all sin.[28]

In the fall of 1840 Brooke had an opportunity to take direct action against slavery. On October 1, he saw wagons with several blacks inside on the Waynesville Road. The suspicious doctor made inquiries and discovered that it was a party of movers from Virginia on their way to Missouri with several slaves. He immediately went into action. He sent some friends to Waynesville to enlist help. Others headed for Lebanon, the seat of Warren County, toward which the movers were traveling. Brooke himself set out after the party, hoping to have a chance to talk with the slaves. In that he failed, but the Virginians, not knowing who he was, doubtless gave the good doctor a bitter satisfaction. They had already told others along the way that in Wilmington several people had warned them to avoid the neighborhood of Oakland, which was a nest of abolitionists who would attempt to steal their slaves. But the Virginians breathed defiance in reply, and greeted those who attempted to converse with the slaves by displaying a small arsenal of loaded guns and butcher knives which they vowed they would use against anyone who threatened their property. They declared, moreover, that they had heard of the abolitionist Dr. Brooke even in Virginia. The cup of his iniquities was full, and they would see that he met his just fate.[29]

Dr. Brooke, however, did not tarry to tempt fate or test the Virginians' resolve. Instead he hurried off to Lebanon to hire two lawyers. He had decided not to bring a suit to free the slaves, reasoning that they had become free when they entered Ohio. Instead, Abraham Allen, another sympathetic Hicksite Friend, filed the necessary affidavit to charge the Virginians with kidnapping. The idea of using the law not just to gain the slaves' freedom, but also to punish their owners, seemed peculiarly appealing to Brooke.[30]

The hearing before a justice of the peace in Waynesville, however, was disappointing and frightening. An antiabolitionist mob had collected, and it frequently interrupted the proceeding with hoots, yells, and applause. Brooke's attorneys argued that since, by the Northwest Ordinance of 1787, slavery was forbidden in Ohio, the Virginians, by attempting to hold slaves within the state, were guilty of kidnapping. The abolitionists also attempted to use a provision of the Ohio Black Laws that required a hearing before an accused fugitive slave could be taken from the state. The Virginians' attorney responded that the Northwest Ordinance did not apply to slaves in transit from one slave state to another and that the Black Laws certainly did not apply, since the blacks were not fugitives. The justice found these arguments convincing and released the movers. Their supporters burst into excited celebration, calling for rails on which to ride the abolitionists out of Waynesville. When Brooke and his friends left the store where the justice's court was held, he was peppered with rocks by the crowd, five or six finding their mark. There were numerous calls from the mob "Kill him!" aimed at Brooke, and when a young black boy, with especially bad timing, came on the scene, he did barely escape from the knives and guns of the Virginians. Then the mob triumphantly escorted the Virginians and their slaves to the county line. Brooke made a final attempt to get a writ of habeas corpus, but could not find any lawyer willing to undertake the case. Later Brooke found out that the Virginians, insecure in their legal victory, had put the slaves in a carriage and had hurried them to Kentucky, where their status could not be challenged.[31]

Afterwards, local abolitionists expressed reservations about Brooke's strategy. Bringing kidnapping charges was absurd, they argued; far better simply to get a writ of habeas corpus, which had been successful in other, similar cases, including one in the same area earlier in the year. Apparently the criticisms left Brooke unsettled, for in a long account of the case for the *Philanthropist,* he concluded with a vision of the nature of law and its relationship to the anti-slavery cause.[32]

Brooke's answer to these charges shows that he was moving to embrace non-resistance. "With such as believe we cannot justly enforce penalties as a punishment for crime, I have no controversy," he wrote. Society could, "*under the control of the moral law,*" use coercive force to "restrain crime, and to reform offenders," but not as punishment. Thus he thought that the current system of criminal justice was completely wrong. But with this Brooke combined the urge for unwavering consistency and the desire for complete simplicity that would distinguish him for the next decade. The letter of the law was clear, he said—kidnapping was a crime. And what was kidnapping but to hold a person against his or her will, the very definition of slavery? In order for society to possess any sort of coherence, laws had to be interpreted not according to speculations about the intentions of their framers but by what they said. To do otherwise was to forfeit, in Brooke' s view, not just legal and moral consistency, but all law and morality. The doctor's determination to follow the implications of his positions to conclusions that even sympathizers found impractical or self-defeating would become increasingly pronounced.[33]

Soon afterwards, Brooke and some associates had the tables turned on them in another case, one that dated back over a year. In November 1839 another group of Virginians, the family of one Bennet Rains, had passed through Oakland with several slaves, bound for Missouri. Brooke and a large party of abolitionists, black and white, had set off in pursuit, overtaking the Rainses near Springborough that evening. By the doctor's account, both sides were relatively restrained. Brooke did threaten that unless the abolitionists were allowed to enter the movers' tent that they would tear it up and pitch it over a fence, while the women of the party were, in Brooke's words, "very abusive and profane." Brooke, knowing that the slaves would be wary of strange whites, sent some of the black members of his party to talk to them. After about an hour of negotiations, the abolitionists left with the four slaves and quickly sent them to a place of safety.[34]

A few days later, however, a large group of men banging on his door awakened Brooke after midnight. It was a party of "ruffians" from Franklin, Ohio, led by the mayor, Samuel Leonard, and Rains. They bore warrants charging Brooke and over twenty others with stealing from Rains four slaves and $1,500 in cash. All were hauled off to Lebanon, where an additional charge of riot was brought against them. After the hearing where they posted bail, a proslavery mob greeted them with rocks and eggs. Despite the fact that many in the mob were easily identifiable, no charges were ever brought against any of the participants.[35]

The trial was, by almost any standard, an extraordinary affair. It was held in the November 1840 term, with Rains and his party as the chief witnesses. Brooke and seventeen of the others accused did not deny having told Rains's slaves to leave; three of the men named in the indictment were, by their own claims, supported by the other participants, not even present. The court, however, even in the absence of any evidence of their presence, refused to release them. During the trial, the courtroom was filled with antiabolitionists, and members of the jury were warned of dire consequences if the "slavestealers" were acquitted. Under the circumstances, it was probably not surprising that the jury, while acquitting all of the defendants of the theft and abduction charges, found fourteen of them guilty of riot. The defendants immediately filed a bill of errors, and so judgment was suspended until the March 1841 term. At that time, after more wrangling among the lawyers for the defendants, the prosecutor, and the judge, thirteen of the party were fined and sentenced to five days in the county jail on bread and water. Abraham's brother James was released because of poor health, but the rest spent two days in the jail before the supreme court in Cincinnati overturned the verdict. They were supposed to be retried, but that never happened.[36]

That Brooke was ready to break the law, when conscience demanded it, there

can be no doubt. On several occasions he violated state and federal law by aiding fugitive slaves. But these experiences with courts and lawyers—courts that
gave their protection to manstealers, that acquitted kidnappers, that accepted
perjured testimony, that sent fellow humans back into slavery, that imprisoned
friends of the oppressed—gave him a sour view of the benefits of law as cur-
rently conceived. Thus, after 1840 Brooke moved increasingly toward a vision
that saw the end of slavery simply as a part of a plethora of reforms that could
remake American society, and, ultimately, the world.[37]

At the same time that he was attempting direct action against slavery, and
suffering disappointments because of it, he confronted the politics of antislavery in other ways. As we have seen, in the spring of 1840, the American Anti-
Slavery Society split. The immediate issue was the role of women, and whether
or not women should serve on the national organization's board of directors
and be sent as delegates to the World's Anti-Slavery Convention that was being
held in London later that year. But there were other elements involved as well.
The conservative abolitionists who withdrew to form the American and Foreign Anti-Slavery Society, often called the "new organization," were also troubled by the vehemence of the radical abolitionists' attacks on the churches and
on political action as an antislavery tactic. As Gamaliel Bailey, the editor of the
Cincinnati *Philanthropist* and Brooke's favorite foil, put it, the main sources of
contention would "be ranged under the general heads of *non-resistance, woman's
rights,* denunciation of the *clergy, personal ambition,* unavoidable sectarian affinities and *prejudice*." The split came not long before the Ohio Anti-Slavery
Society's annual meeting at Massillon. As an affiliate of the national organization, the Ohio group had to choose if it would retain its ties to either.[38]

When the meeting came, a majority of those present chose what they apparently perceived as a position of neutrality. They broke their affiliation with
the American Anti-Slavery Society, on the grounds that not to do so would be
to identify themselves with the positions of Garrison on the vexed subjects of
nonresistance and woman's rights. By not affiliating with the rival "new group,"
the American and Foreign Anti-Slavery Society, the Ohio abolitionists were
showing, according to Bailey, that the divisive squabbles in the East were irrelevant to Western abolitionists, and Ohio antislavery men and women could continue to work in unbroken ranks. Still, Bailey considered the Garrisonians to
blame for the split in the East by attempting to force their views on peace,
women and the churches on all abolitionists; by his own account, he was "itch-
ing to be at" Garrison, but refrained from fear of aggravating tensions. To
Bailey, it would have been comparable for the large number of Quakers in the

Ohio Anti-Slavery Society to insist that all of its members accept the distinctive views of Friends on all subjects.[39]

Abraham Brooke, however, saw the situation quite differently. As Gamble has noted, Brooke's analysis remarkably presaged that of scholarly admirers of Garrison a century and a quarter later. Brooke replied to Bailey that the Ohio abolitionists had not adopted a position of neutrality at all; everyone understood that their refusal to keep up ties with the organization that had nurtured them for five years was a repudiation of it. Moreover, in Brooke's view, Bailey's statement of the issues was backwards. "By refusing to remain connected with the American Anti-Slavery Society, because some of the members of another auxiliary society differed in opinion with them on topics independent of the anti-slavery cause," Brooke wrote, the Ohio majority showed "a disposition so as to narrow the anti-slavery platform, as to render an effective national organization impracticable." If remaining connected was to endorse Garrisonian abolition, Brooke asked, then how could not a withdrawal be anything but a repudiation and condemnation? Most disturbing to Brooke was the thought that by breaking with the "old society," Ohio abolitionists had "virtually sanctioned the doctrine that an inequality exists between the rights of males and females." Bailey and his sympathizers might deny that, but Brooke challenged them to place a woman in an office or on a committee. "I guess her right to serve the society will not only be denied, but the action of the [American and Foreign Anti-Slavery Society] seceders and that of our convention at Massillon will be offered as precedents to justify it," he sadly concluded.[40]

Still, Brooke was not completely in the Garrisonian camp, particularly on the question of nonresistance. At the state meeting in Massillon, he had urged the society's endorsement of the Free Produce movement as the appropriate instrument of moral suasion to wage war on slavery, and he continued to press for that position. He was not ready, however, to give up political action against slavery completely, and that put him strangely at odds with the Garrisonians with whom he sympathized on other points, and in alliance with Gamaliel Bailey.[41]

These events were being played out against the backdrop of the election of 1840. For the first time, an explicitly antislavery party, the Liberty party, had nominated candidates for the presidency and vice-presidency, and had put forward candidates for other offices as well. Since the Liberty candidate, James G. Birney, had lived in Cincinnati, Ohio was at the center of Liberty party politics. The Liberty party was inextricably tied up with the American and Foreign Anti-Slavery Society, however, and was the subject of an onslaught of vituperation by Garrisonians, who insisted that since the Constitution sanctioned slavery in a variety of ways, and since all government rested on the foundation of coercive force, no consistent abolitionist, and certainly no consistent nonresistant could engage in political activity, let alone vote.[42]

Both the editor and the doctor, however, were prepared to break with their natural allies on this question. Bailey opposed the formation of a third party as being counterproductive. Many Ohio abolitionists still retained intense party loyalties, particularly to Whigs, and a demand that they cut those ties would instead result in their loss to the abolitionist ranks. Thus Bailey's commitment to maintaining unity among Ohio abolitionists dictated his tactics. When he issued a call for a meeting of southern Ohio abolitionists at Hamilton on September 1, however, he found Brooke endorsing the project and urging that all Ohio abolitionists attend.[43]

In this Brooke was virtually alone among Ohio Garrisonian abolitionists, who shunned the Hamilton gathering. Brooke, however, apparently still retained an inconsistent faith in the possibilities of the republican foundations of American government. A year later, even after his disastrous tangles with the court system, he was still calling for petition campaigns to eliminate the 3/5 clause that gave the slave states extra members of the House of Representatives. "As a republican, I can never submit to this," Brooke wrote, but instead had to obtain "an equal amount of political power with any other class of citizens." Brooke also took issue with Garrison publicly over the *Liberator*'s attacks on the Liberty party. Whether Brooke himself voted for Birney is unknown. He at this time considered himself a Liberty man, but he thought it inconsistent of the Garrisonians to want to expel from the abolitionist ranks those who saw utility in the Liberty party. After all, they had broken with more conservative antislavery forces because of conservative insistence on expelling those who disagreed with them. Even though he sometimes faltered, Brooke continued the pursuit of consistency.[44]

So by 1841 Brooke had emerged as a major force in Ohio abolition. But, unlike Gamaliel Bailey, he was beginning to explore the radical implications of his thought. And that would take him in extraordinary directions.

Hiram Mendenhall

Ultimately, the person who made the greatest commitment of his means to reform, and lost the most from that commitment, was the third of the Hicksite Quakers, Hiram Mendenhall. He came late to the enterprise. There is no evidence that Mendenhall had any contact with any of the other principals before 1842. But once committed, Mendenhall put all of his substance at the disposal of the cause, and became its foremost victim.

Mendenhall, like Nicholson and Brooke, had roots in a slave state. He was born in Randolph County, North Carolina, February 20, 1801. As a child, he had come north with his parents, Nathan and Ann (Harlan) Mendenhall, in 1807. They settled in the western part of Clinton County, Ohio, in a Quaker settlement on Todd's Fork, known as Springfield. There he married Martha Hale, daughter of Jacob and Martha Hale, of neighboring Warren County, November 27, 1821. Martha Hale Mendenhall, like her husband, was a native of Randolph County, North Carolina, and had come north with her parents about the same time as the Mendenhalls.[45]

We know nothing of the early life of either Hiram or Martha; it is even more shadowy than Abraham Brooke. We have a brief biography put together by his children in the 1880s, the reminiscences of one of his sons, some scattered snippets in newspapers, two letters written near the end of his life, a mass of papers generated by a lawsuit, and a file of bad debts painfully collected after his death. The scarcity of personal materials is all the more exasperating because of all those who committed themselves to the cause of Reform in 1843, Mendenhall was the most notorious; indeed, his name was probably known to every Whig and abolitionist in the United States.[46]

After their marriage, Hiram and Martha settled on a heavily wooded tract of land on Flat Fork in Warren County, not too far from their old homes. There they prospered; fifteen years after starting life in a one-room cabin in the woods, they had a farm of 216 acres, a brick house, and a big frame barn. Hiram and his brother Nathan Jr. had a reputation as skilled mechanics, and Hiram supplemented his farming income in a variety of ways.[47]

The first turning point of the Mendenhalls' lives came in the mid-1820s in the Hicksite separation among Friends. In many ways their experience was similar to that of Valentine Nicholson—the Springfield meeting was an Orthodox stronghold, yet they chose to cast their lot with the Hicksites. Their son Joseph, writing half a century later, said that they were drawn to the Hicksite wing by reading some of Elias Hicks's published sermons. That is plausible; some of the sermons were in print by 1825, and Joseph's description suggests that they had the series that became the first volume of *The Quaker*, a collection of Hicksite sermons that began publication in 1827. In casting their lot with the Hicksites, Martha's influence may have been decisive; while the Hales were Hicksites, Nathan and Ann Mendenhall and the rest of their children were Orthodox.[48]

Religious differences did not sunder family ties in this case, however. There is considerable evidence of continued close links between Hiram and Martha on one hand and his parents and siblings on the other. In 1835 Hiram, his brother Nathan, and their parents began buying tracts of land in Randolph County, Indiana. In April 1836 Hiram and Martha moved their family, now consisting of two daughters and four sons, to the new land in Indiana. Behind them they left twin sons who had died at two months in the autumn of 1835. Two more sons were born in Indiana.[49]

All indications are that Hiram had become a capitalist on a minor scale,with considerable ambitions. The farm in Warren County, which he had bought in two tracts from his father for $700, he sold in 1839 to his brother-in-law Eli Hale for $6,000. Meanwhile he had begun an aggressive land buying campaign in Randolph County. By the end of 1836 he owned 1,000 acres, and for the next few years he continued to buy and sell. On one of the tracts he laid out in 1837 a town that he named Unionsport. He also built a grist mill, a carding mill, a woolen mill, a woodshop, and smithy. By 1840 Unionsport had become a trad-ing point for the surrounding countryside.[50]

In 1838, Mendenhall entered local politics in two ways, and met defeat on both occasions because of neighbors to the south. In the fall of 1838 he orga-nized a campaign to form a new township that had Unionsport at its center. The county commissioners granted the petition, and appointed Mendenhall the inspector of elections. Early in 1839, however, there was another petition campaign organized, this one to dissolve the new township. Apparently the commissioners found the new petitioners more persuasive, since early in 1839 Union Township ceased to exist. The meaning of this episode is unclear. It is hard to see what advantage Mendenhall would have derived from the new township, unless it was the hope that Unionsport would become its polling place and thus, at least once a year, attract more trade.[51]

We know more about Mendenhall's other foray into politics. In the state election in August of 1838 he sought Randolph County's seat in the state legis-lature. It was not exactly a partisan contest; both he and the incumbent, Miles S. Hunt, were Whigs, but the election does tell us much about Mendenhall. Hunt was part of a large family clustered around the village of Huntsville, about three miles south of Unionsport. They had every reason to resent Men-denhall as an interloper whose enterprises threatened their own. There were also religious differences. Miles's father, "Old Billy" Hunt, was a Methodist minister from Kentucky known for his rigid orthodoxy and fire-and-brimstone preaching. He doubtless had no love for Quakers, especially those tinged with infidelity, as which many regarded Hicksite Friends. More to the point, the Hunts were rabid antiabolitionists. "Old Billy" regularly confronted any abolition lecturer coming through the neighborhood, and his house was a favorite resort of slave catchers. The Hunts and their partisans industriously went to work charging that Mendenhall was a fanatical abolitionist who had been circulating petitions calling for blacks to be given the vote. Moreover, Mendenhall intended his new township to become a stronghold of free blacks.[52]

Hunt won the election; no records have survived to show the margin. It is impossible to know whether his charges against Mendenhall were crucial in his victory. He was the incumbent, part of a large and well-connected family, while Mendenhall was a relative newcomer. And while racism was endemic to Indiana throughout the nineteenth century, there is reason to believe that Randolph County may have been more enlightened; in 1851 it was one of four counties in the state to vote against a black-exclusion clause in the new state constitution. But Mendenhall believed that Hunt had slandered him, and with his "gross slander" had won the seat. In a letter published after the election, Mendenhall denied that there had been any such petition; given the provisions of the state constitution, it would have been futile. Moreover, Mendenhall wrote that he had always been opposed "to push[ing] an object not only as being inimical to the citizens but to the colored people themselves."[53]

What is noteworthy is that Mendenhall did not deny the other charge, that of being an abolitionist. His son Joseph later claimed that Hiram embraced abolition in 1837, converted through conversations with two neighbors. If so, they were among the first abolitionists in Indiana. There was no state antislavery society organized until the autumn of 1838; no one from Randolph County was present at the meeting. It was not until the fall of 1839 that the abolitionist cause began to emerge in the state, with the arrival of an embattled and controversial figure from New England, Arnold Buffum.[54]

Buffum came west as the duly accredited agent of the American Anti-Slavery Society, charged with organizing anti-slavery societies and giving new life to the fledgling Indiana Anti-Slavery Society. It was Buffum who shaped the antislavery movement in Indiana. Before his arrival, it had been a fragmented group, mostly Presbyterian. Buffum, however, set up headquarters in Newport in Wayne County, and concentrated his organizing efforts on the Quaker counties of eastern and central Indiana—Wayne, Union, Henry, Grant, Hamilton, and Randolph. He traveled incessantly, lecturing and debating; early in 1840 he began publishing an abolitionist journal, the *Protectionist*, in Newport.[55]

Buffum was a veteran abolitionist. A Quaker from Rhode Island, he had been one of the founders of the American Anti-Slavery Society in 1833, and had been involved in a variety of antislavery activities for the rest of the decade. He had also served for a time as the president of the New England Anti-Slavery Society. In practical affairs, however, he was far from successful. Failing in various mercantile pursuits (at one point he and his family were reduced to working in a cotton mill), he also dabbled in land speculation, sheep-raising, and teaching. He had also sought fortune with a variety of inventions. His business pursuits took him to Connecticut, to Europe, and finally in the 1830s to Philadelphia, where he manufactured and imported hats and tried to perfect an improved steam engine. The Panic of 1837 left him bankrupt, and his tangled financial ruin also brought him disownment by the Orthodox Quakers. His agency in the West, along with the *Protectionist*, provided him with the barest of livings.[56]

When the 1840 split came, Buffum took the fledgling Indiana Anti-Slavery Society into the conservative wing, affiliated with the American and Foreign Anti-Slavery Society. He was a confirmed political abolitionist as well. The chief target of his wrath was the Democratic party which, in his view, had prostrated northern commerce with its Southern-dictated low tariff policies. He also had close ties with James G. Birney, the Liberty party leader. In August 1840, at Buffum's urging, a convention of abolitionists from the Upper Whitewater Valley was held in Newport to discuss political action. Whig Congressman James Rariden, however, appeared at the meeting and apparently was successful in convincing the group that a third party would only work to the benefit of the Democrats. After the election, however, the abolitionists met again in the Wayne County village of Economy to form the Indiana Liberty party. By the spring of 1841, they had a full ticket on the ballot in the Quaker counties in the eastern part of the state.[57]

Buffum and Mendenhall had much in common. Both were Quakers who had suffered disownment by the Orthodox—Buffum was still the center of considerable hostility emanating from the more cautious of the Orthodox group in Indiana Yearly Meeting. Both were small capitalists who had had dreams of amassing wealth, dreams that proved illusory. Both were men of mechanical inclinations and aptitude, fascinated by machinery and technology. Both were interested in politics as a means of advancing antislavery. It seems almost certain that while Mendenhall may have had abolitionist leanings earlier, Buffum brought him into the antislavery movement, including abolitionist politics.[58]

That conversion was gradual. Mendenhall's loss in the 1838 legislative election had not alienated him from the Whigs; he was a delegate to the 1840 Whig state convention. By 1842, however, he was in the thick of Liberty party politics, and that would bring him his brief moment of national recognition.

In the fall of 1842 Henry Clay was touring western Ohio and Indiana. He was the certain Whig presidential nominee in 1844, and the trip through the "West" was designed to kindle enthusiasm comparable to that which the Harrison campaign had aroused in 1840. Clay was the political hero of the Whitewater country; the Whig press already carried his name at the head of its editorial columns. "Clay is emphatically the people's man, and though persons may differ with him on political principles," opined the *Richmond Palladium;* "no man worthy of the name of a MAN, doubts his patriotism, his integrity, his talents, and his ability to administer the Executive duties of the nation." When word was received that Clay planned to be in Richmond, Indiana, October 1 and 2, plans were immediately made for an elaborate welcome by the local Whig faithful.[59]

Others, however, viewed Clay's imminent arrival with an interest that the Whigs found appalling. The Indiana State Anti-Slavery Society held its annual meeting in Newport in September, with the state central committee of the Liberty party meeting concurrently. During the society's meeting a motion was agreed on to circulate a petition, for presentation in Richmond, calling on Clay to free his slaves. Daniel Worth of Randolph County, the society's president and the chairman of the party's state committee, took responsibility for the presentation. The abolitionists had no reason to love Clay. He was not only the owner of fifty slaves but in 1839 had publicly condemned all forms of emancipation, immediate or gradual. The adulation of Clay by most Quakers, who were usually staunch Whigs, was a further source of irritation.[60]

The petition was controversial. The abolitionists circulated drafts in Wayne, Randolph, Henry, and Union counties, gathering almost two thousand signatures. The signers' names are unknown. The *Free Labor Advocate* of Newport, the successor to the *Protectionist,* obliquely described them as "citizens of Indiana." The Whigs countered that a third of the signers were Democrats, whose only interest was to embarrass Clay; another third were free blacks; and of the last third, whom it admitted were probably abolitionists, a good many were women. The Whigs knew about the petition; it would have been almost impossible to keep it a secret. One local newspaper, the Centerville *Wayne County Record,* printed its text five days before Clay's arrival and argued that its presentation would be a "breach of hospitality" and an "insult." Subsequent Whig strategy is unclear, but there is some reason to think that the local Whig leaders, with Whig Congressman James Rariden at their head, chose to use the petition to their advantage.[61]

Saturday, October 1, dawned warm and sunny. Clay arrived at the Ohio-Indiana state line about ten that morning and entered Richmond half an hour later, "to the deafening and spontaneous shouts of the yeomanry of the country"; one probably overenthusiastic observer claimed that eight hundred carriages and wagons accompanied him. When Clay arrived at his hotel he found Worth, Mendenhall, and two others awaiting him with the petition. They were told that he would receive them the next morning and departed. Next followed a council whose proceedings Hiram described to his son Amos: "The pro-slavery politicians saw their chance. A pro-slavery politician from Indianapolis was particularly adamant that the presentation be made in public to embarrass the d——d abolitionists." Hiram's access to such deliberations is doubtful, but the events that followed confirmed that he was probably not far from the mark.[62]

That afternoon Clay addressed a crowd estimated at ten thousand. The Orthodox Friends were holding their yearly meeting in Richmond, so broad-brimmed hats and plain bonnets were much in evidence. His speech dealt with stock issues: the tariff, banking, and Democratic corruption. When Clay finished, Rariden, the president of the day, announced that there was a committee of abolitionists present with a petition to present and invited it to come forward. Considering the circumstances, Worth quickly concluded that this was a Whig trick to stir up antiabolitionist animosity. However, he had become separated from the other three men in the crowd. After consulting briefly they sent forward Mendenhall, who with his height and strength could force his way through the crowd, with the petition.[63]

Events followed quickly after Mendenhall arrived at the speaker's stand. Clay refused to touch the petition, but had Rariden read it to him. He then appealed to the crowd, which had begun to murmur angrily, for calm. Then Clay spoke for about twenty minutes, condemning slavery and abolition as twin evils, complimenting the Society of Friends for its moderate antislavery stance, and concluding with an admonition to Mendenhall and all abolitionists to "go home and mind their own business."[64]

From all accounts, the partisan crowd loved the speech. The Whig newspapers were lost in admiration and unrestrained in their description of the assembly's enthusiastic response. William H. Coffin, a young Quaker himself sympathetic to abolition, wrote of the conclusion of Clay's address: "Then came a mighty and prolonged roar from the excited ten thousand . . . and Mr. Mendenhall went into a hole, pulled the hole, and disappeared." Whigs had a field day representing "fanatical abolitionists" as "assaulting" Clay with the petition, violating the duties of hospitality. Returning to the home of his uncle, James R. Mendenhall, a prominent Richmond physician (and a delegate to the 1839 Whig national convention) with whom he had been staying, Hiram was told that he had disgraced "his name, family, self, state, country, and human nature itself," and to leave immediately and never return. Abolitionists were quiet about the response to Clay's effort, save for acerbic comments about the warm reception given "the high priest of American slavery" by the Orthodox Friends and the telling hope that "there are yet 7,000 in our Israel who have not bowed the knee to the Baal of slavery, nor kissed his image."[65]

For the next few weeks "Mr. Mendenhall, the Quaker" had his name in newspapers across the country. For abolitionists Mendenhall became something of a hero. Virtually every antislavery journal in the country noted and commented critically on Clay's performance. At least one antislavery society in upstate New York forwarded resolutions praising Mendenhall and his conduct under trying circumstances.[66]

Still, the events in Richmond were a point of no return for Mendenhall. His dreams of material success were fading. The Whig newspapers probably were engaging in selective gossip when they said that Mendenhall was a man of very limited means whose affairs were sadly neglected, but he did have debts, including legal judgments against him, that amounted to fifteen hundred dollars. These forced him to sell off land, over half of his holdings. His notoriety did not enhance business prospects. And certainly any hopes that Mendenhall had of political success as a Whig had vanished when he publicly tried to face down the national leader of the Whig party. For Mendenhall, there was little left save to attempt to salvage some of his tangled affairs and pursue his interests in reform. In little more than a year he would find a way to combine the two.[67]

❖ 3 ❖

THE SOCIETY FOR UNIVERSAL INQUIRY
AND REFORM BEGINS

BY 1842 A variety of reformers had concluded that the redemption of the
United States from the sins in which it was enmeshed required reform far more
thorough and far-reaching than they had realized previously. Wattles, Collins,
Murray, Brooke, Nicholson, and Mendenhall were hardly alone in their conviction that slavery was just part of a larger system of evil that required change.
This conviction pointed to ultraism, the perception that American society was
so fundamentally flawed that radical change was imperative in economic, political, gender, and other relations. Ultraism meant that one needed to go farther, to strive for the limits and beyond, to effect the fundamental changes the
social order demanded. With these sentiments growing stronger, these women
and men first began to voice their views collectively in 1841. By the end of 1842,
they had formed the Society for Universal Inquiry and Reform, seeking to
bring in with them the "choice spirits of the age" to consult about the measures
they should pursue for the amelioration of these evils. By 1843 they had reached
a broad consensus on a set of ideas for reform. And by 1844 they were forming
communities to put those ideas into practice.

If the Society for Universal Inquiry and Reform had any one forerunner, it
was a meeting in Boston in the autumn of 1840, a meeting that only one of
those who would play a leading role in the formation of the society, John O.
Wattles, attended. That was the famous Chardon Street Convention, called by
the murkily defined Friends of Universal Reform to discuss the relation of
church and state, particularly Sabbath observance. It was, as one historian of
abolition has put it, "beyond all projects, plans, blueprints, all 'small, sour and
fierce schemes.' "[1]

Ralph Waldo Emerson, in one of his most memorable essays, has left a delightful account of the Chardon Street meeting: "Madmen, madwomen, men
with beards, Dunkers, Muggletonians, Come-outers, Groaners, Agrarians, Sev-
enth-Day Baptists, Quakers, Abolitionists, Calvinists, Unitarians, and Philosophers—all came successively to the top, and seized their moment, if not their

hour, wherein to chide, or pray, or preach, or protest." Emerson's slightly pejorative characterizations of some of the strange participants aside, it was an apt description of the diverse elements that would come together for Universal Inquiry and Reform. No minutes or resolutions emerged—the meeting refused even to be bound by the niceties of parliamentary procedure, in order to uphold the right of free discussion. But it did introduce the note of universal reform, the sense of the connectedness of antislavery, religion, and the general state of American wickedness.[2]

The convention provoked a variety of responses. Reports of it in England complicated John A. Collins's life there in the winter of 1840–41. More conservative abolitionists predictably labeled it further proof of the atheistic, infidel tendencies of the radicals. But it also was watched in the West. Two Hicksite Friends from Columbiana County, Ohio, Samuel Myers and Thomas E. Longshore, wrote approvingly of the meeting. "I fear, to be Christ-like . . . has constituted no part of the concern of the present ministry; and I conclude that it needs a thorough sifting," Myers told Edmund Quincy. Longshore agreed: "tyrants and thrones, ecclesiastical and civil, must be laid low." And in a few months Wattles would be back in Ohio, apparently preaching this new gospel.[3]

Late in 1840, Garrison apparently gave new impetus to this movement by reprinting in the *Liberator* an article from the *Practical Christian,* a nonresistant journal published in Boston. Its assumption was that communitarianism was the logical outcome of reform. It noted the successes of the Shakers and Moravians, which, the anonymous author argued, were not ideal models, but presented much that was worthy of emulation. Like these "peculiar" groups, the "practical Christian" community would be made up of families "dwelling together . . . in love and peace, ensuring to themselves the comforts of life by agricultural and mechanical industry." Unlike the sectarian communities, however, they would not be inward-looking but would devote "the entire residue of their intellectual, moral, and physical resources to the christianization and general welfare of the human race." More than that, they would set themselves apart from other communities by their belief that "perfect *individuality* is a fundamental idea of the *true man.*" By setting man right with God, community would bring society into right relationships. "We therefore go for unabridged *individuality* of mind, conscience, and duty and responsibility—for *direct* divine government over the human soul—and, of course for as little *human* government as possible." Everyone could live by obedience to "the law of God written on his heart, without the aid of external bonds and restraint." The author went on to suggest some guidelines, mostly questions about how such a community would come to be—its membership, obtaining the land, choosing the members, determining the size, writing the constitution. The advantages, it concluded, were numerous. It would "furnish a happy home to many pure-hearted Christians, who are now scattered abroad insulated from each other, and oppressed by the world." They could secure living with less toil and effort, rid themselves of habits injurious to their health, and guard themselves from "corrupt and demoralizing influences." They could establish purified churches, and send out "true hearted, religious moral, and philanthropic missionaries into the surrounding world." They would set up schools for the better education of their children, and asylums for the victims of society. "In fine," the author concluded, "it would be a powerful concentration of moral light and heat, which would make practical Christianity known and felt by the world." If one was set up, it would give rise to others, "until at length the kingdoms of this world should be absorbed into the glorious kingdom of our Lord Jesus Christ."[4]

Early in the new year, some of these Ohio Friends tried to put their reactions into more concrete form. In February 1841, eight Hicksite Quakers in Columbiana County—William and Hannah E. Myers, Owen and Mary F. Thomas, Benjamin B. Davis, Joseph Granetsone, James Barnaby, and Thomas E. Longshore—sent to the *Liberator* a plan for community, a subject which, they concluded, "Must unavoidably assume a more important aspect than the many now attach to it, or can fancy it will ever possess." Most of them would later become part of the community near them at Marlborough. The Chardon Street events had either influenced them, or perhaps simply reflected their thoughts. They envisioned a community with a minimum of restraints—no written constitution, no lists of membership—and large enough to embrace "the whole human family." They called for another convention to discuss "the propriety and practicability of the project."[5]

Meanwhile, in southwestern Ohio, the group that would ultimately take the lead in this enterprise was forming. In January and February, 1841, some of the Hicksite Friends most active in the Garrisonian Warren and Clinton county antislavery societies met in the homes of Abraham Brooke and Abraham Allen. The latter was a Hicksite Friend who had come from New York with his family twenty years earlier. The group consisted almost entirely of four families—Dr. Brooke, his brothers Edward, William, James and Edward's wife, Hannah, and his brother-in-law Joseph Lukens; Abraham Allen, his wife, Cata, and their son David; Thomas and Esther Whinery, brother and sister from a large family from Columbiana County, who were now teaching school near Center; and

Barkley Gilbert, the skeptic who would make such sport of Valentine Nicholson's vision, Gilbert's wife, Mary, and his brother Amos. Nicholson was not
there, probably because he was living in eastern Greene County, a long journey
from Oakland. All, however, were active in the Clinton County Anti-Slavery
Society, and had signalled their devotion to antislavery in a variety of ways.
Allen's big brick house, known as Mud Castle, frequently sheltered fugitive
slaves; on at least one occasion slave catchers invaded it. He had constructed a
new carriage that he had christened "The Liberator," in honor of Garrison,
with a bell attached to an odometer so that it rang as each mile brought slaves
closer to freedom. Esther Whinery was teaching school with the hope of saving
enough to go off to Oberlin that fall, a hope in which she was to be disappointed.[6]

The Allens, Whinerys, Brookes, Lukenses, and Gilberts, while sympathetic
to the reformers whose proposals they were reading in the *Liberator,* were either
more pessimistic or more pragmatic in their approach than their old friends in
Columbiana County. By their own description, they were "practical men and
women" and wanted something concrete, not "abstractions." In their minds,
the key was education. They had despaired of "entire reform in any adult population," and so decided that their efforts would better be devoted to "the right
training of the rising generation." The solution, or at least the natural first step,
was to go back to one of the cradles of the antislavery movement—the manual
labor school, although, for this group, one "free from sectarianism."[7]

Such an institution, they were convinced, was not only practical; it would
also be effective. There was an abundance of potential students, wanting only
a way to attend; there were "competent instructors" willing to volunteer their
services for a "mere support"; there were, perhaps most importantly, "disinter-
ested persons . . . willing to place their means at the disposal of a well-ordered
institution, from motives of justice and philanthropy." All that was lacking was
money, and that, many were convinced, could be supplied adequately only by
"a community of interests in more than school arrangements."[8]

The meeting at the Allens' took up the problems and potential of cooperative living. The discussion began with an attempt to identify the evils plaguing
society and to trace them to their source. The root of all evil, some present
argued, was "the conflict of opposing interests," a social system in which "he
who possesses beyond what he had created has the surplus from the labor of
others, who, of course, are divested of it." The ignorant, the privileged, and the
enemies of progress were committed to such a system. But those present were
hopeful enough to set a second meeting at Abraham Brooke's late in February.

There they decided to seek wider support—calling for meetings at Green Plain Friends Meetinghouse in Clark County in March, and at Oakland again in June, as well as using the *Liberator* to seek support from interested friends of reform in the East.[9]

This first stirring was not to produce much. The school never came to be; indeed, nothing more was heard of the project, and if the meetings at Green Plain and Oakland took place, no record of them has survived. For the next year, from the spring of 1841 to the spring of 1842, these abolitionists were absorbed in other matters, particularly the intricate maneuvers over the fate of the Ohio Anti-Slavery Society. It was those events that would bring Brooke and Nicholson into contact with Wattles and Collins and launch Universal Inquiry and Reform.

In the late summer and fall of 1841 the American Anti-Slavery Society sent two agents, Oliver Johnson and Charles C. Burleigh, out to gauge sentiment in the West. They met the usual reception accorded abolition organizers: mobs, threats of mobs, and eggs. But there was also a warm welcome for them in certain quarters. The warmest came when Johnson visited Clinton County and made the acquaintance of the Brookes, Allens, and Whinerys. Johnson went back to New England heartened by his reception and by a number of new subscribers for the *National Anti-Slavery Standard*.[10]

Meanwhile, Abraham Brooke was feeling a growing sense of disquiet that events in the fall and early winter of 1841–1842 exacerbated. He found himself increasingly at odds with Gamaliel Bailey, and increasingly frustrated by what he perceived as a fundamental misunderstanding of the issues in the split between old and new societies. "It is only the belief that prejudices in favor of some men and against others, govern such of our friends as prefer to join the seceders," he wrote in July. The overwhelming majority embraced the Garrisonian position of "*equal rights and complete freedom of conscience to individuals.*" But few understood the causes of the split in the East; many of those who did still inclined to the "new organization" because of their "zeal for political action," and the baneful influence of sectarianism operated against those who held heterodox opinions, especially Garrison. Still, Brooke thought that Ohio abolitionists had been successful in avoiding sectarian squabbles and divisive battles over voting. "It is a matter of no moment which of our Eastern friends is most popular here. Like ourselves, they are none of them any better than they should be . . . individuals here or there are but drops in the mighty ocean of antislavery feeling," he wrote to Bailey. The whole eastern question was, he admitted, "a jumbled up concern—a tangled web which may not easily be unravelled." "We may as well preserve our joint end of the lever, which we can all pull at."[11]

By the fall, however, Brooke was openly angry with the position of abolitionists. Too many, he raged, were hypocrites. Those who abhorred the thought of owning slaves, nevertheless, were amassing "princely fortunes, by the barter and use of the products, wrung from the toiling slave by the hand of power." Too many of the "industrious yeomanry," even though touched by the sufferings of the slave, were more concerned with adding another field to their overgrown farms. Only purity would redeem the cause—plucking the beam from their own eyes, freeing themselves from all complicity with sin. Then abolitionists would stand ready to rebuke the guilty and move forward.[12]

Early in 1842 Edward Brooke, Abraham's younger brother, opened a new line of attack with a letter to the *Philanthropist* in Cincinnati. Up to this time the battles between Garrisonians and non-Garrisonians had been relatively muted, mainly a question over whether the state society would affiliate with the "old" or "new" organization. Other vexed subjects that had torn apart eastern abolitionists had not been controversial in Ohio, even though some Ohio abolitionists, such as the Congregationalists and Presbyterians at Oberlin or Gamaliel Bailey, were given to private fulminations against Garrison and to public attacks on infidelity. While the Brookes saw themselves as committed to nonresistance, they did not see the Liberty party or voting as evil. Abraham Brooke, for example, regularly acted with the Liberty men until 1843. In Ohio, the position of the Garrisonians was that while abolitionists were free to act with the Liberty party if their consciences led them to do so, they were no more bound to do that than to vote with the Whigs or the Democrats. Bailey, the effective leader of the Liberty party in the state, agreed that the party and the state antislavery society were separate. By late in 1841 that idea was leading him, in his search for support from sympathetic Democrats and Whigs, to certain concessions. Bailey stated, for example, that while he could not obey a law that forbade him to aid fugitive slaves, neither could he actively resist it. Perhaps even more disturbing, Bailey took the ground that while distasteful, the Fugitive Slave Act was constitutional, and that the Liberty party, while committed to the end of slavery, was not committed to immediate action against slavery where it already existed. Politically, this was wise, but for some it was too much of a compromise, and Brooke was among them. Brooke wrote that he and abolitionists at Marlborough, nearly all of them Hicksite Quakers, found the Liberty position morally indefensible. "If we consider slavery to be wrong under all circumstances, why offer to sustain it by legal protections?" he asked. "Are we not bound to withdraw all protection from it?" Brooke concluded by saying that the laws of God took precedence over those of humans. Brooke's stance was endorsed by another group of Hicksite abolitionists, those at Green Plain in Clark County. The society in April passed resolutions that bemoaned the domination of the federal government by the "slave power." "The peaceful union of liberty and slavery is about as practicable as the coalition of fire and gunpowder," they resolved. "A peaceful dissolution of the Union would be preferable to us than the position of bodyguard to slavery." Thus the more radical elements of the abolitionist movement, mainly Hicksite Quakers, were moving toward the extremes of Garrisonian abolition that had been so divisive in the East.[13]

This discussion coincided with the newest organizing schemes of John A. Collins. Now the American Anti-Slavery Society's general agent, Collins wanted to expand the network of state and local societies affiliated with the "old" organization. Already he was laying plans for a new society in Connecticut, but Ohio was a major prize and so Collins set out to attend the state society's annual meeting held in Mt. Vernon early in June 1842. In April Joseph A. Dugdale from Green Plain and Edwin Fussell from Pendleton, Indiana, both leading Hicksite abolitionists, were elected officers of the American Anti-Slavery Society, Dugdale a vice president, Fussell to the board of managers.[14]

At the June meeting, the Garrisonians moved to resolve some of these problems of politics and ties with other abolitionists. Dugdale, Abraham Brooke, and Abraham's brother James Brooke were all members of the business committee, and they brought in a series of resolutions that would have moved the state society away from even a semblance of neutrality. The most controversial would have renewed the state society's affiliation with the "old organization," the American Anti-Slavery Society. They also would have released abolitionists from any duty to obey immoral laws, specifically the Fugitive Slave Act. The convention would not even debate the resolutions, tabling all of them without discussion. Thereupon the Garrisonians left and met the next day to form a new group, the Ohio American Anti-Slavery Society.[15]

Quite naturally, the two sides explained the separation differently. William Birney, the son of Liberty party presidential candidate James G. Birney, explained it simply as "a secession . . . of Garrisonian malcontents, led by Dr. Brooke . . . and incited by the wily arguments and plausible sophistry of J. A. Collins," who, according to Birney, had been "sent out . . . expressly for the purpose of fomenting our dissensions." After their departure, the overwhelming majority of the delegates remained and conducted the business of the organization harmoniously.[16]

Brooke and Dugdale strenuously attacked this account, as did Collins. Collins, according to Brooke, had not been at the heart of the split; indeed, he had barely been allowed to speak at all. Instead, those who were forming the Ohio American group were those who doubted the wisdom of tying the future of abolition in Ohio to the Liberty party. According to Collins, while the Ohio Liberty party was composed of good men trying to do good, it was "dampening the zeal and destroying the faith of its friends in the practicability of affecting the abolition of slavery by moral means." Brooke furiously denied that the new group in Ohio was simply a tool of Garrison, an accusation that Joshua Leavitt leveled in New York. "Does Joshua Leavitt suppose because he has put upon his neck a collar, with the name of James G. Birney inscribed thereon, that there can be no such man as a freeman who dares to call his soul his own, and be *his own* man?" Those in the new group, Brooke concluded, while mostly viewing Garrison as "an able, eloquent, uncompromising, honest friend of the slave," would not follow his dictates in all matters.[17]

The course of the new society in Ohio largely bore out Brooke's statement. It did not pursue a sectarian war with the older group—in its founding statement, while listing grievances going back to 1840, and bemoaning what it saw as a declining moral influence as emphasis on politics increased, it did not fling vituperation at it. The two groups, it concluded, could be "two divisions of the same army bearing down on slavery's castles." The new group, while placing more emphasis on moral suasion than political action, did not condemn the Liberty party. Many of those who had left continued to vote the Liberty ticket. And some Ohio abolitionists chose to be members of both groups. When the Clinton County Anti-Slavery Society decided that fall to affiliate with the Ohio American, it first made provisions to pay off an indebtedness to the old organization. Members continued to support the *Philanthropist* in Cincinnati, which still printed their letters and reported on their meetings.[18]

Still, the new group was different in important ways. Hicksite Quakers dominated it; its executive committee included Dr. Abraham Brooke, his sister-in-law Hannah Brooke, Joseph A. Dugdale from Green Plain, and Abraham Allen. The first local societies to break away and join the new group, in Stark, Harrison, and Clinton counties, were all Hicksite strongholds. And the new society quickly signalled the direction it would take by issuing public invitations to Garrison and Abby Kelley, the New England Quaker abolitionist lecturer who was considered not only a rabid Garrisonian but also a woman of suspect morals because of her public career, to come to Ohio to address conventions to be held at Georgetown in Harrison County, and in Oakland, that fall. The inclusion of women as officers was a break with the policy of the old organization.[19]

As the new society struggled to find a foothold, Abraham Brooke was at a turning point in his life. Heretofore he had been active politically, first as a Whig and then in the Liberty party. But now he had become convinced that it had made too many compromises with slavery. And if this led him to embrace the doctrine of "no human government," he was willing to follow the implications of his beliefs to their logical end. Thus fortified, the Ohio reformers began their new antislavery careers.[20]

Meanwhile, as the Brookes, Dugdales, Allen and other Hicksite Friends were "coming out" of the Ohio State Anti-Slavery Society and the Liberty party, they were faced with a disquieting situation within the Society of Friends. Once again, abolitionists found themselves reacting to events in the East. The divisions among Friends, however, were to be far more bitter and more enduring than the splits among abolitionist factions. The division would mirror the variant strains within Hicksite Quakerism. On one side would be the traditionalists, opposed to anything they perceived as innovation. On the other would be the incipient Universal Reformers (and many others), at first questioning authority in the name of individual conscience, and later challenging both the marketplace and received doctrines and offering radical alternatives.

The Hicksite Friends in Clinton and Clark counties were members of Indiana Yearly Meeting. Numerically probably the smallest of the Hicksite meetings of Friends set up after the separation of 1828, geographically it was the largest, stretching from the Alum Creek Quaker community north of Columbus, Ohio, west to the Illinois prairies. Its largest concentration of members, however, was in southwestern Ohio. The Nicholsons, after they returned to live in Warren County near Harveysburg, became members of the largest monthly meeting, Miami, whose center was in Waynesville. The Brookes, Allens, and Whinerys belonged to Center Monthly Meeting, which embraced Hicksites in the northern and western parts of Clinton County, between Oakland and the county seat at Wilmington. Both were part of Miami Quarterly Meeting, the largest in the yearly meeting. To the north was the relatively new Green Plain Quarterly Meeting, made up of three scattered monthly meetings: Green Plain in Clark County, in the countryside between the villages of Cortsville and Selma; Goshen, forty miles north in Logan County on the edge of the village of Zanesfield; and Alum Creek, fifty miles east of Zanesfield in what was then Delaware County.[21]

The involvement of these Friends in abolition was uneven. There were relatively few abolitionists in the confines of Miami Monthly Meeting. As usual, Valentine Nicholson's was a lonely situation. Center, on the other hand, was with the Brookes, Allens, and Whinerys, an abolition stronghold. And the Friends around Green Plain, led by Joseph and Ruth Dugdale and the minister Elizabeth L. Borton, had been among the first in western Ohio to organize an antislavery society. As a group, the Indiana Hicksites were committed to the traditional Quaker testimony against slavery, regularly referring to it in their exchange of epistles with other yearly meetings. In 1833, for example, they told Friends in New York that "the oppressed African race have also claimed a share of our solicitude, with fervent desires that Friends may not rely on what our predecessors have done to ameliorate the condition of that suffering people." Each Friend, they concluded, should "honestly examine his own heart and know how far he is coming up in the performance of the work of his *own* day, and whether the time is near when truth will require at our hands to abstain from the productions of slave labor." The Indiana Friends were thus following the teachings of Elias Hicks, in a way that would satisfy Abraham Brooke himself.[22]

The rise of immediate abolition, however, left many Friends, Orthodox and Hicksites, suspicious of the antislavery movement. Genesee Yearly Meeting in New York summarized that point of view in its 1837 epistle to Indiana, praying that "Friends may be preserved in the prosecution of benevolent objects from joining in association with others conducted on principles in any degree adverse to those precious Testimonies given to us to bear." Friends must beware of such associations, lest the language of scripture become applicable to them: "Strangers have devoured thy strength and thou knowest it not." Some other Friends were even more vociferous, denouncing abolitionists as "servants of the devil, emissaries of Satan, howling wolves too famished to bite, and reptiles."[23]

It was the preaching of a Hicksite minister who had never seen Miami or Center or Green Plain that would provide the impetus for bringing the abolitionists there out of Indiana Yearly Meeting. George F. White was a middle-aged merchant in New York who had been disowned early in the 1820s for taking advantage of the bankruptcy laws. Cast out by Friends, he had plunged into the thickets of New York City politics in the 1820s. In 1832 he was "favored" to see the error of such ways and return to the society. In the manner of true converts, he was zealous in upholding all of the peculiarities of Friends, and as one who had wandered in the wilderness of "popular associations." To his mind, they "under a profession of being engaged in work of righteousness and benevolence," sought "the rewards of men," and turned sufferers not to Christ or faith but "to man, or to associations of men." Among such suspect groups, White placed antislavery societies. In Rose Street Meeting in New York City, he preached that such associations did wrong, albeit with good motives, by encouraging slaves to look to men for their freedom rather than to God. All those who joined in such groups were hypocrites, blasphemers, and false teachers, led astray by the power of their own wills.[24]

Such a discourse naturally attracted attention. The Garrisonian press, always alert to any signs of complicity of the clergy with slaveholders, gave it considerable attention. The *Liberator* led the way with a furious attack by Oliver Johnson, who had been in Ohio three years earlier. The *National Anti-Slavery Standard* in New York City soon followed suit, copying Johnson's story under the title "Rare Specimen of a Quaker Preacher." It blasted White and defended abolitionists, hurling the same epithets at White that he had applied to the antislavery cause.[25]

The abolitionist attack on White, one of the "weightiest" of Hicksite ministers in the East, had serious repercussions. Three Hicksite Friends—Isaac T. Hopper, his son-in-law James S. Gibbons, and Charles Marriott, all leading abolitionists—were directors of the American Anti-Slavery Society, which owned the *Standard*. New York Monthly Meeting promptly disowned them for defamation, in spite of the fact that they had had no prior knowledge of the article. For abolitionist Friends, the New York actions were outrageous and a source of agitation for years.[26]

Abolitionist Friends in Ohio also responded, and made confrontation inevitable. When the abolitionists at Green Plain read of White's sermon, they felt so strongly about it that they had to take some sort of action to express their disunity with such proceedings. So at their quarterly meeting in May, they agreed that after the close of the regular business they would remain to hold a special convention. Twenty-nine men and twenty-three women wrote "A Disclaimer" for publication in the *Philanthropist*. After noting with "mortification and astonishment" the publication of such remarks by a minister among Friends, they felt bound to call White to repentance, citing 1 Timothy 5:20: "Them that sin rebuke before all, that others may fear." "We feel bound as Friends, some of us standing in the same relation to the society as G. F. White, to utter publicly our solemn protest," they wrote. "In the above emphatic condemnation, we are actuated by no invidious feeling towards the erring individual, but speak the truth in love, for we know that the expression of such sentiments as are attributed to our friend G. F. White will pain the hearts of many who love and cherish the principles as professed by our religious society."[27]

This was an extraordinary proceeding. The signers included some of the most prominent members of the quarterly meeting. Joseph A. Dugdale, his mother Sarah B. Dugdale, and Elizabeth L. Borton were among the most eminent recorded ministers in the yearly meeting. Joseph A. Dugdale had just become the clerk of the men's monthly meeting at Green Plain. His predecessors had included two other signers of the disclaimer, John Shaw and Thomas Borton, the latter an elder; George Hayward, another signer, had been Green Plain's assistant clerk. Shaw, Joseph Dugdale, and Thomas Swayne, another signer, were all members of the meeting for sufferings, the yearly meeting's equivalent of an executive committee and the center of considerable power. For a group of such well-known and influential Friends to publish a scathing attack on a minister from another yearly meeting, a widely respected one at that, was an event that signaled a schism in the making or at best a serious outbreak of disaffection.[28]

The Green Plain Friends, however, were at work for other causes almost as radical, ones that owed as much to Garrisonian principles of equality of the sexes and resistance to authority as they did to Quaker tradition. In the fall of 1840, as the yearly meeting held its sessions, Green Plain Quarter had sent up a proposal "that our Discipline be so altered as to give women Friends equal rights with men in the administration thereof." It is not clear what Green Plain had in mind, unless it was the appointment of women to the meeting for sufferings. The yearly meeting rejected the idea. When the yearly meeting met again late in September 1841, Green Plain not only brought the old proposal back again but accompanied it with an even more radical idea—abolishing the office of elder and the practice of recording ministers. The Hicksites had been founded in large part on the rejection of what they regarded as dictatorialness on the part of ministers and elders, but no body of Friends had suggested such a drastic idea before.[29]

The yearly meeting did not take up either proposal, even for discussion. Instead, the meeting for sufferings reported "a complaint against a number of Friends members of Green Plain Quarterly Meeting for publishing a protest or 'disclaimer' censuring some expressions said to have been made by an approved minister of our society belonging to another yearly meeting." The meeting for sufferings condemned the action as improper and urged the appointment of a committee to investigate the situation within Green Plain Quarter and to labor to bring the Friends who had signed the disclaimer to a sense of their fault. The committee was made up of eleven men Friends, only one of whom, Abraham Allen, was known to be sympathetic to abolition.[30]

Both sides, abolitionist and antiabolitionist, recognized what was at stake for abolitionist Friends in the Green Plain case. George F. White himself had received a "minute" (the Quaker term for credentials) to travel to Ohio and Indiana that fall, and the possibility that he might attend the yearly meeting heightened the atmosphere of confrontation, but ultimately he did not. Oliver Johnson was in the neighborhood, raising funds and doubtless seeing more examples of clerical oppression, even among those who professed not to have a clergy. From Philadelphia, James and Lucretia Mott urged the Green Plain abolitionists to "let love abound" and "let no strife or spirit of bitterness" enter into the proceedings, even though both thought that White's antiabolitionist venom was the fruit of an unbalanced mind.[31]

The yearly meeting's antipathy to the Green Plain Friends' action, however, did not deter their sympathizers from undertaking similar actions. After the yearly meeting, Oliver Johnson was in the Center neighborhood, and the Brookes, Allens, and Whinerys handed him their own protest to be published in the *National Anti-Slavery Standard.* It was even more hostile than the Green Plain disclaimer. They found it "anomalous" and "unaccountable" that White would publicly show himself out of unity with the historic testimonies of Friends against war, slavery, and intemperance. That White had made such statements with "impunity" could be explained, the writers asserted, only by a defection from those testimonies by Friends in New York. White's public statements, moreover, were "evasive, uncourteous, . . . hypercritical, and sadly deficient in the dignity becoming one holding his station." The disownment of Hopper, Gibbons, and Marriott equally outraged the three families, and they contemplated a similar public protest against it. "They are as noble a set of people as I have ever met," Johnson told Hopper. "If a weight of love could break one's back, mine would give way under the accumulated load which I have been charged to convey to you." The Center Friends were doing more than sending condolences to New York. They were publicly accusing leading Friends in New York and in the West of apostasy.[32]

We have little knowledge of what happened over the next year—the records of both Green Plain monthly and quarterly meetings for 1842 and 1843 have been lost, as have the minutes of the meeting for sufferings. Apparently, however, the proceedings of the yearly meeting's committee were such as to inspire little hope among the Hicksite abolitionists. From the beginning, the presumption had been against the Friends who had signed the disclaimer. "I could see nothing but division and discord in the distance," wrote Joseph A. Dugdale. When the committee wrote its report, it told the yearly meeting that Green Plain Monthly Meeting was "in a weak and divided state" and was not "in a disposition to receive or cooperate with our labors." At Goshen the committee found the "same want of openness." The quarterly meeting was thus "in a weak and divided state," and the committee recommended that the quarterly meeting of ministers and elders—the "select meeting," as it was known—be "laid down," the Quaker term for dissolved. Still, there was something of a victory, apparently won by Abraham Allen, for the abolitionists. The committee agreed to recommend further labor toward the restoration of unity; there was no explicit condemnation of the abolitionists.[33]

When the 1842 yearly meeting was held, however, and the report was read, Allen immediately realized that someone had altered it. To the recommendation that the committee visit the dissident Friends had been added eleven words: "and endeavor to convince them of their error . . . in the Truth." This changed the entire thrust of the report—it judged the abolitionists as in error, and the practice among Friends was that those who were in error and could not be brought to a sense of it were to be disowned. The committee was now in a position to drive the abolitionists out of the yearly meeting. Allen immediately denounced the altered document and called for the original, only to be told that it was "lost." Dugdale saw the hand of the meeting for sufferings behind it. The revelation of the alteration was followed with a denunciation from another committee member, who said that had he known this would be the result, he would never have served on it. Two others disclaimed any knowledge of the alteration. "Voices in all parts of the house" were heard in protest, but John T. Plummer, the clerk, pronounced it properly read. Nevertheless, Dugdale was heartened. The previous year, he told a Friend in the East, the "popular current" had been against them, but now Friends were seeing events in their true light. A new committee was appointed, which Dugdale thought "mixed" but more sympathetic to the abolitionists than the previous year.[34]

Two days later, the meeting for sufferings reported, its main product being an epistle "against the Reforms of the age." Plummer opined that it was a sound, admirable work, but, according to Dugdale, those present reacted with protests. One who had denounced the "Disclaimer" in 1841 now told the yearly meeting: "it is evident to my mind that there is a thirst for power, and I do

consider this Epistle one of the grossest impositions I have even known produced upon any body of people." Even Plummer's own father pronounced:
"The minute will not do." "All this *done good*," Dugdale wrote, "it opened the
eyes that were blind." Ultimately, the yearly meeting refused to endorse the
epistle. Dugdale felt that nothing less than a miraculous deliverance had taken
place: "I feel myself humbled, and I think I see the omnipotence of principle."[35]

Others, of course, besides Dugdale watched the events at the yearly meeting
with interest, and among them was Abraham Brooke. Characteristically, he saw
more to disturb than hearten him. The Hicksite battles over the Green Plain
abolitionists coincided with a split among the Orthodox Friends of Indiana
Yearly Meeting, also over abolition. The Orthodox leadership, on the same day
that they welcomed Henry Clay to Richmond and made life so unpleasant for
Hiram Mendenhall, had issued a directive that all active abolitionists were to
be removed from positions of leadership. Brooke heard from Orthodox sympathizers that all of the preaching at their last quarterly meeting at Center had
been against abolition. Within a year Joseph A. Dugdale sadly recorded that
among the Hicksites "the feeling of hostility is not a whit abated." Brooke
wrote bitterly: "Political parties, and religious sects are the principal barriers
which impede the progress of antislavery principles." And now he had been led
to the conclusion that his own Society of Friends was "exerting a *pro-slavery*
influence in Ohio, greater than all other influences put together." It was with
this disillusionment with politics and religion that the Brookes, Nicholsons,
Mendenhalls, and the other Hicksite abolitionists of Green Plain, Goshen,
Oakland, and Harveysburg awaited the arrival of John A. Collins and John O.
Wattles.[36]

In October, the convention called by the Ohio American Anti-Slavery Society met for three days in Oakland. Wattles put attendance between fifteen hundred and three thousand. Collins was back again from the East, "on an Anti
Slavery scout." Wattles had not left Ohio, traveling to visit settlements of free
blacks and gauging sentiment among abolitionists in western Ohio and in the
Quaker counties in eastern Indiana. George Barrett of Delaware County, Ohio,
a Hicksite Friend originally from New York, presided. The meeting began by
deciding to devote its attention equally to six topics: the "inherent sinfulness
of slavery," the relationship of the North to Slavery, the moral implications of
slavery, measures that would bring abolition nearer, the progress of the anti-
slavery cause, and the encroachments of the "slave power" on the rights of the
free North. Most of the time was devoted to debating a series of resolutions.
Wattles and Collins put forward two which condemned as abettors of slavery

all those who were not actively engaged in the abolitionist cause and which called on all abolitionists to "apply their principles to all the political, religious, and benevolent associations with which they are connected." Abraham Allen led a successful effort to table these.[37]

Others equally radical, however, were adopted. After a speech those present resolved "with three cheers" that "every man, woman or child" had the right to run away from slavery, with their *own* bodies, on their *own legs*," and they proclaimed their "determination to assist all such in reclaiming their inherent self-evident right, *by day and by night*." They also condemned the Ohio Black Laws, and all other legislation that legitimized racial discrimination, and called for their repeal. "Negro hatred, or prejudice against color, is the legitimate offspring of ignorance and depravity," they resolved, and they blasted "those in high standing in society, the churches, legislatures, the civil tribunals, and the social circles" who were the cause of "the injustice, oppression, mobs & violence upon the people of color in the nominally free states." Quakers came in for special criticism. The Orthodox and the Hicksites were hopeless; while they retained "the language, habiliments, and rites of John Woolman, and others of the early Friends, they are destitute of the life giving principles of human freedom in which these great apostles of Christianity pre-eminently excelled." With even the Quakers derelict, their meetinghouses closed to antislavery meetings, there was no hope from the churches, until all came to "treat the slaveholders and their apologists as they do other criminals."[38]

One other resolution came out of the meeting, a request to the executive committee of the Ohio American Anti-Slavery Society to hold a "large series of conventions" throughout the state. They invited Garrison, Douglass, Remond, and Kelley to come to Ohio for the convention. The meeting closed on a conciliatory note by again calling for those present to contribute to paying off the debts of the old Ohio state organization, and endorsing the *Philanthropist* and the Newport, Indiana, *Free Labor Advocate*, neither of which was favorably inclined toward Garrisonianism.[39]

During the convention, Valentine Nicholson remembered, "there would be little groups of thinking minds discussing the most feasable [sic] plan for geting [sic] the social reform subject presented to the minds of others." So, in an impromptu manner, it was decided to hold another convention. As the antislavery meeting closed, Collins announced the meeting to follow and its aims.[40]

On October 27, 1842, "a number of those favorable to reform in the present social system" met in Liberty Hall at Oakland. The building was a huge shed that Abraham Brooke had put up on his land to host this convention after it became apparent that Quaker meetinghouses would henceforth be closed. A visitor a year later wrote of how impressive the scene was, to see hundreds gathered, surrounded by the forest.[41]

There was no list of attenders; we know the names only of those who took a leading role. Valentine Nicholson remembered that the meeting was not as well attended as the antislavery convention, but that many remained for it. They included most of the Hicksites who had contended for abolition and reform in Ohio for five years. Edwin Fussell, a Hicksite Friend from Pendleton, Indiana, who was one of the few abolitionists in Indiana sympathetic to Garrison, presided. Joseph Lukens, now grown up and as enthusiastic as his brother-in-law Dr. Brooke, was the secretary. Collins put himself at the center of all of the proceedings, serving on the business, nominating, and drafting committees for the constitution of the new organization. Wattles was also on the business committee. Hiram Mendenhall, fresh from his encounter with Henry Clay in Richmond, was there to arouse the indignation of those present against Whiggery and the Quakers who placed party before the testimonies of Friends. The whole Brooke clan was present. A new addition was still another brother, Samuel Brooke Jr., who, after doing engineering work in the West for the army, had now returned to Ohio to begin a career as a reformer and abolitionist. Then there was Valentine Nicholson, confident that the meeting was another step toward the fulfillment of his hopes. Barkley Gilbert's skepticism did not keep him away; his wife Mary was the only woman on one of the committees. The comprehensiveness of the movement was evidenced by the presence of Aaron L. Benedict, an Orthodox Friend from Delaware County and committed abolitionist. Also there from the East was William Bassett, a leading reformer from Lynn, Massachusetts, whom the Orthodox Friends had disowned for his commitment to Garrisonian abolition and nonresistance. Representing the Green Plain radicals were Joseph A. and Ruth Dugdale. The Allens and the Whinerys completed the delegation from Center.[42]

The three most important newcomers were Samuel Brooke, the brother of Dr. Abraham, Marius R. Robinson, and Edwin Fussell. Samuel Brooke came to the convention with an unlikely background for an abolitionist. He was born in 1808, and educated at the Strasburg Academy. In 1831 he embarked on a career in civil engineering. He worked for the Baltimore and Ohio Railroad, then surveyed part of the James River and Kanawha Canal in Virginia. Thence he went west, working on Illinois's ill-fated internal improvements program. By 1842 his health was declining, so he returned to his family. Separation had not prevented him from imbibing abolition principles. Almost immediately on his return, he threw himself into antislavery work.[43]

Robinson was perhaps the most important recruit to the cause, and John O.

Wattles was probably responsible for bringing him into the group. A native of Massachusetts reared in New York, Robinson had gone south to Tennessee as a young man and had graduated from the University of Nashville in 1827. From Nashville he went to teach in a Presbyterian mission school in northern Alabama. Theodore Weld, raising money and recruiting students for a "great national Theological Seminary on the Manual Labor Plan," had converted him to the cause of reform. By 1832, he was already doubtful about colonization; as an acquaintance put it, he looked "farther than to the colonization of the free blacks." The opportunity to act on his reform convictions came with the opening of Lane Seminary in Cincinnati in 1833. Robinson became one of the converts to abolition in the debates of the winter of 1833–1834. Soon he left his classes to join his close friend Augustus Wattles teaching in a black school.[44]

In 1836 Augustus Wattles and Robinson became two of the American Anti-Slavery Society's agents for organizing in Ohio. Robinson worked mainly in the Western Reserve. He achieved considerable success, but also faced the usual hostility. In the spring of 1837, while he was staying with a family in Berlin, Ohio, a mob dragged him from the house in the middle of the night, badly beat him, tarred and feathered him, and then hauled him ten miles in a wagon and dumped him. He managed to lecture as usual that night, but his mistreatment had lasting effects on his health, and the Oakland convention marked his return to active work.[45]

Fussell, the president of the convention, was another relatively young man, but already experienced in the antislavery cause. Born 1813 in Chester County, Pennsylvania, Fussell was a nephew of Bartholomew Fussell, one of the founding members of the American Anti-Slavery Society. He had been well educated in Quaker schools and at the University of Pennsylvania, and had been active in literary and scientific societies before going west to Indiana in 1836. He made his new home in a community of Hicksite Quakers, most of them recently from Chester County, on Fall Creek near Pendleton. Fussell, despite old friends and neighbors around him, was not happy in the backwoods. He went back to Chester County to marry his cousin, Rebecca Lewis, in a non-Quaker ceremony, which resulted in their being "disowned." Later, however, they made their peace with Friends. She was an equally dedicated reformer who had resolved to give "the holy causes of Peace Abolition and Temperance and Education . . . all the support my little power is capable of giving."[46]

Fussell's letters home to family were full of unhappiness mixed with hopes for change. He worked to improve his community: he founded a debating society, lectured on "the rights and duties of woman," served as one of the trustees of the new county library, and in 1837 took a leading role in organizing a local antislavery society. But he found more to make him dissatisfied. He was lonely and isolated, moping in an "old smoky, drafty log-cabin." He made scarcely enough to live on, and was reduced to working as a carpenter. He was upset by the rampant competition for land and wealth he saw around him, even among Quakers. And politics disgusted him. A visit to the Indiana legislature in 1837 left him thinking that while some of the members were men of talent, others "scarcely have enough sense to turn a grindstone in a proper manner." The avid support of the Fall Creek Friends for William Henry Harrison in the election of 1840 left him skeptical about the commitment of Friends to translating their professed beliefs into action. He deplored divisions among abolitionists, but sided with the Garrisonians. When the difficulties arose within the yearly meeting over the Green Plain statement in 1841, naturally his sympathies, and those of his wife, were with the radicals.[47]

Although the convention spent two days in what it later described as an "excited and deeply interesting discussion," we have no account of the substance of the discussion. We have only the constitution that was unanimously adopted. Its preamble describes succinctly what the group saw as its mission:

Preamble

Whereas it is most evident that it is the design of our Creator, that man should be happy in this state of existence, and that he has given him laws, which, when obeyed, will secure ease, peace, Freedom, plenty and intelligence; and whereas society, as it is now organized, produces toil, anxiety, disease, covetousness, intolerance, poverty, intemperance, slavery, war, and premature death; and whereas the human mind is in its nature progressive, and adapted to truth; and whereas sects, parties, governments, creeds, and Authorities, are by their nature enemies to human progress and human happiness; and whereas mankind should be regarded as an equal brotherhood, the joint proprietors of the soil and of all the products of human industry; and whereas the principle which recognizes the right of one man to ownership in the soil and products of industry, in contradistinction to another, is the fruitful cause of the evils of civilized society, and the great obstacle to reform; and believing that a better state of affairs can exist by organizing the social system in accordance with the principles of God's government, by which equality or rights and interests shall be secured to all, and to inquire into our duties in relation to these subjects, and to enable us to perform them, we associate together

This preamble embraced a considerable body of ideas. In it, the group committed itself to going far beyond abolition to more fundamental reform of society, waging war on all of its ills. It embraced an optimistic, Romantic view of human nature and ability, of perfecting it through progress. It endorsed socialism, viewing private property as a source of social evil. It envisioned "God's government," seemingly simple words, but ones that in 1842 were pregnant with meaning for anyone who had followed the course of reform in the last decade. Finally, it committed itself to inquiry, in the belief that human effort could discover the laws of God's Government that would guide humanity into the world they sought. The constitution went on to describe the workings of the group. "All human beings who desire it, in virtue of their humanity," were entitled to membership, "without regard to sex, sect, condition, color, country, creed, or character." There would be the usual officers, but particular importance was attached to the "associate corresponding secretaries," who were charged with gathering "information in relation to the present social system, and the best way of improving it in their respective vicinities."[48]

The very act of writing a constitution may have been the source of some controversy. Some probably found it too much of a human attempt to define the limits of God's Government, but the articles were simple and uncomplicated, committing the group only to pursuing the goals enumerated in the preamble, opening membership to "all human beings," specifying the duties of the officers in the broadest possible terms, and putting special emphasis on *inquiry:* gathering the information that would be the basis for the society's work of improvement.

The main officers were the men who were the leading spirits in the meeting. Abraham Brooke was elected president, and the corresponding secretary, an important post for any antebellum reform society, was John A. Collins. The always dependable Joseph Lukens was recording secretary, and the executive board was made up of Edward and Samuel Brooke Jr., Abraham Allen, Elizabeth Lukens, and James Romely, of whom nothing else is known. No fewer than fifteen vice presidents were named. Some, like William Bassett and Edwin Fussell, were participants. Most, however, such as Lucretia Mott, Maria Weston Chapman, and Richard Davis Webb, the Irish abolitionist, were named because of their reputations as reformers and because of their presumed sympathy for the goals of the group. That was even more the case with the sixty-seven associate corresponding secretaries. A few, like Robinson and Nicholson, were present and committed to the cause. But for the most part the group had put together a wish list of reformers it hoped to attract—William Lloyd Garrison; Charles L. Remond; Frederick Douglass; Nathaniel P. Rogers, the New Hampshire nonresistant editor; Orson S. Fowler, the well-known phrenologist; Abby

Kelley; Henry C. Wright, the nonresistant lecturer; Parker Pillsbury, a rising young star among Garrisonians; Albert Brisbane, the New York Fourierist reformer; Amos Bronson Alcott, the Transcendentalist with a deep interest in communitarian ventures; and a number of Hicksite Quakers, American Garrisonians, and sympathizers Collins had found during his travels in the British Isles, like the Unitarian feminist and abolitionist Harriet Martineau. Most would show only a perfunctory interest, attending perhaps one meeting and thereafter ignoring it. Others, if not hostile from the beginning, would be within one year. Only a handful would ever take the group seriously.[49]

One of those who did cast an extremely sympathetic eye on the events in Ohio was Orson S. Murray in Vermont. He reprinted the complete proceedings and constitution in the *Telegraph*. He was enthusiastic in his praise, pronouncing the society "the best thing yet, in the shape of an *organization*—because it goes farther towards the *dis*organization of all hurtful organizations." This new movement would be a powerful force for good, Murray argued, a "cause for congratulation to friends of all truth and goodness; . . . cause for terror and alarm" for "the sinful and selfish." "Sectarians and partyists may tremble and quail as they read," Murray concluded.[50]

Murray had one predictable criticism to offer. For him, it was too much of an organization. All organizations, he argued, by their nature engendered exclusiveness and jealousy; they included some and excluded others. And that, in turn, inevitably made for strife, ending in war and bloodshed. "Man was made for self-government," he wrote. The individual, "by going into these organizations, throws away the government of himself, or commits it to the unnatural hands of tyrants." In the various provisions for officers and meetings, Murray saw tendencies in that direction. But he also wrote hopefully that he was not sure that these strictures were appropriate for the Society for Universal Inquiry and Reform.[51]

Early in 1843 Collins and Bassett took the cause east. On the 28th to the 30th of January, a special meeting of the society was held in Lynn, Massachusetts, to examine the influence "which capital, monopolized as it is now by individuals, associations, and governments, exerts upon society and reform." The turnout must have been a hopeful sign to the two men. A stellar group of abolitionists was present: Frederick Douglass; Charles L. Remond, apparently willing to forgive Collins for the misery they had inflicted on each other in England two years earlier; Oliver Johnson, always seemingly drawn to reform schemes with a Quaker flavor; George Bradburn, a member of the Massachusetts legislature and intimate of Garrison; James Boyle, another veteran Garrisonian organizer; the notorious Mary S. Gove, just beginning a career of involvement in communitarianism; and a number of Lynn Quakers, including James N. Buffum, who had stalwartly supported Collins and Douglass in their battle against railway segregation. Bassett presided, with Collins and Sydney H. Gay, another Garrisonian who flitted in and out of the society for the next two years, as secretaries.[52]

The Lynn meeting marked an important step for the fledgling society. While the Oakland convention had committed itself to "universal inquiry and reform," and to fundamental social change, it had not raised the subject of communitarianism. The Lynn convention did that. It provided the specific details of the general critique of American society that Collins in particular had been framing for two years and that the organizational meeting in Oakland had set forth.

The Lynn meeting opened by enumerating the evils of the social system, but the emphasis soon changed. The central question became—as some correspondent, probably Collins, reported it to the *Liberator*—"How much is man indebted to society for the formation of his character?" One faction argued that "men were the victims of institutions." Heredity, and the influence of "virtuous or vicious society" had effects, but it was social institutions that molded humans, "as really as was the foot of the female Chinese into the wooden shoe into which it was pressed." All of these institutions were wrong; "society, as it now exists is all false, with scarcely a redeeming feature," as the critics put it. It was fraught with otherwise inexplicable contradictions: "poverty and riches, scarcity and abundance, intelligence and ignorance, tyranny and servility, slavery, war, deception, fraud, disease, and premature death." Only social transformation could alter this deplorable state of affairs. Others took an opposing view, arguing "with great force and beauty" that since humans were the creators of institutions, they could overcome their influences—"so mysteriously connected with the Infinite, as to enable him, if he desired it, to . . . trample on all human arrangements, and to bring himself into perfect harmony with Divinity."[53]

After debating the nature of humanity, the convention moved on to take up "capital and its rights." Again a basic division emerged. One group argued that "trade and commerce" were the "bane of civilization." Private property, by definition, made for inequality, and from inequality flowed all other evils. Others agreed that the right of "individual ownership in the soil" was wrong, but that there was no inherent evil in trade and commerce or in other forms of private possession. To give all the absolute right to the fruits they gathered from the forest, or the fish they took from the stream was enough to guarantee equality for all individuals. To go beyond that would be to stifle individuality.[54]

All present did agree, however, that only in community life would social reform come. "A community of interests and labor will alone supersede the necessity of competition," the group resolved, "as individuals combined together may resist the aggressions of the present false system of society." Again, however, there was a division. Some in the meeting were drawn to the theories of the Frenchman Charles Fourier, and proposed a system that would recognize individual "possession and accumulation" but avoid the evils of the present social structure by a proper allocation of the returns: 5/12 to labor, 4/12 to talent, and 3/12 to capital.[55]

Collins and the nonresistants responded that while such a system would be a dramatic improvement over the current state of affairs, it would hardly satisfy "the mass of inquiring, intelligent reformers of this country." In lofty terms, Collins argued that just as all were entitled by nature, to "the joint and common tenury" of the sun, the air, and the water, so they were also entitled to the soil. If all were entitled to the products of their own industry, that meant that children and the disabled, the old, and the ill who could not produce were not entitled to any sort of existence, except by charity or sufferance, and that clearly was unacceptable and inhumane. Once more Collins showed the determination for carrying ideas to their logical ends that would distinguish the group. If "the doctrine of appropriation," as he referred to private property, was indeed legitimate, then it was legitimate to allow, "as in Great Britain, only *one* of every eight hundred of its inhabitants the privilege of appropriating soil to themselves, and multitudes from appropriating food sufficient to preserve life." But since the principle produced evil results, it was in itself evil. Collins and his supporters in the Lynn convention were now ready to attribute to private property all of the ills of society—it was not human government, or sectarianism, or slavery, that stood in the way of the establishment of the government of God. Instead, all of these baneful institutions, productive of so many ills, were themselves the products of this *malum in re.*[56]

After the Lynn convention, Collins remained in Boston. He was still the general agent for the Massachusetts Anti-Slavery Society, and took an active part in its meeting in January. Meanwhile, he had three other matters to occupy his time. The first was initiating the work of Universal Inquiry. The Oakland convention had selected the *Herald of Freedom* in Concord, New Hampshire, as its organ, since the Universal Reformers perceived its editor, Nathaniel P. Rogers, as sympathetic to their cause. Collins sent him accounts of the new group for publication. There was also an elaborate questionnaire to send to the corresponding secretaries, informing them of the honor they had been paid and asking them for the information the society needed to advance its work. Collins was so slow in doing this that many of the correspondents doubtless learned of their new duties by reading of them in the *Herald of Freedom,* or in the *Liberator* or *Vermont Telegraph,* which quickly reprinted the account.[57]

Collins's other duty was one to which he was more accustomed: organizing meetings. At the annual meeting of the Massachusetts Anti-Slavery Society in January, just before the Lynn convention, Collins played an active role in the proceedings. Among his main interests was pushing through a proposal for a series of Hundred Conventions to begin in the spring and continue into the fall, to be held in Vermont, New York, western Pennsylvania, Ohio, and Indiana. The scheme was largely his, and as general agent the responsibility for organizing it would be mainly his. He also organized another "property convention" in Worcester.[58]

Finally, and more inextricably intertwined with Collins's plans for the Hundred Conventions than the officers of the American Anti-Slavery Society realized, was the first meeting of the Society for Universal Inquiry and Reform, to be held in New York City in April, immediately following the annual meeting of the American Anti-Slavery Society. And back in Ohio, the Brookes, Allens, Dugdales, and Nicholsons awaited it eagerly. It would be the great adventure of their lives, for they were to attend it.

In April 1843 a company of ten set off from Clark County, Ohio, in Abraham Allen's famous carriage, the "Liberator." It was a distinguished group of reformers. Allen, of course, drove. The other men were Abraham Brooke, doubtless pondering the gravity of his debut in Eastern reform circles; Amos Welch, a young Hicksite Friend from Harveysburg and cousin of Jane Nicholson; and John O. Wattles, returning east for the first time in a year. With Wattles was his brother-in-law David Ripley, and a nephew; Edwin Fussell, torn between regret over leaving behind his wife Rebecca and their children in the woods on Fall Creek and excitement over an opportunity to return to his family in Chester County; Dr. John McCowan, a brother-in-law of Joseph A. Dugdale, traveling on business; and Valentine Nicholson, who approached the whole journey and all of its events with wide-eyed wonder. The women were the distinguished Hicksite ministers Elizabeth L. Borton and Sarah B. Dugdale, who were combining with their reform interests a welcome chance to visit old friends and relations in the neighborhood of Philadelphia. The men left Oakland on April

13, heading north to Green Plain, where Elizabeth Borton and Sarah B. Dugdale joined them. The "Liberator" struck the National Road at Springfield, and then headed east. At Lloydsville in Belmont County another young Hicksite Friend, Rebecca Nichols, joined the party. Her father, Eli Nichols, was, as one abolitionist wrote, a "tried and faithful champion of our cause."[59]

If the brief letters of Edwin Fussell and the memories of Valentine Nicholson half a century later are reliable, it was a happy journey. "The 'Liberator' is fixed up quite in style" Edwin Fussell told Rebecca, "will carry 10 very comfortably—has elliptic springs, patent lock, lamps, etc. has a place to carry luggage behind and on the top, and is fixed so that 8 can sleep on it at night." At Washington, Pennsylvania, they left the National Road and took the Glade Road east through Bedford and York and on to Philadelphia. They probably held meetings en route; at least Fussell had given speeches on abolition all the way from Pendleton to Oakland. On May 2, they arrived in Vincent in Chester County. Immediately they held a meeting to promote communitarianism, then went on to Philadelphia.[60]

There well-wishers gave the group a warm welcome. They were just in time for an antislavery convention in which Nicholson and Brooke spoke. Nicholson and Amos Welch were guests of James and Lucretia Mott. When the rest of the group drove on to New York City in the "Liberator," Welch and Nicholson stayed behind to play tourist. Their special interests were the Liberty Bell and Girard College, then under construction. The next day they went on to New York City on a steam packet. There they joined Brooke, Fussell, Allen, and Wattles as guests of Isaac T. Hopper.[61]

The 1843 "anniversary" was not a seminal occasion in the history of abolition, but for the Westerners it was memorable. The convention opened with an address from James Monroe, a young abolitionist from Connecticut who was making his debut as a speaker and who had accepted a post as a lecturer for the impending Hundred Conventions campaign. Jacob Ferris, another sympathizer, followed. Then came the major attractions—William Lloyd Garrison, Abby Kelley, Frederick Douglass, and Wendell Phillips. Garrison urged the statement with which he was to become permanently identified: "That we cannot regard any man as a consistent abolitionist who, while holding to the popular construction of the Constitution, makes himself a party to that instrument, by taking any office under it requiring an oath, or voting for its support." The real business was being carried on in the executive committee, which considered a proposal to move the headquarters of the group to Boston, recognizing the reality that virtually all of its strength was in Massachusetts. Some of the inner group stridently opposed this as being a virtual surrender to Lewis Tappan and the "new organization." Compromise quietly resolved the controversy.[62]

Still, the presence of the Westerners was remarked, and their ingenuity and dedication in making the long journey praised. In turn, the Ohio visitors were suitably impressed to meet Garrison, Phillips, Douglass, Kelley, and the other luminaries. For Nicholson, however, others furnished the highlights at the meeting. The 1843 meeting marked the debut before the American Anti-Slavery Society of the Hutchinson Family, the siblings from New Hampshire who attained wide acclaim in the next few years for their performances of antislavery songs. For the Quakers, whose Discipline forbade musical performances, this was a new experience, and forty years later Nicholson remembered the "thrilling force and inspiring power" of what they heard. Hearing the Hutchinsons was another step on his journey away from his strict Quaker upbringing— within a year he would be in difficulty with his monthly meeting for organizing a "singing school." Mary S. Gove, the health reformer who had attended the Lynn convention, was one of the speakers at the meeting. When the president introduced her, the audience, one of whose primary reasons for existence was commitment to the equality of women, responded enthusiastically by clapping and stamping their feet. When the noise finally subsided, Gove "very calmly and quietly in a clear earnest voice," spoke: "The greatest respect that could be shown to a woman on this occasion would be to be still and listen to whatever she might have to say." She then sat down and refused to say more. The audience, Nicholson recalled, seemed quite sheepish afterwards.[63]

On May 12, the day after the end of the American Anti-Slavery Society's meeting, came the long-awaited convention of the Society for Universal Inquiry and Reform. From the beginning, there were ominous signs. Almost all of the Massachusetts abolitionists with whom Collins had been working— Garrison, Phillips, Kelley, Douglass, Remond, the Weston sisters—did not linger to attend. Nor did Lucretia and James Mott, despite their kindly hospitality to the group from Ohio. There was some comfort in the presence of some Fourierists—Horace Greeley, William H. Channing, Albert Brisbane—and that of a few well-known abolitionists who had not involved themselves in previous efforts, such as Stephen S. Foster, Thomas Earle, the Pennsylvanian who had been the Liberty party candidate for vice president, and Ernestine Rose, the pioneer feminist from New York City. Also present was Orson S. Murray, now making plans to move his reform journal to New York City and make it the organ of the new society. His influence, before the day was out, had brought about contention and disagreement, a hint of what was to come for the group. Mary S. Gove was also there, making the acquaintance of Henry G. Wright, the Englishman with whom she would be associated the next few years, and there was Jacob Ferris, a young Quaker from Wayne County, New York. The last had already made an auspicious debut. The year before, at age twenty, he had been appointed an agent by the American Anti-Slavery Society; Oliver Johnson thought him "an uncommonly good speaker."[64]

As president, Brooke should have presided over the proceedings. At the opening, however, Murray made a speech in which he elaborated his views on the evils of organizations and advocated turning the gathering into a "free" meeting. This persuaded Brooke, who announced his hope that "each individual present would be left free to act on his own responsibility." He then resigned his office. Wattles was so appalled that he refused to participate further, leaving to lecture in New England and hope that he could revive the cause by finding support there and in western New York. Collins did remain to take part in the debates, but the direction in which Murray and Brooke had moved the meeting unsettled him.[65]

No account has survived of what speakers said, save what Nicholson recorded forty years later. He recalled with approval the advocacy of Fourierism by Greeley and Brisbane. There were the resolutions that condemned the present social system as responsible for all of the evils of the world. One new idea did emerge, however, a resolution Brooke introduced that among the influences that worked to increase the misery of the world "despite of the multiplied efforts of professed reformers . . . a prominent one is perceived to be the circumstances which surround the human mind, and impede where they do not entirely prevent its investigation of truth." This emphasis on the possibilities of knowledge would emerge again and again over the next two years. On Saturday the convention adjourned.[66]

Those present left with varied feelings. Murray was convinced that a new era of reform was about to dawn. "I have had part in many heavenly meetings," he editorialized in the *Telegraph*, "but this exceeded them all." The order, the conclusions, the absence of "violent organization and government," "despotic moderator," "Aristocratic business committee," "Contentions," and of "recognition of color, caste, creed, sect or sex" all heartened him. Edwin Fussell cryptically told his wife that he would have to explain in person, rather than in writing, what had happened. Most of the Westerners, however, were taken aback by what they saw as Murray's fanaticism and Abraham Brooke's surrender to it. "It was quite discouraging," Nicholson wrote, "after we had made to much do about the great things [we] . . . intended and expected to do for the good of the race to have our President back down, resign his office, and join O. S. Murray in destroying the organized form of our Convention, thus throwing all order into chaotic confusion." In fact, the first anniversary was to be the last. Never again would all of these reformers gather together.[67]

Still the trip was a happy one in most ways for the group. A number of luminaries cordially received them. After the convention, Albert Brisbane invited them to call at his home. Nicholson also was received by La Roy Sunderland, a former Methodist minister and leading proponent of phrenomagnetism and other popular pseudo-sciences of the time. Nicholson spent much of this time "looking at the condition of my fellow man." He was especially moved by what he saw when he went "into the lanes and alleys, where live the kind of people whom Jesus loved to visit." There he saw "scenes calculated to move the hardest heart," and "pictures of human suffering, want, and woe, that might distill a tear in the dryest eye." That fall he wrote to Nathaniel P. Rogers: "These things mine own eyes have seen, and I have made a firm resolve to 'Do or die.' "[68]

The one person they did not have an opportunity to meet, however, was one of the people they most wanted to see, Lydia Maria Child. Child had been the editor of the *National Anti-Slavery Standard,* and the Westerners were her great admirers. She had published with kind words letters by Brooke and Nicholson. From this and her "Letters from New York," they felt as if they were already acquainted. When they crossed the Appalachians, Valentine had gathered some trailing arbutus and Sarah Dugdale had put it carefully into her traveling basket, saying "I will give it to Lydia Maria when I see her." They were downcast when they learned on reaching New York that Child had gone away to spend the week in the country, but reconciled themselves to the disappointment. It was especially acute because Child had made arrangements to live in part of Isaac T. Hopper's house.[69]

On the morning that Brooke, Nicholson, and Allen were to leave New York City for Albany, Valentine and the doctor were waiting in the hallway of the Hopper house for Allen to come back from the livery stable with the "Liberator." As he brought down trunks and boxes he met "a small German-looking woman in the hall, bringing a lot of boxes and other articles in from the street where they had just been unloaded from a dray." The two ignored each other until one of Hopper's daughters came in, then the woman asked: "Where's John?" "I think he is at [the] office." "Confound him. I wish the Old Nick had him. Here I've been waiting at the wharf ever since daybreak this morning and have had nothing to eat but a cracker or two. I wrote to him yesterday and I know he got the letter and told him I was coming on the boat this morning and I asked him to be sure to help me get my baggage brought up from the boat. Confound those draymen. I am not afraid of them." Nicholson was incredulous when Hopper came in and said: "Why Lydia Maria, how does thee do? I am so glad to see thee back with us again." Nicholson was stunned that this "vixen" was the revered Mrs. Child. Meanwhile she had got hold of a hatchet and was attacking her boxes and crates.[70]

When Brooke and Allen drew up with the "Liberator," Brooke came in for their baggage. "We are going to get to see Lydia Maria after all," Valentine told the doctor, pointing to the woman hammering away. Brooke looked at her, then turned back to Nicholson: "That ain't Mrs. Child." "Yes it is." "Why don't you introduce me to her?" "I can't because I've not had any introduction to her myself." Brooke approached her, introducing himself as "Dr. Brooke of Oakland Clinton County Ohio." "How do you do, sir," replied Child, not missing a stroke of her hatchet. Brooke tried to pursue the conversation, saying to Child: "I am sorry you was not at our convention." Child, still not even looking up, replied: "I have a great aversion to large conventions and never attend them." Thoroughly nonplussed, Brooke left her and harrumphed to Nicholson: "She gives me the shorts, so I shall let her alone." Nicholson, however, was more understanding, seeing a tired woman constantly harassed by "the flatteries and attentions of the multitudes." He seemed, at least in retrospect, rather to admire her independent spirit.[71]

After the convention, the group split up. Borton and Dugdale, the two Quaker ministers, remained in New York City to attend New York Yearly Meeting, which undoubtedly did not warmly receive the two signers of the Green Plain disclaimer. Nichols remained with them. The Ripleys, of course, returned to Newark, and Fussell went back to Chester County to spend more time with relatives and to await Sarah Dugdale, with whom he planned to travel to Cincinnati. Brooke, Allen, and Nicholson loaded the "Liberator" onto a Hudson River steamer and set out for Albany, accompanied by some New York Friends who wanted to go west.[72]

From Albany the group drove to Syracuse, where Collins was already making arrangements for the purchase of a farm for a community a few miles away. Collins and Wattles had given notice of plans for a meeting for community purposes to be held, but the day arrived and neither had appeared. Allen steadfastly refused to try to speak in public, and Brooke was hardly a rousing orator. So Nicholson became, by default, the speaker of the evening. By his own account, he had "a fair portion of inspiration" and gave an "earnest and animated address" to an enthusiastic audience.[73]

The next day Collins and Wattles arrived in Syracuse. The enthusiastic response to Nicholson's speech seemed to justify another meeting, which was held that evening. This one, however, became a debate between Collins and Nicholson. Collins argued that all private property was an evil, and that from this evil flowed all other evils of the world. Nicholson answered that private property was not evil per se, but that private ownership of land was. This led to monopoly by a few, shutting out many from any chance of providing themselves with the necessities of life. A local newspaper spoke admiringly of Collins, conceding that he was "a thorough-going radical, whose views will be far from pleasing all" but also "a man of talents" who could "impart much information to almost any person whose preconceived notions have not led him to think that the whole world lies in the narrow circle in which he moves." Nicholson, on the other hand, was sure that he had given as good as he had received. His memory was that many in the audience responded positively to his arguments. Two would feature largely in the future difficulties of John A. Collins—a young lawyer named Quincy Adams Johnson, and a Syracuse schoolteacher, Maria Loomis.[74]

After a visit to Skaneateles, where Collins and sympathizers were looking at a farm, the Westerners pushed on to Rochester to call on Isaac and Amy Post, another prominent Hicksite abolitionist couple. In the towns of the Burned-Over District—Waterloo, Seneca Falls, Geneva, Palmyra—they lectured and spoke on social reform. West of Rochester, they reverted to being tourists, admiring Niagara Falls and then pushing on along Lake Erie back toward Ohio. In Stark County they visited the first community to grow out of their efforts, at the Brookes' old home in Marlborough. They found the beginnings there encouraging.[75]

Still, it was a considerably chastened and now divided group that returned in the "Liberator" to Oakland. Brooke had separated from Allen, and Nicholson, and the rest of the Westerners; he was about to start down a path that would lead him, in his quest for complete freedom from private property and coercive human government, to complete isolation from the reform community. Indeed, by the summer he was denouncing abolitionists as a "sect," "practicing oppression themselves" by using the products of "the unrequited toil of others" for the cause of emancipation. Property holding tainted even nonresistance societies. Most of the others who went east with such high hopes also decided against becoming involved; the Bortons, Dugdales, and McCowans went back to Green Plain and devoted themselves to the redemption of the Society of Friends, rather than of humanity.[76]

Doubtless more disappointing was the failure to attract support in the

East. The great figures of the antislavery movement for whom the Westerners had fought for three years—Garrison, Phillips, Child, Kelley—had politely spurned them. The Easterners who had shown an interest—Collins, Murray, and their supporters—had gone off in directions that seemed at best peculiar and at worst disruptive of all that they were trying to accomplish. And Wattles, the one person with strong ties to the Eastern abolitionists who seemed to share both the Westerners' dreams of universal reform and their doubts about Collins, had disappeared into New England leaving them to battle Collins alone, not to mention all of the other doubts. Nevertheless, the remnant, led by Nicholson and Allen, persevered, looking to their own resources, and the hope of help from the East arriving with the Hundred Conventions in the fall.

Collins, meanwhile, pushed ahead with his own plans for a community near Skaneateles. Before Nicholson, Brooke, and Allen arrived in Syracuse, Collins had already held a meeting which committed those in attendance to the purchase of a farm near the "smart little manufacturing town" of Mottville, north of Skaneateles, and presented a provisional constitution. Collins seemed to have a solid group of supporters, in spite of doubts on all sides, who committed money toward the purchase of the farm.[77]

In less than three years, Wattles, Collins, Murray, and the Hicksite Friends in southwestern Ohio had moved from isolated groups, pondering how they could be agents of change in their neighborhoods, to advocacy of a grand vision of "Universal Reform," nothing less than beginning the Government of God. They were convinced that that required not only the end of coercive human government and "sectism," but the end of competitive capitalism as well. Only a complete reordering of society could meet the requirements of divine law.

To accomplish this, the Society for Universal Inquiry and Reform came to be. In its early months, its founders had a grandiose vision of bringing together all of the leading reformers of the age in one grand organization. Instead, their first (and last) national meeting ended in chaos. They found relatively little support among reformers in the East, and in fact by the summer of 1843 they were experiencing a division in their own ranks. The Hundred Conventions seemed to offer the final hope of transforming the abolitionist movement into one for Universal Reform.

❖ 4 ❖

THE HUNDRED CONVENTIONS
Aspiration and Failure

IN THE SUMMER of 1843, the advocates of Universal Inquiry and Reform looked to the Hundred Conventions, headed by some of the nation's leading Garrisonian abolitionists, to attract new adherents and to rebuild some of the enthusiasm lost with the confusion of the New York City meeting that spring. Not only would the conventions advance the cause of nonresistant abolition, but they would also give those who attended a higher vision of reform a chance to articulate that vision to thousands who were yet in "darkness." The plan was to be a project of unprecedented, breath-taking scope, to mount one hundred Garrisonian meetings. It would begin in New England, then move west into upstate New York, Ohio, and Indiana, concluding in western Pennsylvania. It would bring leading radical abolitionists to places in which Garrisonians had never appeared before.

In fact, the results of the Hundred Conventions were very different from what the advocates of Universal Reform hoped to see. The abolitionist luminaries who led them were badly divided among themselves. Nonresistants clashed with those sympathetic to political action. Blacks were exasperated with whites. And those committed to cooperation found themselves in bitter conflict with those who wanted the meetings to focus just on abolition. By the end of the first month, it had become apparent that, even for Garrisonian abolitionists, Universal Reform was a bitterly divisive endeavor. The tour ended in failure by almost every standard. Some of the party dropped out along the way, others refused to work in company with their appointed compatriots, a mob nearly killed some of the group, and, in Indiana, the conventions found themselves dividing the antislavery movement there.

The Hundred Conventions were the brainchild of John A. Collins. He had convinced the board of the Massachusetts Anti-Slavery Society to commit a considerable sum and some of its most effective and highly regarded lecturers and organizers—George Bradburn, Charles L. Remond, James Monroe, and

Frederick Douglass—to their execution. Jacob Ferris, the young Quaker from New York, William A. White, Sydney H. Gay, Collins, and Wattles were also involved, as was Abby Kelley, working on behalf of the American Anti-Slavery Society. Douglass, a fugitive slave, was just beginning the career that would make him the best-known black man in the United States. Remond was another leading black abolitionist. Kelley, an Orthodox Quaker from Massachusetts, was already well known as a Garrisonian speaker and organizer, as were Gay and White. The campaign meshed well with the desires of the Ohio American Society, which had in March published a call to Bradburn, Kelley, Remond, and Douglass to spend three months in the West. The stated goal of the campaign was to hold one hundred conventions to strengthen abolition, recruit members for newly formed affiliates of the American Anti-Slavery Society, and attack the "new society" and political abolition. Collins, Ferris, and Gay, however, by the summer had new interests, interests that the other abolitionists did not share. This group's journey west was to be much like the journey east of Brooke, Nicholson, and company that spring—begun in high hopes, ending in near disaster.[1]

In June 1843 Collins announced the scheme with appropriate rhetorical flourishes in the *Standard*. "The time has come; the men will be with you shortly," he told sympathizers in New York, Ohio, and Indiana. With their help they would reach between three hundred thousand and half a million fellow citizens; they would also have the "opportunity for . . . mutual consent, information, and concert of action." "Let us rouse the ready West to the encounter, and slavery will sink beneath that giant tread. . . . raise the battle-cry for the rights of man, and bid you stand by them in the moral conflict that calls up every noble feeling, and extinguishes every base one." The *Liberator* added its endorsement, predicting that the movement would "create a thrill of admiration and delight in thousands of bosoms" and "prove highly disastrous to the slave cause, and of immense service to the cause of universal liberty."[2]

The conventions were arranged as a double series. Collins, Kelley, Monroe, White and Ferris were to begin in Springfield, Massachusetts, and then go west to Albany and Utica. Douglass, Remond, and Bradburn were to go up into Vermont, holding meetings in Middlebury, Randolph, and Ferrisburgh. Wattles, Nathaniel H. Whiting, and John Orvis followed to agitate universal reform. Both series would begin on July 10, then at the end of the month the two groups would meet in Syracuse and proceed west across New York, before splitting up again for a second double series moving south and west across Ohio.[3]

From the beginning, however, the two groups met with problems. On July

10 Monroe found himself alone in Springfield—none of his associates had yet appeared, and he had been forced to undertake the scheduled convention alone, not a comforting prospect for the youngest and least experienced of the group. Grumbling, he went on to Albany with the hope that the others would catch up with him, but only after sending an angry demand for help back to Boston. The Vermont contingent was at full strength, but the reaction to their work was uncertain. The ever-optimistic Wattles hastily scribbled a note that "the voice of freedom has gone out from the green mountain tops" and "the signal of Liberty has been telegraphed from the high lands." Wattles continued that "the crusades were for the recovery of the Holy Land from the infidel, Ours is for the redemption of the world, from sin." The medieval crusaders had prevailed by the power of the sword, but the new crusade would overcome evil "by the power of Truth. Glory by Truth shall shake the earth." Whiting argued that it was necessary to begin society anew, with governments the first to go. "They commenced by trampling on the most important of all rights. . . . they commenced by butchery," he told a meeting in Randolph. Then: "the right to the earth had to be recognized for every man," for "he that claims the earth to himself is guilty of all the evil that is in the world." Indeed, "the enslavement of the Earth" was the evil that had given rise to human slavery. Collins summed up: "When you allow man to hold property in earth, . . . you sanction robbery & crime & murder." Orvis wrote confidently to Orson S. Murray that the Vermont meetings were a success, a judgment that Murray endorsed. Looking back half a century later, however, Douglass was less confident. He had spoken in all three places with eloquence and power, attacking the churches for compromising with slavery in the South and with racism in the North. Wattles made careful note of Douglass's speeches: "The church is dishonored when she feels for the heathen abroad—upon the authority of [the] apostle he is a liar he cannot love god whom he hath not seen, if he despises his brother whom he hath seen." Douglass, however, remembered that audiences were small and that the group left little of an impression behind in the state. In Middlebury they were the target of eggs and rocks. From Vermont, they passed on into New York, where they held meetings in Keesville, Albany, Peru, Troy, and Utica. Peru proved a hard place; Orvis thought that material success had inured the residents to the claims of humanity. In Albany they found only "apathy and ignorance." Three days in Utica were more successful. There Collins joined them, and he and Wattles "wrought up" a "large meeting of thrilling interest . . . almost to enthusiasm." The Baptist minister had locked them out of the Bleeker Street Tabernacle, which they had planned to use, so they obtained the court-

91
❖ The Hundred Conventions ❖

house instead. But the emphasis at Utica was not on abolition—it was instead on Collins's plans for general reform, particularly his opposition to private property. The result was the formation of a Society for Universal Inquiry and Reform in Utica.[4]

The two contingents met in Syracuse for a convention on August 1, and there controversy broke out between Douglass and Kelley on one hand, whose commitment was to abolition, and Collins, on the other hand, who wanted to make antislavery merely one facet of the cause of universal reform. No church in Syracuse would open its doors for the meeting, so the attenders crowded into a dismal, abandoned Congregational church. Some were ready to give up any effort in the city. A split took place that would not be healed.[5]

Collins turned the Syracuse meeting into a consideration of the "no property question." When the scheduled starting time for the antislavery convention came, only Kelley and Douglass were present because Collins had chosen to remain behind in North Utica to discuss his community plans with sympathizers. Thus Kelley and Douglass spoke the entire day before Collins arrived that evening. The next day, Monday, August 2, there was to be a "property meeting" presided over by Collins in the morning, with an antislavery meeting that afternoon. Collins, Whiting, Gay, and Orvis all held forth, with Collins taking the lead. Much of the meeting was devoted to Collins's stock expositions on the failings of church and state and the evils of private property. Collins bragged about his success in the last six months, the land, livestock, and money pledged to the cause. "I do not war with any man, but systems," he told his audience. "I have no hard feelings toward my [fellow] man but these institutions which make man a wolf to his fellow man." Humanity was not, he said, "made saddled & bridled & the other part booted & . . . made to ride the rest." There was no government in the world that recognized rights of conscience, "not a government in all Christendom that acknowledges a God." Yet in a world being transformed by steam engines and railroads, there was no reason that "the mental world" should not keep pace. But now "man is in such a condition that he cannot [but] be selfish & we must alter his relations." Toward the end he included the abolitionists in his denunciation for "bigotry and narrow-mindedness"; they were guilty of that worst of all sins, they were "sectarean [sic]." Collins climaxed his denunciad by announcing that the afternoon would be given over to another property meeting. This was too much for Remond, who attacked Collins for making abolition a mere "stepping stone" for his own pet theory. Collins responded with a long speech in which he accused abolitionists of "a mere dabbling with effect." Private property was the root evil of which slavery was merely an emanation. Now Douglass answered Collins with considerable vehemence. Kelley was not present, but she characterized the day as a "most disgraceful 'twitting meeting.' " Collins and Remond were openly feuding, and "the proslavery are quite transported and the abolitionists are most dreadfully mortified." It was all "confusion worst confounded."[6]

What was at stake here was a fundamental question of strategy and tactics, one in which Garrisonians like Douglass, Remond, and Kelley saw Collins as headed in the wrong direction. Looking back years later, Douglass summed up his view in words that might have been Lewis Tappan or Nathaniel Colver speaking of the Garrisonians. Douglass was opposed to Collins's actions because they imposed an "additional burden of unpopularity on our cause." Both he and Kelley, moreover, saw a more practical issue at hand, one of basic honesty. Collins was being paid to serve as the general agent of the American Anti-Slavery Society, and had been sent west to create abolition sentiment. But, as Kelley put it, "his soul is not in there"; for him, "the association question is of vastly greater importance." He had shown himself incapable of working harmoniously with his coadjutors, and Kelley was blunt in urging that he be dismissed, threatening that the real "stars" of the campaign—she, Douglass, and Remond—would leave if Collins continued in charge.[7]

Fundamentally, however, the situation was simply one in which Kelley had run out of patience with Collins. "I can say from the depths of my heart that I admire Collins as a man—He is generous, noble, bold, and humane," she told Maria Weston Chapman, the Boston abolitionist leader, but Collins was using his property meetings as a "long tail . . . to whip off the antislavery flies that may have accumulated through the efforts of the antislavery convention previously held." He had "no system." Kelley thought it a "marvel" that "Douglas [*sic*] knowing him so well could consent to be under his keeping." But Kelley was about to rebel. Collins wanted her to continue on to the meetings in Ohio, but she knew that would require systematic planning, of which she saw Collins as utterly incapable.[8]

Collins was not the only source of irritation for Kelley, however. On arriving in Syracuse, George Bradburn had journeyed on to Peterboro, New York, to call on Gerrit Smith. Smith was renowned both for his great wealth, and for his sympathy for all reform causes, including abolition. He had tried to remain neutral in the 1840 split, but by 1843 was becoming increasingly committed to political action through the Liberty party. This was sufficient to damn him in Kelley's eyes, for she considered it synonymous with "new organization," which was trying "to destroy the moral movement which occupies the only broad and catholic ground and which alone has any real vitality for the overthrow of slavery." Certainly New York Liberty leaders had no use for the Hundred Conventions, which they excoriated as full of "no Government men" who had "other axes to grind." Kelley was convinced, moreover, that Smith had tried to bribe her to support his views. Thus she considered Bradburn's overtures to Smith an act of treachery, and was convinced that the two had reached some sort of dark accord. "Since the Hundred Convention movement commenced," she wrote to James Monroe that autumn, the Liberty party and Smith's forces "have been seen to be one," and she blamed Bradburn for it. In fact Kelley had good reason to be suspicious of Bradburn's political leanings. A former state senator, he was increasingly uncomfortable with the disunion sentiments of the Garrisonians, and by the spring of 1844 had publicly embraced the Liberty party. But with the conflict between Bradburn and Kelley the group had still another source of stress, and that was enough to convince Kelley to quit the tour and stay behind in New York to "cut out the tongue of the Chief son of the Father of Lies" by attacking Smith and the Liberty party.[9]

Kelley's departure was ironic, since Collins never made it to Ohio, either. After the meetings in Syracuse he collapsed. Even in the middle of July he had complained of feeling unwell; his wife was unwilling for him to tax himself even writing letters. By the time he arrived in Syracuse, Kelley, admittedly not the most objective of observers, claimed that "his nerves are so entirely afloat he is all confusion." After Syracuse he gave up speaking in public—he had an "inflammation and pain in his side" that lingered for nearly a month. His wife refused to let him speak, read, or write until late in August. His account of the Syracuse meeting showed that the attacks of his associates prostrated him. Bradburn, he claimed, constantly found fault, and was too egotistical to be an effective abolition speaker. Kelley was "intolerant beyond degree"; she hated "the property question, as the slaveholder hates antislavery." As for Douglass and Remond, they met his efforts in Syracuse with groans and sad looks. Remond in particular had attacked him viciously; first he had "disposed of the property question as humbug and moonshine," and then "he came down upon me like a thunderbolt, and hardly left enough of me to give the smell of fire." Collins had tried to be conciliatory, saying that their resentment of anything that even seemed to distract from antislavery was natural and understandable, but they had not responded to his overtures. So he gave up. Soon afterwards he was dismissed as agent. He was not fully recovered until late in September,

when Anne Weston found him with her sister Maria Chapman in Boston, laying out "the plan of 300 conventions in Massachusetts next winter to go for a
dissolution of the Union."[10]

From Syracuse the group passed on west through the familiar towns of the
Burned-Over District. The meetings in Seneca Falls, Rochester, and Lockport
were more harmonious, although it is unclear whether this was the result of
Collins's sympathizers muting their communitarian message, or because Remond and Douglass had swallowed their reservations under orders from Boston. (Douglass remembered later that his complaints to Maria Chapman had
drawn a scathing rebuke, saying that Collins was in charge and he was to do as
directed.) Douglass and Bradburn went on to Buffalo, where Bradburn, finding the accommodations intolerable, left Douglass to fend for himself. His and
Remond's speaking efforts attracted relatively few hearers—Remond saw the
hand of the clergy behind the paucity of the turnout. More to their liking was
the National Convention of Colored Men, held in Buffalo in August. The experience was an important one for Douglass, since it marked his introduction
to such black leaders as William Wells Brown and Henry Highland Garnet.[11]

From Buffalo, the group, now made up of Douglass, Remond, Monroe,
White, and Bradburn, with Wattles following in their wake, set off for Ohio.
Once there, they again split into two groups planning to reunite at Oakland.
Monroe, Remond, Ferris, and Wattles were to speak at Jefferson, Salem, Massillon, and Utica, while Bradburn, Collins, and Douglass were to be at Cleveland, Oberlin, Mansfield, Woodberry, and Green Plain. As in New York, Collins
had arranged for a series of meetings for "the purpose of discussing the right
to individual property," to follow each of the antislavery conventions. Ferris
would join with Wattles, while Whiting and Orvis would join with Collins.
These carefully laid plans fell apart, however, when Collins became ill in Syracuse, and when Remond and Douglass rebelled at the chaos they saw all around
them. They agreed to be at Oakland for the Ohio American Anti-Slavery Society's meeting early in September, but they refused to be the tails of the communitarian kite. So the schedule was hastily rearranged. It preserved the two
series, but with considerably reduced personnel.[12]

Ohio abolitionists had looked to the coming of the Easterners with considerable anticipation. "The fields are beginning to whiten to harvest in this part
of the antislavery field," one had written to Monroe in the spring. And young
Monroe bore the brunt of the speaking. Almost every day he spoke at least
three hours, some days for five or six. Remond would occasionally appear, but
was more often absent. By late in the month Monroe's voice was gone, and new

friends were worrying that he would collapse, just as had so many other abolition organizers. "Stop and rest a while—or you will destroy your usefulness in future day," one ordered him.[13]

The reports that went back to the *Liberator* told of one success after another. When they entered Ohio, Monroe, White, and Gay were received by Joshua R. Giddings, the Whig congressman from the Western Reserve, who was considered one of the foremost abolitionists in the House of Representatives. In Warren their reception was equally friendly; all was "kindness and attention." In Salem they held the largest meeting yet of the tour. It took place in the woods, since there was no building big enough to accommodate all who were there. In the evening, two churches were opened for their use. Then it was on to New Lisbon, and then west to Marlborough, where again no building was large enough to hold all who had come. These were Quaker communities, with large Hicksite elements sympathetic to abolition. From there, however, they went west to Massillon and Wooster, which were considerably less friendly. In Massillon they had their first public confrontation, with a lawyer and "a Methodist priest, named Ambler," who, as White wrote to Garrison, "seems to be most appropriately named, for from his speaking, I imagine he ambles most highly over the sins of his people." White dismissed them as "catspaws" who were an embarrassment. In Wooster they could not even find a meeting place, so they were forced to speak in the town square. There they encountered the congressman from the district, a Democrat who denied that Elijah Lovejoy had been murdered, but argued loudly that Garrison should be, and that everything that Monroe said was a lie. In Utica they met with a certain General Warner, a prominent Whig who branded the abolitionists as "the immediate successors of the Jacobins of the days of terror." Monroe responded with "wit, satire, and reason," and if the general "was not entirely overthrown, it was because like a feather, he was entirely blown away by the first burst of artillery."[14]

The Easterners found much they liked in the West. Marlborough was especially to their taste, since every man, woman, and child in the village had taken the temperance pledge. The outdoor meetings were also a source of pleasure: "Gatherings in God's temple are most beautiful spectacles," White wrote. "In the midst of the noble and lofty trees, the seats are arranged, and a rough stand for those who are to address the meetings." There one would hear the speakers amidst "the glories of God's temple, in which no priest can claim a proscription or shut out any on sectarian grounds." White even liked the mothers who came with their babies: "a little annoying . . . when ten or a dozen set up a shout," it was an encouraging sign of interest on the part of the mothers. Only the towns were not to their liking. "I have been disappointed in the appearance of the Ohio towns," he wrote to Garrison. "Notwithstanding the abundance and cheapness of land, the houses are crowded close together, and look as though they had been built in the woods, and getting frightened had rushed pell-mell together, and stood in compact rows, both great and small."[15]

No account has survived of how the other group did across Ohio, but they joined with Monroe and company at Green Plain, and then went on to Oakland, where early in September a three-day anniversary meeting of the Ohio American Anti-Slavery Society was held. Joseph A. Dugdale presided, and Abraham Brooke chaired the business committee. Bradburn, Monroe, and White all played an active part, and the Easterners were favorably impressed by all that they saw. On the first day, Bradburn counted 470 horses around Liberty Hall, and even more on the second day. "This is a meeting well worth the expense," he wrote to the *Liberator*. "I have seen here the need of goodly number of speakers; for the people desire to hear us almost from the rising of the sun to the going down thereof." They were disappointed, however, since all but Bradburn and Ferris were sick with bronchitis. Douglass and Remond did not arrive until after the anniversary had ended. Abraham Brooke saw some ulterior motive behind the delay, although he did not elaborate on his suspicions. Still, within two hours, almost a thousand people assembled to hear them speak. One hearer wrote that they held forth "with a boldness and power which I have never seen surpassed."[16]

From Oakland the group was to go into Indiana, a doubly hostile place. The antislavery cause was, of course, extremely weak there, probably more so than in any other northern state. The Indiana Anti-Slavery Society was a small group, virtually indistinguishable from the state Liberty party, and dominated by Orthodox Quakers from Hamilton, Grant, Randolph, Union, Wayne, and Henry counties. They tended to view Garrisonians as infidels, so Garrisonian sentiment was limited to a small group of Hicksite Friends and a few scattered New Englanders. It was, as one minister put it, "a hard place for antislavery." The events of the next month would prove that.[17]

The plan for Indiana had the Easterners visiting areas known to be sympathetic to abolition (as much as any part of Indiana could be) and venturing into neighborhoods that had barely been reached by antislavery organizers of any kind. Monroe, Remond, and Gay were to hold conventions among the Orthodox Friends at Cherry Grove in Randolph County and the Hicksites at Camden in Jay County, then go on to the Orthodox Quaker communities in Hamilton County. Thence they would travel on to Indianapolis, the state capital, and then to Greenwood, Sand Creek, and Milan, where there had been stir-rings of abolitionist sympathy. Douglass, Bradburn, White, and Wattles were supposed to cover the Quaker area of east-central Indiana—Cambridge City, Richmond, New Castle, and Liberty, all in the midst of Quaker communities but not especially known for abolitionist sympathies; and Pendleton, Edwin Fussell's home. Remond, however, was thrown by a runaway team as they were leaving Oakland, nearly breaking his wrist.[18]

Remond, Monroe, and Gay stopped first at Newport in Wayne County, a noted center of antislavery sentiment. Israel French, a Hicksite Friend who lived south of town, was their host. From there it was on to Cherry Grove for two days. Gay liked the meetinghouse "placed on a secluded but picturesque hillside, in the midst of God's first temples—the primeval western forests, the gothic groves, on which the devastating hand of man has never yet been laid." Several Orthodox Anti-Slavery Friends were present, including Daniel Puckett, one of their most prominent ministers. The emphasis was on boycotting goods produced by slave labor, a subject on which abolitionists of all persuasions in Indiana were in agreement. Gay thought that they were making progress and winning converts; the presence of Hiram Mendenhall especially pleased him. From Cherry Grove they went on to Camden. Gay noted acerbically that a mob was rumored to be massing, "but the mobocrats, or their leaders, had all gone on to a more appropriate sphere—a camp meeting." Gay considered the Cam-den meeting, in which "the church and the State were thoroughly discussed" a good one. He also liked the Camden Friends, whom he judged to be "true-hearted abolitionists," who were "wielding an influence, which has made itself felt already, and will yet revolutionize this section of the country."[19]

It was Douglass who was to prove the martyr of the expedition. Given In-diana's reputation, both he and Remond had been dubious about attending the meetings that had been scheduled for them, but after long discussions at Oak-land had decided to proceed. The meeting in Cambridge City was uneventful, and then Bradburn, White, and Douglass, moved on to Pendleton, Wattles hav-ing left them to go off with Edwin Fussell and Valentine Nicholson to agitate the cause of Universal Reform.[20]

Pendleton, despite its Quaker residents, was in Madison County, an area that was notorious for its antiabolitionist sentiments. Two years earlier, a meet-ing in the northern part of the county had proposed a new state law: "that no Abolichenor shal be alowed to vote at the poals Bair armes in the Militery servis worke Roads pay pole tax or Bee a witness for or against a white Man or A Dutch Man or to hold any ofice of trust Or Profet." Bradburn, White, and

Douglass were warned when they arrived that they should expect a visit from a mob. But they discounted the warnings.[21]

On September 15 the three opened the convention in the Baptist church. Ominously, its minister was not present; although sympathetic to abolition, he had, he later confessed to Fussell, stayed away out of fear. The morning session was undisturbed, but when the three returned in the afternoon, they found themselves locked out. The minister feared that if the meetings continued a mob would tear the building apart. So Bradburn tried to speak in front of the church, but a sudden downpour forced him to stop after fifteen minutes. Bradburn announced that the convention would resume the next day, September 16, in a nearby grove.[22]

That afternoon the signs of trouble appeared. Bradburn and White saw in the crowd the stereotypical antiabolition mob: "unshaven, lantern-jawed, savage-looking loafers," who filled the air with "their horrible mutterings of murderous threats, and blasphemous oaths, against abolitionists and 'niggers.' " As might be expected, "their courage had been stimulated by the spirit of rum." Bradburn and White tried to talk with them about the effects of slavery on the rights of northern workingmen, but the rainstorm brought that to an end. The mob contented itself with throwing a single stone and few eggs.[23]

The next day the riot took place. That morning White and Bradburn spoke for about an hour and a half to a "good audience," when a local physician named Cook arrived to warn them that the mob was on the way. There were about sixty men from the country east and south of town, "coatless, with shirt-sleeves rolled up, marching in double file, all well supplied with brickbats, stones, and 'evangelical eggs.' " One of the leaders, a brute with a "villainously low" forehead, and wearing a "fantastic coon-skin cap" which "had probably been out in 'the cider barrel campaign' of '40," was trying to look "particularly ferocious." The spokesman for the mob ordered the meeting to disperse. Some of the audience tried to leave, but those on the platform held their ground. The mob then let loose with the eggs and rocks, but for whatever reason their aim was bad. Some moved up to the front and began to argue with White and Bradburn; one named Rix took over the speaker's stand and harangued those still there on how the abolitionists were "anti-republican" and "tories," because they would not vote for slaveholders, and because they insisted on "letting the niggers loose for nothing." But the would-be orator proved a disappointment; "his tongue, refusing, with the most asinine obstinacy, to utter his feelings, the fellow fell into a paroxysm of mute gesticulation, exhibiting such grotesque, and at the same time terrible contortions of trunk and limbs, as perhaps were

never exhibited by any culprit corpse subjected to the action of a galvanic bat-
tery." The assemblage began to laugh, and the mob leaders, seeing their riot on
the verge of becoming a farce, moved quickly to rally their troops. They first
tore apart the speaker's stand, then turned on the speakers. Bradburn was lucky
to escape relatively unscathed with only a scalp wound from a rock.[24]

Douglass and White bore the brunt of the mob's wrath. When several fell
on one of the abolitionists, a "general melee" began. Thinking it was White,
Douglass rushed to his rescue, picked up a club, and set on White's attackers.
He soon lost the club, however, and, now unarmed, tried to run. The mob
caught him quickly, shouting, "kill the nigger, kill the d—n nigger." One struck
him on the head with a rock, raising a bump "nearly as large as a hen's egg,"
besides leaving him sore and bruised on his side and his right hand broken; he
was maimed for life. White probably saved Douglass's life. Ironically, he had
not been the mob's initial victim after all, and when he saw Douglass run, he
followed. Just as one of the thugs was about to strike Douglass a blow that probably would have killed him, White sent him sprawling with a swipe from a
stick he had snatched up. White himself emerged from the fight with his head
bleeding profusely, and several of his teeth knocked out. Douglass was carried
off unconscious to the house of Neal and Elizabeth Hardy, Fussell's sister and
brother-in-law, who lived on a farm outside town. Some feared that he was
dead, but, nursed by the gentle Elizabeth Hardy, he was soon back on his feet.[25]

That night the abolitionists waited in fear. There were rumors that the mob
would return to demolish Edwin Fussell's house and office, so a number of the
town's non-Quaker residents had armed themselves. The abolitionists scattered, further alarmed by reports that the mob had been reinforced and was
regrouping for another attack. As night fell, Rebecca Fussell and her three children were hurrying out of town, a scene that deeply moved Bradburn: "that
dear woman, the doctor's excellent wife, taking her leave of friends and relatives . . . hurrying out of [her] own house . . . to avoid being buried beneath its
ruins by an infernal mob." As Bradburn went to his own hiding place, he saw
a young man with a rifle, hurrying to the town's edge. "I was half tempted to
stop him," Bradburn wrote, "and beg his acceptance of my thanks for this humanity; for, after all . . . it *must* be humanity, to shoot down, like mad dogs,
such infernal enemies of our race."[26]

The affair in Pendleton had lasting effects. It made Indiana's already awful reputation in antislavery circles even worse. It sealed Douglass's friendship
with White; the memory of Pendleton would haunt him for the rest of his life.
It also marked the end of Edwin Fussell's association with universal reform.

Returning from his tour with Nicholson and Wattles to find mobs still threatening, he packed up Rebecca and their children and returned to the more civilized confines of Chester County.[27]

From Pendleton, Douglass and his companions went on to the Indiana Anti-Slavery Society's annual meeting at Jonesboro in Grant County, a small town in the midst of another Quaker neighborhood. The Indiana society was not likely to prove a sympathetic audience—its convention coincided with that of the Liberty party, and the Orthodox Quakers who dominated it were mainly concerned with the upcoming state elections. Bradburn, predictably, with his sympathy for political action, found the Liberty men in Indiana and Ohio "to be worthy of [the] name. Truer abolitionists one need not ask for." Indiana abolitionists, moreover, tended to look on Garrisonians as infidels—their sympathies were firmly with the "new society." Gay sensed it; from the beginning he thought that the convention was haunted by a "lurking suspicion in the minds of some of the Indianans, of the eastern agents." But he liked the Westerners, especially for their aid to fugitive slaves.[28]

Thus it was probably inevitable that the Garrisonians from New England would find themselves involved in controversy, and they did. Ironically, its seeds, in the words of one of Abraham Brooke's correspondents, had been sown through "want of harmony of feeling among our Eastern friends who were with us." Bradburn, who had begun a long speech in a morning session, wanted to conclude in the evening. Douglass objected; he was irritated because he thought that Bradburn was dominating the convention, and angry because Bradburn had made what Douglass considered to be racist remarks. The society's president, Daniel Worth, the Wesleyan Methodist minister who had been Hiram Mendenhall's comrade in confronting Henry Clay, ruled that Bradburn could finish. That set off Remond, who demanded the floor, called Worth a "jackass," and "made a hot speech" appealing to the convention to overrule Worth. When it refused, Remond stormed that "they must be a set of monkeys out here in the West." Monroe, apparently disgusted, refused to speak at all. Douglass completed the round of controversy by getting into a "difficulty" with Benjamin Stanton, the editor of the *Free Labor Advocate*. The Indiana abolitionists were not happy with the Garrisonians. William Beard, a Quaker from Union County, Indiana, told another antislavery man "if they do not do more hurt than good before they get out of the state he shall feel thankful." The two were, in Beard's mind, "a disgrace to abolition." Beard was a stalwartly Orthodox Friend who might be expected to be fearful of Garrisonians, but Abraham

Brooke expressed similar fears. "As near as I can find out Remond and Douglass choose to be the lions of the party and are unwilling to be directed by others or restrained by parliamentary usage" (a strange worry for Brooke, the avowed enemy of all such restraints on liberty). Remond, however, came away from the convention in a happy mood. He thought Stanton "rather sectarian" but "a true friend to the slave," and pledged to obtain five new subscribers for the *Free Labor Advocate*.[29]

After Jonesboro, the two parties continued on schedule. Douglass was subjected to a few eggs in Richmond, but little more. In Noblesville, Remond and Monroe faced what Remond called "the coolest act of the kind within my recollection of mobocratic history." They had planned to speak on September 25 in the courthouse, but a group from the countryside came in and ordered them and the audience to leave—and the audience quickly did. "No damage was done—nor lives endangered, but liberty was murdered by the cowardly surrender of unquestionable rights." Remond wrote to a friend in the East. From there they were to go to Indianapolis, which Remond considered one of the chief strongholds of the slavocracy. "If reports are to be relied upon sad scenes will take place there," he predicted. "Two hundred men have been drilling for the past week on horseback with the avowed determination to burn, kill and destroy if the attempt shall be made to hold the assembly." But the convention passed without incident.[30]

In early October the Easterners returned to Clinton County, Ohio. There Abraham Brooke had an opportunity to talk with them, and revised his opinions. He was pleased by their efforts in Clinton County. "Frederick has been doing a grand work in this neighborhood the past week—The people hear gladly," he wrote to Maria Weston Chapman in Boston. "Proslavery politicians and religionists are perfectly rabid and frothing at the mouth at every——."[31]

From Oakland the group turned east toward home. In New Lisbon Douglass proved so effective that the Ohio American managers offered him a year's contract. Bradburn was unhappy with their reception in Pennsylvania; he thought that there was less enthusiasm there than in Ohio. The last convention was held in Philadelphia in December.[32]

The impact of the Hundred Conventions was uncertain. In the autumn, observing from a distance, Abby Kelley thought it all a grand success. "I throw up my bonnet and give three cheers for the 'Hundred Conventions' " she wrote to Monroe. "Every where we have been misrepresented—This refutes the slanders and gives us the advantage of our lying enemy." But Kelley was almost alone in her optimism. The conventions may have reinforced the Ohio Garrisonians, but they made no inroads on the commitment of virtually all Indiana abolitionists to the "new organization" and the Liberty party.[33]

More than that, the conventions reinforced the distance between the "universal reformers" and many of the radical abolitionists to whom they had looked for support. The Westerners' trip east in the spring, and the work of the Easterners in New York, Ohio, and Indiana had shown that even radical abolitionists looked askance at the communitarian dreams of universal reform. Their rejection did not weaken the adherence of Nicholson, Brooke, Wattles, and the others to abolition. It was but another sign of how much work had yet to be done. As Brooke had written to Maria Chapman when Douglass and Remond were in Oakland in October, while they were "talented and glorious specimens of the 'fallen' humanity," they were still but "unregenerate men." In other words, they were creatures of the unregenerate world that the devotees of Universal Reform were attempting to transform. But now they knew that they had to proceed alone.[34]

The result of the Hundred Conventions was to blast the last hopes of the Universal Reformers that they might be able to bring abolitionists and kindred reformers en masse into their association. Instead, Universal Reformers like Collins and Wattles had found themselves isolated, regarded as distractions and pests by their colleagues. Attempts to use the Hundred Conventions as a vehicle for attacks on private property and competitive capitalism had yielded uncertain results. Separate meetings drew some attention, but attempts to introduce these topics into antislavery conventions, like those of Collins at Syracuse, failed. After the summer of 1843, the advocates of Universal Reform apparently gave up on winning adherents through such means. No longer would they depend solely on words to win the world to their cause. Instead, they would proceed to the establishment of communities, to begin the transformation of the world and usher in the Government of God.

THE COMMUNITIES

"COMMUNITY," WROTE John O. Wattles early in 1844, was "the embodiment of all good, and the consummation of all Reform."[1] After the Hundred Conventions had failed to create a broad-based movement for Universal Reform, advocates turned to another strategy. Instead of using agents and lectures as the primary vehicles for turning the world away from competitive society, the reformers would now show the way by actually living in community. There they would live according to the demands of God's Government, showing that what skeptics and scoffers said could not be done was indeed possible. They would begin to "redeem the Earth" for Humanity, establishing homes in which Humanity could escape the oppression of robbers and slave masters of all types, Southern and Northern.

Eight communities attempted to make Universal Reform a reality. The largest and best known was that at Skaneateles, New York, which John A. Collins headed. Three were in Ohio—Marlborough, which actually antedated Universal Reform agitation but was intimately tied to it, and the closely connected Prairie Home and Highland Home communities near West Liberty and Zanesfield (not Zanesville), Ohio, respectively. Four were in Indiana: Union Home in Randolph County, West Grove or Fraternal Home in Jay County, Kristeen in Marshall County, and Grand Prairie in Warren County. All but Marlborough and Kristeen came to be in 1843 or 1844, and all had collapsed by the autumn of 1846.

Founding communities based on nonresistance was almost unprecedented. Of course, there were nonresistant communities not linked to Universal Reform, Adin Ballou's Hopedale being the best known. But Universal Reform does provide an opportunity to study the problems inherent in nonresistant communitarianism. As this chapter and the next will show, the Universal Reformers faced problems from the beginning. Some of these problems were common to almost all utopian communities: debts, lack of capital, conflicts over membership and leadership. This aspect of the communities' history will hold few surprises for historians. Others, however, were inherent in nonresistance and the Universal Reformers' ideology and thus were peculiar: How could they have any sort of order without some means of coercion of the recalcitrant and disorderly? How could they raise the funds they needed to survive without engaging in commerce and compromising with capitalism? How could they welcome all of humanity without being victimized by the lazy and shiftless? How could they be committed to what was essentially a religious vision without some sort of shared religious commitment? As this and the following chapter will show, these problems continually vexed what may have been the most ambitious attempt in America to usher in the Government of God.

Marlborough

"The Marlborough community seems, as I think of it, to have had its existence so entirely in the dreams of human advancement and the generous wish to promote it, and also in ignorance of all but the better part of human nature, that it is hard to speak of it as a *bona fide* portion of our plodding work-a-day world." So wrote Esther Ann Lukens, the wife of Joseph Lukens, late in the 1840s.[2]

It was the first of the communities to come into being, preceding the actual formation of the Society for Universal Inquiry and Reform. The Brookes and their relatives, the Lukenses, were the moving force behind it, and it was the Brookes and Lukenses who ultimately were responsible for its dissolution.

The community formed in 1841. It was the product of the discussions among the Brookes and their friends around Oakland. Finally Edward Brooke, the member of the family who had remained in Marlborough, offered his farm as the site for a community. Abraham and Elizabeth Brooke, who had held on to a tract of land near brother Edward's farm when they moved to Oakland, offered it for the use of the enterprise.[3]

Relatively little is known about the people who made up the community. Its leading spirit was Joseph Lukens, the younger brother of Elizabeth Brooke, who joined it in the summer of 1842. Apparently saved from the bad companions his brother-in-law had feared, he had become a dedicated reformer, "zealous . . . for the spread of science, and a just appreciation of the rights of man." Most of the rest who can be identified were Hicksite Friends who were also active abolitionists. Jonathan and Hannah (Thompson) Thomas came from nearby Salem. From New Garden came Owen and Mary F. (Myers) Thomas; she was just beginning the career that would make her one of the Midwest's first woman physicians and a leading advocate of woman's rights. Jacob Ferris found a home there at least for a time, as did Amos Gilbert, a schoolteacher from Columbiana County who had left a deep impression on Esther Whinery, John O. Wattles's wife-to-be, both for his dedication to teaching and for his encouragement of his students to question and challenge. Also joining were Marius Robinson, the old Lane rebel, and his wife Emily.[4]

When the group reached its height early in 1845, it had about fifty residents, about half of them adults, the adults equally divided between men and women. Amos Gilbert, who, as will be seen later, was nothing if not a hardheaded realist, thought that the physical situation was encouraging. The purchase of another tract of land had given the community about five hundred acres, two hundred of them cleared, "though but a patch of that is in good farming order." The soil was good—oats and wheat flourished, potatoes were plentiful, and orchards promised abundant fruit in time. There were good springs, and two small creeks usually provided enough water power for two sawmills. The timber—beech, sugar maple, oak, hickory, and poplar—was enough for at least half a century of rail fences and building lumber.[5]

There was relative harmony among the residents of the community, at least initially. Most were old friends and neighbors. Several were "skillful mechanics," but that proved to be of little use. In Esther Ann Lukens's view, they were thoroughly "honest, philanthropic, warmly social" and "eminently moral and intellectual." In their religious views, they had advanced beyond Hicksite Quakerism, and some did not take offense at the label of "Free Thinker." Abraham Brooke labeled them "a very liberal little sect." Every Sunday they held conferences for "improvement and domestic counsel," but religion, according to Lukens, was not a subject of discussion. They were also united in a commitment to the "plainest vegetable diet." There was "much time" for discussion and "social and mental improvement," and the discussions were never quarrels. "Love and good fellowship reigned paramount."[6]

We have only a vague picture of how the community operated. There were originally two large houses on the farms the Brookes had donated, each accommodating three families, and two log cabins each housed another family. By 1845 two more houses had been built, and only two families shared living quarters. Community seems to have consisted in large part of these common living arrangements. There is conflicting evidence about the division of labor. Amos Gilbert wrote in 1844 that while "there may have been, on the part of some a sickly anticipation of hope—an over-wrought anticipation of immediate, perfect results," the inhabitants had become more realistic. They had settled down to "hard knocks"—"rolling logs, excavating stumps, plowing, sowing, etc. . . . precisely as other industrious intelligent men perform the same operations."

They were confident that soon "their labors will ensure them with a supply of all their necessities with less dependence of commerce than is now practicable." Then their work would be "comparatively light, leaving sufficient leisure for intellectual and social culture." Esther Ann Lukens was less sanguine. The residents were "willing to perform what appeared to them the right amount of labor belonging to freemen in a right state of society." That, in her view, was invariably less than the needs of the community required.[7]

In keeping with the vision that originally united them, the group elected no officers. They believed that "rights are based on wants," but they still regulated admission, much in the manner of a Quaker business meeting. They had no written rules except what Lukens called "a brief statement of principles," which new members were invited to sign. There was no requirement that a new member make any kind of financial contribution, and many came in without contributing anything. New members had to be acceptable to everyone already in the community, however, and they were admitted only if there was some suitable employment or "the means of living" available at the time. After a time, the community appointed a finance committee to oversee its business affairs.[8]

In 1844 the group began to disintegrate. The death of Joseph Lukens from a spinal injury in August 1843 was a terrible blow. Although he was only twenty-two, he had been the central figure of the community, the glue that held it together. After his death, the community found itself increasingly tense. It attempted to deal with the problems at least in part by writing a constitution, but that only irritated those like Abraham Brooke who saw all such documents as instruments of tyranny.[9]

Economics, however, proved the downfall of the community, both in reality and perception. As was the case with all of the communities, capital was always short—most of those involved brought little into the experiment. The growing membership forced the community to buy more land, in this case at a high price from a neighbor who had no interest in "the cause of humanity." So a debt was incurred that could be paid off only through more commerce with the world. Some were willing to resort to this as a temporary expedient, others saw it as a betrayal of principles. By 1845, this had grown into an open conflict between the brothers Edward and Abraham Brooke. Edward Brooke had become convinced, either from a commitment to the growth of the experiment, or a desire to protect his investment, that the community had to be put on a surer financial footing. Thus he favored more carefully controlling admission, giving preference to those who had resources to commit to the venture, or who were clearly committed to community principles. Otherwise, he feared that those who wished to be supported without working and who had a vague commitment to communitarianism, but did not share the beliefs of the founders of Marlborough, would overwhelm the community. Edward Brooke, moreover, with the mortgage hanging over the community, wanted to emphasize activities that would bring in the cash it so badly needed. Within the community they would have "everything free among themselves," but "traffic in the common way with those outside."[10]

For Abraham Brooke, however, this was a betrayal of the whole principle of community. He had agreed to leave his land in the hands of the Marlborough group, but he and Elizabeth Brooke never lived there, and he contributed nothing more. Abraham Brooke was becoming increasingly radical to the point of eccentricity. He objected to any kind of organization. A traveler who visited him in the fall of 1844 found a "tall, thin man with gray hair and beard quite unshaven," barefoot in only shirt and pantaloons. He lived in a small neat house filled with books, but refused to compromise with coercive government in any way. By this time he had even given up the *Liberator*, since he received it through the mail, and the mails were a function of the coercive government.[11]

Abraham Brooke had become equally unyielding in his attitude toward commerce. His only principle, he said, was "to do what he considered right." He dispensed his medical services free of charge, and whenever he needed something, he simply asked for it, whether it be of merchants or neighbors. In one case, he wanted a brick building put up in back of his house, so he simply made his need known and five men appeared to build it. "Many looked upon the man himself as being *crasy* [*sic*]," the visitor concluded, "though he was much respected in this neighborhood in which he lived."[12]

Faced with this sort of split, the Marlborough community began to break apart. What future the community had lay largely with three families who were in a position to contribute capital. All three were supposed to sell farms and then turn the proceeds over to the community. Two of the families, after living at Marlborough for a year, came to dislike the place, and decided to leave before turning over the funds that they were supposed to contribute. The third was unable to sell its farm.[13]

Thus it became apparent that Marlborough was no longer viable, and the ever-practical Edward Brooke decided to pull out. With him would go a large part of the community's land. Thus the "true socialists" were left in an impossible situation—only Abraham Brooke's farm and some mortgaged land, no capital, and the departure of some former enthusiasts who now thought that community lost. And so, early in 1846, it came to an end. Esther Ann Lukens provided Marlborough's epitaph: "the experiment failed at the time it did through lack of faith in those who had the funds, and lack of funds in those who had the faith."[14]

Prairie Home

The most ambitious of the communities in the West was Prairie Home, located in the Mad River Valley north of Urbana in Champaign County, Ohio. We also know more about it than any other, save Skaneateles, since its affairs were widely discussed in Orson S. Murray's new newspaper, the *Regenerator,* and since Valentine Nicholson was one of its promoters, and he was careful to record its history.

When Valentine Nicholson and Abraham Allen came back from New York in the summer of 1843, they were still committed to community life. As has been seen, Wattles also kept up the cause in Indiana and Ohio, speaking at meetings and conventions in the traditional Quaker antislavery centers like Green Plain and Newport. In December 1843 or thereabouts Wattles spoke about community in Zanesfield, a small but vibrant community of Hicksite Friends in Logan County, Ohio. Wattles found so much interest there that he scheduled another convention a few weeks later. It attracted the curious from all over western Ohio, especially from the Hicksite Quaker communities where radicalism was always strongest: Oakland, Green Plain, and Harveysburg. It lasted three days, and, as Nicholson remembered, "awakened so much interest by the pictures we presented of the possibility of enjoying Peace, Harmony, more advantages for mental improvement and intellectual culture, that the entire neighborhood . . . seemed ready to unite in the enterprise."[15]

By the spring of 1844 the enthusiasts had decided that the time had come to select a place to put theory into practice. After considering various places, they decided on a farm of five hundred acres on the Mad River near the line between Logan and Champaign counties. The owner was one Israel Pim. Pim is a shadowy figure, and most of what we know of him comes from Nicholson, who, as will be seen later, had every reason to dislike him. There was a large and prominent Quaker Pim family in Columbiana County, but it is unknown whether Israel was related to them; it appears that he was not a Friend. Pim's landholdings were large, but he was overextended, and eager to sell. He himself was not interested in community (although he told the buyers that he was), and he may have seen in the Prairie Home group some likely prospects of whom he could take advantage. But the group agreed to pay five thousand dollars for the farm. Nicholson signed the contract, along with Friends from Clinton and Warren counties—Abraham Allen and Elihu Oren—and at least three from Zanesfield, Horton Brown, Thomas Pennock, and Benjamin Michener. "We had not the least thought of any danger about failing to raise the money by the time we agreed to make the payments," Nicholson remembered, "because we had the names signed in good honest faith of enough well to do farmers, mechanics, and others to have easily paid twice that amount."[16]

All were enthusiastic about the location. It was (and still is) a beautiful place. John O. Wattles had liked to sing of the paradise on earth in which Humanity would find its home:

Lo, down in the beautiful valley
Where love crowns the meek and the lowly
And the land storms of envy and folly
Shall ne'er find those regions of peace.
Lo there, there the Lord shall deliver
And souls drink of that beautiful river
That flows peace for ever and ever
Where love and joy shall ever increase.

At Prairie Home the surroundings seemed to Wattles to fulfill the vision of his song. "This location is in one of those '*beautiful* vallies,' mentioned in the song and which can only be found in the Western world," he told the readers of the *Regenerator*. "Its natural advantages are only exceeded by its unrivalled beauty." "It varies in width, from one to several miles," he continued. The four small streams seemed "so enraptured by its beauty" that they wound and meandered, reluctant to leave "the enchanted vale." "And the four rivers, the Euphrates and its tributaries, that flowed from *primeval* Paradise that was planted 'eastward in Eden' could scarcely have afforded more beauty to the beholder and more utility to the dwellers there, than these that run through this 'beautiful valley.'"[17]

Actually, the land was a pleasant combination of bottom land along the Mad River, and part of the gentle hills that overlooked it on the west, to rise two or three miles east. Wattles was again moved to romantic ecstasy. "On their majestic brow, Hope and Fame, hand in hand, and side by side, sit in holy contemplation and talk of other Homes and other Edens to be planted there." Thus, "the homes for Humanity's sons and daughters shall look upon each other from hill to hill, across the extended prairie—and as the ancient statue on the Egyptian temple made music at sunrise, so these shall make melody, one to the other, at the rising and the setting of the summer's sun." On the hills and in the valley the world would be shown the better way.[18]

The men who selected the site were practical, experienced farmers, however, and practical considerations were paramount. The soil was rich; the uplands clay, bottoms alluvial loam on top of clay and gravel, so that they drained easily. About half of the land was still in timber—oak, walnut, hickory—not particularly well-suited to building, but lumber was plentiful and cheaply obtained from neighbors. It also had water power from Mad River; a grist mill and a saw mill were already in operation on the farm. A distillery and a brewery were also on the land, and that also attracted the communitarians—they would "sink these infernal engines so deep into the sea of eternal oblivion, that even the bubbles shall never rise over them again."[19]

The modernizing tendencies of the group were apparent in the emphasis they placed on "Intercourse with the World around." The farm was about twenty-five miles north of Springfield and the National Road. More important, at least for Wattles, it lay on the line of a projected railroad from Cincinnati to Toledo. "This will put the community within three or four days journey of the Atlantic shores; thus bringing the inhabitants of the Valley and those of the eastern states into neighborly proximity." Certainly this would not have left Nicholson, Allen, and the others unmoved, but the more practical benefits of good transportation doubtless held attractions for them as well.[20]

Forty years later, Nicholson remembered the purchase as "verry [sic] cheap," but as not without problems. There was a "fair sized dwelling house" on the place along with several old log cabins. The mills, however, were "sadly needing repairing and the entire farm suffering for want of wise industrial care and attention." But since they could supply that care, and seemingly had the resources to make the necessary improvements, they agreed to take possession from Pim, who indicated his willingness to allow them considerable time before they began making payments.[21]

Ironically, none of the purchasers ever lived at Prairie Home. Among the first residents to arrive were Lee Bennett and his wife Mary, a sister of Joseph A. Dugdale. Bennett was something of a ne'er-do-well lawyer. Nicholson remembered them as "a verry [sic] good and well meaning pair" who unfortunately "had not the gift of accumulating property and so had not much beside their own industrious hands to help with." They thus did not contribute toward the purchase. Although Abraham Allen never moved his family to Prairie

Home, he was, in Nicholson's words, "one of the best and most ingenious of mechanics," and he spent weeks on the farm trying to fit up and repair the log cabins so that they would be fit to live in. Another early arrival was Stephen Mendenhall, with his wife Mary (Thomas) Mendenhall and their children. He was a millwright, and joined Allen in repairing the grist and saw mills, soon putting them into operation. About the same time there also came William H. Hilles and wife Hannah, his brother Elihu and wife, and their sister Ann. They also met with Nicholson's approval as "good industrious people as could be found anywhere." They arrived with little money, but they did own land in Jay County, Indiana, which they promised to mortgage to help pay the debt on Prairie Home.[22]

All of these families were Hicksite Friends, and all came with high hopes. In the next year others joined them. Nicholson in the 1880s made a list, and a memorandum left by Wattles preserved the names of others. Many of those Nicholson remembered were Hicksite Friends from New Garden like the Hilleses and Mendenhalls. Most were connected by family ties as well. Benjamin B. Davis had been interested in community since at least 1840. He had married Mary B. Ingram, the sister of Robert Ingram, who with his wife Hannah and children did the cooking for the entire community. Also there was Eli Davis, Benjamin's brother, and Robert Whinery, a cousin of Esther, the wife of John O. Wattles. Esther was there to teach. Eli and Deborah (Dutton) Cleaver had also come from New Garden; Deborah was a sister of Hannah Hilles. Although the impetus for the community had come from Friends around Oakland, only two families came from the area, only one of these Quaker: Dr. Jacob Barton, his wife, Sidney, and two children. Joel P. Davis was a young abolitionist, born in Clinton County in 1822, whose family had come from Kentucky; he was not related to Benjamin B. Davis, and was not a Friend. Moses and Jane (Foulke) Allen were originally from Belmont County, Ohio, and came to Prairie Home from Jay County, Indiana.[23]

Most of these had long-standing interests in reform. Joel P. Davis had become interested in abolition as a teenager in Clinton County. His father had left Kentucky because of his opposition to slavery. Davis later remembered his parents as "continually hounded by slave catchers." The academy he attended near Oakland had by some murky means become tied to Lane Seminary. On the outside, to declare their sentiments to the world, they emblazoned on the side of the schoolhouse: "Free Discussion. Abolition. Temperance. Woman's Rights." The Hilleses had helped to form the first antislavery society in their part of Indiana, and the Whinerys had been involved in radical abolition since at least 1839. Benjamin B. Davis had long been an enthusiastic abolitionist; "no man was more active than he," a neighbor remembered. He had committed himself to nonresistance by 1841, and was by then already interested in what he called "Fraternal Communities." In their constitutions he saw an "approximation to equal and evenhanded justice between man and man." But he was skeptical of associations and organizations generally. In Prairie Home's loose community his doubts would be assuaged.[24]

Not all who came to Prairie Home were Hicksite Friends. Wilson D. Schooley was an Orthodox Quaker from Spiceland, Indiana, a stronghold of unbending Orthodoxy, who had just married Caroline Taylor; her brother George was also a resident. Another Orthodox Quaker, Clarkson Puckett, came from Randolph County, Indiana. There was one German, "the Dutchman," as he was known to all, Frederick Schulling, who had been involved with communitarian ventures before he came to Prairie Home. A. J. MacDonald, the wandering visitor to communities who came to Prairie Home in August 1844, described him as "a gaunt figure about 50 years of age who looked singular with a large stubbly beard and an ill-tempered countenance." There were at least two Englishmen, one a young cabinetmaker from Bond Street in London named Howlet Thompson, the other John Wood, in MacDonald's words, "a pretty good specimen, blunt, openhearted and independent." He had had ties to Owenites in England. From Concord, New Hampshire, came John B. Chandler and wife Mariah and infant son Henry, along with his sister Judith and another reformer, Mary Ann French. Chandler was a clockmaker and former deacon of a Congregational church in Concord who had been excommunicated in 1840 for his radical abolitionist views. A close associate of the ultraradical Nathaniel P. Rogers, he and Mariah Church had created a minor uproar when they refused to be married by a minister, instead marrying themselves in a Quaker-style ceremony at the breakfast table. French was an equally radical reformer who had not been afraid to exhort her Congregational church in Manchester about its sins. In the summer of 1844 arrived Dr. Harlow Hard, a Water Cure physician and Free Thinker who had wandered from the Western Reserve to northern Indiana, before he came to Prairie Home. There are some about whom we know nothing other than their names—Daniel McLean "and wife," Charles Gardener and his sisters Emily and Irene, Enoch Haskell. There was also at least one black woman, whose name Nicholson had forgotten, and a few others.[25]

The best known arrivals in the community in 1844 were Orson and Catherine Murray and their family. Late in 1843 the Murrays had moved to New York City, where he began publishing a new reform paper, the *Regenerator*. By spring of 1844, the Murrays had decided to come west to Prairie Home, and make it the

Regenerator's new home, solely on the basis of the marvelous descriptions that Wattles had sent, and without writing to anyone connected with the venture. In July Catherine Murray and her six children set out from New York via the Erie Canal and Lake Erie. Orson remained behind in New York City to close out his affairs, and then follow the same route with the *Regenerator's* press and the family's furniture. Catherine and her family arrived safely at Prairie Home, only to be crushed by the primitive conditions that awaited them.[26]

Orson Murray's trip was more eventful. He left Buffalo on the steamer *Robert Fulton* about 7:00 P.M. on October 18. Late that night a tremendous storm blew up that nearly swamped the ship. With unusual understatement, Murray labeled the night "exceedingly distressing." In fact the storm drowned the engines and carried away one mast. The upper deck was nearly destroyed, and much of the cargo was washed overboard, along with several passengers. Murray himself survived only by spending most of the night clinging to a rope. About 4:30 that morning the ship finally ran aground about twenty miles north of Buffalo at Dibbles Bay, fortunately on a gentle beach that made escape easy.[27]

Murray spent the next month wandering around western New York and Pennsylvania. For a week he roamed the lakeshore between Buffalo and the site of the wreck, trying to find property that had washed ashore. Then he wandered down into Pennsylvania, where at Warren he got passage in a skiff with two hunters bound for a winter in Iowa. With the three men and their baggage, the boat was so overloaded that "it sunk to the level with the surface of the water, in passing rapids the ripples would frequently dash, in." With no pilot, the danger was increased, but, as Murray cheerfully concluded, "my companions were both swimmers and I felt confident there would be some way for me to gain the shore in case of any difficulty that might reasonably be expected." But it appealed to Murray because "we were free. Were not under the tyranny of the ignorant, licentious and mercenary who have too much to do with controlling the travelling conveyances generally in this country." At Pittsburg and New Brighton he found new friends for the *Regenerator* and held at least one meeting. Then it was down the Ohio on a steamboat to Cincinnati. From there he made his way to Harveysburg, where Valentine Nicholson and Jane's brother-in-law Henry T. Butterworth took him in. Finally, on November 24 he found Catherine and their children at Oakland, living with Abraham Brooke. They had taken refuge there from the wreck of Prairie Home, which by November, scarcely six months after it had come into being, was no more.[28]

Signs of trouble had already begun to appear in the spring. One was the eternal problem of money. While the farmers who had made the agreement with Pim easily owned enough property to meet Pim's demands, like most

Western farmers few had ready access to cash. By May the first payment was due, and the hard-pressed Pim was demanding it. Nicholson and a friend managed to come up with almost half of the purchase price, $2,200, but there seemed to be no prospect of finding the rest as readily. In May, Nicholson approached the Shakers at Union Village for a loan, depending both on past friendly relations and the knowledge that the Shakers often lent large sums at interest. The Shaker brother that Nicholson approached, Charles D. Hampton, responded sympathetically that "there is no where on earth we should sooner grant it, than in an institution whose object is to make better the condition of the human family." But, Hampton, gently assured him, they had not the means.[29]

The purchase price was not the only financial burden. There were also necessities of life to provide. The first few families who had come to the community were almost destitute, lacking even bedding. The grist mill could provide them with enough meal and flour once the corn and wheat were in, but until then all had to be fed. Nicholson used his own money liberally to buy dried fruit and beans and bolts of cloth and muslin and send them up to the community in the "Liberator" with Abraham Allen.[30]

The supplies were needed, since throughout the spring and summer there were new arrivals. Most were not old reformers, like the first enthusiasts on the place, but were the fruits of John O. Wattles's missionary labors. With the same fervor he had once hoped to expend on the heathen in distant lands, Wattles now traveled with the glad news of Prairie Home and the new order of things that it would inaugurate. Looking back years later, Nicholson thought that Wattles's "benevolence, and his sympathy for the suffering poor in general," made it impossible to him to do otherwise. As one who had known poverty and had seen from his father what alcohol could do, "it would be natural for him to wish the blessing of home, friends, and better opportunities should come speedily to such women and children as had been rendered destitute by men addicted to the habit of intemperance." So Wattles took to the road, and everywhere, from Dayton even to the jails of Pittsburgh, his message was the same to his hearers. "We have now got five hundred acres of God's beautiful green Earth redeemed from the curse of man's folly and it is as much your right to enjoy it as it is that of any others," he told them. A new dispensation was come to earth, and by the time that Prairie Home was filled up, there would be other homes prepared. And soon poor men and women who took Wattles at his word began to arrive.[31]

At least one communitarian early realized that Wattles was courting disaster, and that was Amos Gilbert, the Marlborough schoolmaster who had that community's experience to draw on. He seemingly was the only one of the communitarians at the time who accurately took Wattles's measure, and he tried to warn the rest. "Colors are more vivid; odors more delicate, flowers more beautiful, and music more thrilling when tested by the senses of J. O. W. than by those of ordinary men;—he transcended transcendentalism." Although those intimately acquainted with him knew Wattles to be "an almost inimitable model of peace and purity," one usually found that his plans were "decidedly unearthly in their character," Gilbert warned readers of the *Regenerator*. "I have never been to any of the localities described but suspect the hills are rather too well formed on paper, the soil too fertile, that the streams have too much fall for a level country, and that those who are throwing their all in to the lap of humanity are rather too just and generous for plain facts."[32]

Gilbert was right; there were people at Prairie Home who from the time of their arrival proved to be problems. Nicholson thought that the situation was summed up simply: there were too many "who loved to talk more than they did to work." And there was no lack of subjects for discussion at Prairie Home.[33]

The community was formed with no constitution, no officials or framework for government of any kind. That meant that no one directed the work to be done. Meetings were supposed to make such decisions, but there was no mechanism for enforcement. There were enough people on the place by the fall to meet normal needs. There were two shoemakers, a hatter, a weaver, a tailor, several carpenters and wagonmakers—everything needed, in fact, but a blacksmith. The mills were well operated. Some approached their tasks with dedication and labored hard to make the community succeed. But there were many others who did not. When MacDonald came in August, he estimated that perhaps half of the labor that one would ordinarily expect of such a group was being done in the fields. Many of the men, he noted, seemed to be constantly eating, cutting fresh melons and anything else that might be at hand.[34]

There were some attempts to oversee the various departments of labor. Moses Allen looked after the stables, horses, harness, and related affairs. Daniel McLean and the Davis brothers were in charge of the livestock, and had authority, subject to approval by the rest of the community, to buy, sell, and trade. Clarkson Puckett was in charge of the farm implements, and had discretion to loan them to the neighbors. Robert Ingram looked after the mill, and Frederick Schulling, "the Dutchman," was the librarian. There were even specific individuals designated to select the vegetables for the communal table and to go to West Liberty for the mail. But while they apparently were to lead, no one would have to follow.[35]

Food, however, was the one subject on which nearly everyone at Prairie Home was in agreement, at least initially. Nearly all of those there were advocates of diet reform, and practiced a strict vegetarianism. They lived mainly on fruits and vegetables; corn, apples, potatoes, sweet potatoes, and graham bread were their staples, along with whatever fruits happened to be in season. Some would carry ears of raw corn in their pockets and gnaw on them for a snack. A number gave up milk as well, holding entirely to cold water. There were a few meat-eating holdouts among them. John Wood, the old English socialist, kept three pigs penned up on the farm, telling MacDonald that he liked "a bit o' meat," and that no one would keep him from it. Mary Mendenhall and Ann Dutton, who had come together from New Garden with their families, found that there were wild chickens about the place, roosting in the woods. Occasionally they could catch and roast one, eating their chicken dinners stealthily in the timber.[36]

Even food, however, became a subject of contention eventually at Prairie Home. Some thought that salt was a poison; Harlow Hard was particularly opposed to its use. Some of the young men in the community eventually became convinced that cooking was wasted, unnecessary effort. They would come to the table eating apples or raw ears of corn, or gnawing on unground wheat, complaining about the waste of milling and cooking.[37]

The community did not neglect education; there were 44 under the age of 16. Esther Wattles was "companion" for those aged 4 to 9, while Joel P. Davis served the "second class," those aged from 9 to 16, who were in the "literary department." William Hilles was in charge of the "manuel class." Wattles preserved a plan drawn up by one of the teachers, although he judged that it "did not seem to correspond with our idea of brotherly love and angelic purity." Children under 4, of which there were 12, were to be under their parents' care, although they and their mothers were to meet together frequently at the various houses. Those from 4 to 9, who were 14 in number, were to be with their parents when not in school. Those 9 to 16 were, when out of school, to be with the "manuel [*sic*] labor superintendent"—there were 18 at the community. It is not clear whether the community saw effective family control ending at this age or not. All 16 to 25 were to engage in "manuel labor" with the farmers and mechanics. Finally, at times, the whole community would gather for instruction. Just why Wattles was unhappy with this scheme is unclear, but he noted that the community wanted to improve it, thus furnishing another subject for contention.[38]

Still another source of trouble was the image that Wattles and the other

Prairie Home enthusiasts presented. The community naturally attracted attention, and the curious often came to see this new thing for themselves. There was, in Nicholson's words, "such a constant stream of visitors calling there for meals and lodging and to talk, talk, talk." Even correspondence proved a burden. Already by May, Samuel Larned, one of the early arrivals, was asking readers of the *Regenerator* to pay the postage themselves on letters sent to the community, since "the great number of letters which arrive with every mail, most of them the highest postage, in one week amounts to a considerable sum, more than we shall at present be able to meet."[39]

Throughout the spring and summer brave reports went from Prairie Home to the *Regenerator* and the *Communitist*. In June Larned reported that crops were in, and fruit trees planted; with the mills already in operation, and the artisans collected in the community, they would soon be self-sufficient. There was school every day for the children, and for the adults every other evening, there was a meeting for lecturing, reading, or conversation. "I have not half the time now, or room in my sheet to say a word on what I would say much, that is, the beautiful union, harmony, and love which exists among us.—We are living like one family, whose Father is the universal one," he wrote happily.[40]

A more realistic glimpse into life at Prairie Home was provided by A. J. MacDonald, the Scot who visited in August. When he arrived in the nearest town, West Liberty, he was almost astonished that "life in the every day style" went on. "From what I had heard of the community my imagination had grown large," he recorded, and he was surprised that the inhabitants were more interested in the election and politics "when a community which appeared to me to be all the talk was so near at hand." But the evident lack of interest of West Liberty's residents enlightened him.[41]

Walking down the Urbana Road, he found his way to Prairie Home. Instead of a garden, he first encountered a gaunt, rough-looking but polite Quaker, then found the "community"—two houses, a log cabin, the flour mill, and "an old saw mill, looking very rough." The porch of one of the houses was filled with women and girls carding wool, but since it was noon the men and boys soon came in from the fields to eat. Dinner was brown bread, potatoes, potato soup, and melons.[42]

MacDonald left to go to the Highland Home Community, but returned the next day to Prairie Home. He spent the night in one of the houses. He did not like his accommodations. "There appeared too much confusion too many people and too many idlers among them," he opined. While the young women were industrious, getting supper, "in a very steady business like manner," the young men "were mostly lounging about doing nothing." When night fell, there were not enough beds for everyone, so all slept spread out on the floor with what bedding was available.[43]

The next morning, a Sunday, the members met in the mill. "The sight touched me almost to tears. I felt that taking the mass of people as they are with their good and evil this was a piece of it which contained much of the good," MacDonald wrote. "There was honest simplicity and generosity some intelligence and enthusiastic industry mingled with a proportion of ignorance, indolence, and coarseness." No one presided. In the manner of a Quaker meeting for worship (and unlike a Quaker business meeting), men and women spoke as they felt led, mentioning the work that had to be done and what they would do. As the meeting closed, "singing was attempted but it was poor indeed," much what one would expect of a group of Quakers reared to regard music as a danger to religious life.[44]

The central point of Prairie Home's existence was cooperative labor, and MacDonald found much to praise, but also much to deplore. On Monday morning he watched a number of the men at work, thinking, "If you fail, I will give it up, for never did I see men work so well or so brotherly with each other." But there was also "evident disorder, showing a transition state toward either harmony or anarchy." That afternoon, a plow had to be repaired. A dozen men spent an hour or so discussing the matter before deciding that it would have to be taken away. But there was no money on the place, so it was decided to send a sack of corn to be sold to pay for the plow. By the time the decision was reached, the corn and plow loaded on the wagon, a team hitched up, and the whole thing sent on its way, the entire afternoon was gone.[45]

Common property was also a source of tension. The English cabinetmaker told MacDonald how he had brought with him a chest of fine planes, chisels, and other tools. While he was off on a visit to friends in Indiana, some of the other men decided that they needed them and knocked the lock off the chest. When the cabinetmaker returned, he found large pieces gouged out of several, "all innocently and ignorantly done by the Brothers who scarcely saw any wrong in it." In another case John Wood was blacking his boots one Sunday morning when "the Dutchman" asked for the brushes. Wood handed them over, but kept the blacking, which he had bought himself. The Dutchman was outraged. "Do you call this Community . . . I ask him for de prushes, to blacken my poots, and he give me de prush and not give me the placking."[46]

Throughout the summer, people kept arriving. While MacDonald was there, one day four men came from Indiana, while soon afterward a large wagon loaded with household goods drove up. A farmer and his family had arrived, "having given up the world to come to what was heaven in idea but was subsequently discovered to be *Utopia*." By the fall, even John O. Wattles was acknowledging that people had to be turned away for lack of space.[47]

Throughout the summer and fall conditions gradually deteriorated. The overcrowded houses and cabins soon made community wear thin even in the eyes of enthusiasts. The influx of people with no particular disposition to work proved discouraging for others. Many of the original residents departed, although Wattles claimed that this was due only to the overcrowding and that they would return in the spring when more houses had been built.[48]

Meanwhile, the debt on the property continued to hang over the community, and all summer Valentine Nicholson continued his scramble to find the next payment. As some of the original backers saw the conditions, and others heard of them, their initial enthusiasm waned. Ultimately, only one of the Center or Green Plain Friends who had pledged to pay the debt—Dr. Jacob Barton—brought his family to live in the community. And as their desire to live at Prairie Home waned, their wish became more and more just to escape with as little financial loss as possible. A few staunch supporters, Harlow Hard among them, indicated their willingness to dispose of property they owned and contribute the proceeds to Prairie Home, but, as MacDonald put it, "times were so hard, there was scarcity of money, and the lands would not sell."[49]

During the summer, Nicholson and Allen had raised another $1,000 by borrowing it from Jacob Pierce, leaving only $1,800 to be paid on the debt. This Elihu Oren was willing to pay by selling his farm. Then a series of events followed that brought the final collapse of Prairie Home.[50]

When Pim learned that the last payment was about to be made, he visited Nicholson, Oren, and Allen. He advanced the same argument to all three, that even with the land paid for, it was impossible for the community to succeed, and that it was unwise to keep it up. Nicholson, by his own account, thought that the worst problems could be solved through a more regular organization of the work and some limits on the admission of members. But when Oren came to him for advice, Nicholson was unwilling to advise him to put all of his property into the hands of "the shiftless, the indolent, and mentally unbalanced," and so told him "to be his own judge."[51]

In October, Allen, Oren, and Nicholson went up to the community to consult with the members as to what should be done. It is not clear just what happened at the meeting. MacDonald later recorded that he heard that on October 25 the members decided to end the experiment, implying that it was a community decision. Nicholson's version was somewhat different. He recorded that most of the discussion involved himself, Allen, Oren, William H. Hilles, Robert Ingram, Lee Bennett, and Horton Brown from Zanesfield, along with Pim. The last, according to Nicholson, "was not in a pleasant mood and was finding all the fault he could." Even as they were meeting, however, a new company arrived, displaced English weavers, destitute and utterly lacking any knowledge of farming, all drawn by Wattles's invitation. So the men brought the community to a close. Nicholson had handbills printed and sent notices to numerous newspapers to prevent any more arrivals.[52]

All that remained was to settle the financial affairs. Horton Brown suggested following standard Quaker practice and submitting the matter to arbitration, but Pim refused. That left only taking the case to court, or, as Brown put it, submitting it "to the court of Israel's own conscience." Since most of those present were Quakers, and since Nicholson, who had invested the most in the undertaking, had, as he put it, "a perfect horror of going to law or depending upon lawyers," the latter was decided on.[53]

Morally, the course was consistent, but financially it proved to be a mistake. Pim's unwillingness to accept Oren's final payment should have made Nicholson and the others suspicious. When they returned the land to Pim's possession, they assumed that he would allow them something for the amount they had already paid for it, not to mention the improvements they had made. Pim showed every sign, however, of keeping both land and money. In this case, however, Nicholson overcame his aversion to lawyers and sued Pim. It took years, but finally the case was decided in Nicholson's favor. Nicholson recorded with grim satisfaction that it proved Pim's ruin, but his fears of the law proved well founded: his attorney took most of the judgment.[54]

So in the fall of 1844 Prairie Home came to an end. The fate of many of the participants, such as the two Englishmen and "the Dutchman," is unknown. Most of the Hicksite Friends went back to their old homes, although, as will be seen, Elihu Hilles insisted on participating in at least one more community before settling down to farm in Indiana. John B. Chandler returned to New Hampshire. Orson S. Murray never made it to Prairie Home, instead remaining in Warren County for new experiments.[55]

Murray was responsible for the last chapter of Prairie Home's public life. By the spring of 1845, he was settled at Fruit Hills in Warren County and in April began publishing the *Regenerator* again. He opened with a postmortem on the community in which he had expected to make his home. "My own opinion to the causes of the failure at Prairie Home, as well as of any other like failures, is, that *ignorance* was at the foundation. There was too much confidence in *money* and too little confidence in *manhood*," he opined. "Much of the remains of erroneous habit. Something of sectarianism and superstition. Not enough of self-knowledge—but especially not enough knowledge of each other among the members." That was too much for Nicholson, who responded that the problem was just the opposite—too much confidence in men, and not enough in money: "For certain I am that people generally put forth the most effort to acquire whatever they have the most confidence in; and there were very feeble efforts made to provide money for the enterprise at that place, and the consequence was a disastrous lack of money." In contrast, there was no lack of effort to secure men, and "there efforts were answered by filling up every nook and corner of every house, mill, cabin, or shanty on the premises, all being liberally packed with *layers and rows of manhood*." The great problem, Nicholson argued, was that too many came who could not help pay the debt, and who lacked even tools for work. But when some who had entered into the original agreements came to have doubts, and others with property, like Abraham Brooke, refused to exchange it for money so that Prairie Home could be truly "redeemed," the end was certain. Nicholson concluded with a broad swipe at Murray, charging that his vague comments showed that he had not escaped "his former training among the priesthood."[56]

Murray was never one to shy away from argument, and two issues later he responded with a like attack on Nicholson. Murray wanted to discuss Prairie Home only so that future communities might learn from and avoid its mistakes. The fact that Nicholson admitted that those involved in the community had property, and yet allowed it to fail for lack of money, showed that they had "too much confidence in money." "It is nothing strange or unaccountable that a man of brother Nicholson's acquiring propensities, after losing so much in such an undertaking, should be found clinging to the old grabbing system, and blinding himself to things as they were and are," Murray argued. "It must be his falling into contempt for manhood, if in fact he has not always been in it, that has led brother Nicholson into the apprehension that others have 'too much contempt' for 'dollars.' "[57]

Neither Nicholson nor Murray, as will be seen, had lost faith in the cause of community. "If they tell you that 'Prairie Home' *is* given up, they shall also tell you that Community is *not* given up. If they tell you that distant friends are somewhat disappointed touching *some* things, they shall tell of their exceeding great encouragement touching *other* things," Nicholson wrote. "We have had in this beginning some essential and useful lessons of experience ever profitable to contemplate upon the next effort." Of these, he thought, the foremost was balancing "Love" with "Wisdom." But they drew sharply contrasting lessons from the failure of Prairie Home. Nicholson would come to rethink many of his older ideas. But Murray was convinced that Prairie Home's principles had been sound from the beginning, that persevering in them would bring success.[58]

Humanity's Highland Home

Closely linked to Prairie Home was Highland Home in Logan County, Ohio. It grew out of the same meeting at Zanesfield in which Prairie Home had its beginning. It opened in the spring of 1844, and, like Prairie Home, came to an end in the autumn of the same year. For almost all of its existence, it was considered to be the sister community to Prairie Home, the "Upper community," as many referred to it. In few particulars did its career differ from that of the group on Mad River nine miles to the south.[59]

Highland Home was located in one of the most picturesque parts of Ohio. East of the Logan County seat of Bellefontaine, the hills rise along the headwaters of Mad River and Darby Creek. Here early in the century a number of Quakers had settled around the villages of Zanesfield and Pickerelltown. They formed a monthly meeting called Goshen. When the Hicksite separation came in 1828, there was a sharp split. About a third of the meeting became Hicksites. After a lawsuit over possession of the monthly meeting's property and records, the Hicksites built a small brick meetinghouse on the east edge of Zanesfield. The two groups settled down to an uneasy coexistence, and, in fact the Hicksite meeting flourished, as new members moved in from eastern Ohio.[60]

It was in this little meetinghouse that, early in 1844, Nicholson, Allen, and their coadjutors held their convention. Nicholson recalled a large attendance, but unless it spilled out into the burying ground it cannot have been too large, since it is doubtful that more than one hundred people could have crowded into the little meetinghouse. But many of those from Zanesfield were favorably impressed, and resolved that in the spring they would form a community.[61]

Four families took the lead in forming Highland Home: the Browns, Micheners, Pennocks, and Taylors. The families, like those at Marlborough, were interconnected by marriage. Aaron Brown, the patriarch of the large Brown family, had married Ann Stanton, a sister of Abigail Stanton, the wife of Benjamin Michener. Martha, daughter of Benjamin and Abigail, was the wife of William M. Taylor, whose brother George was one of the most enthusiastic supporters of the community. Only the Pennocks were not connected to the other families, but they had recently arrived from New Garden in Columbiana County, that fertile breeding ground for all reforms.[62]

These families had been active in Hicksite affairs. Horton Brown was a recorded minister, and, in Valentine Nicholson's estimation, a "strong minded" man, noted for his brief but impressive preaching. Nicholson remembered one of his "deep" discourses. "It is a great attainment, we have made, when we have learned to unlearn that which we had learned amiss." Benjamin Michener was a member of the Meeting for Sufferings. He and Thomas Pennock were both elders, and with Horton Brown had been active in the affairs of the Hicksite yearly meeting since the separation, as had Abigail Michener. Benjamin Michener had been one of the signers of the Green Plain disclaimer against George F. White, while Sarah Michener and Horton Brown had been active in opposition to the yearly meeting's leadership since 1840. They also apparently took the lead in Goshen Monthly Meeting's rebellion against the yearly meeting's dissolution of Green Plain Quarterly Meeting. In August 1843 the yearly meeting's committee visited the quarterly meeting at Goshen. It reported that the predominant group there was in rebellion against the yearly meeting, and that its ministry had become mostly "unsound and lifeless." Thus they were quite similar in background to the Hicksites at Prairie Home.[63]

The enthusiasts entered the experiment full of idealism. Nicholson remembered that the whole neighborhood was so taken with the "pictures we presented of the possibility of enjoying Peace, Harmony, more advantages for mental improvement and intellectual culture" that after the convention he expected all to come to it. In fact most must have had second thoughts, but those who remained were, in Nicholson's words, "men of property and standing."[64]

Highland Home was on the farms of Horton Brown and Benjamin Michener at the edge of Zanesfield. Like Prairie Home, it began in the spring of 1844. Its picturesque situation moved Valentine Nicholson to poetry:

Come, ye fathers and ye mothers
Come, kind sisters, and kind brothers;
Neighbors, come, and come all others
Home to the "promised land."

In good faith we now invite you;
Come and share the love we plight you;
Where temptation will not excite you—
Here in the "promised land."

Hand in hand, with perfect union,
Long we've sought to find the true one
Now we can enjoy communion
Here in the "promised land."

Now we'll leave the past behind us,
And invite mankind to join us,
Then may Satan come in minus,
Here in the "promised land."[65]

We have no indication how many people became part of the Highland Home community. According to A. J. MacDonald, there were some prospective members from Indiana who came during the summer, but it is unclear whether they remained. Apparently they lived together in Horton Brown's house, with some in temporary buildings that were put up on the farm. Some spilled over onto the farm of Benjamin Michener. Michener had a large, comfortable house that became part of the community.[66]

Most of what we know of Highland Home again comes from MacDonald, who visited it during his trip to Prairie Home in August. He seems to have liked things there more than at the other community to the south. He stayed at Benjamin Michener's, which he pronounced a "comfortable and pretty looking" place. That evening, he put a series of questions to the residents.

1) Do you make laws? No!
2) Does the majority govern the minority? No!
3) Have you any delegated power? No!
4) Any kind of government? No!
5) Do you express opinions and principles as a body? No!
6) Have you no form of society or tests for admission of members? No!
7) Do you assist runaway slaves? Yes!
8) Must you be Grahamites? No!
9) Do you object to religionists? No!
10) What are the terms of admission? "The land is free to all. Let those who wish, come and work!"
11) Any particular trades? No!
12) Can persons take their earnings away with them when they leave? Yes!

MacDonald recorded that "they repeatedly told me" that the leading principle of the community "was to endeavor to practice the Golden Rule of 'Doing as they would be done by.'"[67]

In at least one respect this was a departure from the original vision at Highland Home. Edwin Michener, a son of Benjamin, wrote that they did not want "any of those who are not redeemed from the perverse and ungodly ways of men." Instead they would bring in only those who were "prepared to live out the laws of their being, as fast as they come to a knowledge of them." But the Highland Home people ultimately came to leave such judgments in the hands of the individuals joining, rather than those already in the community.[68]

There was a little industry at Highland Home: a stone quarry, a lime kiln, and a saw mill. There were orchards, which supplied both communities with apples. MacDonald found that the farm had been well managed but now there was "a little disorder." "The workers appeared to be without clear ideas of the duties they were going to perform." But they had no lack of subjects for discussion. Many of the residents were devotees of diet reform, which they credited with improving their health. They were also students of phrenology and a variety of other reforms. MacDonald found it unsettling to see "rude looking men, almost ragged ploughing, fence making or such like employments" talking knowledgeably about phrenology, physiology, magnetism, and hydropathy.[69]

Highland Home came to an end shortly before Prairie Home disbanded in October. Of all the communities, the reasons for its disruption are the least clear. There is no evidence of dissension, and the members had incurred no debts. It is clear, however, that the residents of Highland Home saw themselves as the partners of Prairie Home. It may be that, anticipating the imminent collapse of the larger community, those at Highland Home also decided to give up. Thus, they simply returned to their own farms. They did not lose their passion for reform, but their dabbling with community was at an end.[70]

Fraternal Home or West Grove

The history of this community is shadowy. It was made up of an isolated group of Hicksite Quakers living around the little town of Camden in the western part of Jay County, Indiana. What we know of them suggests that their story paralleled that of the communities elsewhere.

The Hicksite Friends around Camden had been among the first in Indiana to organize an antislavery society in March 1840. After that almost all record of it disappears. The names of its officers do not appear in the proceedings of the Indiana Anti-Slavery Society. That, and subsequent activities of some, suggest that their sympathies may have been with the Garrisonians in the split of

1840. They were sympathetic to fugitive slaves; Joseph H. Mendenhall, Hiram's son, wrote of them: "Truer hearts to the flying fugitive never lived."[71]

These Friends also had ties to the Hicksite Friends at New Garden in Columbiana County, Ohio. Seven families were at the heart of the enterprise—Hilles, Dugdale, Lewis, Irey, Sumption, Mendenhall, and Williams. All but the Sumptions, Williamses, and Lewises had come from New Garden, which had been a fertile ground for radical reform in the late 1830s and 1840s, and would continue to be down to the time of the Civil War. Some of the first stirrings of communitarian interest had come there in 1840 from the Davises, Longshores, and Myerses. Most of these families were bound together by family ties as well. Four Lewis brothers—Enos, Syra, Emry, and Hervey—were actively involved. All were Hicksites in their thirties and forties from Harrison County, Ohio, who came to Jay County late in the 1830s. Enos had married Margaret Grissell of New Garden, while brothers Hervey and Syra had married, respectively, Elma and Sarah Ann Grissell. Their mother and grandmother, Martha (Dingee) Grissell, was the second wife of Hugh Hilles Sr. Jonah Irey and William R. Dugdale were married to Rachel Hilles and Ann Hilles, respectively, daughters of Hugh Hilles Sr. And William R. Dugdale was a brother to Joseph A. Dugdale, the minister at Green Plain. Another son of Hugh Hilles, William H. Hilles, was one of Valentine Nicholson's correspondents vitally interested in the Prairie Home community; he later married Mary Ann French, who had come to Prairie Home from New Hampshire. John Sumption had married Susannah Lewis, a connection of the other Lewises. Only William and Joseph Mendenhall (whose relationship to each other is not clear) and George and Rachel Williams were not related to the others, and only the Sumptions and Williamses were not Friends.[72]

Fraternal Home is unique among the western communities in that its constitution has survived (see appendix). It apparently dates from late in 1844. The constitution declared its goal to be to "unfold and unite all affections of mankind, and to harmonize isolated interests in the mutual and general good." It described humans as "septenary in nature," with seven "natural rights or wants"—land on which to work, a house in which to live, food, clothing, tools "where with the produce," a "knowledge of his physical being and its surroundings," and "a knowledge of his spiritual nature and the being by which it is governed."[73]

To realize this vision, the inmates at Fraternal Home committed themselves to a series of principles. In commerce, cost would be "the limit of price." They would educate "in all the arts and sciences," and give "a thorough knowledge of the laws of life and health." They would "render labor honorable and attractive" by giving members "such occupations as harmonize with their organic inclinations." Each family would have its own home, with all of the buildings in seven "circular teers [sic]," with a school in the center. Work would be done in groups. Each member would be compensated according to time and value of labor and would "be entitled to all the resources of life and comfort, at cost, making their interests mutual." The community never elaborated on this rather vague formulation. There would be an "Instructor," whose duties were undefined, and a clerk to keep records. The members left themselves open to new revelations of progression, however, by agreeing to "change and adopt any new and better system of government, when made tangible to our understanding."[74]

We know relatively little else about the community, particularly how much its life reflected the vision of its constitution. Certainly no buildings were ever erected. The tradition survived for many years in the neighborhood that the "Fraternal Brotherhood" was essentially a group of families that wished to live near each other in a "huddle." Each retained its own land. "The idea seemed to be to have a good social time," one who heard about the group in his boyhood remembered. "They got along fine as long as the provisions lasted."[75]

The constitution itself was a source of contention among the faithful. Those who proposed it thought it necessary to have some test of sincerity to keep out those who were not really committed to community and instead sought only an easy living. John Dugdale of Green Plain voiced their sentiments in a letter to his son William, in which he criticized the plan of the Prairie Home community to admit all comers: "This appears to me to be opening the door almost too wide, inasmuch as humanity is [in] an unregenerated state and prone to schemes and selfishness." William H. Hilles and his sister-in-law Matilda Irey Hilles spurned Fraternal Home for that reason; however, Matilda rejected "a great long Constitution to make me do what a majority might dictate." "Just burn your constitution and give up your rights of property and see if we do not come and join you," she told her sister-in-law Rebecca Hilles Irey in 1845.[76]

The experiment ran out of provisions in June 1845. In October 1845 William H. Hilles reported that, just as he expected, the Fraternal Brotherhood had come to an end. There was nothing left to do but settle up the debts, most of which William R. Dugdale and George Williams assumed. The interest in reform did not cease; the West Grove group became Progressive Friends, and they continued their interest in abolition. But there would no longer be a Fraternal Brotherhood among them.[77]

Union Home

After Hiram Mendenhall found himself a hero among abolitionists and other reformers for his confrontation with Henry Clay, he seems to have become increasingly interested in radical reform. He did not completely eschew his capitalist enterprising. He became interested in at least one new venture, the Whitewater Canal, built to connect east-central Indiana with the Ohio River. But Mendenhall became attached to the sort of communitarian venture that the advocates of Universal Inquiry and Reform advocated.[78]

In the summer and fall of 1843 Mendenhall came into increasing contact with the radical Garrisonians. He was at Cherry Grove for one of the Hundred Conventions as one of the celebrities of the occasion. His family was also there, and apparently John O. Wattles moved them deeply. One of Hiram's sons, according to Wattles "when he got home, went and got his pen and ink and a piece of paper and lay right down upon his face by the light of the fire he was writing down what he had heard." Wattles then went on to Economy in Wayne County, where he found that reform-minded abolitionists had been discussing community for two or three years, inspired by some passing lecturers and a Fourierite tract that one of them had obtained. "The people turned out 'en mass,' " Wattles wrote. "All seemed so interested . . . and some of the most choice of them gave us their names as ready for action." "An old widow woman," Mary Macy Maulsby, and her children, who owned large tracts of land around Economy, were so moved that they urged Wattles to stay and begin a community on their farms.[79]

The turning point, however, apparently came in a meeting in Newport, in Wayne County, October 20 and 21. Wattles was there to acquaint abolitionists with the principles of Universal Inquiry and Reform. The meeting, after considering the state of the world, the rights of humanity, the problems of religion, and the sources of evil, took up "the immense work to be done before the brotherhood of the human family is fully realized." Having reached agreement on this foundation, it then turned to the solution—"commencing the great work of building a home for humanity." It was to be in the West, and a committee was appointed to canvass for "a suitable location for a community somewhere in the great Mississippi Valley." They were also to determine "from the several friends of community what amount of land or other property they had ready to return to humanity."[80]

The men on the committee are an interesting group, since they suggest that, at least for a time, Wattles had succeeded in reaching out beyond the usual circle of Hicksite Friends. Some, to be sure, were of that persuasion. Nicholson was on the committee, as was Edwin Fussell, although he would soon be back in Pennsylvania. Another member was Israel French. French was a well-to-do landowner who lived between Richmond and Newport. He had come from Belmont County, Ohio, in 1832. In Ohio, he had been one of the most prominent figures in the Hicksite separation. For two years he had been the clerk of the Hicksite yearly meeting, but after coming to Indiana he had been much less active in Quaker affairs, almost invisible. His only child, Julianna, however, had been prominent in abolitionist activities, serving in a number of posts in the local and state female antislavery societies. Charles Atkinson was another Hicksite Quaker who had moved from Center in Clinton County, Ohio, to Marion, Indiana, where his family may have been the only Hicksite Friends in the county. He had been an active abolitionist, however, one of Arnold Buffum's early converts. In 1841 he had made the sixty-mile journey from Grant County to Newport over miserable roads with his wagon to bring Buffum to Grant County to lecture. Buffum found himself and Rebecca sharing a one-room log cabin with Charles and Lydia Atkinson and their ten children. Family connections may have played a part here again: Lydia Atkinson was a sister of Elihu Oren, one of the chief financial backers of Prairie Home.[81]

At least three of the committee, however, were Orthodox Friends, albeit of suspect status. David Winston Jones was the youngest, born in Miami County, Ohio, in 1821. He had come to Grant County with his parents, Obadiah and Ann (Pearson) Jones. Old grandfather Abijah Jones, still alive in Ohio, was a highly respected minister, but son Obadiah and his family were less inclined to conformity. David Jones had been disowned when he married a non-Friend late in 1840. Such a proceeding was routine, but David had taken the extraordinary step of appealing his disownment to the quarterly meeting. He had no chance of succeeding, and perhaps for that reason decided to drop it. At the time of the Newport convention Obadiah and Ann Jones were being disowned for joining the Anti-Slavery Friends. By 1844 Obadiah was publishing an abolitionist newspaper in Grant County.[82]

Two other Anti-Slavery Friends from Westfield in Hamilton County were also on the committee, James P. Antrim and Asa Bales. Antrim and his wife, Mary, had been among the leaders of the Anti-Slavery separation in Westfield Monthly Meeting. Judging from the books he bequeathed to his children, he was interested in a wide variety of reforms. Asa Bales was one of the leading Friends in Westfield. A founder of the town, he was one of those men the nineteenth century liked to call "public-spirited": teacher, active in local affairs, generous to the unfortunate. He and his wife Susannah were childless, but took in a number of orphans. He had already made his will, which ordered that his property be used to establish a school "to educate orphants [*sic*] and other poor children" of the neighborhood. If there was enough money left, it was to be used to open a boarding school "on the manual labour system." Although he provided that the school was to be under the control of the monthly or quarterly meeting, Bales significantly ordered that "no sectarian principles shall ever bar any child or children from attending said school," a departure from the usual Quaker pattern of keeping schools "select," for members only. The presence of men like Antrim and Bales could not help but add to the respectability of the venture.[83]

Of the three other members of the committee, Wilson Schooley, an Orthodox Friend, and George W. Taylor, a Hicksite, found homes at Prairie Home and Highland Home respectively. John D. Cooper of Pendleton was the only non-Quaker in the group. He was not heard from again.[84]

In the spring of 1844 Mendenhall and numerous other Indiana sympathizers had committed themselves to a community about half a mile south of Hagerstown in Wayne County. It was a peculiar choice. The nearest Quaker settlement with sympathizers of any kind was five or six miles north around Economy. But it was on the line of the Whitewater Canal from Cambridge City to Hagerstown, whose construction Mendenhall was superintending. Like the other Universal Reformers, Mendenhall was a great believer in the benefits of improved transportation, and the canal was doubtless an attraction. The site, Mendenhall claimed, was in every way equal to Prairie Home, save "only in the quantity of land." "If we had a little ready cash," Mendenhall told readers of the *Regenerator,* they would be able to buy one of the best farms in Wayne County adjacent to "our little spot of ground." Mendenhall offered "one of the best bargains in real estate and machinery" ever offered in Randolph County, for the two thousand dollars he needed.[85]

The community was conceived in the broadest possible terms. In admission, there was "no respect of persons," as they did not expect anyone of bad morals to be interested. They would offer accommodations to all who came. They asked only that they bring what they needed. There were no written laws or constitutions, although Mendenhall did not seem completely opposed to the idea. The great need was for a school, and for another community lecturer to offer more guidance.[86]

By late that spring, Mendenhall had apparently abandoned plans for the community at Hagerstown. He was at a three-day convention in Greensboro the first week in June 1844. Greensboro, in Henry County, was another stronghold of Quaker abolitionists, "only a little less notorious than Newport," in the judgment of a contemporary. Previously it had been impervious to the blandishments of Garrisonians, although Douglass had spent the night there after the attack at Pendleton. The meetings were held in Liberty Hall, put up in the winter of 1841–42 "for conscience sake" after the Orthodox meetinghouse was closed to abolitionists. The crowd overflowed it, and the meeting adjourned to a nearby grove. The first two days were devoted to a convention of the Indiana Anti-Slavery Society and the Indiana Liberty party. George Taylor, who reported on the events at Greensboro to Orson S. Murray, disliked these "organized disorganizations," but hopefully opined that they were "preparing men to take another step in reform." Many of the Liberty men, Taylor thought, were "now ready for something better."[87]

That came on the third day, when the largest community convention in the history of the state was held in Liberty Hall. It was, Taylor noted with approval, "in the fullest sense of the word, a 'free meeting.' No chairman, secretary, order of the day, or any other of those refined machines usually made use of for the purpose of suppressing the freedom of speech." The meeting took up all of the standard topics of reform, ranging from human depravity to "associated action." Prairie Home was the subject of considerable discussion.[88]

The meeting ended with a decision that a community on the model of Prairie Home should form somewhere in Indiana. Showing a realism that was somewhat out of character, they recommended that it not commence until the fall, since farmers were unlikely to want to relocate until they had their crops in (and were unlikely to have cash to put into the community until that time, too). There was considerable enthusiasm. Those present offered to donate three thousand acres of land for the cause: one thousand from Mendenhall, a thousand from Charles Atkinson, the rest scattered at various places belonging to several individuals.[89]

The committee to visit the proffered land and recommend a site was again an encouraging sign of the appeal of communitarian principles to an increasingly broad spectrum of abolitionists. The committee included familiar people like Mendenhall, Taylor, Atkinson, and Harlow Hard, but it also took in a number of Orthodox Anti-Slavery Friends. Edwin, Irena and Emily Gardner were young people (twenty-three, twenty-one, and eighteen, respectively) and siblings from Union County. Edwin was to have been the teacher at Hagerstown. Huldah Wickersham of New Castle, a first cousin of the Gardners, was also young, twenty-eight. A schoolteacher and unmarried, she had been active as an abolitionist since 1840 and had acquired something of a reputation as a writer. Her cousin, Moses R. Wickersham of Greensboro, was another abolitionist who had acquired a considerable reputation in Indiana antislavery circles. Also from Greensboro was Enos Adamson, an Orthodox Friend originally from Tennessee. An important new convert from Westfield was Micajah C. White. He was the son of Isaac White, who before his untimely death in 1840 had been one of the most prominent Orthodox Friends in Indiana. By 1844 Micajah was becoming well known as a minister in the Anti-Slavery Friends. He was joined by William Frost of Westfield, the other non-Quaker on the committee.[90]

Taylor was apparently as effective as John O. Wattles in painting enchanting pictures of the possibilities and prospects of community. If all who agreed to join the committee were as taken as Emily Gardner, he was successful indeed. She wrote almost rapturously of the "joyous time" at Greensboro. "Many who had heard much of the subject of community went away satisfied that it was the plan the true way of living while those who were before convinced of the necessity of a reform had their faith strengthened and their hearts cheered by the promise of the future," she exulted. Taylor apparently waxed particularly eloquent in his account of life at Prairie Home. "Most sweetly did it chime with my highest aspirations after a true life," Gardner told her friends. Those not in community knew nothing of freedom, Taylor argued, and Gardner was convinced of that, but "rejoiced that there was one spot at least on this broad and beautiful earth as free as the air and sunlight which play around and beautify it." The Gardners, at least, "look[ed] forward with bright anticipation to the time when the western prairies and forests shall be dotted over with free homes for free minds."[91]

The second Saturday in July most of the committee met again in Greensboro and called a meeting for "Universal Inquiry" at the Mendenhall farm on Cabin Creek on July 18. No record of this latter convention has survived, but apparently it was then decided to accept Mendenhall's offer.[92]

In August the community, now christened Union Home, was underway. Mendenhall gave 315 acres of his land, and the community purchased another hundred adjacent. By early October there were about twenty people on the place. They lived in the Mendenhalls' five-room house, or in the five or six other, smaller buildings on the place. Amazingly, a correspondent of the *Communitist* said that they could accommodate another twenty people.[93]

Among the first arrivals at Union Home were Kersey and Lydia (Michener)

Grave, the latter the daughter of Benjamin and Abigail Michener of Highland
Home. Kersey Grave was another Orthodox Friend who was beginning an exceedingly unorthodox career as a radical reformer. Born in Brownsville, Pennsylvania, in 1815, he had come to Richmond, Indiana, as a child. He began
teaching at age nineteen. By the late 1830s he was traveling as a lecturer on various reforms: phrenology, health, temperance, and abolition. In 1842 he had
been elected the corresponding secretary of the Indiana Liberty party. He resigned in August 1844, just as he and his wife prepared to go to Union Home.
In the same month the Orthodox Whitewater Monthly Meeting had disowned
Kersey Grave for not attending meeting. He had by this time begun his journey
toward atheism.[94]

In all of these distinctions ex-Friend Kersey was not alone. Writing to the
Communitist, Grave described the little group as "a few sectarians, several
infidels, some religious nothingarians." All were dedicated to diet reform, although, Grave acknowledged, "we have a few who are sighing for the 'flesh-pots
of Egypt.'" But it was, according to Grave, a happy group, "a band of true-
hearted reformers." "I never before enjoyed such pure unsullied pleasure—
never before felt so perfectly at home," he told John O. Wattles.[95]

In December, Mendenhall struck a deal with the other members of the community. In return for money enough to pay his debts, which amounted to about
$1,000, Mendenhall deeded 246 acres, including his carding and fulling mills,
to the other members of the community. The deed, fortunately, listed those
who had taken up residence at the time, and gives us a portrait of the "true-
hearted reformers" of whom Kersey Grave was so enamored. Significantly, few
of the committee that had agreed on the location were among the first residents; in fact almost none of them ever came to Union Home. In some cases
this may have been due to second thoughts. By 1846 James P. Antrim had gone
back to the sureties of the Orthodox Friends. David W. Jones, who retained a
firm commitment to most Christian orthodoxies, may also have been given
pause by the vagaries of inhabitants like Kersey Grave. And by this time Asa
Bales and Huldah Wickersham both had less than a year to live. But many of
the others—the Gardners, Israel French—retained an interest in communitarianism. If they were staying away, it was for other reasons.[96]

There were forty-nine people at Union Home in December, twenty-five
adults and twenty-four children. In addition to Hiram and Martha Mendenhall and their adult children Joseph and Martha, and Kersey and Lydia Grave,
there were at least two refugees from Prairie Home, Harlow and Margery Hard,
whose stay apparently was short. The rest were a diverse group. Andrew and

Fanny (Hopson) Spillard were the veteran reformers. He had been part of Robert Owen's New Harmony experiment. Little is known of their life in the 1830s, save that they were in another community in Illinois in 1836, but by 1840 they were in Economy in Wayne County, involved with the organization of the Economy Anti-Slavery Society. The others were connected by intricate family ties. Pusey Grave was a cousin of Kersey Grave. Pusey's wife, Jane Witchell, was the daughter of John and Bathsheba (Foulke) Witchell, who were among the older members of the community. They were Hicksite Friends who had come to Wayne County from Belmont County, Ohio. Mark and Mary (Jones) Patty were originally from Miami County, Ohio—she was an aunt of David W. Jones. Samuel M. Ruble was originally an Orthodox Friend; his wife Rowena was the Mendenhalls' daughter. Enos Adamson was the young Orthodox Friend from Greensboro. Of the other three couples—Richard and Jane Warwick, Thurston and Jerusha Conant, and Samuel and Lydia Mitchell—we know little else. The Warwicks may have come from Clinton County, Ohio, and Samuel Mitchell had been an active abolitionist in Randolph County.[97]

In the spring of 1845, four more families joined the community. Three were part of the complicated network of Hicksite communitarian reformers. Moses and Jane (Foulke) Allen had been at Prairie Home; Jane was a sister to Bathsheba (Foulke) Witchell. Talbert Garretson had two sisters who had married brothers of Moses Allen. Jesse and Sarah (Dutton) West were from New Garden in Columbiana County. Two of Sarah's sisters, Deborah Cleaver and Hannah Hilles, had been at Prairie Home. Only Joshua and Nancy Ballinger are not known to have had any connection with others at Union Home or one of the other communities.[98]

Union Home, like the other communities, was based on farming, along with some primitive industry. Early in the community's life, the members traded the carding mill machinery to a neighbor for an adjacent tract of land. The group cultivated about a hundred acres—"corn, wheat, oats, meadow, potatoes, Irish and sweet potatoes, pumpkins, beans, and a variety of garden vegetables, too tedious to mention." There was timber in abundance, and the saw mill and grist mill turned out most of the products that the group needed. Members sometimes hired themselves out for neighbors. Their pay went into the community treasury.[99]

We know little of the internal workings of the community. Every Friday afternoon there was a lecture. The business was usually the province of a committee, made up of Mendenhall, Mary Patty, and Pusey Grave. Grave also acted as the community treasurer. By all accounts, there was little trouble with the division of labor.[100]

For the first year, things went on harmoniously at Union Home. Relations with neighbors were friendly. "I know of none in the neighborhood round-about, but wish us success," Mendenhall wrote to Wattles in June 1845. W. Rufus Merine, a sympathetic neighbor, was favorably impressed; he thought the group at Union Home, "a band of brothers, in the true sense." They were "vigorous," with a "full maximum of virtue and wisdom." They were fortunate in their location, "retired from the gorgeous taste of a city; from the trappings of state . . . and at the same time in the very heart of the country, embracing a good farm land, as any in the state." They were "generous and obliging neighbors, opposed to selfishness, persevering in all their various pursuits, full of enter-prise making substantial and durable improvements." Already the community was having an effect. "If the social reform system should fail here," Merine told Wattles, "it would fail in almost any other location on the globe."[101]

Hanging over Union Home, however, was what Mendenhall called "the in-cubus of indebtedness, which nightmare like rides communities to death." In fact the finances of Union Home were hopelessly entangled with Mendenhall's. Apparently having learned from the experience of Prairie Home, several of the members wanted a deed made that would leave no doubt of their right to the property, to avoid what Pusey Grave called "after-claps." Grave and Patty later claimed that they wanted to pay Mendenhall the full value of $5,000, but Men-denhall insisted that he wanted only enough to pay his debts, which he put at about $1,000, and would donate the rest. So all agreed that Mendenhall would receive $1,000 immediately, and that the members would, twenty-one years later, pay Mendenhall an additional $3,500.[102]

The situation was complicated, however, by Mendenhall's involvement in the Whitewater Canal. Mendenhall had bought $1,000 worth of canal stock, secured by a mortgage on part of the land deeded to the community. Menden-hall's position was that by occupying his land, and benefiting from it, the community assumed the obligation to disencumber it. Mendenhall apparently originally believed that the money paid by the members and the income from the community's endeavors would be more than enough to relieve his obliga-tions. In the spring of 1846 he confidently reported to Wattles that great pro-gress was being made.[103]

Instead, money once again proved a community's undoing. From the adult members came only $623—one hundred dollars each from Patty and Pusey Grave, and the remainder from Thurston Conant. The members refused to aid Mendenhall in raising the mortgage held by the canal company, since Menden-hall still had other property. There was contention over the amount of work contributed by the members. Andrew Spillard, for example, was apparently in poor health and spent much of the time in bed. Mendenhall was also unhappy with the Wests, Garretsons, and Allens. As tensions increased, several families left—first the Spillards, Warwicks, and Mitchells, along with Adamson, then the more recent arrivals, the Allens, Wests, Garretsons and Ballingers.[104]

The final disintegration came in March of 1846. The Graves, Pattys, Conants, Witchells, Rubles, and Mendenhalls were still trying to live in community. According to Mendenhall, the other families decided to abandon Union Home and thus brought it to an end. The version of Mark Patty, Pusey Grave, and Thurston Conant, however, was that Mendenhall had become dangerously irrational, making "threats and menaces of bodily injury, published in . . . various speeches and declarations." Mendenhall also accused some of the others of cheating him—the Allens, Wests, and Garretsons of selling some of his mill machinery and pocketing the proceeds, Pusey Grave of doing the same with some accounts he collected, the rest with failing to meet their debts. And so the last families left, leaving the Mendenhalls in possession of the land, the mills in worse condition than when the community began, and Hiram's creditors still pressing him.[105]

It was "mammon," John O. Wattles opined, that brought Union Home to its end. Remarkably, however, at least some of the residents had not lost their interest in community. As Union Home disintegrated, Conant, Mitchell, Patty, and Kersey Grave endorsed a new Wattles project, a manual labor school that would preferably be based in a community. Their verdict on their experiences seemed to be that they had given the fainthearted too many chances for escape. "We think at least to place as great a barrier against retreat as the present contingencies will admit of," they told Wattles. They would thus put control in the hands of "the more elevated philosophers," and force out "the more poisonous dregs."[106]

The last word of Union Home, like Prairie Home, came in the courts. In June 1847 Mendenhall sued most of the former members, both for possession of his land and for the money and property he claimed they had taken from him. The case dragged on for three years before the defendants prevailed—Mendenhall was left only with his encumbered land.[107]

Kristeen

After the collapse of Prairie Home, at least some of the faithful there did not give up the cause of community. One of them was Harlow Hard, the physician from Plymouth in northern Indiana. The history of short-lived Kristeen community in Marshall County, Indiana, is largely that of Dr. Hard. Indeed, we know little else about Kristeen other than what he told of it in the *Regenerator* and John O. Wattles's *Herald of Progression.*

Harlow Hard was a New Englander, born November 10, 1804, in Franklin, Vermont. His father, Lysander Hard, was a Methodist minister, who in 1816 brought his family to Wadsworth in Medina County, Ohio. Lysander was, in the words of the county historian, "an unsettled sojourner among men," who had "inherited all the poverty that an unsuccessful Methodist preacher is entitled to possess." He "wandered up and down, in to Pennsylvania, New York and Eastern Ohio." Only by "streaks of luck" was Harlow able to study medicine. He then moved east to Trumbull County, Ohio, where on February 27, 1834, he married Margery McFarlane. They were the parents of four children: Francis, Felena, Calantha, and William Lloyd Garrison, born between 1835 and 1842.[108]

The Hards had an ambulatory life after their marriage. From Trumbull County they moved over into Pennsylvania, then back to Wadsworth, then south to Delaware County, Ohio. Finally, in 1841, they went west to Marshall County in the days of its earliest white settlement. Hard was one of the first physicians in the area.[109]

It is unclear how and when Hard came to the antislavery movement. He does not appear in any of the accounts of the first conventions of Garrisonians in Ohio, or in the first years of the Indiana antislavery movement, or in the early agitation of Universal Inquiry and Reform. He initially was a reluctant activist. When Stephen S. Harding, an abolitionist from southern Indiana, attempted to enlist his aid in an organizing tour for the state Liberty party, Hard begged off, telling Harding that his "limited practice of physick" was "the sole dependence of his family," and besides, he was "but an indifferent speaker." Still, he concluded, "I do what I can in my own county." In the spring of 1844, just before the Hards went to Prairie Home, he was active in a Liberty party meeting in Plymouth.[110]

After Prairie Home dissolved, and after a brief stay at Union Home, Harlow and Margery Hard went back to Plymouth; they had never sold their property there. By this time Hard had largely renounced traditional medicine ("has now out-grown it and got to be *a man*," as Orson S. Murray put it) and gone in for the water cure. Harlow, at least, had still not given up on community. Joel P. Davis, also late of Prairie Home, joined them. They had also become connected with a certain Charles Mowland, who purchased a tract of 370 acres along the Tippecanoe River west of Plymouth. He named it for the Christianna River, along which he had been reared in Delaware. It was pronounced "Kristeen," he told the doctor, but Mowland was unhappy when Hard spelled it thus.[111]

From the beginning, Hard kept one lesson from Prairie Home firmly in mind—he and his compatriots were "determined to keep out of debt." They owned the main tract outright, and Mowland deeded it to a familiar group of trustees: Wattles, Murray, Nicholson, Hard, and himself, along with Joel, Benjamin B., and Eli Davis; Emily Gardner, Huldah Wickersham, and Howell D. Thompson of Clinton County, Ohio. All but Thompson and Mowland himself had been involved in some way with either Prairie Home or Union Home. The site was chosen at least in part because there were other lands nearby that could be cheaply purchased, if the funds could be raised. In June 1845 they bought another tract of 148 acres nearby, because they thought it better for mill purposes. This time, however, they had to choose between owning the land outright or shepherding their capital for other purposes.[112]

As was the rule with any community, Hard had to wax lyrical about the location. It was conveniently located to the Wabash and Erie Canal. It was the site of "one of the best springs in northern Indiana, and also an abundant water power furnished by the river." Timber, mostly poplar, was abundant, and the soil "not easily surpassed; not yielding to that of Prairie Home."[113]

In the spring of 1845 Hard, with a hired team and two or three others, began the back-breaking work of clearing the land, all but fifteen or twenty acres of which was heavily timbered. One of the attractions of the land purchased later was that it had forty acres of land under the plow. Their goal was to plant as much wheat as possible, in addition to setting out potatoes, corn, and the usual varieties of garden truck. They had enough seed, but very little else. In the *Regenerator*, Hard listed the types of people and other items needed: "8 or 10 efficient hands immediately," along with carpenters, millwrights, blacksmiths, horses, and a wagon, all kinds of farming, carpentry and millwright tools, grain, and hay." After the second farm was purchased, Hard sent out an appeal for a set of millstones. Obviously, the endeavor was beginning with little besides land and people. Hard warned the interested, moreover, that there was only one cabin on the place, although by the fall a story-and-a-half frame house had been put up.[114]

Hard was equally specific about the sort of people who would be part of Kristeen, and he seemed to echo the sentiments of Valentine Nicholson. A community, he wrote, should be based on "persons of similar habits and modes of thinking." He had no desire for those who sought wealth, or those "yet under the influence of superstition and bigotry," or those who claimed to be interested in reform "while they constantly stimulate their bodies with animal food, and all the usual condiments and stimulants which are found in civilized life." Instead, he invited "any who feel willing to give up all property for the general good, who feel disposed to be industrious and prudent in their habits, who will not be a burden upon the brethren, who are not more attached to any sectarian creed than they are to principles of goodness and propriety, who feel disposed to adopt any reform in diet that is consistent with health, and who have no special predilections for me and mine instead of thee and thine." Hard promised initially a life of privation, but the result would be to show that "the flame of love to man still burns" and that it would "yet burst forth with resplendent effulgence, to enlighten man in relation to the advantages of associated action."[115]

We do not know how many ultimately came to Kristeen, or how long they stayed. The community followed Prairie Home in not celebrating its first anniversary. Early in the fall of 1845, Wattles came up the Wabash from Grand Prairie to visit, but when he arrived at Kristeen, he found it deserted. He conjectured hopefully that its residents had gone home for the winter or were away nursing sick relatives "as there was a great deal of sickness in the country." But they never returned, and skeptics were free in advancing explanations. "I understand that the great *reformer*—the spotless and knowing Harlow, differed with some of the head, and wise ones, at the community, and the contention grew so sharp that he parted asunder and came to Plymouth," Libanus Allen, one of Hard's relatives back in Ohio and a Methodist preacher, charged in a letter to Hard in October. This exchange, which Hard sent to the *Regenerator*, provides us with our sole hint of what lay behind Kristeen's expiration. Hard denied that there were any contentions in Kristeen. "I know of no human being with whom I feel the least disposition to quarrel," he told Allen, "much less with those dear friends, who, with me, are doomed to the constant contumely of our fellow men." He had other reasons, not specified, for leaving and going back to Plymouth. There may have been contention over Hard's ideas about religion and marriage. In the former he was verging on infidelity—"a belief in certain books and men as devine [*sic*] persons and things is the greatest barrier in the way of human progression." As for marriage, he judged it "as now practiced" to be "favorable to impurity rather than to purity." Thus he advocated that married people live apart "if they would by doing so live pure."[116]

So Kristeen came to an end. Hard stayed on in Plymouth, still sending letters to the *Regenerator*. By 1849 he was dead.[117]

Grand Prairie

Some of the participants in Universal Reform were persistent communitarians. When one community, like Marlborough or Prairie Home, failed, they moved on to another, like Fraternal Vale or Kristeen. The participants in the

Grand Prairie community, however, were the most persistent of all. As early as 1817 they had attempted to form a community in Warren County, Ohio. They moved to Indiana to further their commitment. And as late as 1860, long after almost all of the other participants had abandoned their hopes, the little group at Grand Prairie kept an interest alive.

Grand Prairie's story actually began in Red Lion, Ohio, near Lebanon, and not too far from the haunts of Valentine Nicholson around Harveysburg. There a group of families, mostly from New Jersey, had about 1820 become interested in the communitarian ideas of William Ludlow. Ludlow was a surveyor who had surveyed much of western Ohio for the federal government, and somehow he had come into contact with James M. Dorsey, the principal of the school at Oxford, Ohio, that later became Miami University. Together, Dorsey and Ludlow put together a plan for a group they called "Rational Brethren." It was avowedly dedicated to free thought, with the manufacture of pearl and potash as its economic basis. The group had lasted little more than a year when it dissolved in 1817. Ludlow, however, remained interested, and after giving up hope of reviving the "Rational Brethren," joined forces with the families of Jonathan Crane, Isaac Romine, Enoch Bowling, Oliver Osborn, and Mathias Dean in Warren County. Osborn was Crane's son-in-law; Romine was married to his niece. They apparently were attracted to the Shakers at Union Village, but instead cast their lot in a new venture with Ludlow. This one, however, was to be free of any taint of infidelity. An attempt to combine their farms failed when they were unable to acquire intervening land. So they sold out in Ohio and in 1824 moved to Fountain County, Indiana, on the Wabash River. There they entered a thousand acres on Coal Creek and in the same year formed the Coal Creek Community and Church of God. The goal of the society was "to ameliorate the condition of man by destroying individual aspirations for wealth, and establish a system of equal rights and privileges upon that estimable principal of doing to others as we should do unto us." By holding all property in common, they believed that they would "increase the sum of human happiness in this world of strife and conflicting wants."[118]

The experiment proved short-lived. Ludlow had received the blessing of Thomas Jefferson himself before setting out from Ohio, but in little more than a year, Ludlow went off to join Robert Owen at New Harmony, 150 miles down the Wabash. He came back in October 1826, but withdrew again in 1830. He went back to New Harmony before he deeded a tract of land to his wife in Fountain County and himself returned to Ohio, where he lived until his death. Ludlow's departure was the signal for the dissolution of the group and the division of its land.[119]

Unlike so many other people involved in such ventures, however, the Cranes and Romines were not discouraged. By early in 1844 they had learned of Universal Inquiry and Reform, and were in touch with Orson S. Murray. Ruth (Romine) Crane, Isaac's daughter, wrote in April that they were being guided by prophecies they found in Scripture and believed applicable to contemporary society. An uncle, she told Murray, had seen a vision of an iron lamp shining brightly above him, which he took to be "the light of truth which is breaking upon us." Now, she concluded, "the light of reformation which is rising in the East shines even to the West, and may well compare with the star of Bethlehem." They were "now ready to come out from under the law, and live by grace."[120]

The Fountain County faithful had the resources to support their hopes. They owned seven hundred acres, most of which had been part of the Coal Creek Community. Beyond that they were uncertain about their direction. They considered becoming Fourierists, but they knew so little of Fourierism that they had to ask Murray to explain it to them. They hoped that Murray would join them, and watched anxiously the progress of Prairie Home as a model. With hopes of expansion, however, they decided not to launch the experiment in Fountain County, but on the other side of the Wabash in Warren County, on what was known as the Grand Prairie.[121]

In April 1845 four families, headed by Abraham R. Crane (Ruth's husband), L. O. Wilcox, and A. Smith, along with Thomas Evans, a single man, began the community. More Cranes and Romines expressed an interest in joining. They paid $1,200 for 200 acres, 120 of prairie already broken and 80 of woodland. There was convenient waterpower, and considerable prairie land adjacent for pasture. Like his compatriots in other communities, Evans waxed eloquent about the physical surroundings: "The situation is truly delightful, surpassing anything I have seen in the west, lying as it does on the edge of the broad and ocean like prairie, which is here dotted with some fine groves and single trees which convey a most vivid idea of islands and ships on a sea coast," he wrote to Wattles. On a low ridge in the midst of one grove they were building their house, a two-story frame with basement and attic 15 by 48 feet, each floor divided into three rooms.[122]

The summer went well for the little group. No one else joined them, but the crowded condition on the farm made that desirable; twenty people were in one small house. They put out twenty-seven acres of corn and another twenty-acre field of oats and corn, along with two of potatoes. They had set out a hundred apple trees, but lost any hope of fruit to a late frost. The fall harvest was good with fifty bushels of corn to the acre.[123]

The winter, however, was a hard time. Although the frame of the new house was up, it was not finished, and the inmates had to face it with twenty people in two rooms. Writing to Murray in October, Thomas Evans invited letters from interested parties, but emphasized that there was no room for anyone else. When Orson Johnson, one of Wattles's correspondents, visited in December he sent back a grim portrait. "Our friends here are all in good health and spirits, but, O dear, in regard to house room and other conveniences. Twenty-one persons in two rooms and a loft for sleeping over one of them, and one of the rooms so open that you could write in the snow on the beds where it had blown in!" The weather was miserable; Johnson arrived just in time for a blizzard. He kept Christmas at the community because of foul weather, but the next day was perfect for sleighing, with "a clear plain of snow, and grass, interrupted only by one or two houses, bounded at the distance of fifteen miles by a long wood."[124]

The group at Grand Prairie was determined to avoid the mistakes of previous experiments, and to learn from those that appeared to be successful. Thus in letters to the *Regenerator* and the *Herald of Progression*, they emphasized that they could not take in families for lack of space; indeed, for that reason, they wanted young, single men who could aid in the early work that needed to be done. They were careful to avoid overextending themselves; one member wrote that they had founded their experiment on the surest foundation possible, ready money. Thus, although they eyed adjoining land, they purchased none of it.[125]

We know but little about the daily arrangements at Grand Prairie; what we do know comes from Gilbert F. Bailey, the schoolmaster, and visitors like Orson Johnson. Bailey, a brother of Gamaliel Bailey, the Liberty party editor, arrived in December 1845 to teach eight or nine students, aged six to fifteen. Bailey was quite content, finding his students amusing and himself with ample time for reading. One of his pleasant duties was to read to the community each evening. His arrival with what he described as two or three years' supply of reading material was probably doubly welcome, since in the late summer Thomas Evans had sent out a plea for books and periodicals. Almost all of the other work centered around the farm, even so far as to neglect the completion of the house. Unlike the other communities, Grand Prairie was not committed to strict Grahamism. Ruth Crane saw nothing wrong with butter or milk, since they did not involve violence. When he visited in December 1845, Orson Johnson was horrified to find "the carcase of a DEAD HOG!!" Even worse, some of it was on the supper table that night.[126]

All of the surviving accounts give no indication of dissension at Grand Prairie. Bailey thought that "a more charitable company does not, I believe, exist, nor one more conscientious—no matter by what other authority another may be guided." He judged them "each and all independent, and as I conceive, upon the whole liberal and true thinkers and actors." Wattles, who contemplated joining the group, told readers of his *Herald of Progression* that there was no place that he would rather live out his life. But by the late summer of 1846 the community was on the verge of disintegration.[127]

The cause may have been their prudence in discouraging new members for whom they had no room. But the result was that the community remained tiny, incapable, in Gilbert Bailey's words, "of obtaining many economies and surpassing advantages of every kind." Two of the families left, one to join a Fourierist group a few miles away. In August Gilbert Bailey sent out a last appeal for new members, else, he predicted, "ere autumn's leaves shall all have perished," Grand Prairie would have come to an end. And by the end of the year it had.[128]

Skaneateles

The Skaneateles Community was the largest and best known community to grow out of the agitation for Universal Reform and, after Marlborough, the longest-lived. It was also the only one east of the Appalachians. The home of John A. Collins, for three years it mirrored his enthusiasms and interests. By almost any standard the most successful of the communities, it is also the best documented. Its failure in the spring of 1846 marked the effective end of the communitarian impulse that grew out of Universal Reform.

The experiment at Skaneateles had its origin in a series of meetings held in Skaneateles and Syracuse in the spring of 1843. The initial enthusiasm had nothing to do with Universal Reform or with John A. Collins. Instead it apparently grew out of the Fourierist agitation that was reaching its height early in the 1840s. The leaders in these meetings, residents of Onondaga and surrounding counties, all were sympathetic to reform.[129]

What is significant, however, is that there appears to be little overlap between those who first conceived of a community at Skaneateles and those followers and associates of John A. Collins who later created it. The first accounts in local newspapers proposed forming an "Industrial Association," and published two versions of a constitution for such a group. In its provisions, it resembled those of other Fourierist phalanxes. Government was to be by a president, secretary, and treasurer, in conjunction with a council. Stock was to be sold, and dividends paid. There was an elaborate set of bylaws. All of these would have been anathema to Collins and his coadjutors. Moreover, of the five men named at a June meeting to interview prospective members, none was associated with Collins or the community that ultimately assembled at Skaneateles. The one thing that the two groups did have in common was location— by late April the Fourierists had already determined to purchase the Elijah Cole farm at Mottville, two miles north of Skaneateles, the place where Collins and his Universal Reformers took up residence.[130]

It was not until May that Collins, John O. Wattles, Valentine Nicholson, and Abraham Allen arrived in Syracuse. They doubtless took advantage of the interest that the Fourierists had already aroused, and may well have attracted some of their supporters. By August, Collins's group, who in contrast to the earlier group called themselves "social reform" advocates, had perfected an organization and were searching for a community site.[131]

The critical meeting was held on August 17 at the Unitarian chapel in Syracuse, some two weeks after the explosive confrontation there between Collins on the one hand and Abby Kelley, Frederick Douglass, and Charles L. Remond on the other. A committee of four men and two women, from Syracuse and Waterloo, had visited possible sites at Oak's Corners, Unionville, and Vienna in Ontario County, and in Skaneateles. They had decided on the Cole farm at Skaneateles, the same place that had attracted the attention of the Fourierist group. The committee waxed eloquent in praise of the location. "It unites the useful and the beautiful in admirable proportions," it told the gathering. The three hundred acres of the Cole farm adjoined several other farms that could be purchased for forty or fifty dollars an acre; all were fertile and well cultivated. At the conclusion, Collins announced that the group had bought the Cole farm for $15,000. A financial committee was named to raise $5,000 as a capital stock for improvements. A business organization was also set up, with Quincy Adams Johnson, a Syracuse attorney, as president.[132]

After the meeting in Syracuse, the backers of the Skaneateles group began to solicit money and members. Trying to draw Valentine Nicholson to Skaneateles, Johnson wrote glowingly of the prospects ahead. "I confidently hope and anticipate that a community of men will congregate on this chosen spot from all parts of the world," he told his new friend in Ohio. Skaneateles, being near the Erie Canal, "the great highway of the nation," would not only be "a stopping place for the traveller" but also a "resort for the Philanthropist of any land, and the museum of Moral and Mental philosophers of all nations." There would be "all the great Spirits of the age congregated."[133]

Before such a congregation could assemble, however, there was much work to be done on the new property. The farm lay on the western edge of the village of Mottville. Quincy Johnson moved his family into the house, along with his brother Solomon and two single men. With some other friends, they put out thirty acres of winter wheat and made other improvements.[134]

Meanwhile, the work of trying to build up support and enthusiasm continued. Several local meetings, all well attended, took place on the farm. In September, a council of twelve members was chosen to make the final preparations to initiate the experiment in community. They fitted up an old log house to accommodate two or three families. The carriage house became the home of a printing office, harness shop, shoemaker and tailor, as well as living quarters for others. With these preparations complete, more families moved onto the property.[135]

On October 14 and 15 the largest meeting yet took place on the farm. Bad weather forced it into the barn, the only building on the farm large enough to hold it, instead of out-of-doors, as was first planned. Collins opened with an address on the evils of present-day society. Ernestine Rose, who had come up from New York City, followed, arguing that all of the evils of the contemporary world stemmed from the isolation of human beings and their removal from their natural state of association. She was greeted with "astonishing" enthusiasm. Nathaniel P. Rogers, the radical nonresistant from New Hampshire, wrote that this acclaim "was the breaking forth of humanity in concentrated form." Rogers followed, declaring that it was worth a journey of five hundred miles just to hear it said that no human being could be happy when even one other was miserable. He struck a blow for egalitarianism by denouncing formal introductions of speakers. Arnold Buffum was also present, indicating his qualms about some of what he had heard but expressing his support for association generally. Light "would go forth from this community," he said, "to enlighten the world." The meeting reached a crescendo when an "unlearned" young man named Rector spoke. His remarks on how he had come to the community "came so direct from the heart of an unlearned man, that a feeling of freedom was created in the audience which we seldom or never witnessed before," Rogers wrote. He described it as "an interchange of feeling and sentiments where heart answereth to heart." Many other speakers from the audience, including Thomas McClintock, a prominent Hicksite Friend from Waterloo, Ezra C. Smith, and John B. Chandler, followed.[136]

The next day saw a business meeting. The first subject was whether or not to take a deed for the farm. Some opposed it as inconsistent with the principles of the community—how could a community of interest found itself on private property? However, the practical need to have clear title, at least in a transitional state, prevailed. The convention concluded that afternoon with an appeal for funds. Some eighteen thousand dollars in cash and property were pledged. Rogers was clearly moved; "the separation which took place after the meeting, was that which is felt only by brethren and sisters of the same family; it was the severing of natural ties," he wrote. "We never before witnessed such intense feeling in any meeting."[137]

The October convention was in many ways the high point of the community. Although it would exist, and in many ways prosper, for another two and a half years, almost immediately dissension set in.

It is unclear how rapidly the community grew. In November, Johnson and Collins made a deed in which they stated that there were 36 people connected with the community. In December, Johnson wrote to Nicholson that there were 30 men, 18 women, and 21 children on the place. We know little about most of the inhabitants. Nathaniel H. Whiting lived at the farm in the beginning, along with John Orvis, the former Hicksite Quaker from Vermont who was, initially, Collins's loyal lieutenant. Also newly arrived from Vermont were Nathaniel and Marenda B. Randall, late of Woodstock. Nathaniel Randall was a jeweler, a member of a prominent Woodstock family, and one of the original trustees of the community. Marenda B. Randall was to be one of the most active and articulate people at Skaneateles. Equally prominent in the community was a schoolteacher from Syracuse, Maria Loomis.[138]

The first controversy, however, centered on the young lawyer, Quincy A. Johnson. Almost everyone who has studied Skaneateles has cast Johnson as a villain, and there may be merit to the charge. A contemporary, later a member of John Humphrey Noyes's Oneida Community, described him as "a long-headed, tonguey lawyer." When Johnson died in 1855, his obituarist agreed to some extent. Johnson was a man of "great intellectual capacity and extensive educational attainments," but he was also one whose "temper was peculiar." As the writer put it: "His indomitable will, strong passions, and taste for debate, often led him into discussions in which considerable acrimony was displayed." This is certainly consistent with the account we have of Johnson's dealings with Collins over the next few months.[139]

The first crisis came in November, apparently precipitated by Collins's desire for increased control over the community and for more rapid progress toward achieving its goals. Johnson claimed that until Collins took up permanent residence after the October convention, all was "peace, quiet and progression." But after that, Collins seemed to change: "he was restless and uneasy," haranguing the inmates every evening, "determined to force every one to follow him." The result, according to Johnson, was chaos. With Collins urging speed above all else, and impatient of opposing ideas, much of the work was sloppy and had to be redone. Even with all thirty men "drove to the utmost extent," by the first of December the sawmill that was supposed to be the first community enterprise was still months away from completion. Even before Collins's return, there was one defection: Nathaniel H. Whiting left for home and did not return. Johnson reported that others were dissatisfied, but that only he would openly oppose Collins.[140]

All of this was preliminary to a meeting on November 17, evidently called to confront the growing dissension in the group. The only full account we have is Johnson's which, needless to say, presents Collins in the worst possible light. According to Johnson, Collins asked that "all of us surrender our rights as men and women and place them in the hands of Collins and call him the Community." John Orvis and Maria Loomis followed in support, saying that Collins possessed "the great idea" and that it would be realized in the community only if he had complete, unfettered control. Others followed in the same vein; one actually laid hands on Collins and proclaimed *him* the community.[141]

Johnson, needless to say, strenuously opposed the proposal. He confronted Collins, asking him if he desired such powers. "Yes I do. It is my right, and I ought to have assumed it long ago," Collins answered, continuing that only out of weakness had he refused to do so earlier. Johnson responded by pointing out the consternation that would result in the broader reform community. That enraged Collins, who jumped to his feet and furiously denounced Johnson as a monster. Others joined in, shouting down the argumentative lawyer.[142]

His control of proceedings assured, Collins told the group that unless he was given complete control that he "would leave them to their own destruction." He then asked each person if he or she would assent to his control. According to Johnson, "some gave flatt [*sic*] worshipping answers," while others equivocated or asked for more time—no one said no save Johnson and his wife Josephine. Collins declared that this was the declaration of confidence he needed, and that the next morning he would identify those with the "great idea." They would be placed on three months probation, with full membership afterwards; the rejected would be free to leave immediately. Johnson responded that Collins "had neither the bodily, the mental or moral ability to maintain such a position for a week." Surely enough, the next day Collins announced that he was tired and ill and that he would announce his selection on Sunday, November 19.[143]

That morning, the adults assembled in the dining room to hear Collins's decision. He shocked almost everyone present by instead presenting an elaborate creedal statement of "fundamental principles." There were but few, "in consequence of their original organization, structure of mind, education, and preconceived notions," who were, he said, "at the present time adapted to work out this great problem of human redemption." Those engaged in the task had to be united, and he considered what he was about to present to them the basis of unity. There were eight propositions.[144]

Collins's propositions were the most succinct statement we have of his vision of what the Skaneateles Community would become and, by extension, what sort of world he envisioned with the inevitable triumph of Universal Reform. The first was a declaration of religion that repudiated almost every standard evangelical Protestant belief: miracles, the Sabbath, the authority of Scripture, the divinity of Christ, the Atonement, even the necessity of any kind of worship. The church and the clergy were condemned as breeders of strife. The second article committed the community to complete nonresistance. Governments were "organized bands of banditti." The only relation those in community were to have with them was to demand that they disband. Private property was repudiated. Marriage was expressly sanctioned, with "licentiousness, concubinage, adultery, bigamy, and polygamy" explicitly condemned. Divorce, however, was also sanctioned when "parties have outlived their affections and can not longer contribute to each other's happiness." Collins went so far as to say that spouses should have complete freedom to break off any union that they found unacceptable for any reason. The rest of the articles dealt with the practical workings of the community, guaranteeing children an education and "parental care," endorsing a "vegetable and fruit diet," establishing a probationary period for new applicants, and making explicit the right of the group to exclude unsuitable persons. The members were to sign it as a covenant.[145]

When he concluded his remarks, Collins asked for responses. Johnson naturally began an attack, but, by his own account, was shouted down by Collins's supporters with cries of "liar," "fool," "pettifogger," and "lawyer." Collins and Orvis spoke again, then all those present indicated their acceptance of the statement, save five: Johnson with his wife Josephine and brother Solomon, William Kennedy of Syracuse, and William C. Benson, who had come to the community from Lynn, Massachusetts. Collins then named a committee of seven, including Orvis and Loomis, to select the candidates for probationary membership.[146]

That evening Collins read the list of successful applicants. Johnson sniffed that the accepted were "several women and boys," with "some of the weaker portion of the men." As he described it, "a dreadful sensation followed": some of the rejected women wept, some sat hanging their heads in silence, while "the most intelligent and forcible laughed aloud." A torrent of questions and protests poured down on Collins; when he attempted to answer, some sneered while others tried to argue with him. Finally Collins left the room, but someone went after him and brought him back. Faltering, he promised to reconsider all of the rejected, then, pleading fatigue, adjourned the meeting and stalked out, calling for the "true hearted" to come with him. Behind followed his committee of seven. The rest stayed behind to listen to Johnson exhort them to hold firm.[147]

The next evening, Collins held another meeting. He retreated almost completely from the day before. Everyone, save for Quincy and Josephine Johnson and two women who had been at the farm only a short time and had not spoken with Collins, would be admitted without probation or restriction. The community would vote on future applicants, with one "dissenting voice" being enough to block admission.[148]

This confrontation apparently divided the community irreconcilably. The smaller faction, which looked to Johnson for leadership, found itself faced with a solid majority loyal to Collins. There may have been other factions as well; Johnson complained that one of the group, Joseph A. Whitemarsh, had formed a "sect" and held secret meetings. Johnson was convinced that Collins's supporters would go to any length to drive out opponents; he told Nicholson that they had "treated my wife worse than ever civilized man was known to treat his brother before this day." In December, however, Johnson was determined not to yield, and thought that "we are now in a fair way of reforming this new sect."[149]

For some, however, the growing tension was too much. Early in the year, some of the faithful began to drift away or withdraw. N. H. Whiting had already left before the first crisis. Early in 1844, three of Collins's chief lieutenants, Orvis, Whitemarsh, and Ezra C. Smith, departed. By spring they were at Galen, New York, attempting to form what they called the "Attractive Community." Soon afterwards Orvis was at Brook Farm, the Transcendentalist community outside Boston, where he became a convert to Fourierism.[150]

Also departing were the Johnsons, under circumstances that are far from clear. The version that Collins broadcast was that Johnson was a "scheming" lawyer, who, through legal trickery, had "got half of the estate into his own hands, and well nigh ruined the concern." No elaboration of this has been found, and it is impossible now to know just what Collins had in mind in making this charge. The deed of sale for the Cole farm had been made to Collins and Johnson, but they had immediately in turn conveyed the property to seven trustees. Johnson boasted that the deed embraced principles "liberal and full," and that they had "made it just what we preached." A reading of it bears out Johnson's claim. It seems just as likely that Collins used Johnson as a convenient scapegoat for the community's rocky beginning.[151]

Indications are, however, that by the spring of 1844 progress was being made. The community found a secure economic base. Although some dissension continued, the membership seemed more harmonious. There also seemed to be considerable unity about the principles by which the community would be governed. From 1844 to 1846, Skaneateles was probably the most successful of all of the communities that grew out of the movement for Universal Inquiry and Reform.[152]

This progress came in spite of doubt and criticism from other reformers elsewhere. Collins spent much of the month of December in Philadelphia and in the surrounding countryside, apparently trying to capitalize on the tenth anniversary meeting of the American Anti-Slavery Society. He collected a few donations, and won enough support for the organization of a society there to support the Skaneateles experiment. Late in December 1843 a "Convention of the Friends of Association" was held in the Tremont Temple in Boston. It attracted an impressive array of radical reformers. William Lloyd Garrison was there, as was Frederick Douglass, who, despite his experiences with Collins, was a member of the Committee of Business. Among the most prominent communitarians present were Adin Ballou, the founder of Hopedale; Charles A. Dana and George Ripley of Brook Farm; the Fourierists William H. Channing and Albert Brisbane; the Transcendentalist Amos Bronson Alcott; George W. Benson of Northampton, Massachusetts; and the Jacksonian labor reformer Orestes A. Brownson.[153]

Although the correspondent reporting on the meeting for the *New York Tribune* reported that "the spirit of Love and Harmony was strikingly manifested" in the convention, it is clear that Collins's position was an awkward one. The *Tribune* writer thought that while Collins's ideas "created the strongest excitement in the convention," it was also clear that "the Convention generally had little sympathy with his peculiar opinions." Indeed, although Collins defended his views ably, he came under more attacks than anyone else. At the conclusion of the meeting, although the convention refused to endorse any particular community or communitarian system, its resolutions had a clear Fourierist tinge.[154]

Collins found some support in Boston, however. Sympathizers there held a meeting on January 31 to form the New England Social Reform Society. An organization of officers and councilors was effected, with Tyler Parsons as president. The group specifically committed itself to supporting the Skaneateles community, and to that end they pledged themselves to raise $150,000 to pay off the mortgage on the property and to finance improvements. Skaneateles, in turn, would serve as a model of "the principle of a community of property and interests, whose government is based not upon physical force but reason and moral suasion, unencumbered by organised churches, sectarian priests, and the authority of all books and creeds." The meeting announced an equally ambitious plan to hire agents, circulate pamphlets, and support the Skaneateles organ, the *Communitist*. Collins continued to hold meetings in Massachusetts and New Hampshire, but there is no indication that they brought in new members or money.[155]

Meanwhile, as news of the difficulties at Skaneateles in the autumn of 1843 spread, consternation grew, much as Quincy Johnson had predicted. E. Gould Buffum, Arnold's son, was outraged by Collins's statement of principles, which he labeled a "creed." "Far better to drag out a miserable existence in the mines of Mexico, or on plantations of Carolina, and have soul free, than enjoy all of the comforts a rational, social system could afford, and have it chained," Buffum fulminated. It seemed impossible that Collins could have fallen so far; "better it had been for Humanity that he had remained a barefooted boy among the bleak hills of New Hampshire." Orson S. Murray joined in, predicting that Skaneateles's days were numbered, lost in "self-confusion and self-dissipation," if it based itself on the "chaff" of a creed.[156]

Nevertheless, Skaneateles showed hopeful signs in the spring of 1844. The community continued to grow. In March the population was 75—39 men, 18 women, and 18 children. By the summer the number was still larger; the number of men remained the same, with an increase in the number of women and children. The community remained at about this level for the rest of its existence.[157]

One of the sources of stability was economic success. Unlike the other communities, Skaneateles seems to have been self-supporting throughout its existence. In the summer of 1844, the editor of the Syracuse *Onondaga Standard*, who was not unfriendly toward the group, visited and was impressed by what he found. Of the 300 acres of the farm, 230 were "well fenced and in a fair state of cultivation." Forty were in wheat, and 130 in the staples of other communities: Indian corn, broom corn, and potatoes. There were acres of vegetables, and orchards, one recently set out by the community.[158]

While farming provided enough for the community's subsistence, the economic success of the community was founded on the small industries on the place. There had been a tremendous struggle to put them into operation in the winter of 1843–44; one of the many battles between Collins and Johnson had centered on where to place the sawmill. Several of the men, not accustomed to carpentry or raising buildings, found themselves bruised and battered. By February of 1844, however, the sawmill was running. That winter the community also advertised that it would do blacksmith, cobbler, printing and saddle and harness work, and would take payment in cash or kind. When the editor of the *Onondaga Standard* called in the summer of 1844, he found the sawmill to be "of the most substantial character: 80 × 60 and two stories, with a number of buzz saws; for sawing lath, etc., and lathes for turning iron and wood." At that time the community also planned a tannery, a lime kiln, and a foundry. Some of the women made men's caps and braided palm-leaf hats. With abundant timber, good water, and proximity to the railroad, the situation was indeed hopeful.[159]

A year later, John Finch, an English Owenite, also visited the community and came away equally impressed. Apparently the plans for the tannery, lime kiln, and foundry went unrealized, but the saw mill and turning shop flourished. There was so much demand that both worked twenty-four hours a day.[160]

Finch provides us with a unique glimpse into the finances and the economics of the community. He found that the crops produced had a market value of about $3,000, and that the sawmill turned out products worth about $6,000 annually. Expenses—interest on the mortgage, living costs for members, seed, etc.—came to a little under $4,000, leaving $5,000 to be applied to the debt. Finch thought that if the community kept up its present pace that it would pay its debts in two years, three at most.[161]

Like most other communities, Skaneateles initially went through a period of struggle over matters of work and labor, although separating fact from the self-serving accounts that Collins may have provided to visitors is difficult. Visitors like A. J. MacDonald and Finch recorded that because Collins "refused to appeal to the government to aid him in expelling imposters, intruders, and unruly members. . . . the Community soon swarmed with an unprincipled, indolent, and selfish class of 'Reformer,' as they termed themselves." Quincy A.

Johnson, one of these "imposters," of course painted a very different picture of men and women, all diligent and hardworking, but with limits to their willingness to be driven by Collins without apparent direction.[162]

Once the community was reduced to Collins's supporters, however, few discovered signs of sloth or indolence. Finch wrote that "the whole of the members, male and female, labor most industriously from 6 to 6." The editor of the *Onondaga Standard,* Marcellus Farmer, noted how in the fall of 1843 there had been dire predictions that the community was doomed because of the laziness and incapacity of its members. Instead, he found "their wants supplied, their crops put in, a mill erected, engagements promptly met, the sum of $4,000 paid on their property," all in the space of eight months. "Is it too much to expect that they will soon prove to the world that their efforts will be crowned with entire success?" he asked his readers.[163]

Skaneateles did decide to regulate admissions on the basis of ability to contribute to the community. When Finch visited, he found that the group had hired fifteen men—in fact hired hands accounted for over half of the work force, something that some at Skaneateles found troubling. The success of the community ultimately depended, they thought, on what its members did for it themselves.[164]

To this end, late in the summer of 1845 the community began to advertise in the *Communitist* for new members. There was enough work for 400 men and women on the place, but with living space limited, the community specified openings for 56 people in 22 categories. Almost all were crafts or manual trades—carpenters, blacksmiths, chairmakers, teamsters, machinists, masons, and mill wrights. Only three—cook, dressmaker, and milliner—were traditional women's roles.[165]

The community was also quite explicit about the personal characteristics it desired, and there they showed a hardheaded realism not characteristic of the other communities. "The vicious, the sick, the infirm, the indolent, cannot at present be serviceable to our cause," a circular in September stated. A community was neither "a poor-house nor hospital." "Our object is not so much to give a home to the poor, as to demonstrate to them their own power and resources, and thereby ultimately to destroy poverty," it continued. The poor were not automatically excluded, but neither did poverty guarantee admission. Neither were men nor money rejected "simply because they happen to be united." Character was paramount; above all Skaneateles sought people with "stability of character, industrious habits, physical energy, moral strength, mental force, and benevolent feelings." There was not room for "non-producers." They wanted single men and women, since they thought that it would make for the strengthening of the enterprise to have only children who were born there, so that they would grow up with an "undivided community feeling." "A man with a large family of non-producing children, must possess extraordinary powers, to justify his admission."[166]

We do not know as much about the people at Skaneateles as in most of the other communities. No membership list is known to survive. From other sources—the *Communitist,* the deed of establishment, accounts left by visitors—about fifty adults have been identified. From these we can make a few generalizations, although they should be regarded as highly tentative for two reasons: first, the incompleteness of the information, and second, the high rate of turnover in the community, perhaps greater than in any of the other communities. Many apparently stayed for only a short time.[167]

An historian of Skaneateles, writing in 1902, described the people in the community as "People of high moral tone, cultured and refined persons . . . doctors of divinity, college professors, lawyers, and physicians." Lester Grosvenor Wells, the most careful student of the community's history, thought that they were "substantial citizens of various portions of New York State" with "well-known names to anyone acquainted with residents of New York State and New England." What we know about the background of residents confirms this impression. The first leaders, Collins and Johnson, were a college-trained minister and attorney, respectively. John Orvis, Collins's chief lieutenant, came from a prosperous Vermont Quaker farming family; he had been a student at Oberlin. R. S. and Jacob Orvis were probably relatives. Ezra C. Smith had been at Andover with Collins. Joseph Savage, another one of the original trustees, was a well-known Syracuse salt merchant. William C. Benson of Salem, Massachusetts, one of Johnson's few supporters, was a cousin of Helen Garrison, the wife of William Lloyd Garrison. Samuel Sellers came from a prominent family of manufacturers near Philadelphia. Maria Loomis, one of the colony's most prolific writers and an editor of the *Communitist,* the community newspaper, came from a prominent family who lived at Cicero, north of Syracuse. Darius R. Stone was an abolitionist and come-outer from Sennett, New York. But in most other cases, we have only names.[168]

We also know that at least some of the men and women had long been involved in reform. Collins and N. H. Whiting were, of course, veteran abolitionists, and Orvis had been active in the Hundred Conventions. Joseph A. Whitemarsh had been involved in nonresistance since 1838 and had edited at least two radical reform journals. At least one of the inhabitants, Thomas Varney, had ties to Robert Owen's New Harmony Community in Indiana. Again, however, we know little else of most of those there.[169]

One indication of previous reform commitments is the firm commitment of the community to diet reform. "This is the beginning place for reformers," wrote Maria Loomis. "I have little confidence in any very considerable reform that does not begin here." Marenda B. Randall, whom Valentine Nicholson remembered forty years later as a particularly thorough radical, boasted that at Skaneateles she found "a less objectionable table than I have ever before found, not to except any private table in any reformed family in Vermont." Writing to the *Regenerator*, she described meals at Skaneateles: "We all sit down together, to a purely vegetable diet. Very much do we enjoy our meals. At least I do, and the rest seem to." She noted with satisfaction that only a few women used black tea; otherwise she had seen "no animal food, alcohol, tea, coffee, butter, cheese, pastry, or anything of the kind." The community folk did bake pies, but Randall begrudged the time that it took. "For this reason I would gladly have dispensed with, and pure unleavened bread and uncooked apples substituted in their place," she wrote to Orson Murray's *Regenerator*. Collins told A. J. MacDonald that "not a bit of flesh meat, or a glass of intoxicating drink, was used during the whole time of the experiment."[170]

This may have been true of the community in its earlier days, but toward the end, at least, it tolerated deviations. They may have been for the benefit of the workmen in the mill. But other members recalled considerable tension. H. J. Seymour, an Oneida Community member whose brother was at Skaneateles for a time, remembered that "the question of diet was one about which the community was greatly exercised." Among some, it worked with such "special violence" that they partook only of boiled mush. Other visitors found two tables at meals, one that had "ordinary food," and the other "boiled wheat, rice, and Graham mush." A disillusioned applicant recalled that "they kept butter, sugar and milk under lock and key, and in fact almost everything else." Another reported that he was told "it was usual for them to give visitors that they were accustomed to," which meant tea and bread and butter. The faithful subsisted on bread and milk. This visitor also found some meat, although the committed still made clear their disdain. One commented at the sight that he "guessed they had been to some grave-yard."[171]

Surviving accounts provide only fragmentary information about how the community governed itself. At times, they contemplated drawing up a constitution, but there is no evidence that they finished or published it. When the community began, it established two committees to transact business. A year later, there were five: agricultural, mechanical, domestic, education, and publishing. Each had a head, and the five made up a supervising committee. There were also various subcommittees. The community appointed other officials; Collins mentioned a secretary, treasurer, and business agent. An article in the *Communitist* early in 1846 mentioned a Mrs. Abbott as the matron.[172]

Many of the mechanics of decision-making within the community are unclear. There were regular meetings for business, sometimes every evening, but no account says whether the decisions were made by voting or by a Quakerly search for consensus. Collins, describing the selection of officers, said that they were chosen by "general consent." On the other hand, Quincy Johnson's description of his confrontation with Collins implies that votes were being taken.[173]

Whatever the method, however, it is clear that the dominant voice in decision-making was Collins's, and that was a source of conflict. Others besides Quincy Johnson came to find that intolerable. Darius R. Stone, one of the projectors of the Skaneateles undertaking, soon came to realize that Collins was a "Dictator," who insisted on fitting all of humanity within his own exceedingly narrow bounds. Marenda B. Randall agreed; Collins had, "in his practical character, the elements of a perfect tyrant," she wrote to the *Working Man's Advocate*. "It is true, he binds with silken cords—but none the less sure; when the hour of trial comes, they are found to possess all subtility [*sic*] of iron bolts and bars."[174]

More is known about the social life of the community mainly from accounts in the columns of the *Communitist*. There were regular lyceums, lectures, and "literary meetings," with discussion of reform prominent. One resident thought the Friday evening lyceum "perhaps the happiest meetings we have—instrumental and vocal music, compositions, dialogues, scenes from the best dramatic authors, recitations, etc." The music and dancing, and even some card playing, were much to the disquiet of some of the Hicksite Friends. At least two, George and Margaret Pryor, left out of disgust at "singing, dancing and card playing." Collins defended such amusements, however, particularly dancing. "It has contributed much toward making our home attractive to the younger members of our family," he wrote in the *Communitist*. Another resident boasted that he had never heard an obscene or vulgar song in the community: "There is scarcely anything in vogue of the light, the frivolous, and the low." Besides, Collins claimed, all such entertainments ended by 9:30 P.M. New Year's Day appears to have been the major holiday, observed with numerous speeches and the visit of a Santa-Claus-like figure called "Philanthropos" to the community children.[175]

One of the reasons that we know so much about some, although by no means all, elements of life at Skaneateles is its journal, the *Communitist,* which began publishing in January 1844. It was interested in all aspects of reform. Articles on diet, dress, antislavery, women's rights, education and property were staples. Opposition to sectarianism and "priestcraft" were prominent. The *Communitist* also gave liberal coverage to other communities, exchanging only a few barbs with Fourierists. The journal was originally free of charge, but because of the need to pay printing costs the price gradually rose, first to a dollar a year, and then to two dollars.[176]

In the spring of 1846, Skaneateles came to an end. The last known issue of the *Communitist* was dated March 10. Up to that time, the accounts from the community had been rosy; typical was a report in February that "the increase of our numbers is steady, and the applicants more numerous, than we can at present decently accommodate. Upon the whole our position and prospects were never more flattering than they are now."[177]

The immediate cause may have been the failure of the community to obtain a charter of incorporation from the New York legislature. Collins had announced the application in November 1845. Acknowledging that incorporation was certainly at odds with the beliefs on which the community was founded, Collins pleaded pressing necessity. Without a charter, the community could not hold property. Thus it would be at the mercy of unfaithful or dissatisfied trustees like Quincy Johnson.[178]

The Skaneateles communitarians faced an uphill battle. As Collins himself admitted, most of the group's neighbors looked on them as "fools and fanatics, knaves and hypocrites." Opposition had been prominent, ranging from newspaper attacks to refusals to extend credit. Moreover, there was considerable popular skepticism about granting any kind of charter of incorporation, as conferring privileges that were antithetical to republicanism. When these prejudices were combined with charges of infidelity and "Fanny Wrightism," it was probably inevitable that the attempt would fail. And it did in the lower house, 62 to 35.[179]

The last issue of the *Communitist* noted the failure to secure a charter of incorporation from the legislature. The community went on for two months, until May 1846. The end was apparently unexpected. One evening, according to MacDonald, Collins called all of the residents together and announced that he was leaving the community. He would deed the property over to the other members, but he himself would depart.[180]

Collins gave no reason for abandoning the community, other than a conviction that the world was not yet prepared to live out his theories. MacDonald noted that the value of the property had doubled. But Collins apparently was passing through still another crisis, coming to think that his beliefs were "false in theory and pernicious in their practical tendencies." By the end of the summer he would be editing a Whig newspaper in Dayton, Ohio, esconced, as one observer put it, "in the decencies and respectabilities of Whiggery."[181]

Since the crisis with Johnson in the late autumn of 1843, Collins had been the heart and soul of the community. When he departed, it disintegrated quickly. Those who remained drifted back to their old homes or to new communities. The farm fell into the hands of Samuel Sellers. But an evil fate seemed to hang over the property. In 1847 an incendiary fire destroyed the barns, and in 1850 Sellers lost it through a mortgage foreclosure. Once more the "Community place" became a prosperous private farm.[182]

Some Conclusions

The experiences of these communities probably hold few surprises for anyone familiar with general trends in nineteenth-century American communitarianism. It is a story that Edward K. Spann has called "melancholy," one of blasted hopes and failure. But a number of generalizations, based on what happened in these eight communities, are possible, and they tell us something about how communities came to be and how they failed.[183]

All of these communities grew, of course, out of the agitation for Universal Reform. Their homogeneity is striking. Marlborough, West Grove, and Highland Home were made up of Hicksite Quakers who had been neighbors previously. Grand Prairie consisted of a group of families long connected by blood and marriage and long living in the same neighborhood. Kristeen drew its inmates largely from Prairie Home. All of these apparently experienced harmonious relationships—with the possible exception of Kristeen, strife and contention were not major problems. When disagreements did come, they involved the nature of community life and the Government of God.

In contrast, three communities attracted a more diverse membership, and in all three there was divisive controversy involving personalities that either weakened or killed the experiment. Skaneateles took its membership from all over New York and New England, and the result was explosive contention. Only after many of the early members had left did it end. Prairie Home drew most of its members from the Hicksite Quaker communities of Ohio and Indiana, but there were also New Englanders, British Owenites, and all of the paupers, debtors, and bankrupts John O. Wattles could find. Harmony quickly disappeared. Union Home was a diverse collection of Hicksite and Orthodox Quakers from Ohio and Indiana, along with a variety of non-Quakers. They also found themselves crippled by personality clashes.

All of the residents of the communities shared a common commitment to ultraist reform. Many had been active in abolition since the early 1830s. From that they moved on to other reforms: diet, health, education, woman's rights, nonresistance, come-outer religion. They thus came to a vision of life that would embrace all of these reforms, and more, under the Government of God.

A few of the reformers, like Collins, Whiting, and Ernestine Rose, had been close to the centers of radical reform previously, and, in some cases, would continue to be. For the most part, however, those who entered these communities came from places far from the centers of intellectual life or reform. From isolated communities, especially in Ohio and Indiana, came the most radical visions of reform and change.

Finances were a common downfall of nineteenth-century communities, and, in some of those that grew out of Universal Reform, they were a problem. Marlborough found the need to raise money to buy land a source of trouble. West Grove failed "when the provisions gave out." Debts haunted Prairie Home, and divided those at Union Home. Yet this was not true of all of the communities. Highland Home and Grand Prairie apparently lacked for nothing material. And by 1846 Skaneateles was by all accounts profitable. Thus the reasons for failure lay elsewhere.

Over twenty years ago, the sociologist Rosabeth Moss Kanter ventured some speculations about the characteristics of successful, long-lived communities. She saw them as characterized by what she called "commitment mechanisms," and argued that six were vital: sacrifice; investment; renunciation of the outside world; communion, or communal unity; mortification, or diminution of the self, and transcendence, or finding meaning in the community.[184]

The communities that grew out of Universal Reform failed on most of these counts. They required relatively little in the way of sacrifice on the part of members—nothing like the celibacy of the Shakers, for example. While the communities usually embraced Grahamite dietary practices, that was hardly a sacrifice for most of the inhabitants, who were committed to diet reform before they came. Similarly, it was an article of faith at all of the communities that monetary investments were no requirement. Thirdly, the Universal Reformers did not require renunciation of the outside world. Members were free to come and go, to associate with nonmembers as they chose, and to maintain a variety of ties. No commitment to the community exclusively was ever asked.

The Universal Reformers' communities did, in some ways, develop a strong sense of communal unity. They did share certain experiences that Kanter sees as critical—common property, and, to some extent, homogeneous backgrounds. Work was shared, and there were no wages. On the other hand, the communities had nothing that would qualify as rituals, and did not face anything that might fairly be described as persecution.

Kanter asserts that "mortification," or the lowering of the self, was critical to the success of communities. The mechanisms she describes: sanctions, mutual criticism, uniformity, and differentiated status were utterly foreign to everything that Universal Reform advocated. Indeed, most involved some degree of coercion. Their employment would have been, for the Universal Reformers, a compromise of fundamental principles. While they sought community, it was as a place in which humans would be completely free of all restraints, save those imposed by God's Government. And those restraints apparently were few.

Kanter's final characteristic is "transcendence," a sense of purpose. That the Universal Reformers certainly had. They were, after all, ushering in the Government of God, redeeming the land for humanity, inaugurating a new order that was to transform the world. They began certain of success, certain that the divine plan for the ages and Natural Law were on their side. They had to succeed, for God willed it.

The communities failed. Finances, internal strife, and ideological contradictions and problems probably all played a part. But the Universal Reformers did have a vision, a vision they articulated fully while attempting to carry it out. If they left a legacy, it was that.

❖ 6 ❖

THE IDEOLOGY OF UNIVERSAL REFORM

Universal inquiry and Reform was at its heart a vision, a vision of a world remade anew. As Maria Loomis, one of John A. Collins's lieutenants at Skaneateles, put it, this was "an enterprise which contemplates the complete overthrow of the whole base and super structure of the present system." Loomis did not understate the case. Collins, Wattles, Mendenhall, and those at Skaneateles, Prairie Home, Marlborough, and the other communities looked to nothing less than a complete remaking of society.[1]

There was, as will be seen, some diversity of views about how this would be accomplished. In some cases, there would be such conflict that, instead of overthrowing the base of society, the communities themselves were undermined. But whatever the contentions that ultimately came to plague them, at the time of their founding the communities did share certain common experiences and a wide range of ideas.

These communities came to be, in large part, because their residents had known isolation—spiritual, intellectual, physical. Community was, to some degree, an end in itself. But it was primarily a means to an end, the way in which society would be transformed. Both by the power of their example and by their growth, the communities would propel universal reform forward. First and foremost, they would usher in the Government of God, the end of government based on coercive force. With the Government of God would come a religious revolution—the end of priestcraft and sectarianism, a return to simple Christianity, or something even more basic. Poverty and want would disappear, as the competitive, "grabocratic" capitalist economy gave way to one based on cooperation and the sharing of the earth's plenty. Education would be critical; all involved agreed that much depended on the rising generation being raised up with the proper habits and being saved from the destructive schooling that was found in contemporary society. Community would also bring liberation and new freedom for women, indeed new understandings of marriage, although there was nothing else close to consensus about all of the implications of this reform. Diet and health reform would also be critical, although the communitarians were not different from other reformers in this respect. For many, the culmination of their labors would be nothing less than the establishment of the Government of God throughout the earth—the arrival of the millennium.

The Experience of Community

One of the striking common strains apparent in the writings of many Universal Reformers is their sense of isolation. Looking at the seven communities in Indiana and Ohio, one fact stands out. Community interest, and interest in radical abolition generally before 1845, tended to be strongest in small isolated Hicksite Quaker communities. Both Prairie Home and Highland Home were in the vicinity of the scattered Hicksites who made up Goshen Monthly Meeting in Logan and Champaign counties in Ohio. They were at least thirty miles from any other Hicksite group and were regarded with suspicion and hostility by their Orthodox Quaker neighbors. The Union Home community in Randolph County, Indiana, Hiram Mendenhall's group, formed around what probably was the only Hicksite family in the county. The Marlborough community in Stark County, Ohio, similarly grew out of a small group of Hicksite Quakers, the only one in the county, in a Quaker community badly split by the separation of 1828. The West Grove community in Jay County, Indiana, was made up of Hicksite Friends who were two days travel from the next community of Friends of the same persuasion. In contrast, in places where there were large, relatively stable Hicksite Quaker communities, such as Wayne, Washington, and Madison counties in Indiana and Warren, Belmont, and Columbiana counties in Ohio, there was comparatively little interest in the movement. The Friends at Center in Clinton County and those at New Garden in Columbiana County were exceptional.[2]

There are similar themes of self-conscious isolation in the writings of many of the Hicksite Friends who were drawn toward the society for Universal Inquiry and Reform. Valentine Nicholson experienced it again and again. At the time of the Hicksite separation, his had been one of only a handful of families at Caesars Creek not to go with the Orthodox Friends. He spent most of the time between 1834 and 1841 living far from any group of Friends. Dr. Edwin Fussell, the Chester County, Pennsylvania, physician who settled at Pendleton, Indiana, in 1836, and his wife Rebecca as well, missed the society that they had left behind. On the Indiana frontier, the good doctor found his non-Quaker neighbors backward and boorish, while even the Friends around him were so committed to Whig politics that they lacked sympathy for social reform. "I have perhaps been more accustomed to more society than any of our friends who came here before me," he wrote home in 1836, "and here there is none, or worse than none, or what is next thing or worse, except in a few families." Israel French, one of the few Wayne County, Indiana, Hicksites with communitarian interests, wrote of similar feelings after moving there from Belmont County, Ohio. "I am now with all my family in a strange land among Strangers," he wrote to a Philadelphia Friend. "I feel very much striped and some times fear I shall be counted as a deserter." Charles Atkinson, another promoter of Union Home, was the only Hicksite Friend in Grant County, Indiana. Perhaps the most poignant testimony was that of Joseph Allen, a Hicksite Friend from Michigan. At age 17, he had read Paine's *Age of Reason* and had lost faith in Christianity. The result was that, as he wrote to John A. Collins's *Communitist*, "I lost my most intimate friends." To want friends was only natural, he told Collins, and to be alone was dangerous to anyone's morals. Thus infidels often fell: "They are as speckled birds, without mates, and looked upon by the generality of people as poor castaways; the poor unbeliever feels that it is unmerited abuse, and it tends to wither the feelings of his nature."[3]

This experience of isolation was not unique to the Hicksite Friends. Wilson D. Schooley, an Orthodox Friend who joined Prairie Home, was the only member of his large family to take an interest in radical abolition and reform. Kersey Grave, one of the founders of Union Home, had found himself at odds with fellow Orthodox Friends around Richmond, Indiana, in a variety of ways, most notably in his support for abolition and his religious heterodoxy that would eventually lead him to atheism. Huldah Wickersham, another one of the early supporters of Union Home, was another abolitionist Orthodox Friend who found herself at odds with almost everyone else in her monthly meeting. David W. Jones, who came from a stalwartly Orthodox family in Grant County, Indiana, found himself regarded as an infidel and treated as something of a pariah because of his interest in Universal Reform.[4]

Perhaps no one knew the experience of isolation better than the men who had led the loneliest of lives—traveling antislavery and reform lecturers and agents. John O. Wattles had known social isolation for much of his life—as the son of a drunkard in Goshen; teaching school in a remote area of north-central Pennsylvania; spending most of the years from 1839 to 1843 traveling, without a permanent home. Marius Robinson, one of the founders of the Marlborough community, had left New York for the lonely life of teaching in Alabama and Tennessee, then had known isolation from the world of reform after an attack

by an antiabolitionist mob left him badly hurt and forced to give up most activities for five years. Emily, his wife, had been disowned by her family for marrying him. John A. Collins had certainly been, for a time, part of the inner
circle of Garrisonian abolition. But his wretched experiences in England, his
perception of lack of support from home, and the discomfort of many of his
old friends with his ideas about economics and society led to a search for a new
circle of intimates. Community may have been a way of finding again the fellowship he had once known.[5]

The Universal Reformers did not see this as a problem peculiar to their own
situations, however. It was, in their view, inherent in a malformed society. Wattles articulated this view most fully. Isolation was, he wrote, in his journal, the
Herald of Progression, "the penalty incurred for the violation of social laws."
Because humanity would "not come together and live in unity and contentment, and yield in harmony and humility to the great principles of universal
right and bring the *will* under the control of the understanding, they are shut
up in solitary cells, and sentenced to hard labor life." Wattles saw this as a particular problem in the West: "See a single individual settled on one of these
large prairies, how lonely he looks; like a toad on a log 'Monarch of all he surveys,' to be sure, but how lonely." "This western country," he wrote in some of
his memoranda, "should not have been settled in this isolated manner. The
social relation has been violated, and man is driven from his fellows." Traveling
along the Wabash River in western Indiana, Wattles found that it "was made
for association." Isolation brought inevitable penalties: "Sickness, Pain, . . .
premature Death, Ignorance, Poverty, and Solitude," which would give rise to
"a generation of pimpering, puny, pale, puking pygmies, dwarfish runts, whose
existence would be a curse." John Orvis, the Hicksite Friend who began his
community career at Skaneateles and ended it at Brook Farm, summed up the
feelings of his compatriots: "Man is not [an] individual—to us is made for society."[6]

After pondering isolation, it was pleasant to turn to contemplating the experience of community. Rebecca Fussell wrote how wonderful it would be to
study what she wanted, read what she wished, "learning freely of the works of
the creator," all the while knowing that it was being done in the service of humanity and a higher vision of human life. Emily Gardner, an Orthodox Friend
from Union County, Indiana, wrote to Esther Wattles, waxing poetic after attending a community meeting at Greensboro, Indiana, in 1844. "'Tis pleasant
indeed to be acquainted and hold converse with such minds," she exclaimed,
for how would anyone find pleasure "with those whose ideas and conversations

[are] confined to dress and fashion [and] good things to eat." Pondering a letter from Esther Whinery, who would marry John O. Wattles, and Joel P. Davis, a fellow resident at Prairie Home, Gardner described "a wave of joy across my soul while hope and fancy pointed to the time not far distant when we shall dwell and labor side by side in sweet unity together in behalf of bleeding outraged and crushed humanity." John O. Wattles agreed. "All those happy hours we spend together are so many arguments and motives for us to labor and plead for the suffering and dumb to endeavor to get society into that state where all can feel what we feel, and be as happy as we are, that all minds may be married and joined to God."[7]

Once communities were established, their experience, at least initially, fulfilled these hopes. Valentine Nicholson's doleful memory of those at Prairie Home, that they loved to talk much more than they did to work, says as much about the pleasures of, and opportunities for, conversation as about the sloth of the residents. An editorial in the Skaneateles community's newspaper, the *Communitist,* painted life there in the most glowing terms. "We enjoy ourselves *much* beyond what is possible for most people to do, even the most favored of mankind," one of the members wrote. They lived not in "little isolated dwellings," where it was "hard even to accommodate a visiting neighbor." Instead they had spacious quarters for all occasions, and they would "not have to ride half a dozen miles in the cold afterwards."[8]

None of the advocates of Universal Reform would have been surprised at such a happy experience, since it was the inevitable culmination of Progression. Emily Gardner was moved to poetry:

> We are children of one Father
> And we're made to love each other
> And in friendship dwell together
> In a great community.

Community was, in Wattles's view, "the embodiment of all good, and the consummation of all Reform." Humans were social beings, and they could not escape from that. "If we ascend to heaven we shall be in community. And if we stay on earth we are in community," he wrote to Orson S. Murray's *Regenerator.* "The only question for us to settle, seems to be, what *kind* of community shall we have?" From Collins, Wattles, Murray, Mendenhall, Brooke, Nicholson, and the others, as we will see, would come different answers on subjects ranging from religion to constitutions to finance. But all would have agreed that the foundation for any community must be the Government of God.[9]

The Government of God

The advocates of Universal Reform faced the future with confidence because they were certain that they had irresistible forces on their side. They intended, through their communities, to replace flawed human governments, based on the evil of coercive force, with the Government of God. Human laws, which had proved a miserable basis for guiding or controlling human actions or society, would give way to natural laws. On this basis, a new society would rise.

As we have already seen, many of the Universal Reformers had been politically active Whigs. By the time they committed themselves to Universal Reform, they had sworn off parties as not only useless, but irrelevant. John A. Collins thought that the democratic process was inherently flawed. "All elections create parties, which produce strife, jealousy and war," he wrote in 1844. "It opens a false road to the ambitions. It disheartens and degrades the masses. It makes them fit tools for the crafty and designing." The Skaneateles *Communitist* described the reaction of residents to the exceedingly close presidential race of 1844: "The great political convulsion which this country has just past through has gone by us like the idle wind.—We heard its footsteps but like the rustling of the forest leaves it has passed off, leaving us unmoved and uninterested, save in sorrow for their strife, and compassion for their delusion." All indications are that those at the other communities were equally indifferent.[10]

Part of this antipathy derived from feelings that any Garrisonian abolitionist would have understood and accepted: to participate in government under the constitution as it stood would be to support slavery, since the Constitution explicitly sanctioned slavery, and that was something that no consistent or conscientious abolitionist could do. Abraham Brooke apparently thought most deeply on this. "Now we find the constitution grants a premium to slavery, by the political power it confers on the slave owner; it pledges the whole physical force of the nation to perpetuate the system," he wrote to Gamaliel Bailey late in 1842. "The individual who exercises political power at all, therefore, *does actually uphold and support slavery.*" Even were a Liberty party president elected, supported by a Liberty party Congress, not only would he be unable to do anything effective against slavery, but would be forced to support it. Brooke posited the scenario of James G. Birney, the Liberty candidate, being inaugurated. The slaves, naturally, would regard "the jubilee as close at hand"; some from Maryland and Virginia, he was sure, would march on Washington, only to be told by the new president, just sworn to uphold the Constitution, "Why my good boys, I can do nothing for you. The general government has no power over slavery in the states. You have nothing for it but to go home and obey your masters." True, Liberty men might say that they would never take up arms against slaves, but that would clearly violate the Constitution that they were swearing to uphold. And if they condemned the Constitution, as it deserved to be condemned, they would have no chance of being elected. Brooke concluded that Liberty party success could come only through "jesuitical doctrine" and sophistry. "Unless the 'end sanctifies the means,' I believe that no man can, in innocence, act politically under our government."[11]

Universal Reformers, however, did not see the matters as one simply of a flawed United States Constitution. The problem was more fundamental—all human government rested on the use of coercive force. Like nonresistant abolitionists elsewhere, they believed that violence was fundamentally wrong. "Let the passage be found, if it can, where Christ declares ye shall make laws and enforce them by the sword and bayonet," wrote Benjamin B. Davis, a Hicksite Friend who lived at Prairie Home. Wattles reasoned that if combativeness was a quality of God, then the more the better, and it would increase until it covered the earth, "and hurls the Great I Am from the center of existence." Force was "the progeny of the dark ages." Wattles looked forward to the day when "monuments erected to the memory of some renowned battle will be the moral of human folly and sadness." Indeed, he looked forward to a time when "the whole vocabulary of reform, including the language of Christendom must be expurgated, and the warlike figures, metaphors and hopes set aside." Wattles thought that "*battling for the Right*" was "really an incongruity, as 'holy sinning' or 'righteous wickedness.'" Collins wrote in the *Communitist* that "governments of *brute force and violence,* with their countless engines of Oppression," would be the first casualties of the growth of community.[12]

Instead, the true Christian and reformer looked to the establishment of the Government of God. Wattles put the basis of community government succinctly: "God exists—He maintains the Elementary Principles of his government, Eternal, universal and unchanging." A true social condition would be "the harmony of characters with the principles of God's government." Concluding an editorial in his journal, the *Herald of Progression,* Wattles summed up: "God maintains the principles of His government, Omnipotent, and Eternal, and if the nations dash against them, like the waves against the butting cliff, they only dash themselves to pieces."[13]

Wattles, Collins, and their compatriots saw the Government of God extending into all facets of life: government, diet, education, religion, health, marriage, child-rearing, gender relations, economics—all subjects that will be examined in greater detail later. The starting point, of course, would be the end of human government. Naturally, advocates were somewhat defensive about what this would mean. Wattles noted that some thought that this would entail the end of all law, that "God has retired from the universe and has thrown reins on to the neck of confusion." Patten Davis, the Vermont abolitionist who was one of the founders of Skaneateles, recorded that in 1838 he had decided that he could not use the courts to collect debts, yet he had never lost a cent. If the world would do likewise, it would be the end of courts. Maria Loomis, the schoolteacher at Skaneateles, wrote in 1844 that "nothing short of anarchy would result from abandoning physical governments faster than men outgrew them." Despotism, she said, would be preferable to anarchy, but "neither are necessary where men are sufficiently enlightened to govern themselves." But a year later she wrote confidently that she believed that "the most perfect order may be maintained without the intervention of physical governments." "We have nothing to hope from the forceful principle," she told readers of the *Communitist*. "Our fear is from its existence."[14]

How, then, was anarchy to be avoided? How would humanity govern itself in the absence of all restraints of coercive power or force? Fortunately, the advocates of Universal Reform saw God as having provided for guidance as the world was reduced to obedience to his government. "Submission, or obedience to the principles of God's government is required of all beings in the universe for the universal good of all," Wattles wrote in 1846, "and a mental principle is given as a consistent part of the Mental Constitution."[15]

The reformers thus were believers in Natural Law, which they thought would prevail when communities opened the way for them. "The principles of a community are the Laws of Nature," Wattles wrote. "It is but the government of God begun on the earth. It is doing on *earth* as it is in heaven." As Prairie Home opened in the spring of 1844, Wattles described it to Orson S. Murray as "a congregation of minds who aim at being in harmony with the principles of God's government; to live out the Laws of their being; or in other words, it is designed to be based on NATURAL LAWS." Thus they sought to create their own version of the nature religion that took many forms in nineteenth-century America.[16]

"Natural Law" was a term popular with all of the Universal Reformers, but they never were precise in its definition. Their writings make it clear that they saw their agenda—abolition, temperance, education, health and diet reform, woman's rights—as based on it. They thought that such knowledge was innate in humanity. "What laws are to govern us?" asked the *Communitist* in 1844. "The laws as we find them written on every lineament of our constitution, by the finger of God." The human soul, N. H. Whiting told an audience at Vergennes, Vermont, in 1843, had in it "the great law of the universe." "Each individual carries the Constitution in his own nature," concluded Wattles, "and will, eternally, for the principles of God's government are unchanging."[17]

There was also general agreement about the source of this innate knowledge—it was divine. The Quakers in the group spoke in terms that evoked the traditional Quaker doctrine of the Inner Light. Emily Gardner wrote that if humans would only rely on "the divine image within" instead of the "strong arm of the law" they would make the world infinitely happier. John Orvis, the Hicksite Friend from Vermont, told readers of Murray's *Vermont Telegraph* that all people had within them a "sense of the good, the beautiful, and the true, which manifests itself in the soul." During the Hundred Conventions he went even farther. "Man is not depraved, . . . he is divine," he told an audience. Emily Rakestraw Robinson, a resident at Marlborough, longed for the time when all people "would give heed to the revelations of the spirit of God in and through their moral nature."[18]

Those who came from more orthodox religious backgrounds were explicit in affirming that human nature was good, and utterly rejected the doctrine of the depravity of human nature. Collins and two of his lieutenants at Skaneateles, Joseph A. Whitemarsh and George Pryor, wrote to Horace Greeley: "Rejecting the hoary doctrine of man's natural depravity, we assert that human nature is pure, noble, divine." Wattles thought that if Christians really believed that man was made in the image of God, they would see that God had none of the attributes of depravity, and therefore when they appeared in man they must be the result of circumstances rather than the nature of humanity. Orvis summed up this view well in a lecture in Randolph, Vermont, in the summer of 1843: "Man is not depraved as the religious dogmas of the age make him to be, he is divine." It was a "slander upon man, and calumny upon God" to assert that.[19]

Orvis, Wattles, Collins, and the others did not deny the evil in the world; it was the knowledge of it that drove them to Universal Reform. But they saw error and evil as the result of a flawed social order, not innate depravity. The cure was to put people into right relations. "Error is to be removed by the prevalence of truth," wrote Wattles. Collins pointed to the power of circumstances. "One has a good organization and a good education and good circumstances—

what praise to him?" Collins asked while lecturing during the Hundred Conventions. "Another has a bad organization, a bad education and bad circumstances—what blame?" Social evils were the result of the violation of social relations; so long as society was so fundamentally flawed, nothing good could come of it. One resident of Skaneateles wrote that in the present social arrangements, the more knowledge man gained the worse he would become.[20]

This, then, was the point of community—to live in such a way to bring the Government of God, to create a society in which its members would come to understand natural laws and thus usher in a better way, to set an irresistible example for the rest of the world. When humans returned to "the primeval order," wrote the Hicksite reformer Thomas McClintock, one of the promoters of Skaneateles, "justice will supersede injustice, benevolence cruelty, truth perfidy; men will be brothers, and God will be glorified." It was an extraordinarily ambitious undertaking, all acknowledged, but nothing less would suffice. "It is a great work, it is true, but there is a Great God at the head of the Universe, and he carries on great affairs," Wattles wrote. He was almost defiant. "If there is not power in the gospel to redeem the slave, put an end to war, put an end to monopoly of the earth, and bring man into love with his brother, and all mind into harmony with God . . . a system of humanity should be taught that *will* do it, for it must be done."[21]

Thus those who embraced Universal Reform saw themselves as beginning the Government of God on earth, the end of human governments of coercive force and man-made law. Instead it would found itself on the will of God, Natural Law. It was only because of false social relations that humans had departed from it. Placed in the proper ones, they would return to following God's laws. And in a variety of vital ways, community would do just this.

Economy

It was not commitment to change in government alone that drove the proponents of Universal Reform. They knew that there were other, more insidious manifestations of coercive power than those that emanated from political governments. Communitarians saw the economic order as being as badly flawed as the political; they had come to view most forms of property, particularly land and the means of production, as violations of natural law and threats to the Government of God. Thus community would be the foundation of a new economic order.

The Universal Reformers lived, of course, in a time of change in American society, what many historians now call "the market revolution." In the Northeast and Midwest, it affected both town and country, as urban areas became increasingly involved in manufacturing and trade with other parts of the country, and farming became increasingly commercial and market-oriented. This transformation had a profound impact on all facets of American society—political, economic, even religious. It is not clear, however, whether the advocates of Universal Reform were benefitting or suffering from these changes. Some, like Wattles, certainly found their families increasingly marginalized in the new economic order. Others, like the Nicholsons and Brookes, apparently were prospering. Still others, like Hiram Mendenhall, had known both success and failure. Perhaps as a result, the Universal Reformers were deeply ambivalent about the changes taking place around them. They embraced some—for example, they wanted to reap the full benefits of labor-saving technology. But in most respects, they were profoundly skeptical about what they saw taking place in a new market economy.[22]

In challenging so profoundly the new economic order, and in particular the fundamental bases of competitive capitalism, these radical abolitionists parted company with most of their compatriots, even most Garrisonians and nonresistants. As several historians have observed, most abolitionists shared widely held assumptions about the virtues of economic competition and the value of poverty as a stimulus to work. Wendell Phillips, Garrison's close associate, wrote that "wholesome poverty, is no unmixed evil; it is the spur that often wins the race; it is the trial that calls out, like fire, all the deep great qualities of a man's nature." Few brooked comparisons of the situation of wage workers with slaves. As another wrote in 1853: "The irreligion of slavery consists in the absence and banishment of the soul itself. . . . The exigencies of Poverty stimulate the mind if they do not elevate it."[23]

Collins, Nicholson, Wattles, and their fellow communitarians took issue with these assumptions. They began by arguing that a competitive economy was a violation of Natural Law and therefore of God's Government. Private property was likewise. Even when there were "winners" in such a situation, those who accumulated wealth and lived by the labor of others suffered in other ways; thus competition brought misery to all. In some ways, as in their embrace of technology, the communitarians accepted enthusiastically the changes taking place around them. But in others, such as their deep suspicion of cities and praise of the rural, they looked backward. The fruit of community, they argued, would be a new economic order that brought a comfortable living to all with a minimum of work.

Looking around them in the early 1840s, the advocates of Universal Reform found ample evidence of deranged economic arrangements. "Already, vast numbers of our people are paupers, and multitudes have no employment by which to secure their bread," editorialized the *Communitist* in 1845. Wattles's *Herald of Progression* agreed the same year. "The piercing cry of needy millions has gone up," he wrote. "Beggars are multiplying, incendiarism is rife, healthy men, women and children throng the streets for labor and bread, and the boarding houses are already stacked with regular daily applicants for the 'cold victuals,' " sadly observed Eliab W. Capron, one of the inmates at Skaneateles.[24]

Even as the poor suffered, however, the growing disparity between rich and poor made society's problems worse. "Wealth and squalor, the hovel and the palace, the millionaire and the starving mendicant, already begin to reproduce themselves," wrote Capron. "The lines of demarcation between the aristocracy, the middling classes, and the laborers, grow more impossible each year." Collins claimed that 99 out of 100 Americans were being robbed of the right of the land. "For the paltry privilege of being allowed to toil upon the soil, the poor delve and delve, to sustain their lordly oppressors, in wealth, extravagance, prodigality, and tyranny," he told a convention of sympathizers in Boston in 1844. Wattles agreed, writing that a visit to any city would bring home the vivid contrasts between wealth and poverty.[25]

The reformers were united in agreement as to the source of these evils. In Randolph, Vermont, in the summer of 1843, Collins made the most extreme statement; "the rich," he claimed, had "entered into a conspiracy against the weak." But this was extravagant even for Collins. Even he usually agreed that the real problem was competition. Samuel Sellers, one of Collins's most enthusiastic supporters at Skaneateles, wrote that "Civilization is based upon *competition* in trade, business, and all things. This is its soul or life-giving principle. This stimulates exclusive selfishness to the highest pitch." Nathaniel H. Whiting, lecturing with Collins and Wattles in Vermont in the summer of 1843, summed up the situation:

> Society makes us do misery to each other—
> Not a trade but that grows fat upon the necessities and
>   miseries of his fellows—
> The carpenter gets business by fire and conflagrates and
>   the tradesman to be glad when a member of the trade expires.
> He must rejoice at every misfortune that makes his trade
>   better.

It was the same for all trades and professions: the farmer took heart from other farmers struck by drought, lawyers from contention and difficulty, doctors from sickness and suffering, ministers from sin. The result was simply summed up. As the *Communitist* editorialized, modern society had as its mottoes "Every man fits himself for the devil take the hindmost" and "Get what you can when you can."[26]

Most Americans, including most abolitionists, would have seen this in terms of the classical economic tradition going back to Adam Smith: people were inherently selfish, and only the "invisible hand" of the marketplace kept their selfishness within bounds. This the communitarians denied. "The present state of social arrangements compels every body to be selfish," Wattles wrote in 1846. Modern society, by rewarding acquisitiveness, encouraged its development, "until it lays its voracious grip on every thing that comes in its way." The Golden Rule might be to love one's neighbor, wrote Abraham Brooke, but that was impossible in a competitive economy. Collins agreed. "The interest of every man is antagonistical to the interest of his neighbor," he wrote. "With his present knowledge and relations, he is forced to prey upon his species. His interests are necessarily antagonistic and hostile to those of his neighbors." Thus the Universal Reformers concluded that a competitive economic system did not grow out of innate traits of human nature. Rather the greed and selfishness that it supposedly controlled were its fruits, the results of disobedience to Natural Law and the Government of God.[27]

As they were opposed to competition, they were equally skeptical about trade. Almost every act of commerce, claimed Nicholson, was an act of mischief; buying low and selling high was inherently unjust. "The whole system of trade is a genteel and common form of robbery," wrote Collins, morally equivalent to slavery. The Fraternal Home Community in Jay County, Indiana, condemned the profit system by making one of its rules "equitable commerce" with "cost the limit of price." Jacob Ferris thought that competitive trade inevitably led to abuse. The power to buy wheat in excess of what was needed for individual or family consumption, for example, meant that capitalists would "send out agents and secure all in the market store the flour and make a panic, then raise the price and treble their money." A Skaneateles resident wrote that "to accumulate wealth through the ordinary channels of trade is to *cheat, rob, and steal.*"[28]

Some of the most radical of the communitarians carried their opposition to commerce to its logical end and condemned the use of money. Some may have been influenced by the antibanking agitation that had been a mainstay of Jacksonian politics in the 1830s. J. M. Beckett, one of Collins's coadjutors at Skaneateles, condemned paper money as making the country "drunk with artificial stimulus." He predicted that a banking collapse would be the "secret spring" that would reveal the rottenness of the whole competitive system. Beckett was probably the author of another piece in the *Communitist* that argued that all who used money in any form participated in "commercial piracy." Almost every piece of coin or paper "in the circulating medium representing value, represents also some individual crime growing out of its most wanton shame." Any act of charity, "every donation in coin or its immediate representative, is literally gratifying benevolence through avarice, crime, and despotism." Joseph A. Whitemarsh, another Skaneateles resident, labeled money "the greatest war and slave-making, gagging, bribing, and corrupting instrument ever known, or that ever will be known." For Abraham Brooke, the question was one of consistency. Money was not inherently evil, but had to be avoided because it was part of the competitive system. "If the competitive system be wrong as a whole, it is wrong in its parts," Brooke wrote to Orson S. Murray's *Regenerator*. "The practice of any part of it being wrong, can not produce right." Thus Brooke refused to use money in any way, giving up his newspaper subscriptions and depending on the good will of friends and neighbors for things that he could not do or make himself.[29]

The communitarians looked askance at wage industries as well. In part they saw them as a dangerous new extension of the competitive economic system, in which employers set wages low while selling at the highest possible price. "Whoever uses the labor of other men without rendering a full equivalent therefor, is an extortioner," wrote Nicholson. William H. Whinery, a brother-in-law of John O. Wattles, agreed. "At the *north*, the master has a lash more potent than the whipthong to stimulate the energies of his *white* slaves—*the fear of want*." Abraham Brooke thought long on this, and concluded that nearly all wealth came from the "uncompensated labor of others." Profits, he argued, "more or less belong to the employed, because they do not include all of his production save that which is needed to support animal life. To substitute a wage system for slavery, Brooke wrote, was "wickedness." Not surprisingly, communitarians looked with special concern at conditions in the emerging factories. Such workers, wrote one resident at Skaneateles, were "enslaved to capital." Collins, of course, had first come to question capitalism from his experiences in English factory towns. Wattles approvingly quoted Milo A. Townsend, an erratic Pittsburg Fourierist, on the evils of employers of women and child labor. "These grabocrats care not if every dollar they make snapped a heart string. To make money is their object, no matter what havoc is made of humanity," Townsend raged. To keep them in sinfulness, "poor little children, and youthful; maidens, and rugged men are forced to wear out their lives." Collins, Wattles, and Murray gave attention to the labor movement in their papers, and supported strikes and unions.[30]

While they looked askance at industrialism, the communitists were not opposed to technology. Wattles especially was enthusiastic about machines as a
means of progression. Writing about an ideal community in 1845, Wattles envisioned: "Inventions and useful improvements of enginery and labor-saving
machinery, discovery of facilities for mental development and social enjoy-
ment." Wattles was sure that humanity would "eventually throw the burden of
drudgery from the shoulders of Humanity, on to steamhorses, iron mules, and
wooden dromedaries. . . . The genius of steam and the wind shall be yoked to
his machinery and turn his wheels and do his labor."[31]

The problem was that a competitive economy inevitably perverted technology. "Labor-saving machinery, which in a true state of society will perform
man's labor, and exonerate him from the pack-horse load to which he is subjected is now his greatest foe—his deadliest enemy," wrote Collins in 1844.
William H. Whinery agreed. Laborers suffered, he wrote, "not because they
have been *idle*, but because they have over*worked*." Through their labor they
had overproduced, and thus reduced, if not eliminated, the demand for their
labor. The *Communitist* observed in 1845 that "the power to add to our wealth,
which we already possess, peoples our alms-houses, increases crime, multiplies
prostitution, expels from the field of honest industry the hardy operative and
reduces the wages of those having employment."[32]

If they abhorred economic competition, the communitarians were adamant
in their condemnation of the private holding of land. Abraham Brooke was
typically blunt: it was "wicked to monopolize the soil." The land was, he wrote
Orson S. Murray, "all in the hands of robbers and pirates, made such by ignorance, education, and habit, whether they know it or not." Whiting pronounced
it an offense against the laws of God. "In order to recognize your right to the
Earth, I want a bill of sale from the Almighty," he told listeners at Randolph,
Vermont, in the summer of 1843. He demanded nothing less than "the signa-
ture of Immanuel." The earth being God's, humans had no right to appropriate
it. On the other hand, humans had a right to exist, and they could not do that
without the right to cultivate the land. "He has a right to till—and of course
has a right to the means of life—has a right to the earth—and in taking from
him the Earth and in that you have taken away his *all*." As Whiting put it, "he
that claims the earth to himself is guilty of all the evil that is in the world."
Wattles was equally certain. "If one Man, to the exclusion of another may hold
the earth," he told a convention at Skaneateles, "he may hold the whole if he
can get it and the almighty committed the trespass in allowing human beings
into the world."[33]

The group disagreed, however, about whether *all* property holding was evil.

Brooke thought it was "at war with God's government, consequently a prolific parent of misery to the race." Brooke, in fact, argued that individual property was the basis of "involuntary as well as voluntary servitude" as well as "human government, war, and the church," along with the evils that grew out of each. Darius R. Swezey, a Skaneateles resident, wrote that he had long thought that "Christianity required the giving up of all individual property and holding it in common, as the primitive Christians did." Collins thought that "laws of property" were only "conventional usages" that kept humanity "from retaking a part of the right that was taken" from it. John O. Wattles, as usual, took an extreme view. When a friend wrote to apologize for having inadvertently kept a pencil belonging to Esther Wattles, he responded in the pages of the *Herald of Progression:* "But the pencil is just as much yours as ours, it belongs to those who need it most." He did not go as far as Jacob Ferris, however, who denied that individuals had even the right to keep their talents to themselves. "Men have a right to enjoy the benefit of each other's ability," he wrote.[34]

Others, however, were unwilling to go this far. William H. Whinery thought that private property had been abused by monopolists, but that was no ground for its abolition. He advocated that in a community "the tools of a family or individual, house departments, furniture and apparatus thereof, the clothing, and all things that are applied for family or individual use, should be held sacred" to individuals. Whinery's view may reflect his experience with the failure of the Prairie Home community, but Valentine Nicholson had reached the same conclusion before Prairie Home got underway. Nicholson wrote to Murray that all individuals had a sort of sacred sphere around them, and that certain objects—"clothes, books, papers, tools, which invariably receive their texture and their form from our several loves and inclinations" should be held sacred to them.[35]

The communitarians also found themselves in disagreement about attitudes toward landed property in the transitional state from "grabocracy" to a communal world. In the case of Prairie Home and Skaneateles, where the communities began by buying land, the question had to be confronted immediately; could those who believed that private landholding was contrary to the will of God begin the redemption of the earth by purchasing it? Abraham Brooke, at least, in his quest for absolute moral consistency, condemned this course with the argument that no good could ever come from violating God's law, even with the best of intentions. "If it be *right* for us to purchase of others access to the soil, then it is not wrong in them to sell it, nor to monopolize it, for the purpose of rent or sale," he wrote to Murray. "By our proposition to purchase that which no man has a right to sell, we proclaim our want of faith in the principles we profess." He refused to go to Skaneateles for that reason. Most, however, were willing to compromise. Murray argued that buying land was like giving one's purse to a robber—to preserve life, one had no choice. Valentine Nicholson replied to Brooke that purchase was a concession to gradualism, and the result would be redemption. "We do not claim to own it, any more than we did before," he wrote to Murray's *Regenerator*. "We only pay for that which humanity shall, humanity ought to and will one day have access to, *free*." Their intentions were indeed different: "We are buying off one robber's title, but not aiming to put another in its place." Wattles was blunt but hopeful: "To be obliged to do what we condemn, to contemplate buying and selling and land-holding as wrong, and yet, for a time, be compelled to practice them, will require the utmost stretch of watchfulness and cautiousness, as well as the full exercise of judgment." In fact the communities settled the question in a variety of ways. Skaneateles bought land and went through all of the formalities of recording deeds; Prairie Home also purchased land, but refused to make any record of it. Marlborough began on donated land, but when it bought an intermediate tract, it also refused to further its rights by proving the deed in court. At Highland Home, Grand Prairie, Kristeen, and Fraternal Home, owners apparently donated the land without making deeds. Only at Union Home, located on land given by Hiram Mendenhall, did a donor make any kind of formal deed; in this case it may have been due to Mendenhall's debts and fears of the claims of creditors.[36]

In many respects, however, the Universal reformers were carrying on older strains that abolitionists and nonabolitionists alike would have affirmed. One was the need of all to engage in productive labor. This was an old theme in reform literature. Even before the rise of abolition, many antislavery advocates had endorsed manual labor schools, where intellectual training would be tied to physical work. Wattles had been a student at Oneida Institute, which was one of the best-known manual labor schools. And, as seen earlier, the whole Universal Inquiry and Reform enterprise had begun in an attempt to found such a school in southwestern Ohio. Wattles was involved in efforts to set up at least two others after 1845.[37]

For the Universal Reformers, work was a matter both of obedience to Natural Law and fundamental morality. Wattles argued that it was its own reward, vital to the preservation of good health. Labor was "man's redemption and the world's redemption." Nicholson argued that aversion to hard work was but another rotten fruit of the competitive system. It was this delusive spirit, he wrote, that "makes us desire to keep our sons clothed in costly apparel, and training in colleges, or sauntering along the streets, behind a smoking cigar," while the poor were denied an education. It was corruption that desired to see daughters of the well-to-do "passing from the boarding school to the splendid parlor, to visit and be visited, attend 'parties' and give 'parties,' moving in the gay circles of what we term 'high life,' " while daughters of the "poor were kept toiling, washing, and brushing, and scrubbing, and cooking, and cleaning," doomed to remain "ignorant and degraded." George Taylor, one of the residents of Prairie Home, wrote that he "used to think that labor was loathsome and degrading." Once in community, however, freed from "the old mercenary system," he found it attractive and rewarding. Marenda B. Randall, one of the most active and articulate members of the Skaneateles community, wrote of her experiences there:

> See those whose fine intellects must formerly have been reserved for the "professions," coming in from the plough, clothed in "stout homespun," hands soiled and rough, faces brown from exposure, and then observe the enthusiasm kindled in the eye which none can mistake. See them sit down and partake of their simplest fare; listen to spirited jokes, retorts, and pleasantries of each other, and then, as they assume a graver tone, listen to the high-toned morality, virtue, purity, and intelligence which speak out in almost every sentence, but above all, the stirring Humanity breathed through every word, look and action.

Labor would thus be a redemptive force.[38]

Running through the thought of the communitarians was a strong strain that exalted productive labor, another prominent feature in Jacksonian thought. The professions, especially law, medicine, and the ministry, were particular targets, since all were seen as the fruit of disobedience to God's Government that would disappear with the coming of community. "The Lawyer is the offspring of social discord. Peace and Harmony would be his death-warrant," Collins told a Boston audience in 1844. Similarly, obedience to the laws of health would remove the need for physicians, and a true knowledge of religion would make the ministry obsolete. As Collins put it: "True social relations will execute the professions, and all the non-producing, but consuming classes, will be converted into active producers."[39]

Finally, these communitarians shared the long-standing American fear of cities. For some, it was because the city was the stronghold of the forces that they feared. When Orson S. Murray moved to New York to publish the *Regen-*

erator in 1844, he drew protests from readers. "I should as soon think of setting up the concern in Tophet," sputtered Abraham Brooke. By his own account, he found the city utterly oppressive; "the moral atmosphere so pressed me down, I seemed hardly able to have any moral life within me." The "luxury, magnificence, and waste," drove him to despair. Nicholson agreed that New York City was "a den of corruption," but that was to be expected. "Large cities *always were, now are,* and as long as they exist, *will remain to be,* places of vile wickedness," he wrote. Nicholson opined that "scatteration" was necessary for the success of reform. "I believe reformers will soon learn that entirely too much of their influence is *absorbed, used up, countered* by city life." Only Murray was willing to plead that the city was not alone in its corruption. "The world is full of perversion and wretchedness. The city is a concentration of it." Only the coming of community could redeem it.[40]

With the coming of community, the Universal Reformers argued, these evils would pass away. They waxed lyrical in imagining the state of affairs when the competitive system was no more. A writer in the *Communitist* imagined a kind of paradise: "perfect equality in the soil and its products; health, peace, right of labor, education, development, variety of occupation, guaranteed harmony and love for the social basis."[41]

The reformers did add a few specific details. They were confident that technology, in community, would be a source of great good. "The aid of machinery," wrote Wattles, "would afford such an abundant supply that no one would think of laying up wealth in the shape of gold, clothing or money." Collins agreed. "Labor-saving machinery, which now cripples and destroys man, will then perform his labor, and be a great instrument for this redemption." The products of the earth, he claimed, would "be as abundant as the air, and more so than water." Wattles saw community farms worked by steam engines, and William H. Whinery, who looked toward a world in which there were no domesticated animals, saw communities connected by wooden railroads, and, incredibly, "very light constructed plows with men substituted in sufficient number to make it light and easy."[42]

There were other features, of course. They foresaw great advantages from consolidating isolated farms; Collins did foresee the future to some extent when he prophesied that, "properly cultivated," there was enough land in New York State alone to feed everyone in the United States. Collins prophesied that with the coming of community, so little labor would be required to meet basic needs that everyone would be free to "follow the bent of his peculiar genius," whether in art or philosophy, "invention or the mechanic arts." Nicholson attempted to woo Garrisonian abolitionists with the argument that community would speed abolition by making the North so wealthy that infinite resources would be available to fight slavery. William H. Whinery agreed; "the whole fabric of southern and northern slavery will totter to the ground."[43]

Otherwise, the Reformers were remarkably vague about how the competitive economic order would come to an end. Only Collins gave much thought to the question of how and why the rich and powerful would give up their wealth and advantages. He saw it as a matter of self-interest: once the well-to-do saw the richness, the harmony, the limitless advantages of community, they would willingly enter into it. For the rest, however, community was in large part an act of faith. Confident that they were opening the way for the Government of God, and living obedient to Natural Law, which they saw as the ordinances of God's Government, they were confident that community had to be.[44]

Diet and Health

If the Universal Reformers were at odds with many other abolitionists and reformers in their views of economics, they found common ground in their advocacy of diet and health reform. Both would be prominent features of each community, in accordance with what the reformers perceived as Natural Law and the Government of God.

It was not surprising that health was a primary concern of reformers, since alternative systems of medicine flourished in the United States in the 1830s and 1840s. Pain and physical discomfort were probably a given in the lives of most Americans; with sanitation and means by which disease was spread but poorly understood, it was natural that millions sought relief in a variety of new medical theories and systems. And given the primitive state of "professional" American medicine, they were probably at least as well off for having done so; this was a time when a sick person was probably safer avoiding a physician than consulting one.[45]

By far the greatest influence on the Universal Reformers, and a seminal figure in the history of American health reform, was Sylvester Graham. Probably best remembered now as the inventor of the graham cracker, Graham was a Presbyterian minister from Connecticut turned temperance lecturer. In 1832 he created a sensation in a series of lectures in which he linked most diseases and illness to irritation of the stomach. This was, he claimed, caused by the ingestion of rich foods, especially meat, sauces, spices, tea, coffee, and alcohol. He urged adherence to a bland diet of fruits, vegetables, and home-made wheat bread. He combined this with an emphasis on close attention to fresh air and cleanliness with an abundance of exercise. It was mainly, in short, what would be regarded today as sensible preventive care. Less "modern" was Graham's horror of any sort of sexual "excess." He regarded sensuality as inherently debilitating. As will be seen, the theories of Graham and his associates and disciples deeply influenced the Universal Reformers.[46]

The Universal Reformers apparently encountered diet and health reform at varying times in their lives and at varying stages of their reform careers. According to Esther Whinery Wattles, John had been a sickly child and youth. Searching for a cure, he gave up meat, tea, coffee, and butter even before Graham's lectures were published. He quickly became a convert, seeing in them the theoretical basis for what he already knew from experience. Thereafter he actively proselytized for the Grahamite way of life. The Brookes, Nicholsons, Whinerys, and other reformers around Oakland and Harveysburg apparently were unaware, or at least unconverted, until about 1840; Nicholson later theorized that they had been slow to grasp the truths of community because they had been fouling their beings with "hog meat." According to Esther Whinery Wattles, Joseph Lukens, Abraham Brooke's brother-in-law, was the first to introduce them to the subject. Her brother William then obtained some of Graham's writings. Then Wattles came among them to lecture on the subject. Murray was an early convert; articles on diet often appeared in the *Vermont Telegraph*.[47]

Wattles was probably the most articulate and forceful advocate of health reform. "Much of the happiness of man depends upon his obedience to the laws of Health," he wrote, and he enumerated them as pertaining to "Diet, Labor, Ablution, Atmosphere, Purity, Sleep." What he called "Physiological Reform" was, in his view, the foundation of all others, since "the body must be purified before a pure mind can dwell in it." Wattles saw a craving for animal food and other stimulants as a sign of the fall. God had created Humanity to live on fruits and grains, but, becoming "earthly and sensual" in their appetites, humans had first begun "preying upon the animal tribes about [them], to appease [their] hunger and thirst by blood." When that did not suffice, they distilled "liquid fire." So people had "eaten till the floods of grease and gravies like the rains of the deluge have closed over them; and drank till intoxicated by their sensual indulgences . . . they have staggered off to hell."[48]

Virtually all other reformers agreed. Thomas Michener, a resident at both

Marlborough and Highland Home, wrote to the *Communitist:* "I have but little hope of social regeneration, disconnected with dietetic reform." The residents at Skaneateles were of the same mind. "I have but little confidence of any considerable reform that does not commence here," wrote one of diet, while another thought it "lamentable" that "professed religious reformers" filled themselves "with decease [*sic*]." Marenda B. Randall blasted evangelical women who advocated "moral reform" while ignoring the impact of diet. "As well might we expect sweet waters from the very fountain of bitterness," she wrote, "as to expect a stream of pure thoughts from one who uses his stomach daily as a sepulchre for all uncleanness, in the forms of alcohol, tobacco, coffee, meats, gravies pastry, condiments, etc." Emily Gardner, one of Wattles's Indiana converts in 1844, argued that diet reform lay "at the foundation of all other reforms: for the mind can never be pure and free while the body is corrupted with all manner of uncleanness." Once freed from corrupting foods, she argued, "the world will not long continue to be cursed with slavery and licentiousness and the untold miseries resulting therefrom."[49]

A variety of concerns led the communitarians to embrace diet reform. The primary one was that described by Wattles, Gardner, and Randall: humans were what they ate, and sensual food created sensual, impure people. As Harlow Hard, a physician himself and one of the founders of the Kristeen community wrote, "I cannot look for a pure manifestation in a body filled with the carcasses of dead animals." William H. Whinery linked dietary reform to the millennium. "The mind cannot unfold the living fruits of its Creator, without the temple being first made pure," he wrote. "There is not the least doubt in my mind, but that this has been the great barrier to the mind, hindering the realizing of the kingdom of heaven on earth."[50]

There is some evidence of a link between the communitarians' nonresistance and an aversion to taking the lives of animals. Valentine Nicholson asked reformers to compare a flowering field or flourishing garden with a slaughterhouse, and then reflect on their products. Gardner agreed. "I'm tired of living among squealing hogs and squalling chickens and bawling cows and murdered calves and slaughtered lambs and barking dogs and where even the free birds of heaven hardly dare come near while chanting their sweet song," she told friends who lived at Prairie Home. "The idea of taking the life of innocent animals always appeared so horrible that I abandoned the use of their flesh before I knew there was such a person in existence as Sylvester Graham."[51]

Others put forth other arguments against the use of animal food. Wattles and Whinery both argued that domestic animals took far more land and care and human effort than did the raising of fruits and vegetables. Wattles saw this starting a chain reaction—using up their energies in animal husbandry, people transmitted "diseased and debilitated constitutions" to successive generations. Whinery was a particular critic of cattle, which in his view took labor, hay, feed, barns, sheds, fences, milking, and milk houses. One cow took up for grazing land that would grow fruits and vegetables for four people. Whinery argued, moreover, that "cow's milk is not adapted to the alimentary organs of adults. It is not consistent enough for the physiological demands of the body," he claimed. Moreover, he told Orson S. Murray, "It seems to depress the organs so that the mind cannot unfold in that easy, calm, and elevated manner as it can without it." Whinery, however, seems to have won relatively few converts to this particular view, other than at Prairie Home, where he lived.[52]

There were other differences as well. Some of the communitarians condemned the use of salt. Others would admit milk to their tables, but banish butter and cheese. There was a raging but brief debate in the *Regenerator* over cooking. Some, like William H. Whinery, thought that it was by its very nature unnatural, producing changes that caused the food to deteriorate. Cooking, moreover, "enslaved women." Marenda B. Randall at Skaneateles agreed. "Oh how ardently do I desire to see this whole system of cooking become obsolete," she wrote. "Then sentences like the following would have no meaning—'I have no *time* to read.' 'I have not *time* to study the sciences.' 'I have no *time* to educate my children.'" In this Randall and Whinery went far beyond anything Graham advocated. Indications are that cooking continued in all of the communities.[53]

On the subjects of alcohol and tobacco, predictably, the reformers did achieve unity. "Hell Broth and Hell Cabbage," one resident at Grand Prairie labelled them, foul narcotics whose effect on humans was "to stimulate their animal propensities, and drive them on to licentiousness and to commit all manner of crime." One of the attractions of the farm that became Prairie Home was that it had on it a distillery. The communitarians stipulated that all of the "evil porridge" on hand was to be included in the purchase, so that they might "pour it into the race and make it do something for humanity, by turning the mill wheels." Neither drinking nor smoking ever appears to have been an issue of contention in any community, although one resident at Prairie Home obstinately continued to use tobacco, to the mortification of others there.[54]

The communitarians were convinced that by following natural laws of diet and health they would banish almost all debility and disease. And that would make the medical profession obsolete. Physicians were not really interested in preventing illness, some argued; "their business is to cure the sick, when we have been so careless as to allow them to violate the laws of their health," wrote one resident at Skaneateles. "That is their trade, and if none were sick their trade would not support them." Wattles agreed. "The world has been Doctored for since its childhood even so that disease is incorporated into its very condition," he wrote. But Universal Reform attracted even physicians, like Abraham Brooke and Harlow Hard, the founder of Kristeen. Dr. Mark D. Stoneman, a sympathetic abolitionist from Greensboro, Indiana, wrote to Wattles that he was "sick" of his profession. Physicians were necessary, but he was "sick of seeing individuals violate the laws of health—be restored to health and soundness, and again pursue the same rounds."[55]

In some ways those committed to Universal Inquiry and Reform were narrow in their vision of health. They concerned themselves almost entirely with diet, to the exclusion of questions of exercise, hygiene, and environment that concerned other reformers. (Their concerns over "amativeness" and sensuality will be considered in relation with marriage.) This may have been the result of who they were and where they lived. Since, with the exception of a few residents at Skaneateles, they had come from farms, they had had no lack of fresh air. And since almost all had been farmers or farmwives or farmchildren, they had scarcely been concerned about enervation from being chained to desks in shops or counting houses. The Universal Reformers showed far more awareness of the dangers of overwork and backbreaking toil than they did of lassitude and indolence. Indeed, their warnings against the dangers of idleness were usually directed at a "them"—none looked back to such an experience even to repent of it and to warn others not to fall into their old erroneous ways. On the other hand, they would have been well aware of the problems of diet from everyday living.

From health reform, then, would come great things. As one resident of Prairie Home put it, having healed themselves by obedience to the laws of health, they would then be able to turn to "the lame, the sick, and the blind, and by an atmosphere of light and penetrating love, win them back in to the true life." The Government of God required nothing less of them.[56]

Women, Marriage, and the Family

Questions about the rights and status of women were of great concern to almost all Garrisonian abolitionists. The inclusion of women in public roles in the abolitionist movement had splintered it late in the 1830s. In the 1840s it would be women abolitionists with ties to the Garrisonian wing, such as Lucretia Mott and Elizabeth Cady Stanton, who would begin the modern woman's rights movement in the United States. A disproportionate number of early woman's rights advocates were Hicksite Friends, as was the case with the Universal Reformers.[57]

Thus it is not at all surprising to find that woman's rights was a part of Universal Reform. The communitarians saw the oppression of women as one of the evils of competitive society, and saw it passing away with the achievement of community. Of particular concern to Collins and Wattles was the institution of marriage, which they saw as being particularly prone to evil in competitive society. For most of the communitarians, freedom for women would come within a conventional framework of marriage and the family, freed from drudgery and toil and from the economic pressures that forced so many into loveless marriages. Thus they would be free to realize their "natural" roles as sensitive guardians of morality and the mothers of the rising generation. By modern standards, this was hardly liberation, but in the 1840s this was very much in line with incipient feminist thought.

Even by the standards of the times, however, these reformers' view of women's roles was somewhat limited. Universal Inquiry and reform was very much a man's enterprise, with a few exceptions. What remains unclear is whether this was because it seemed the natural way of doing things to Wattles, Collins, Nicholson, Mendenhall, Murray, and the others, or whether women were more skeptical, and thus less likely to enter into the discourse that was shaping the communities and the new society that was to emerge from them.

On New Year's Day in 1846 the Skaneateles community celebrated with speeches and readings. For the children there were some un-Grahamite cakes, pastries, and candies; for the adults, a round of toasts (in cold water, of course). Sarah H. Crowell made hers pointed: "Woman—the slave of man—may the day soon come when she knows the sweets of Liberty."[58]

The woman's rights movement began with the realization of some women abolitionists that they were bound in many of the same ways as the slaves they sought to liberate. Apparently at least some of the women involved in Universal Reform had similar experiences. Slavery was very much like the status of women, wrote Marenda B. Randall, "the only difference in the slavery of the sexes seems to be, the males bind themselves, while the females quietly submit to be bound." A Prairie Home resident agreed. Women were "in every part of the world oppressed." The *Communitist* approvingly quoted Ernestine Rose, a major figure in the early feminist movement, who had attended the society's organizational meeting in the spring of 1843 and who was for a time interested in Skaneateles: "What rights have women? Are they not the merest slaves on earth? What of freedom have they?" Rose asked a convention of Collins's sympathizers in Boston in the summer of 1844. Women were punished for breaking laws in which they had no hand in framing; "all avenues to enterprize [*sic*] and honor" were closed to them. If poor, they were condemned to drudgery; if wealthy, they were "dressed dolls of fashion—parlor puppets." Single, they were the dependents of parents or brothers, and, when married, "swallowed up in their husbands." Rose thundered out her conclusion: "Nothing of nobleness, of dignity, and of elevation is allowed to exist in the female."[59]

To this description of the status of American women, the communitarians added other injustices. Maria Loomis was a particular critic of the follies of fashion, writing scornfully how it kept women absorbed in following the nonsensical whims of "leaders" of society. Her chief target was tight lacing of corsets which, like many other contemporary feminists and not a few male physicians, she viewed as harmful to women's health. Emily Gardner was also a critic of "society," mourning how women would "flutter away their short lives in ministering to the follies and vitiated tastes of a corrupt community." (One has to wonder how much of "society" the young Quaker had seen in Union County, Indiana.) John O. Wattles worried about the lack of educational opportunities for women. "Because by the present arrangements and structure of the social organization, woman is hindered in her Mental Progression, and circumscribed in her Intellectual immunities," he wrote in his *Herald of Progression.* "The race can never advance, as a whole, while a part are left in the rear." Collins focused on the toll that the chores of housekeeping took. "Observe the one or two female drudges and slaves . . . shortening their days by toil, and benumbing their minds by monotonous servitude," he told a group of sympathizers in 1844. "Look at the weekly expenditure of female strength over the washtub, and her labor upon the ironing-board. Mark the desponding saddening look of the poor man's wife, as she is bound to the unchanging round of household drudgery."[60]

The reformers were quite certain that all would change for women in community. Knowledge of Natural Law, and the commitment to live by it, would cause such nonsense as tight lacing to disappear. The technological innovations, and the centralization so beloved of the communitarians would make household drudgery a thing of the past; Collins called the use of labor-saving machinery the "enactment of the first bill for female emancipation." Wattles, planning arrangements at Prairie Home, saw "washing, ironing, knitting, cloth-making, etc. done by machinery," with "the cooking done by men in a building specially for the purpose." Thus they would "take a vast amount of labor from the shoulders of *woman*."[61]

The reformers' commitment to the Government of God, however, limited their vision of equality of women. Much of the focus of the early woman's rights movement was on attaining certain kinds of legal rights: the vote, the right to hold property, the right to enter certain professions. These would have no meaning in community, since they were based on an absence of laws and the abolition of all offices, elective or otherwise. Marenda B. Randall saw this clearly—women were enslaved, but equality before the law was no answer, since laws were but a refined form of oppression. It was true also of the professions. Given the reformers' view of lawyers, doctors, and ministers as fruits of corruption, they would have considered it a questionable victory to have women join their ranks.[62]

The Universal Reformers were like many of their contemporaries in seeing women as morally superior, and they saw community as a means by which to give that gift free rein. "Whether woman *rules* the world or not," wrote Wattles, "it is certain that they exert a very great influence—her generous heart and sympathizing nature make her heart swift and her hand strong [in] deeds of love and kindness." For him, the archetype of womanhood was still the Solomonic one from Proverbs: "Far above rubies." Marenda B. Randall agreed. Women's strength was not, she wrote, in mind or body but "in persuasion, gentleness, kindness, and affection, combined with virtue and intelligence."[63]

It is difficult to determine much about the roles that women played in the various communities. There is evidence that at Skaneateles, at least, women took positions of leadership, either in unwavering support of Collins, like Maria Loomis, and, for a time, Ernestine Rose, or in opposition, as Marenda B. Randall eventually found herself. They and other women were frequent contributors to the *Communitist*. Most of what we know about the Grand Prairie Community comes from the pen of Ruth Crane, who seems to have been its primary link with other reformers. There were other women, such as Rebecca Hilles at Fraternal Home or Esther Whinery Wattles at Prairie Home, who were as fully committed to Universal Reform as their husbands. On the other hand, their occupations usually were the traditional ones: cooking, housekeeping, child care.[64]

Yet it is striking that Universal Reform was an enterprise that men dominated. Jane Nicholson, the wife of Valentine, and Elizabeth Brooke, the wife of Abraham, had been involved in antislavery work, but they wrote not a word on communitarianism, nor is it clear that they ever attended the Universal Reform conventions or accompanied their husbands on speaking tours. Eunice M. Collins, the wife of John A., Catherine Murray, the wife of Orson, and Martha Mendenhall, the wife of Hiram, are even more shadowy. Catherine Murray did briefly edit the "Woman's Department" of John O. Wattles's *Herald of Progression,* but that is the extent of her involvement in community. We have no record of anything on the part of Martha Mendenhall, or Eunice M. Collins, or Margery Hard, the wife of Harlow Hard of Kristeen. The proselytizing, the lecturing, the publicity through letters and pamphlets, were mostly the work of men.[65]

There are several possible explanations. One is the simplest: that many of the wives of Universal Reformers were more skeptical about the enterprise than their husbands. The evidence is less than conclusive, but we do have some tantalizing hints. Maria Mendenhall Michener, who first was at Prairie Home and then Marlborough with her parents, remembered that her father was the enthusiast for community; her mother undermined the enterprise in various ways, particularly with chicken dinners. Although Jane Nicholson was a committed abolitionist, she apparently always refused to go into community, and particularly after the failure of Prairie Home she refused to allow any of the property she had inherited from her father to be used for such purposes. Hannah Ingram reportedly wept whenever she spoke of her experiences at Prairie Home—she was convinced that the motley company there had corrupted her children. Esther Wattles finally put her foot down and told husband John that, after her experience of community, she would not try to raise children in one. She demanded that they purchase their own farm, even if it was in proximity to a community.[66]

Thus Universal Reform saw itself as a force for the liberation and equality of women. And it certainly shared many of the concerns of the emerging woman's rights movement; the differences were due almost entirely to the communitarians' commitment to nonresistance and the Government of God. And in the ways that they affirmed fundamental institutions like marriage and the family, they also shared the views and hopes of other reformers, feminist and otherwise.[67]

One of the worst problems that the communitarians faced was the charge that they were advocates of free love. A century later, Lester Wells found remnants of that belief still current in the neighborhood of Skaneateles. Abraham Brooke reported that his neighbors around Oakland read Orson S. Murray's *Regenerator* "clandestinely and furtively" in hope of finding food for scandal. In the spring of 1844, a Baptist minister named Mason descended on Harveysburg, Ohio, to unloose a series of blasts at the "infidels, hypocrites, vipers and murderers" of the Society for Universal Inquiry and Reform. In the course of his lecture, as Nicholson recounted it, Mason "emphatically declared that he would rather have his daughters raised in a brothel of some large city, than to have them live in such a community as John O. Wattles and others are advocating."[68]

The reputation was undeserved. The Universal Reformers adamantly opposed promiscuity and argued for infrequent sexual intercourse even within marriage. The closest things to heterodoxy in sexual matters to survive in anything related to the communities is a single piece in the *Communitist* in 1845 on the views of Fanny Wright, a figure of considerable notoriety because of her association with unconventional views on marriage, and an obscure comment made against Harlow Hard. There were, of course, some communitarians who *did* embrace controversial views of marriage. Mary S. Gove, present at the convention in New York City in the spring of 1843, was later involved in such activities. But there is absolutely no evidence of anything unconventional in any of the communities established as a result of Universal Reform. Collins spoke for his compatriots in his condemnation of "bigamy, polygamy, adultery, concubinage, and licentiousness."[69]

All indications are that the communitarians found "sensuality" an evil, growing out of depraved appetites that were the unhappy result of the present social arrangements. "Idolatry, war, slavery, and landholding, licentiousness, gluttony, intemperance, all are but necessary consequences arising from the sensual direction, and attempted sensual gratification of the faculties, given for higher and more exalted purposes," wrote Wattles. Licentiousness was a "scarlet colored beast with the cup of filthiness in her hand caressing the nations to drink it." In community, according to Wattles, there would be "no sensuality, or lust or licenscious [sic] desire, or sexual coition." There were strong overtones of perfectionism in some of Wattles's essays. "The soul can never meet God in purity and love, until it is redeemed from under the influence of the body," he wrote. "Apetite [sic] Lust and passion must be cast out, the temple must be cleansed, all the earthly and sensual feelings must be turned out."[70]

In the present social arrangement, it was unsurprising to find that sensuality had reared its ugly head within the marriage relation. "Marriage, also, has been abused most shamefully. Lust and Licentiousness with thongs of torture, have driven the Angel of Purity from the soul, and taken up their abode in her apartment," Wattles wrote. Harlow Hard of Kristeen told one of his relatives that "as now practiced, marriage is favorable to impurity rather than to purity." He argued that "when parties lived together in a licentious state they might better be separate if they would by so doing live pure." Marenda B. Randall argued that it was hypocritical to have laws against prostitution when "the condition of the mass of the married [was] aught but a state of legalized licentiousness." John B. Chandler thought that "the propagation of the species" was the only moral occasion for sexual relations. "A man has no right . . . to have sexual intercourse with his own wife, except for the purpose of procreation, than he has to cohabit with another man's wife."[71]

The reformers were convinced that the evil effects of licentiousness in the competitive system manifested themselves in reproduction. One writer for the *Communitist* argued that abortion was a natural outgrowth of relations in a competitive society. An expectant mother "who has not received a license from God, or from the registrar, for the generation of the embryo she carries," was compelled "to take means to create abortion, endangering her own life and most probably injuring her offspring." Such unfortunate women, forsaken by "heartless seducers," were thus forced "to confine themselves unnaturally, and eventually to commit murder on the produce of her own womb."[72]

Those children who did come in to the world found its inhabitants in a parlous state. "Wallowing in filth and pollution," claimed Abraham Brooke, they ignored "true physiological laws." Not surprisingly, it was John O. Wattles who thought most deeply (or extravagantly) on the subject. Sexual intercourse was not inherently sinful, he argued; one could perform "the duty of reproduction and pro-creation" in a state of purity. Indeed that was a duty, he wrote; "if we cannot keep our minds pure and wholly exempt from *lust and carnal indulgence*, we are wholy [*sic*] unfit for marriage and parental relation." By his understanding of physiology, the mind controlled the nervous system, and through that the rest of the body. Thus the state of mind of the parents at the time of conception would be conveyed to their offspring; "monsters and idiots" were the products of excessive lasciviousness and lust. By correct diet and ways of life, physical perfection would come closer.[73]

Wattles went beyond this to argue that the Government of God would necessarily make for a healthier race. "The passions of parents have lived over again in their progeny," he told a group of sympathizers. "Fathers engage in wars and blood and their children grow up after them to re-enact the same dreadful deeds." Those children would in turn "transmit the same feelings to their children, who also grow up to perpetuate the same deeds of carnage." Wattles saw proof throughout history, especially American history. Children born in the violence of the Revolution were fated to fight the War of 1812, although it was less destructive because "peace principles had been disseminated." Now the fruits of 1812 were being seen "in the riots and mobs and tumultuous gatherings" that were "the premonition of the gathering storm."[74]

The reformed explained this wretched failure in various ways, but most linked it to the economic necessities of all, but especially women, in the present system. Wattles argued that men put off marriage to lay up wealth. As a result, they would forgo first loves, and, when rich, they married not for love, but out of lascivious desires that they could now indulge. A Skaneateles resident countered, however, that the problem was early marriage—women especially accepted first suitors, compatible or not, out of economic necessity. Maria Loomis saw the problem in society's view of marriage as a matter of "arbitrary law," when it should be based on the "affections." If marriage was seen as fundamentally a contract, it was unsurprising that women found themselves treated as property.[75]

Perhaps the fullest exposition we have of the nature of marriage is an essay that John O. Wattles composed and read when he and Esther Whinery wed in Clinton County, Ohio, in May 1844. (With a true reformer's instinct, Wattles promptly had it printed and circulated.) Marriage, Wattles told the assembled company, was "a union of two spirits of the two sexes." The basis of that union was love, something that Wattles thought undefinable and almost indescribable. "Love refuses to be written; it proclaims its own authority and utters its own mandates unawed." It was the highest gift of God.[76]

Marriage, however, was more—it was a matter of Natural Law as well, the law that "one mind can be *married to but one other mind*." Much evil came from misunderstanding this truth, according to Wattles, from confusing the feelings that were the basis of marriage with affection, friendship, or kindness. God intended that marriage involved two minds that could be tied only to each other. "Could several minds be married to one," Wattles opined, "then must infinite confusion follow, to know which of the many was the married one. . . . endless unhappiness must be the result." Indeed, as Wattles saw it, such a marriage would extend beyond the grave, "during the continuation of the soul's immortality."[77]

The reformers' view of marriage was also clear in the ways in which they themselves married. We have records of at least five marriages that took place in communities, four in Skaneateles, and that of John O. Wattles and Esther Whinery, both residents of Prairie Home but who married at her father's home near Wilmington, Ohio. All were modeled after the Quaker marriage ceremony, in which the couple repeated short, simple vows to each other in the presence of friends and family. This had attracted other reformers, like Theodore Weld and Angelina Grimke and Stephen S. Foster and Abby Kelley. It involved no clergy, a particular virtue at Skaneateles. It also denied the power of the state, since Quakers did not obtain marriage licenses or record their marriages with civil authorities. "Where the band of connubial love twines, no other power is needed—when true spirits gather themselves under the shelter of Jehovah's throne, no other protection is wanted," Wattles told the company at his wedding. "If martyrdom be required to re-instate the purity and simplicity of the primeval matrimony, then welcome the prison, the rack or the stake." He married Esther by stating that "in the person of Esther Whinery exists the mind, of the union with which I have no more doubt than of existence; and according to the *laws of mind,* which are the laws of God, we are married." Couples at Skaneateles wed in much the same way. When Maria Loomis, one of the leaders of the community, married Thomas Varney on New Year's Day in 1846, they wrote their own vows, which Collins read. Marriage, they said, was the result of attraction and affinity. Only they could marry each other, and no "priest" could give what they were doing any further legitimacy. Later the same month, when Henry Hawley and Eliza Smith wed, they read a statement that their commitment to each other was based on "strong affinities, sympathies, and adaptations."[78]

Once in community, the reformers were convinced that marriage would be conformed to the requisites of God's Government, and the evils that characterized it under the competitive system would pass away. A wife, wrote John O. Wattles, would be "an *equal,* and not a menial, a companion, and not an appendage—an intelligent being, and not a mere reticule to hang on to a man's arm." All families, he claimed would be "united in one great community of families." They then would know the "connubial felicity" of the "true family relation."[79]

Education

The Society for Universal Inquiry and Reform originated in an attempt to found a school. Thus it is not surprising to find that its adherents gave careful thought to education. This was doubtless reinforced by the backgrounds of the reformers; Quakers and New Englanders had traditionally been supportive of schools. Many in the group—Murray, John O. Wattles, Esther Whinery, Emily Gardner, Maria Loomis, Harlow Hard, Marius and Emily Robinson, and doubtless others—had been teachers, some for several years.[80]

When the reformers looked at education as it was in the 1840s, they found little to praise and much to arouse anger and concern. Their criticisms were numerous. Like Transcendentalists such as Amos Bronson Alcott, they were critical of what they saw as the dogmatism of most schools. Schoolmasters were, in their view, "Petty tyrants," who instructed children in "words" rather than "facts" and in "dogmas" rather than "principles." Emily Gardner, the Quaker teacher, mourned the school environment, where children were "confined to the school room which seems almost like a prison to them, obliged to sit still for hours together." Instead they "should be out on the hills in the fresh air and sunshine, singing with the birds, sporting with the lambs, and plucking the first flowers of spring, or twirling winter's hoary locks." John A. Collins agreed; most schoolhouses, he told a Boston audience, were "illy ventilated, and crowded like a slave ship." John O. Wattles thought that the common schools were "moral murder mills"; in them children learned more evil than parents could begin to counteract. "Do you not often trust your children with a man whom you would not trust your horses with?" he asked. Collins probably spoke for nearly all when he said: "Our present education is as false as our religion—as barbarous and inhumane as our governments."[81]

In contrast, the reformers promoted educational views that are clearly indebted to Transcendentalists and to the Romantic movement. Education would be, in large measure, self-knowledge, the process of discovering truths about self and about Natural Law and God's Government. Collins put this most clearly at one of the Hundred Conventions when he asked: "How [can] we attempt this instruction when the child knows more than us all—we must go to him to learn."[82]

None of the other reformers' views was quite as extreme as this, but they agreed that education as it existed in their day reflected the disarrangement of society. Wattles called it a mark of the fall. "Had our predecessors lived in obedience to all the laws of their being thro' all past time and thus been competent to have transmitted perfect constitutions—Education as now performed would not have been necessary," he wrote in an unpublished essay. "But by the violation of all the principles of government of God . . . the laws of our being as well as the physical 'foundations of Nature' are 'out of course' and an effort must be made to bring the mind back to its original destination." Thus education would be self-knowledge, what William H. Whinery called "the knowledge of the elements of our minds." A writer in the *Communitist* summed up this outlook: it was human responsibility to "become scholars of ourselves, and understand the laws of our own being."[83]

The reformers, as befitted those committed to "Universal Inquiry," thought that increasing knowledge and education had the potential to remake society. "The hopes of communitists are based on the increasing knowledge—the growing intelligence of the race," wrote one resident at Skaneateles. "As man is seen to increase in knowledge, he is seen also to be breaking away from . . . superstitions, traditions, and authorities, meritorious for their antiquity alone." If ignorance had been the evil, the writer concluded, "so knowledge must and will be the remedy." Maria Loomis agreed. "I expect communities to become schools, in which the world is to be educated in all that is pleasing to good taste—all that is good, beautiful, pure, noble, and refined," she wrote. Communities would "embody not only the atmosphere of peace and good will to men, but a love for the orderly, the beautiful, the tasteful, the grand, the magnificent, and the sublime." Man "must ever be a student," wrote Collins, and communities would be schools in which humanity would learn "from the cradle to the grave," to live by natural laws.[84]

The reformers were, for the most part, realistic enough to believe that educating the world would take some time. There was even some disagreement over what would come first: would certain people come to a knowledge of Natural Law and then inculcate it in the rising generation, or would, properly guided, the rising generation gradually erode the evils of competitive society? John O. Wattles thought the former; "if we would 'train a child in the way he should go,'" Wattles argued, "we must go in the way we would train up the child." Collins, however, disagreed. Community, he told the sympathizers, would be "like a wall of fire like the mountains around Jerusalem," throwing "a protecting sentiment around the infantile mind." Ultimately, of course, neither had a chance to prove himself.[85]

While waiting for community to transform the world, however, communities would have children to educate, and reformers had definite ideas about the form that that education should take. They agreed that teachers were the key—John O. Wattles thought that they were second only to God in their impact on the world. Collins said that they would be people who would "have an attraction for children of every age." Working with parents, they would blend home, schoolroom, and family as places for learning.[86]

In deciding the curriculum, the reformers blended practicality with Romanticism, and with some orthodoxies of reform. The *Communitist* set the tone by calling for teaching "reason and common sense." They were not, "like the mysterious dogmas of religion, shrouded in mists and darkness," but were "so simple and evident that whomsoever [sic] will may learn." Nonetheless such a curriculum aimed to approach perfection by exercising "*all* the attributes of the mind and each one in due proportion." At Skaneateles, students learned astronomy, drawing, sketching, botany, philosophy, and geometry. Collins hoped that eventually physiology, physics, and mechanics would be added. Wattles thought more in terms of character traits and abilities that he wished to see developed. He listed no less than thirty, ranging from individuality to "vititiveness," which he defined as "due regard for the preservation of life." Notably missing were the classical languages and scripture exercises that most would still have regarded as the foundations of a respectable education.[87]

Community education would differ from that of "the world" in other ways as well. All assumed that it would involve some combination of intellectual endeavor with manual labor. It would also govern itself by the principles of nonresistance. "Governments, the simplest in their arrangements, and mildest in their legal code, are the best regulated, mildest, and happiest," wrote Collins. "The best regulated schools, the most happy families, are those whose forceful regulations are swallowed up in reason and moral suasion." Elizabeth L. Dyer, an Abington, Massachusetts, teacher whom Wattles had converted to nonresistance, noted that teachers who embraced the cause found parents criticizing them for giving up corporal punishment. "I have recently heard it remarked, that the doctrine of nonresistance 'is going to spoil the children,' " she wrote to Wattles. "I should delight in seeing them thus spoiled, if they were to become non-resistants." And that, of course, was precisely what the reformers hoped to see.[88]

Religion

"Religion," John A. Collins told a convention in Boston in the summer of 1844, "is essential to darkness." Almost all of the Universal Reformers agreed; "sects" and "priestcraft" were part of the system that was oppressing the world. The church as it now existed would inevitably disappear with the triumph of community. But there agreement ended. Some of the reformers, led by Collins and Murray and strongest at Skaneateles, came to repudiate organized religion entirely and to glory in the label of "infidel." Others, including Wattles and the Quakers, saw their task as the reclamation of Christianity from degeneration and the ushering in of the millennium. Many would ultimately come to find a comfortable home in the Progressive or Congregational Friends, one of the most thoroughly radical sects in antebellum America. The Congregational Friends would carry to their ultimate conclusions the radical strains of Hicksite Quakerism, especially the liberal and deistic strains, the questioning of authority, and the emphasis on individual conscience. Whatever forms faith took in Universal Reform, however, the strains of nature religion would be prominent: yearnings after mastery, innocence, and purity.[89]

Many abolitionists found themselves in conflict with their churches in the 1830s and 1840s. As has already been seen, the Garrisonians had particular problems. A variety of issues had brought them into conflict with the leaders of the evangelical churches—woman's rights, nonresistance—and, in the case of the Quakers, the very question of cooperation with non-Friends.

What information we have suggests that almost all of those involved in Universal Inquiry and Reform had had some sort of church tie. The communities in the West consisted of Hicksite Friends like the Nicholsons, Brookes, and Mendenhalls; occasionally an Orthodox Friend, always with abolitionist sympathies, would be drawn in. The exceptions were the Kristeen and Grand Prairie communities. Little is known about the views of those at Kristeen; Grand Prairie, as has been seen, was made up of families who had formed an independent church in the 1820s.

At Skaneateles, we know less about the religious backgrounds of residents. Some, like John Orvis and Eliab W. Capron, had been Hicksite Friends. For those whose ties are known, only one, Joseph Savage, came out of a Universalist church. The rest were evangelicals: Collins and Patten Davis, Congregationalists; Maria Loomis, a Presbyterian; Quincy Johnson and his wife, Methodists.[90]

No matter what their backgrounds, the Universal Reformers had come to see the churches as the supporters of slavery, and thus as evils. The "diabolical church and priesthood," wrote Abraham Brooke, were "a bulwark of slavery." John Orvis agreed. Slavery was not the creation of law, he told an audience at Ferrisburg, Vermont, but of the mind and spirit, which were shaped by religious sentiments and institutions. "No stupendous system of iniquity ever long existed, unless the church and clergy cherished it," he wrote. "O what a curse they are to deathless nature. How they damn the world, rather than save it." Wattles approvingly recorded the words of Frederick Douglass in one of the Hundred Conventions that by being false on one thing—slavery—the church was not true in any. "Tell me not of the soundness of your revivals," Douglass thundered. "It will not give bread to one hungry man, or liberate one poor slave."[91]

These were, of course, sentiments that most abolitionists shared to some degree. By 1842, many were acting on them in "come-outer" movements, in which abolitionists repudiated their old churches as morally flawed by compromise with the sin of slavery. Probably the best known of the secession movements was the one that created the Wesleyan Methodist Connection in 1842 and 1843. Other denominations saw similar secessions. Not surprisingly, the Universal Reformers endorsed such movements. By 1843, virtually all of those of an evangelical background had either resigned, or, like Collins and Murray, been disfellowshipped or excommunicated. Patten Davis, a Vermont abolitionist and a founder of Skaneateles, wrote proudly that he had left his church in 1831; Marius Robinson had resigned from the Presbyterian church in 1837. The Hicksite Friends among them were rapidly moving in a similar direction, especially in Ohio and Indiana, driven by what they saw as the unbearable provocations of the conservative Friends at the head of the Indiana Yearly Meeting.[92]

In the summer and fall of 1843 there was a split among the Indiana Hicksites in which Universal Reformers played a prominent role. The battle began in the spring when Center Monthly Meeting disowned Abraham Allen for publicly criticizing George F. White, the New York minister. That summer a committee from the yearly meeting visited Green Plain and Goshen meetings, both strongholds of abolition. Both defied the committee; the Green Plain Quarterly Meeting, setting aside the yearly meeting's advice, replaced a clerk sympathetic to the yearly meeting with an abolitionist. The yearly meeting responded at its session in September by, over the protests of abolitionist Friends, dissolving the Green Plain Quarterly Meeting. Torn between sorrow and anger, the abolitionists in the yearly meeting met in the Green Plain meetinghouse early in November and resolved to resist. For their "feeble efforts to promote the work of reformation," they wrote, they had "been proscribed as unworthy, and sinister motives imputed" to them. So they would leave Indiana Yearly Meeting in order to uphold what they saw as the good order and traditional testimonies of Friends. They invited all those in sympathy to join with them. Of the twelve Hicksites who signed the statement from the Green Plain conference, nine had been interested in Universal Inquiry and Reform, and five—Nicholson, Horton Brown, Lydia Whinery (the mother of Esther and William), Sarah Michener, and Hannah Ingram—were connected with Prairie Home.[93]

In some cases the Universal Reformers were disowned for "disunity" by the Hicksite Friends, like Abraham Allen and Abraham Brooke. Some were disowned by their monthly meetings on other pretexts; strangest perhaps of all was Valentine Nicholson, who, amidst all of his heterodoxies, was "read out" for organizing a singing school! Still others went out with ringing denunciations of the fading glory of Friends. Esther Whinery Wattles was perhaps the most notable. She renounced her membership in a letter to Gamaliel Bailey's

Philanthropist. "I most sincerely believe that were the sentiments taught and practised by early Friends, in our country acted out at the present day, slavery would not now be in existence," she wrote. Now, however, Friends, instead of pleading the cause of "*God's poor,* they are found in direct hostility to them." They closed their meetinghouses, advised members to shun abolitionists, and disowned those who supported them. They oppressed people of conscience, and gave their influence to support governments based on force. Were she to remain a Friend, Whinery concluded, she would "be on the side of the oppressor, and be found fighting against God." And God was calling her to obey the commands of the Scripture: "Come out from among them, and be ye separate, that ye be not partakers of her sins, *and that ye receive not of* her plagues."[94]

The advocates of Universal Reform sought more than just a purified church, however. They wanted nothing less than a new religious vision, comparable to the new government and economic order that they thought would emerge from community.

The communitarians saw little to admire in the church as they knew it, and were ferocious in their denunciation of it. "What are the church and priesthood ... but the *scabs,* with which humanity has attempted to heal over the sore which is gnawing at her vitals?" asked Abraham Brooke. John B. Chandler, the New Hampshire abolitionist who moved to Prairie Home, wrote that he would prefer a graveyard to a church—"the devil's parlor," as he called it. "Religion—pure religion—and *nothing but* religion is the worst curse I know," stormed E. W. Capron of Skaneateles. Ernestine Rose urged women to come out of *all* churches. "I call upon you, then as you venerate truth and reason, as you love yourselves, your children, and race, never to enter a *church* again," she told a Boston convention. "Countenance them not. They oppress you. They prevent progression. They are opposed to reason."[95]

The reformers did not lack specifics to support their attacks. They included doctrine and practice, theology and worship, lay people and clergy. Some even went so far as to discard Christianity entirely.

The reformers directed some of their fiercest blasts at the clergy or "priests," as they were wont to call them. "The priest is the creature of mental and moral darkness," Collins told his followers. "In ignorance and prejudice he lives, moves and has his being. Science and philosophy are his deadly foes." Maria Loomis called them "a set of arrogant spongers, preying upon the lifeblood of society." Wattles thought them interested only in popularity: "make sheep stealing popular and we would have hard work to keep the ministers ... out of our sheep pens," he told an audience at Middlebury, Vermont. Marenda B. Randall agreed. "If I believed in especial providence (which I do not)," she wrote in the *Communitist*, "I would sooner think the office of the priesthood was sent as a scourge to punish man as any other evil I know of."[96]

It was not just clergy, however, who were targets of the reformers' scorn. Their churches were filled with hypocrites as well. "I wish to be saved, 'with an everlasting salvation,' from the kind of self styled 'Christians,' who make great professions of how much they believe . . . and yet are scarcely . . . willing to permit an honest minded person to live on the same earth at the same time," wrote Valentine Nicholson. Nicholson listed the faults that he saw in the church members around him—they were "fretful and peevish, doubting and distrustful of everybody and everything about them." While "many of these loud-professing, self-styled Christians . . . were loud and long in their prayers—or rather in their *lectures* to God—telling them what in their opinion he had better do," they were less kind to the poor and unfortunate than many infidels. Most church members, argued Harlow Hard, himself the son of a Methodist minister, were caught up in "the poisonous influences of sectarianism."[97]

Sectarianism was an evil because it set Christians at odds with each other. Even worldly people would combine to gain their ends, wrote Wattles, while professed Christians occupied themselves "trying to pick some flaw in each other's creed." Thus the religious press was filled with "controversies about names and forms, and unimportant tenets," instead of articles that would help to produce "holiness in the heart." A prison was to be preferred to a seminary, Murray wrote; in fact, the former was the product of the latter. Even nondenominational organizations were guilty. Thus the *Communitist* fulminated against the American Board of Commissioners for Foreign Missions, one of the bulwarks of the evangelical Benevolent Empire, as a "gray headed lump of Calvinism for propagating Christian heathenism among the foreign nations, and perpetuating it at home."[98]

The reformers also had little use for many historic Christian doctrines. Wattles considered the doctrine of the Fall irrational. "I do not believe that the sins of one man, however enormous they might be (much less the mere eating of an apple) could doom the whole human race," he wrote. "This is the most unreasonable of all fables ancient or modern." E. W. Capron blasted "the abominable old hack of *total depravity*." Abraham Brooke wrote scornfully of the orthodox view of the Atonement: "The God of their invention has placed men in a situation where they cannot avoid the commission of sin, and then sits in judgment upon them for their deeds and saves such of them as he fancies . . . on account of the sufferings and death of another—His son and a part of himself." David Winston Jones, an Orthodox Friend in Jonesboro, Indiana, attacked "the preaching of wrath and vengeance to impel men to do right" as "unphilosophical" and "anti-Christian." Orson S. Murray agreed and went beyond that—he could not accept any god guilty of the acts of cruelty in the Old Testament, and he thought the Mosaic laws full of "hellish features." One of the contributors to the *Communitist* dismissed hell as a silly delusion. Maria Loomis went even further; to her, the Bible was "but little less than a compound of ignorance and superstition inconsistency and unnaturalism." Rebecca Lewis Fussell agreed; to her the laws of the Old Testament "appear[ed] to be too very ridiculous to have emanated from the Holy One." Collins thought that the apostles had been captives of their time who did not understand human rights, "All bigoted men and narrow minded," he told a Syracuse audience.[99]

Not surprisingly, the reformers also dismissed many of the accepted practices of the churches. Marenda B. Randall attacked the observance of the Sabbath. What was worse, she asked, than that on a hot July day a man who had worked hard all week would "put on a thick 'Sunday suit,' ride then, four or five miles in a scorching summer sun," to arrive at church and sit "with several hundred fellow sufferers, all cooped upon hard benches," sitting for hours listening to a minister, "dealing out words which to many are big with sound, or anything but meaning." The Sabbath was really "Priest's Day," when the clergy labored "to make their hearers believe themselves unable to do their own reading and thinking." Another contributor to the *Communitist* dismissed revivals as exercises in the power of magnetism: "Why, bless you, you can get up a revival any time by paying a good magnetizer a few dollars," wrote the skeptic. "Your good, effectual preachers are but good magnetizers, and your prayer meetings and protracted meetings are regular magnetic experiments, in which the magnetism of the whole church is employed."[100]

Religion as it existed was, then, a failure. Wattles saw the proof of it most clearly in the fact that there were no communities; it was "a poor compliment to the labors of 40,000 ministers, and 55,000,000 *professors of Christianity*, and the preaching of the gospel for 1,800 years." If in an age that claimed to be dedicated to proclaiming the gospel at least one community could not come into being, then it was "time we had another gospel, or another set of gospel expounders, or something." A Skaneateles resident agreed: "Religionists have been trying for thousands of years to make the world happy by converting them to their religion," and yet "their object is no nearer accomplished than it was five thousand years ago." If communitarians showed "the same devotion," they would quickly succeed.[101]

The reformers were sure that religion was in its last days. One of Wattles's compatriots believed that "men are progressive beings," and that "progression both in mental and physical science" was advancing at a rate that made "Priestcraft and all its concomitant crafts quail and shudder as though they were in their last agonies." John Mitchell, a Skaneateles resident, predicted that the "numbers who are now throwing off the falling chains which bound them to a stand-still church" would turn public sentiment rapidly against it. Collins agreed; the church, by "disgusting the mind with creeds and authorities," was "preparing it for science and philosophy."[102]

If the churches as they then existed would disappear with the coming of the Government of God, what form would religion take? Here the reformers found themselves in sharp disagreement. Some, especially in the West, found the answer in a reformed variety of Hicksite Quakerism. Some, like Wattles, embraced a vaguely Christian religion of progress and reform. And some, led by Collins, renounced faith entirely and came to glory in the name of infidel.

Quakerism held attractions for many of the reformers, regardless of their backgrounds. Wattles had embraced a number of Quaker peculiarities, such as renouncing physical communion, by 1840. He later began to use the Quaker plain language of "thee" and "thy." Maria Loomis found much to admire among the Hicksite Friends—honesty, simplicity, neatness, good nature, purity. "Hicksite Quakerism is much the best religion in the world," she wrote, but that was because "it has the least religion in it." By refusing to be bound by biblical infallibility, they were open to guidance by common sense. Loomis was especially moved by her experience of the "deep and silent meditation" of a meeting for worship. What we know about religious worship in the communities suggests that it was closer to the Quaker model than anything else.[103]

The Brookes, Whinerys, Nicholsons, Allens, and nearly all of the Quaker communitarians in Indiana and Ohio found a new religious home in the Congregational Friends, or "Friends of Human Progress," as they were often called. These were Hicksites who split off from Indiana, Ohio, New York, and Philadelphia yearly meetings and who eventually came to include such reform luminaries as Sojourner Truth, Susan B. Anthony, and Oliver Johnson. The Green Plain group began the split, however.[104]

Most Congregational Friends, even at Green Plain, had not been involved in community, but a look at their statements shows why Universal Reformers like the Brookes, Nicholsons, and Allens became leaders among them. David Evans, a prominent Hicksite opponent of abolition from Waynesville, Ohio, described them as having "a platform broad enough to embrace infidelity and even atheism, and subject to all degrees of anarchy and ranterism that can be named." Joseph A. Dugdale responded by quoting the Progressives' statements: humans had "the law of God written on the conscious power of [the] soul," and thus could know what God would have them do. They would associate together in small meetings, "avoiding extraneous uncalled for church arrangements." There would be no disciplinary regulations as such, as yearly meetings would concern themselves with "the removal of the existing evils of the day, war, Intemperance, Licentiousness; or in whatever form, cruelty injustice and other perverted principles may operate." Thus they carried forward the rebellion against authority and the openness to ideas, no matter what their origins, seen in some strains of Hicksite Quakerism since the 1820s.[105]

David Evans was not alone in charging the Universal Reformers with infidelity; it was one of the most common attacks that they had to face. Typical was the comment of one recipient of Wattles's *Herald of Progression*, who returned it with a note: "I am sorry, John, that you have got to be an infidel." A minister appeared at one of Collins's meetings to warn him that he had fallen into "an infidel trap" that would lead, if unchecked, to the horrors of the French Revolution repeated on a larger scale. Abraham Brooke dismissed the charge as a worn-out bogeyman: "This old scarecrow has been used so long it nearly lost its power," he wrote to Orson S. Murray. "Free minds there are now, and I am thankful that in this region they are numerous, and daily increasing, who venture to examine an opinion even if advanced by one scouted at as infidel." Valentine Nicholson agreed. "Infidels" were, in his experience, usually "Practical Christians" of "honest hearts and discerning minds" who were bringing woe to hypocrites and pharisees. "Infidelity," was "only another name for 'Honesty.' " The real infidels were those professed Christians who did not live up to the ideals they proclaimed.[106]

But there were some reformers, most notably Collins, Murray, and their followers, mainly at Skaneateles, who *were* atheists. "We abjure all religions," wrote Maria Loomis in 1844. Collins agreed in his assessment of the first year of the Skaneateles community's life: "skepticism," he wrote, "has taken a deep and strong hold on the minds of nearly all." In a convention in Boston in the summer of 1844 he forthrightly avowed his doubts. The obituary of one member there doubtless described the ideal for many; the deceased was a "fearless, independent Free Thinker." The *Communitist* held up Thomas Paine as a model for reformers.[107]

Skeptical reformers explained themselves in various ways. Harlow Hard thought it unreasonable "to pray to, or worship a being of whom I know nothing." Gods, he argued, were the result of human needs, and societies created them to meet their needs. A resident at Skaneateles agreed; no one knew what was the "real true church of God"; the search for it was simply a sign of human longing for escape from the world's problems. Another writer in the *Communitist* argued against the divinity of Christ on similar grounds—almost every religion put forth some sort of savior. Collins professed "a profound admiration for the holy precepts and principles of the Saviour," even as he "denied the authority and divinity of their author." One of his doubts was based on what he saw as Christ's ignorance of Natural Law. "Jesus did I believe not know all our physiological laws," Collins told a Syracuse audience. "He consumed flesh it is said—He told the apostles to catch fish. He did not exhaust the soul's possibilities." Others saw religion as superfluous. "With me, *morality* pertains more to *doing* than to *believing*," one wrote. "With me, proper practices are quite sufficient." Joseph Allen, the Michigan Hicksite turned freethinker, agreed. "I am satisfied that if the pains taken by the teachers of the people to fix their attention on the unknown, were employed in developing social principles, and teaching man known truths," he wrote, "a vast improvement in the condition of man would soon be effected."[108]

The Skaneateles skeptics had numerous opponents among the communitarians, however. Within the Skaneateles community, Valentine Nicholson's friend, the lawyer Quincy A. Johnson, took the lead. "Religion is an innate principle to man, and forms part of his organization," wrote Johnson in the *Communitist*. David W. Jones in Grant County, Indiana, agreed; "I believe that no reformer can succeed without integral faith in God," he wrote to Wattles's *Herald of Progression*. Edwin Michener at Highland Home community thought that without faith in a God of justice, it was absurd to speak of living according to the requirements of the Government of God; infidelity was sapping the foundations of community, he warned. Wattles wrote that God must be the center of all mind, all endeavor. Only God could satisfy human longings for "Wisdom, Knowledge, Thought, Mental Wealth, Intellectual Treasure." Abraham Brooke was sure that community would usher in "a realization of true christianity."[109]

Beyond this the reformers were often vague about their vision of religion.

Wattles agreed with Milo A. Townsend that communities should operate on the principle: "By their fruits shall ye know them." Wattles also wrote that as people became subject to natural laws, they would come to understand and practice "true worship," and all would naturally go in the same paths. They would have no clergy, of course; "man would be his own priest," worshiping in the open air. Valentine Nicholson refused to consider even excluding infidels; he thought them far less dangerous than hypocritical professing Christians. Whatever forms their vision took, however, it embraced the yearnings after purity and certainty that other advocates of nature religion in nineteenth-century America sought.[110]

Many of the communitists were confident about the ultimate outcome of their efforts—the dawn of the millennium. This was much on the minds of many reformers in the 1830s and 1840s. Since the eighteenth century, many Americans had been drawn to the belief that the millennium—the thousand years of perfect love and peace on earth—would dawn in the United States, before the return of Christ as foretold in the book of Revelation. They were thus known as postmillennialists. In the late 1830s, however, a new view of the coming of the millennium was put forth by a Vermont Baptist minister, William Miller. On the basis of a complex computation of certain Scriptural texts, Miller predicted that the world would come to an end in the fall of 1843 (later revised to the fall of 1844). His theories attracted thousands of followers, who became known as adventists.[111]

A few of the reformers may have had slight Millerite inclinations, at least in the 1830s, and perhaps later. During one of the Hundred Conventions at Vergennes, Vermont, Collins told his audience that "Miller's doctrine is great in meaning." In the 1830s Wattles had seen the United States as a Sodom, ripe for the awful judgments of an angry God. Darius R. Stone, one of the founders of Skaneateles, saw judgment as imminent. "God is turning and overturning, and the kingdom and glory of it under the whole heavens promises to be soon vested in Him whose right it is to reign. The saints of God are coming out of Babylon."[112]

By the 1840s, however, Wattles had come to a different vision of the millennium, one that community would usher in, beginning at Prairie Home: "The gate shall not be shut; and into it shall throng the reformed and the Reformers, the redeemed and the Redeemers, till all the nations of the earth shall be in one great community—and heaven and earth shall touch together. The Tabernacle of God shall be with men, and He shall dwell among them." His brother-in-law William H. Whinery agreed. "All the works of the Creator seem to in-

vite us to community action. His spirit says come. His creation says come," he
wrote in the *Regenerator*. "Why should any hesitate to labor for the kingdom
on earth?" Emily Gardner, the Quaker schoolteacher from Union County, Indiana, awaited "the dawn (at least) of the morn of millennial glory." She saw
a world in which people would "return to paradise and live like our parents
before the fall," a time in which "not only all mankind but all animated creatures existing in God's Government and into which he had breathed the breath
of life shall live in perfect harmony and peace." Joshua W. Engle, a Green Plain
Progressive Friend and another of Wattles's correspondents, foresaw that "the
ambitions of man shall be changed from his beastly pursuits, and shall 'learn
war no more,' and when the 'swords shall be beaten into pruning hooks.' " At
that time "shall the powers of the devil be chained, and the ruling of Christ
commence in the world." Another one of Wattles's contributors sketched a
world where "the rich and the poor, the kings and the subjects, the inheritors
and the servant will feast alike on the good things of the earth, and all will be
order and harmony and blissful security forever."[113]

As with all other aspects of society, the Universal Reformers saw much to
dislike in contemporary religion. The clergy were self-serving and corrupt, and
many church members were hypocrites. They were bound up in sectarianism
and primitive doctrines at odds with natural law. They agreed that the church
they knew must disappear, but there agreement ended. Most of the Hicksite
Friends embraced a variant of Quakerism, shorn of the strictures of the Discipline. Others, especially at Skaneateles, renounced faith entirely. And a third
group looked toward a vague religion of humanity, akin to Quakerism, and
toward the dawn of the millennium.

Ideology in Context

As befitted a group dedicated to nothing less than a complete transformation of human society, the advocates of Universal Reform had a wide-ranging
vision of social change. Economic, political, educational, religious, and gender
structures would all undergo transformation in the world that they hoped to
create. But they were not the only reformers with visions of social transformation in the 1840s; competing with them were Fourierists, Owenites, and Perfectionists, not to mention Shakers, Mormons, and a variety of other groups of
uncertain origins and brief duration.[114] The Universal Reformers were eclectic,
drawing on a variety of sources, including other types of communal thought.

Nevertheless, one looks in vain for extended dialogue between those re-formers and other communitarians. Most of the other communal groups apparently gave little attention to the Universal Reformers, either from lack of knowledge of them or lack of interest. And for the most part the communitarians returned the sentiment. The columns of Collins's *Communitist* or Murray's *Regenerator* or Wattles's *Herald of Progression* are relatively free of controversial pieces aimed at other communitarian theorists. Not infrequently they reprinted pieces from other communitarian journals, such as the Fourierist *Phalanx* or the Owenite *New Moral World,* but direct attacks on other groups were the exception rather than the rule. Apparently they were much more interested in analysis of the problems of competitive society than in challenging other reformers.

The largest and most influential communitarian movement in the United States in the 1840s was Fourierism. Based on the theories of the Frenchman Charles Fourier, these communitarians advocated a complex system of socialism that attracted many followers, some of them well-known and influential, like Horace Greeley, the editor of the *New York Tribune.* Actually, Fourierism in the United States was mostly the product of Albert Brisbane, who, in Ronald Walters's words, translated "into American terms the French utopian's awkward vocabulary and intricate system of social relationships." Fourierism of the Brisbane variety centered around life in communities called phalanxes and a central building called a phalanstery. Private property remained; indeed, the phalanx was based on investment. Fourier argued that all persons were a mixture of twelve different passions; the particular mixture determined the work for which the person was best fitted. At its most basic, Fourierism would usher in happiness by allowing people to do what they were best suited to do. In its American variety, it was not necessarily tied to radicalism on slavery, religion, or women's rights, although many Fourierists embraced those causes.[115]

The Universal Reformers were aware of the Fourierists and made it clear that they wished them well, even while articulating their points of disagreement. An editorial in the *Communitist* summed up this attitude of good will: "So far as we have been concerned, we do now, and ever have entertained the kindest feelings towards the advocates of Association. . . . They constitute a bright galaxy—a constellation of stars of the first magnitude."[116]

On the other hand, the Universal Reformers made clear their differences with Fourier. Valentine Nicholson spoke for them when he wrote that Universal Reform was on "higher ground." Fourierism, he claimed, did not "contemplate or advocate the equality of the human race. It makes provision to enable the capitalist to live without labor, if he wishes and thus thrust the burden of his maintenance upon those who have less wealth than himself." Fourierism was good, Nicholson wrote, better than the present system, but only for those who were not prepared for Universal Reform. Abraham Brooke was disturbed in 1843 when some Fourierist pieces written by Albert Brisbane appeared in the *Liberator* signed only with the initials "A. B."; a number of readers had assumed that Brooke must be the author, and that pained him. Fourierism, he wrote to the *Philanthropist*, varied from "Divine law," and thus was "false philosophy," because it allowed for people to have "separate interests." Maria Loomis praised Fourierists, but concluded that they erred in allowing for "a divided interest and inclination." It is probably significant that, even after the collapse of the communities, but few Universal Reformers, such as John Orvis and his future wife Marianna Dwight, are known to have moved on to a phalanx, in their case Brook Farm.[117]

Surprisingly, the Universal Reformers had even less discourse with a variety of communitarians with whom they appeared to have much in common, the perfectionist communitarians like Adin Ballou and John Humphrey Noyes. At the same time that the Skaneateles, Prairie Home, and other communities were beginning, Ballou was founding the Hopedale community at Milford, Massachusetts. And even before the conventions of 1842–1843, Noyes had begun to gather at Putney, Vermont, the nucleus of the group that would flourish as the Oneida Community in Madison County, New York.[118]

There were important differences between Ballou and Noyes—Hopedale was utterly conventional on sexual matters, while the Oneida Community would become notorious for its embrace of "complex marriage" and birth control. But the two groups did share a commitment to the possibility and reality of human perfection: that, through divine grace and favor, humans could be redeemed from the power of sin, immune to its temptations, living sanctified lives of holiness and perfection.[119]

Certainly the Universal Reformers were no strangers to perfectionism. We have seen how Wattles became committed to it while at Oneida Institute (unconnected with Noyes's Oneida Community). The Quakers came from a strong, albeit different, holiness tradition. They would have been reared under the view that the goal of religious life was not an instantaneous conversion experience, but gradual growth into holiness, by which they would achieve salvation. As readers of the *Liberator*, the reformers certainly would have been familiar with Ballou, who shared their commitment to the Government of

God. Ballou did attend one of Collins's "no property" meetings in the summer of 1843, but came away convinced that Collins's hostility to private property had led him astray. Noyes had traded barbs with Murray, but the only comments we have from Noyes about Universal Reform deal only with Collins and Skaneateles, and date from many years afterwards.[120]

The primary difference between the perfectionists and the Universal Reformers was captured well by William Lloyd Garrison in 1843, writing about Collins. "He holds . . . that man is the creature of circumstances, and therefore not deserving of praise or blame for what he does." Garrison, Ballou, and Noyes held, in contrast, as Garrison put it: "it is an internal rather than an outward reorganization that is needed to put away the evil that is in the world." As has been seen, the Universal Reformers thought that internal transformation was impossible until society had changed to allow it.[121]

The communitarian thinker with which the Universal Reformers were most often associated by others was Robert Owen, but that was only with Collins and the group at Skaneateles. Collins had, of course, met Owen, the Scots industrialist and philanthropist, while in England in 1841. Collins claimed that he had arrived at the same conclusions as Owen without reading any of Owen's writings. But, as one historian has recently put it: "In all aspects, John Collins sounded like an 1840s version of Robert Owen, and his community duplicated with flawless fidelity the same problems that beset New Harmony."[122]

Certainly the group at Skaneateles was unrestrained in admiration of Owen. An editorial in the *Communitist* late in 1844 called Owen a "truly great and distinguished philanthropist." The writer concluded: "There is no man living whose acquaintance we are so anxious to make." Maria Loomis, writing about a convention of infidels in the spring of 1845, noted Owen's presence: "this is sufficient guarantee that good will be done." The *Communitist* ushered in the year 1846 with a salute to "the delightful schemes of the greatest philanthropist ever yet presented to the world, Mr. Owen, of New Lanark." Perhaps the grandest occasion in the history of the Skaneateles community was May 16, 1845, when Owen visited and was feted with speeches and a tour. He genially gave his approval to everything that he saw.[123]

In the West, however, there was no corresponding interest or admiration. Two residents of the communities, John Wood at Prairie Home and Andrew Spillard at Union Home, had previous Owenite ties; Wood had been "acquainted" with Owenite groups in England, and Spillard had been at Owen's New Harmony Community in the 1820s. But they were minor figures of relatively limited influence. In the West, Owen held little fascination for Nicholson, Wattles, Brooke, or their compatriots.[124]

As several historians of Owen's ventures have noted, he was not always precise about the shape that he expected the "new moral world" to take. But he was clear on two points. First, he saw environment as critical; if humans were supplied with education, appropriate work, and a decent standard of living, then they would become moral. Degraded circumstances made for degraded people. This was very close to the position of the Universal Reformers that evil existed because social structures would not allow people to live according to natural laws.[125]

Owen's second critical contribution was to separate community from religion. Owen was a notorious freethinker, and Owenism was usually associated with infidelity in the popular mind. This may explain why Owen was so popular at Skaneateles and viewed with less enthusiasm in the other communities. By the end of its first year of existence, Skaneateles was populated mainly with freethinkers. Thus Owen would have been all the more attractive to them. In contrast, the westerners (with some exceptions) remained committed to a religious vision of community as the Government of God. Infidelity did not necessarily repel them, but neither did they consider it favorably. Thus few apparently drew heavily, or at least openly, on Owen's ideas.[126]

The ideology of Universal Reform was, then, an amalgam. Those who shared it also tended to share certain common experiences. The most striking was the experience of isolation. They had led lives that put them at odds with their neighbors, whether from religion, or occupation, or frontier necessity. At its most basic, their desire for community came out of a desire to live with and share the experiences of like-minded people.

Once in community, there was general agreement about the shape of the new world that would result. It would be based on the Government of God, with human government banished and the only laws natural laws, as inscribed by the creator on the human heart. Economic competition and private property, the bases of current society, would disappear, replaced by cooperation and commonly held goods. Women would achieve equality and be freed from lives of drudgery. Education would be based on knowledge of natural laws. Only on religion was there significant disagreement. All rejected "sects" and "priestcraft." Some took up the cause of reforming Quakerism, others embraced a vague religion of humanity, others went on to infidelity.

In the context of their times, the Universal Reformers were eclectic. They differed significantly with the Fourierists. With the Owenites they shared an environmental outlook that saw people as the creatures of circumstances, to be transformed by transforming the world around them. But with the Perfectionists they, for the most part, shared a commitment to the Government of God. Universal Reformers took ideas from a variety of sources, sometimes independently arriving at conclusions other communitarians had reached. They were guided by a commitment to, above all, what they thought was God's will and what they thought would work it.

THE FATES OF REFORMERS

"AND NOW AT almost 89 I see little to regret in life." So wrote Esther Whinery Wattles, probably the last survivor of the Society for Universal Inquiry and Reform, not long before her death in 1908. It was a feeling that most other fellow reformers apparently shared.[1]

The Society for Universal Inquiry and Reform had disappeared as an organization after the failed attempt at a national convention in New York City in the spring of 1843. When Valentine Nicholson and Abraham Allen parted company with John A. Collins in Syracuse afterwards, it represented a cutting of ties between the Westerners and those in the East with whom they hoped to form common cause. They still communicated with each other through journals like the *Liberator* and Nathaniel P. Rogers's *Herald of Freedom*, and, later, the *Communitist*, Orson S. Murray's *Regenerator*, and Wattles's *Herald of Progression* in Cincinnati. With the exception of the ever-irascible Orson S. Murray, individuals in the various communities seldom had hard words for other communities (in contrast to how they often dealt with fellow residents where they lived). But if there was other communication, no record of it has survived. Late in 1848, a reader of the *Regenerator* asked plaintively what had become of Wattles and Collins, who had roused such hopes in the spring of 1843. Murray could only respond that both were still living, but leading very different lives.[2]

These reformers would, in fact, take various paths after 1846. Most continued to be active in abolition, woman's rights, and liberal religion. Some remained committed to communitarianism. But they would pursue their concerns in different ways, and for the most part separately from each other.

Probably none of the Universal Reformers underwent such a radical transformation as did John A. Collins. In 1846, over half of his life lay ahead of him. In the minds of other reformers, the latter half was consistent with his earlier life only in its erratic course.

After leaving Skaneateles, "out of money, business, credit, and health," Collins went to Dayton, Ohio, where he became the editor of a Whig newspaper, the *Daily Daytonian.* He opened his new career with a brief sketch of his intellectual progress that received wide attention in the Whig and reform press. He had been a Whig until 1837, he wrote. Then for almost ten years he had devoted himself to "works of philanthropy." From nonresistance he had passed to infidelity, and finally to "a Community of Property." To the last he had sacrificed money, health, his own comfort, and that of "a feeble wife and many helpless children." But finally he had realized that his beliefs were "false in theory and pernicious in their practical tendencies." Nonresistant theories were exalted, and might "do very well if men were angels, and angels Gods; but human nature is too low, too selfish and too ignorant for relations so exalted." He was still committed to the "great cause of virtue, equity, temperance, freedom and the brotherhood of mankind." But now he sought to advance them through "the two great institutions" of Religion and Government.[3]

Collins's course naturally drew the plaudits of more conservative reformers and the execration of his old associates. Orson S. Murray unloosed the harshest blasts, accusing Collins of extravagance, greed, laziness, and misappropriation of funds. He was using his personal failures in practice to discredit a whole system of theory, "always a failing with brother Collins." The truth was simple, Murray concluded: "John A. Collins wanted bread, and must have it or starve, and being unable to obtain it in an unpopular movement, without more labor with our hands on the soil than was agreeable, felt compelled to return to church and state and sue for Salvation."[4]

Collins did, in fact, return to the church. In 1847 the *New York Tribune* reported that he was "now a member of an orthodox church and a student for the ministry therein." In the spring of 1849 he lost his wife. Anne Weston sourly reported to her sister that Eunice Collins had "died of consumption and in the bosom of the proslavery Orthodox church."[5]

Collins's stay at the *Daytonian* was relatively short. By 1848 he was lecturing agent for the Sons of Temperance, advocating the death penalty for selling liquor. Murray attributed his change of heart to giving up diet reform for meat— "the flesh pots are having their legitimate effects on him, in making him savage and ferocious." In 1849, however, he joined the Gold Rush to California. There he found no gold, but became involved in trying to design and build machinery to mine quartz. By 1855 he had become a traveling lecturer again, presenting a series on geology "illustrated by brilliant Philosophical experiments" and paintings that took up 3,000 feet of canvas. He drifted to Nevada and then back to California, where he settled to practice law in San Francisco. An abolitionist friend encountered him in 1864 and mourned that Collins was "belying his whole better nature—conscience, principle, conviction, and habit," and was "devoting himself to the use of the 'muckrake,' the gross worship of mammon, the brazen-faced denial of his earlier better life."[6]

This was probably unfair, since there is evidence that Collins had held to at least some of his old ideals. In 1853 he was an independent candidate for governor of California. By the 1860s he was a spiritualist, and was at his death in 1890 president of the Society of Progressive Spiritualists. He was a founder of the National Cooperative Homestead Association, which aimed at change in the industrial system through workers' cooperatives.[7]

In 1879, Collins reestablished ties with William Lloyd Garrison, just before Garrison's death. He sounded much like the Collins of the 1840s. "In our barbarous competitive system, the man of average ability, has no possible way to be more than a wage slave, however honest, industrious, and frugal he may be," he told Garrison. Industrialism had brought a "complete revolution," with wealth for a few and helplessness for workers, "a frightful chasm" as bad as in the Old World. Industrialism was leading to such overproduction that a search for foreign markets was inevitable, and that in turn would lead to imperialism—a prescient assessment, in the view of some historians. Two years later Collins wrote to Frederick Douglass to rejoice over the success of the antislavery cause, and to predict that defending the rights of Chinese immigrants would be the next great reform cause.[8]

Collins was not alone among the Universal Reformers in criticizing the direction of American industrial society after the Civil War. John Orvis especially kept up a commitment to cooperation until late in the century. He championed cooperatives and labor organizations, helping to found the Sovereigns of Industry in the 1870s and serving as an officer of the Knights of Labor. At Orvis's death, he was involved with Edward Bellamy's nationalist movement.[9]

If John A. Collins found some measure of contentment after his communitarian effort failed, that was in stark contrast to Hiram Mendenhall. The few years that remained to Mendenhall were filled with disappointment.

The collapse of Union Home left Mendenhall's finances more precarious than ever. His debts still remained, his mills were decrepit, and much of the good will of his neighbors had vanished. After 1846, Mendenhall concentrated on a desperate struggle for financial survival, putting aside almost all of his reform interests. His health was also uncertain. He did give some attention to spiritualism, however, and had by 1850 become a convert.[10]

In April 1850 Mendenhall and his son Amos set off for the California gold fields. He hoped to recoup his fortunes, and, even if that failed, to restore his health through travel. And if California was not to his liking, then he would go on to Oregon. His experiences crossing the Great Plains and Rockies moved him deeply. "It is a magnificent sight to behold at the same glance such a mighty contrast as those snow capt mountains . . . and the broad green valleys below." Salt Lake City depressed him—the Mormon "cystem [sic] of bigamy . . . would have caused men to blush in darker times."[11]

California also was a disappointment. He found the inhabitants "a motley crew . . . whose morral [sic] cultivation has been greatly neglected." They were "gambling and drinking, carousing and swearing almost every breath they draw." Mendenhall blamed "indolence concequent [sic] upon the spontanious [sic] productions of a rich soil and salubrious atmosphere." Mendenhall was convinced that "if any man whose soul was never sickened for the want of full opportunity to see how low man can descend, let him come." Given a choice between two years in the Indiana state prison or in the California gold fields, Mendenhall concluded, he would choose the former.[12]

Mendenhall's gloom deepened as the year passed. He found a paying claim near Sacramento, but fall floods destroyed his machinery. His son Amos fell sick, and Hiram himself had forebodings that he would never see his family again. He was unable to send any money back to his hard-pressed family in Randolph County, and was reduced to hoping that they would be able to collect some old debts owed to him.[13]

In the spring of 1852 Hiram and Amos set out for home. They sailed from San Francisco to Panama, then took another steamer across the Gulf of Mexico. Cholera broke out, and Hiram fell victim to it. He died June 30 off Key West. One day earlier Henry Clay had died, a coincidence in which abolitionists found great meaning.[14]

Orson S. Murray remained the radical reformer to the end, even though after 1845 he was distant from centers of intellectual life and reform thought. On a few issues he shifted or retreated. But on most he remained uncompromising.

One cause that Murray refused to abandon was community. When Prairie Home collapsed, the Murrays found a new home near Valentine Nicholson in Warren County. Orson soon obtained possession of a farm that he named Fruit Hills and promptly proceeded to another attempt at community. About twenty people joined. As always, those on the place were hopeful about their prospects. The land was fertile and well-timbered. It was also a stop on the Cincinnati and Sandusky Railroad. The principles were those of Prairie Home—common property, nonresistance, and diet reform.[15]

The community proved as short-lived as Prairie Home. A. J. MacDonald wrote its epitaph: "all the necessaries of life could be raised in abundance, but the laborers were mostly unused to agriculture and in too many instances lacked industry so that disappointments took place . . . leaving the burden of the place on Murray." Within a year, the Fruit Hills community had ceased to be.[16]

Longer lived was the *Regenerator*. In April 1845 Murray resumed publication. The journal was little changed. There were withering attacks on those who incurred Murray's displeasure, such as John A. Collins or Valentine Nicholson, with a lengthy postmortem on Prairie Home. Murray continued to advocate diet and health reform, woman's rights, nonresistance, peace and socialism, and to attack orthodox religion and slavery. Murray's vitriol excited the wonder of the Transcendentalist George Ripley, who mourned that Murray was "literal and unimaginative to the large degree of rigidity," but used "words with the most remarkable caution and precision of any popular writer we know."[17]

Gradually, however, Murray flagged in the struggle to keep up the *Regenerator*. In 1846, he changed its publication to semimonthly. There were never enough receipts to do much more than barely cover the costs of printing. Murray depended on his children to do most of the work on the paper. Eventually the *Regenerator* became a monthly, and then came out irregularly. Finally, in 1856, when Murray's son Carlos, who had borne the weight of the journal for several years, died, it stopped forever.[18]

For the next thirty years Murray lived on his Warren County farm. He softened some of his views. He gave up strict vegetarianism. Supporting himself as a farmer, he necessarily was caught up in the marketplace, "to buy cheap and to sell dear with the best and the worst of them." (In one of the great ironies of Universal Reform, Orson's son Charles used the experience he gained on the *Regenerator* to publish the *Cincinnati Price Current*, a leading Midwestern source for crop prices.) In other ways, however, Orson S. Murray remained very much the nonconformist. Since moving to Ohio, he had refused to cut his beard. And he remained a religious skeptic.[19]

Murray died on his farm in Warren County in 1885. His mind remained active to the end. His death left only three of the charter members of the American Anti-Slavery Society still living. On his deathbed, he dictated an essay to be read at his funeral, perhaps to forestall any rumors of his final return to religion, definitely so that his voice, and not that of some priest, would have the last word. And that last word was uncompromising. "The Christian religion is an organized conspiracy against human nature; against all other religions, and against salutary scientific knowledge," he told his hearers. It engendered "uncharitableness," "animosity," "rancor," and "hate." "The 'God' of Christendom is money, and the power it gives to reduce and subordinate."[20]

Thus Murray saw nothing to regret. "Mine has been a life of endeavors not to have the world the worse for my having lived in it." He had tried to appeal to "consciences and common sense." And he felt vindicated in all. "The philosophy which has fully and constantly sustained me . . . , I now rely upon unwaveringly," he concluded. "It enables me to feel that this perpetual end is rest from toil and trouble—is an entrance upon sleep which knows no waking." Unconventional to the end, he left instructions that his body be cremated.[21]

Universal Reform had led Abraham Brooke on a lonely path. His drive to free himself from any connection with sinful, coercive power had by 1844 placed him in almost complete isolation. Eschewing the mails cut him off from correspondence and even from subscribing to reform journals, although he apparently read those that the Murrays, Nicholsons, Allens, and other less scrupulous neighbors passed on to him. For a time, he even managed to live without money. Needless to say, his eccentricities made him almost legendary throughout southwestern Ohio.[22]

By 1848, however, Brooke was reconsidering some of his views. He again was comfortable subscribing to the *Liberator*. Apparently he was willing to send letters (at that time the recipient compromised with the coercive power by paying the postage). Early in 1847 he directed a blast at William Lloyd Garrison. Although he took pride in being "called a Garrison abolitionist," he feared that Garrison had been carried away by the praise and adulation he had received. He still remained firmly committed to nonresistance, and with his wife was a firm disunionist. He and Elizabeth had also become antisabbatarians, opposed to "coercion of obedience to 'an ordinance for the better observance of the Lord's Day as a day of rest.' "[23]

Brooke, however, was coming to doubt his course in other respects. For several years he had tried to resist "the power of grabitation," but he gradually concluded that he had gone too far. He needed time to work his way back, but over the next few years he began a return to reform work.[24]

Brooke's religious affiliation in these years is uncertain. The Hicksite Center Monthly Meeting had disowned him in 1843. A similar fate befell the radical abolitionists at Green Plain, West Grove, Goshen, and other Hicksite communities. They began to hold their own meetings; in some places they were strong enough to keep possession of the property. There were similar separations among Hicksite Friends in New York, Michigan, eastern Ohio, and eventually in the Philadelphia area. Eventually they came to call themselves Progressive or Congregational Friends.[25]

In 1848 the Congregational Friends in western Ohio and Indiana came together to form Green Plain Yearly Meeting of Friends "who have adopted the Congregational Order." There was no Discipline, each meeting being free to make its own rules and regulations, which would be minimal. Instead they pointed Christians to "the *divine laws of God* written in our being," believing that "man should never concede to any combination or order of men, his *individual freedom*." Abraham and Elizabeth Brooke, with the Allens, Nicholson, and many other Universal Reformers, were present at the convention that organized the yearly meeting. By 1850 Abraham Brooke was the co-clerk.[26]

The Green Plain Friends apparently held only three yearly meetings. They concerned themselves mostly with reform. A stream of letters and memorials went forth, demanding equal rights for blacks and women, endorsing temperance and the abolition of capital punishment and slavery, and calling for an end to the army and navy and their academies at West Point and Annapolis. The 1850 yearly meeting preached defiance of the newly enacted Fugitive Slave Act. "If it be really a constitutional obligation that all who live under the government shall be kidnappers and slave catchers, for southern tyrants," they wrote in a public letter, "WE GO FOR REVOLUTION, by such instrumentalities as are in accordance with the laws of God."[27]

The Brookes did not confine their work for woman's rights to the deliberations and statements of the Green Plain Yearly Meeting. Congregational Friends in New York had played a leading role in the first woman's rights convention in Seneca Falls, New York, in 1848, and when the second such convention was held in Salem, Ohio, in April 1850, Congregational Friends, and the Brookes and their relatives, played important roles. Abraham and Elizabeth did not attend, but he sent a letter of support, and the convention elected her a member of the standing committee to continue the convention's work, along with her sister-in-law Esther Ann Lukens of New Garden.[28]

Congregational Friends and Universal Reformers would, in fact, play prominent roles in the woman's rights movement for the next half century. Mary F. Thomas, who with her husband Owen had been among the founders of the Marlborough community, was one of the first woman physicians in Indiana, the editor of its first woman's rights journal, and the leader of the movement in the state until her death in 1888. When the first woman's rights convention in the state was held in Dublin in 1851, former Universal Reformers—Thomas, Joel P. Davis, George and Eliza Taylor, Clarkson Puckett, and Wilson D. Schooley of Prairie Home, and Lewises, Wrights, and Dugdales from West Grove— played leading roles. Joseph and Ruth Dugdale helped inaugurate the movement both in Pennsylvania and in Iowa. Hannah Myers Longshore, one of the founders of Marlborough, was in the first graduating class of the Woman's Medical College of Pennsylvania. Marenda B. Randall, the pioneer feminist at Skaneateles, became one of the first woman physicians in Vermont.[29]

In 1853, Abraham and Elizabeth Brooke left Oakland and returned to Marlborough. They moved to advance their interest in reform. "The change which had been going on in society at Oakland had left but very few of reformatory tendencies and intellectual activity," Abraham wrote to the Nicholsons. "Here we are surrounded by those who think and feel with us upon many important questions." The Brookes bought part of the old community farm adjoining his brother Edward.[30]

One of the causes into which the Brookes plunged themselves anew was abolition. After 1845, Salem in Columbiana County, about twenty miles east of Marlborough became the center for Garrisonian abolition in Ohio. The Ohio American Anti-Slavery Society had faded away, replaced by the Western Anti-Slavery Society. For most of the 1850s Abraham Brooke served as an officer, contributing articles to the society's organ the *Anti-Slavery Bugle*. He continued to look askance at government and politics, and became increasingly disenchanted with what he saw as William Lloyd Garrison's temporizing on those subjects. About 1855 Abraham, at the request of a black neighbor, went secretly to Tennessee to try to rescue her daughter from slavery. He failed, and barely escaped himself back to Ohio. In 1859, however, he took a leading part in the rescue of a young slave girl from a train in Salem.[31]

The Western Anti-Slavery Society and the *Bugle* both collapsed in 1861, after which all mention of the Brookes disappears from view. He died in Marlborough in 1867.[32]

If the failure of Skaneateles, Prairie Home, and the other communities discouraged the majority of Universal Reformers, it did not discourage John O. Wattles. For the decade after Prairie Home's collapse, he remained committed to the cause of community, and he continued to agitate its principles for the rest of his life.

After Prairie Home dissolved, John O. and Esther Wattles went back to Clinton County to make their home with Esther's family, the Whinerys. They had a vague idea of beginning a new community called Fraternal Vale, but it remained little more than a name.[33]

Instead, in the spring of 1845 the Wattleses moved to Cincinnati. A female antislavery society there hired John to act as a teacher and lecturer, while Esther took a position at a black elementary school. John also began publication of a journal, the *Herald of Progression,* its terms, "read and circulate." It was "devoted to the cause of God and Humanity, in the Redemption of the 900,000,000 *Physiologically, Mentally* and *Socially.*"[34]

John, however, was ever ready to consider other communal experiments. Up the Ohio River from Cincinnati in Clermont County was a failed Fourierist phalanx known as Utopia. Several communitarian sympathizers from Cincinnati—Moses Cornell, Lucius A. Hine, Hiram S. Gilmore, Pascal B. Smith, and Wattles—had begun to meet in 1846 to discuss reform. Gilmore was the principal of a black high school in Cincinnati. Hine was a lawyer and editor of the *Quarterly Journal and Review,* which in January 1847 had merged with the *Herald of Progression.* Smith was a well-to-do merchant. Together, they and other sympathizers formed what they called the "Universal Brotherhood." In Smith's words, its intention "was to establish a Christian Church, on the broad principles of the gospel of Christ, with a view to remedy the great evils of society."[35]

An ill fate pursued the community, which took the name Excelsior. The group, with Smith's money, began to put up a large brick building to house the residents. In December 1847, however, a flood destroyed the entire community. Cornell and sixteen others, over half of the residents, drowned, and the Wattleses barely escaped. The survivors, after the waters receded, tried to begin again, but when the frame building where they lived burned in May 1848, the group broke up.[36]

After Utopia, John and Esther found themselves in conflict. "We have been tried by water by whirlwind and by fire. *I* would like to try something else," Esther told him. He, however, had heard of a new community at Lake Zurich near Chicago that Seth Paine, a reformer after his own heart, was forming. "He was so charmed that I saw I was to try again," she remembered sixty years later. She returned to her parents' house while he went to visit Paine.[37]

Esther, however, still had doubts, and left by herself in Wilmington she finally wrote her husband a remarkable letter. "The more I try to persuade myself that I have been serving God and Humanity the more I see it as untrue," she told him. "What have I done but serve those whose devilish passions and appetites have brought disgrace on themselves on us and all reformers?" When he spoke of community, she saw only "pleasure and delight." But their experiences had taught her only of "man's deception and cold heartedness." She was hopeful that "our efforts may hasten the day and the time may come when coming generations can enjoy a true state of society," but they were not yet ready for it. And although it was their duty to aid in preparing humanity for that, she concluded, "It don't seem to me that this makes it necessary that we should sacrifice everything that might add to our comfort."[38]

Esther, moreover, had other worries. "I am not a fit companion for thee as I am, as everybody knows," she told him. "Thee asks me now and then to write and want I should mingle with the educated, but if I do it I have to show my ignorance and thus am a disgrace to thee, and this grieves me so that I feel I cannot endure it much longer." She yearned to complete her education: "I must devote a year or two to my own mental training or I shall not be able to inherit the kingdom or capable of enjoying it if it is presented to me." But her experience of community had convinced her that it would always mean such unrelenting work and toil that she would never have time for learning in one.[39]

Esther had one other fear. By this time she probably knew that she was pregnant—the first of her three children, Celestia, was born in February 1849. (Years later, Esther told her daughters that she and John had had sexual intercourse only three times, each occasion producing a daughter.) Apparently she had not told John about the pregnancy, so she appealed to him in more general terms. "Suppose thee had children, would thee be willing to take them to a state of society like at Excelsior?" she asked. She was convinced that he had erred in deemphasizing the family. "A true state of society does not convey to my mind a scene of constant stir and commotion," she wrote. "Let us enjoy the family relation in connection with our attempts to redeem society, or we shall fail to realize it."[40]

Esther's plea made an impression. John had gone to Chicago to explore Seth Paine's incipient community. He responded quickly to Esther's protests. "I have not done my part—I have required too much of you," he wrote. "I have made your happiness *secondary* to that of the world." But while conceding that, he was not willing to give up on communities. "I can make a home and a good one too in *Isolation* if it comes to that," he told her. "But let us try to do it the best way first."[41]

Won over at least temporarily, Esther made the journey to Paine's land at Lake Zurich north of Chicago, possibly persuaded by promises that she could have her own house and that Paine would deed her a tract of land. Once there, however, she became skeptical. The community had attracted a number of adherents, but Paine soon expelled most of them. Mrs. Paine's opposition to the whole project further complicated matters. The Paines invited the Wattleses to remain, but they refused. When there was enough snow on the ground, they left in a sleigh for Warren County, Indiana, where the Cranes and Romines contemplated reviving the Grand Prairie Community. Three days after their arrival, their oldest daughter, Lucretia Celestia, was born in the midst of a howling snowstorm. By the autumn, John found himself in conflict with the others over crops and money.[42]

Esther was by now ready for a home of her own, indeed, insistent on it. This time John gave in, purchasing a small farm on the Wea Plains near the village of West Point in the summer of 1849. Esther's father purchased and deeded an adjoining tract to Esther, and John and Esther bought an additional 350 acres with the idea that it someday might be the site of yet another community.[43]

Instead of a community, the land became home to a school, the Grand Prairie Harmonial Institute. Various accounts put its founding in 1851, 1853, or 1854; the Wattles formally deeded the land late in 1853, although classes could have started there earlier. The constitution that John drew up was in keeping with what he had advocated for over a decade. The constitution of humanity, he wrote, "was designed to harmonize with the government of God, or Laws of Nature." Disobedience brought "Misery, degradation and crime." So, "to afford an opportunity to those who are desirous of living a harmonious life," Grand Prairie was established. Horace Greeley himself consented to serve as one of the trustees.[44]

The school was short-lived. Initially it attracted some support from neighbors, who enrolled their children. Two teachers, formerly part of the Universal Brotherhood, A. L. Childs and D. E. Eldridge, came from Cincinnati. Within a year, however, "community principles" caused the school's downfall. Eldridge fell in love with Cornelia Childs, the principal's daughter, and they decided to marry themselves in Quaker fashion, just as the Wattleses had wed in 1844. The ceremony, without minister or justice of the peace, mystified the neighbors, however, who soon broadcast that the school was a haven for "free love." Parents quickly withdrew their children, and the Grand Prairie Harmonial Institute closed.[45]

John in these years did not bury himself on the Wabash. Two more daughters were born, Harmonia in 1851 and Theano in 1853. (John and Esther apparently timed the births in some way—Celestia was born February 11; Harmonia, February 10; and Theano, February 4.) Esther chose their names. He traveled;

in 1853 he made a long trip east to New England and New York, returning to his boyhood home in Goshen, discussing affairs at Grand Prairie with Horace Greeley, and seeing his mother, who was living with the Ripleys in Newark. He returned in 1854. In October that year he was in Philadelphia for the Fifth National Woman's Convention as the guest of James and Lucretia Mott, taking a prominent part in the proceedings.[46]

Wattles continued his interest in reforms of all kinds—woman's rights especially—but from 1849 until his death he focused much of his energy on spiritualism. Even in the days of the Universal Brotherhood in Cincinnati he had anticipated aid from supernatural sources; the Brotherhood claimed "to have discovered the laws of spiritual communication, and to be governed in all their movements by information received from the world of Light." Wattles even claimed clairvoyant powers, that he was "a spontaneous clairvoyant—that is, he enters the clairvoyant state by the power of his own will." Wattles did not record any of these clairvoyant experiences before 1850, but such affinities may explain the attraction that spiritualism held.[47]

Spiritualism began to sweep the nation in 1848, when two sisters in upstate New York claimed to receive messages from the spirits of deceased people, ranging from friends and family to public and historic figures. Certain favored mediums were believed to have particular gifts for receiving such messages, either through rappings or through writings that the spirit dictated by guiding the medium's hand. By 1851, hundreds of mediums had appeared and the movement had gained thousands of adherents.[48]

Spiritualism held special appeal for reformers. As Ann Braude has noted, it drew activists who "felt oppressed by the traditional roles assigned to men and women, found the entire social order in need of revision, and condemned the churches as perpetuators of repressive conventions." Virtually all of the Universal Reformers embraced the cause—the Brookes, Nicholsons, Mendenhalls, Collinses—along with many of the ultraists and the Progressive Friends of the 1840s. William Lloyd Garrison, Thomas Wentworth Higginson, Henry C. Wright, and Theodore and Angelina Grimke Weld were among the best-known converts.[49]

For the Universal Reformers, spiritualism held special meaning. Robert H. Abzug has written that one of its functions was to "reduce the heavy load of guilt emanating from failed expectations." Wattles and his compatriots were sure that they were advocating what God wanted the nation and the world to be, yet all of their efforts had failed. What was more reasonable than to expect divine guidance from angels and good spirits to lead humanity into the state that God intended? "Things are in a mighty turmoil—one great event follows another like mighty Rail Road trains rushing to some great center," John wrote to Esther late in 1854. But through the spirits were being revealed not only celestial laws but even the essence of celestial things. "I expect it is just what I have been wanting to get at for so many years," he concluded. "The future is pregnant with great events; great thoughts on their way to the world; good spirits are even now bending over us."[50]

The Wattleses remained longer at West Point than any other place, but by late in 1855 John again was restless. That spring his brother Augustus had moved his family to Lawrence, Kansas. Determined to keep slavery out of the territory, Augustus was a stalwart Free State man, and in fact for a time served as an assistant editor for the Lawrence *Herald of Freedom*, the territory's leading antislavery newspaper.[51]

John, however, for reasons that are unclear, took up residence in Linn County, where Augustus joined him in 1857. It was not a promising place for them, dominated by proslavery "Border Ruffians" and other Southern sympathizers. The Wattleses did not mute their abolitionist sympathies; Augustus had dealings with John Brown, although he condemned Brown's violent ways. It appears that John had drifted away from nonresistance himself, although there is nothing to indicate that he ever bore arms in Kansas. In October 1857 John returned to Indiana and brought Esther and their daughters back to Kansas.[52]

David M. Potter has noted how by 1857 the "war" in "Bleeding Kansas" had come to an end, as combatants on both sides threw themselves into land speculation and building fortunes. To the end of his life, John O. Wattles was wary of owning land, but he did devote considerable time to "improvement." In February 1857 he and Augustus had laid out a town that they named Moneka. John put up a substantial building to house an academy in which he taught. Confident as ever about the advantages of technology, in 1858 he became involved in a project to build a railroad from Jefferson City, Missouri, to Emporia, Kansas. Almost single-handedly he obtained a charter and directors and made the surveys. He spent the winter of 1858–59 in Washington, lobbying Congress for a land grant and to approve the right of way. In this he proved successful.[53]

Wattles did not put aside his reform interests entirely. In February 1858 he played a leading role in the formation of the Moneka Women's Rights Society, which was probably the first in the territory. Esther was its vice president, and their niece Sarah G. Wattles was the secretary. The group committed itself to

Esther Wattles and her daughters, ca. 1865. In author's possession.

Prohibition and to equal rights for blacks and women. In the spring of 1859 the Kansas Woman's Rights Association was formed in Moneka, with John as its president.[54]

The immediate stimulus for the formation of the state organization was the impending state constitutional convention. There was no hope of obtaining woman suffrage, but the reformers hoped for other gains, such as the right to vote in school elections and a married woman's property law. John planned to give a series of speeches throughout the territory to aid the cause. But early in September 1859, just before the first work on the railroad was to begin, he fell ill with what Esther called "brain fever." He died at Moneka on September 20.[55]

Esther survived him nearly half a century, until 1908. She never married again, apparently content with her memories, her letters, and occasional communications from her husband through a variety of mediums. In 1865 she moved to Oberlin, Ohio, where she kept a boarding house. All three daughters, aided by Uncle David Ripley, became Oberlin graduates. Esther continued her interest in spiritualism and woman's rights, although almost entirely outside of the public view. When she died in Theano's home in 1908, she was probably the last adult survivor of Prairie Home.[56]

Only one of the organizers of the Society for Universal Inquiry and Reform lived to see the twentieth century, Valentine Nicholson. He survived the collapse of Prairie Home by almost sixty years. He continued a life that was devoted to reform, but that was to be fractious, uncertain, and unhappy.

The dissolution of Prairie Home did not end Nicholson's interest in communitarianism. In 1845 and 1846 he tried to bring some of the former residents of Prairie Home together around Harveysburg in a new experiment—the Murrays, William H. Hilles and his new wife, Mary Ann French, from Prairie Home. But this new community never became reality. Later he began corresponding with Josiah Warren, the anarchist theorist who had been involved in a variety of communities since the 1820s. He also drifted away from nonresistance, but gradually, apparently without leaving behind any record of how he did so.[57]

Nicholson also continued his work on behalf of other reforms. From 1845 to 1847 he traveled through parts of western Ohio and east-central Indiana giving abolitionist lectures. His themes were the iniquity of slavery, the perfidy of the Liberty party, and the necessity of disunion. In the fall of 1845 he played host to Abby Kelley; other abolition lecturers found their way to Harveysburg and the Nicholson house. He and Jane continued to shelter fugitive slaves, on one occasion aiding an entire orchestra who had fled from playing on a riverboat. On the outskirts of Harveysburg he set up what he called his "post office," a stand filled with radical reform literature free to passersby.[58]

Nicholson was especially interested in the problems of free people of color in the 1840s and 1850s. When Frederick Douglass broke with William Lloyd Garrison and started his own newspaper, the *North Star*, Nicholson became an agent for the new journal. He was anxious to see black women as antislavery lecturers, both because they could speak with personal knowledge of oppression, and because of the example that they could set for other women. "It seems to me that examples of this kind will do more than almost anything else, toward reminding females in general that they should not be burying the talents entrusted to their care."[59]

In 1849 Nicholson's commitment to racial equality brought him new controversy. He was one of the directors of the Harveysburg Academy, a secondary school that had gained a reputation for excellence. Its headmaster was Wilson

Hobbs, an Orthodox Friend from Indiana. Conflict between him and Valentine Nicholson was probably inevitable. Hobbs came from a family well-known for its antipathy to abolitionists, and he was the son-in-law of Achilles Williams, a leading Whig and Orthodox Friend in Richmond, Indiana. At Nicholson's urging, a young black woman, Margaret Campbell, had entered the school. Because she was extremely light in complexion, at first no one realized that Campbell was not white. When Hobbs did, he not only ordered her out of the school but prevented her entry into the academy at nearby Waynesville as well.[60]

Nicholson was outraged. Hobbs's actions, he wrote, were "looked [on] with loathing and disgust by the better part of [the] community in every part of the state." He took the lead in organizing a protest meeting in Harveysburg at which he, in his own words, "made some tolerable severe remarks upon the hipocritical [sic] character of persons who proferred to be the immediate followers of the meek and lowly Jesus and yet could crouch and grovel before a corupt [sic] public sentiment becoming the veriest lickspitles [sic] of Despotic Tyrany [sic]." Afterwards Hobbs showed signs of retreating, but finally refused to admit Campbell or compromise. The controversy eventually broke up the school.[61]

Nicholson matched his heterodoxy on racial matters with his continuing assaults on "sectism." After his disownment by the Hicksite Friends in 1844, he continued his attacks on what he saw as a "proslavery" church. "Most of the professing denominations in existence are . . . *holding back* and *hindering* their members from remembering the disfranchised millions 'as in bonds with them.' " For consistent abolitionists, the only possible cause was "Comeouterism." Writing to the *Anti-Slavery Bugle* in 1846, Nicholson concluded that: "History leaves no record of any reformation or advancement ever having been made without the persons engaged in it came out." " 'Comeouterism' is only another name for progression." That naturally led him to the Green Plain Congregational Friends. Jane, however, remained with the larger Hicksite body.[62]

Even the Congregational Friends, however, did not satisfy all of Valentine Nicholson's religious longings. Ultimately, he found that satisfaction in spiritualism.

In retrospect, Valentine's attraction to spiritualism has a sort of inevitability about it. Its attractions were multiple. The death of their fifteen-year-old daughter, Ruth, in 1846 left both Valentine and Jane longing for some kind of continuing link. The failure of Prairie Home left Valentine uncertain about his future direction. The involvement of virtually all of his old compatriots—

the Brookes, Dugdales, Allens, and Wattleses—in spiritualism would give him ample opportunity to test its claims. And there was, of course, Valentine's long-standing fascination with the supernatural. A believer in a clairvoyant like Dr. June would have little difficulty accepting the possibility of communication from a spirit.[63]

Thus, from the beginning Valentine was interested in the spiritualist out-pouring. He obtained a copy of one of the earliest spiritualist works, Andrew Jackson Davis's *Principles of Nature.* He subscribed to the *Univercoelum,* a re-form periodical that was one of the earliest to commit itself to spiritualist phi-losophy. He was a close follower of the Fox sisters and other early mediums in western New York. "I have watched with deep interest every thing which has come into print relative to the phenomina [*sic*]," he wrote to Isaac and Amy Post, two fellow Congregational Friends and spiritualists in Rochester, New York. "I am pained to the heart at every coarse and vulgar remark which I *see* or *hear* made in relation to the subject."[64]

Spiritualism was, in fact, the answer to many of Valentine Nicholson's long-ings. Joseph A. Dugdale, the Green Plain minister, was also an enthusiastic be-liever in spiritualism, and his confidence inspired Nicholson. According to Dugdale, "our guardeen [*sic*] angels seem to manifest a willingness to impart instruction and give us salutary and wholesome advice . . . pertaining to what would be the most useful *occupations* and *stations* for certain individuals to be permanently engaged in." For Nicholson, it was what he had awaited without knowing, and, as he put it, "it seem[s] easy and natural . . . to believe these things."[65]

When Nicholson wrote to the Posts late in 1849, he had no direct experience of communication with spirits—in fact he asked the Posts if it was possible for anyone in Ohio to make such contacts. But within two years there were circles in the Nicholson home and in other places in Harveysburg and from the spirits came guidance. In February 1851, for example, a seance contacted the spirit of Hiram S. Gilmore, one of the Cincinnati Brotherhood. The putative Gilmore came with "an offer from the friends in the spiritual world to furnish us in this, with the necessary rules and regulations to enable us to form *circles* or *socie-ties* which should be in *harmony* with each other and the members of which should be raised above *conflict* or strife and should all mutually labor to benefit and assist each other."[66]

Gilmore's advice spoke to one of Nicholson's continuing concerns—living in community. When he wrote to the Posts in 1849, he was seeking advice about "sometime in the future of becoming united with or somehow situated *near* more congenial neighbors than surround us." Jane Nicholson, however, was adamantly opposed, preferring to remain in Harveysburg near her mother and family. She prevailed, as the Nicholsons did not leave for any community.[67]

As the interest in ultraist reform around Harveysburg declined, Valentine found himself more and more isolated. The Brookes' move back to Marlborough was a particular disappointment. So it was natural that when a new radical reform enterprise appeared nearby, it drew him into it.

The new community was at Yellow Springs, and its leaders were Dr. Thomas L. Nichols and his wife, Mary Gove Nichols. Valentine had first encountered Mary Gove in New York City in 1843, when she had attended both the American Anti-Slavery Society's annual meeting and the convention of the Society for Universal Inquiry and Reform, and had so impressed him. Mary Nichols had had a wildly checkered life that had led her from Presbyterianism to Orthodox Quakerism to health reform, abolition, and Fourierism as well as some fame as a writer of novels and short stories. Estranged from her ne'er-do-well husband Hiram Gove, she had taken up with an English communitarian, Henry G. Wright. After his death, she married Thomas L. Nichols, an editor and writer who subsequently acquired a medical degree. They ran a water-cure establishment for women and became firm adherents to spiritualism. In 1854 they arrived in Cincinnati, where they began publishing a journal and formed a group, the Progressive Union, to advocate their views.[68] All of this would have raised questions in many minds, but what made the Nicholses notorious was their commitment to free love.

It is difficult to describe the depth of horror that "free love" evoked for most Americans in the 1850s. It conjured up sexual promiscuity and unbridled lust, the end of marriage and the family. Its advocates were, in fact, typical health reformers who often saw sexual intercourse as inherently debilitating, and thus to be engaged in with restraint. But they did see the institution of marriage as inherently flawed; Thomas Nichols proclaimed that "it is by marriage that the great evils of civilization are produced and perpetuated." Natural Law had inclined humans toward "passional attention" with more than one person; denying this led to declining health and disease. And marriage itself, with its oppression of women and unwanted children, was a fertile source of evil. On this basis, in 1856 the Nicholses arrived in Yellow Springs, Ohio, to convert an empty water-cure establishment into the Memnonia Institute, a boarding school in which their ideas would be taught.[69]

Valentine's precise involvement in Memnonia is uncertain, but it is clear that he became a close associate of the Nicholses. By the autumn of 1856, he was one of the publishers of *Nichols' Monthly,* as well as its financial agent. He saw the Nicholses as one of the instrumentalities for "the healing of the nations." The *Monthly* would spread the glad news of "the progress of a new society" which was being formed. "The numbers are being found," Nicholson told readers, and "angels and spirits are writing, impressing, advising and encouraging every one . . . [to] become truly the recipients of heavenly knowledge and wisdom." Nicholson's own involvement in Free Love is not clear. Memnonia, however, was short-lived. In 1857 encounters with the "spirit" of a Jesuit led the Nicholses to convert to Catholicism, an unlikely end for two such ultraist reformers.[70]

After the collapse of Memnonia, Valentine apparently went into a period of depression and conflict with his family that culminated with his departure from them in 1864. The immediate issue is unknown, but Jane Nicholson and the three surviving daughters, Martha, Mary, and Elizabeth, were deeply alienated, seeing Valentine as disturbed, perhaps even insane. After Martha married Horace McKay, they all moved to Indianapolis. Horace McKay established himself there as one of the city's leading bankers and businessmen, a friend of President Benjamin Harrison and an active Republican. Neither Mary or Elizabeth, (Libbie, as the family called her), ever married. Mary Nicholson became one of Indianapolis's best-loved educators, while Libbie Nicholson became well known after study abroad as an artist and teacher. All three sisters, with Jane, became pillars of the woman's club and state woman's rights movement. Jane made a deep impression on the clubwomen, attending their meetings in her plain Quaker dress.[71]

Valentine, in contrast, began twenty years of wandering. From Wisconsin to Indiana to Illinois to Ohio to Missouri he moved, seldom remaining in one place long. At one time he bought a small vineyard in Missouri, but soon gave up raising grapes. In 1871 he considered becoming a Shaker. "The fact is that I have for years been a Shaker in faith and principle," he wrote to Jane and Martha. He changed his mind about joining, but did live for a considerable time at Union Village near his old home in Ohio. Occasionally he visited Jane and his daughters in Indianapolis, occasions that usually brought them pain and frustration mixed with pleasure.[72]

In all of his wanderings, however, Valentine did not give up his reform interests. He remained an enthusiastic spiritualist—most of his diary entries for the 1870s and 1880s are accounts of seances. One of his favorite neighborhoods was Fountain County, Indiana, where still lived the Cranes, Romines, and others who once had supported the Grand Prairie Community and John O. Wattles's Harmonial Institute. They kept up one of the last yearly meetings of Congregational Friends, now calling themselves Friends of Human Progress. He remained a fast supporter of woman's rights, soliciting subscriptions for Susan B. Anthony's journal, the *National Citizen*. His nonresistant principles had slipped away, but in politics he was still a radical, in the 1870s and 1880s, a Greenbacker. "The Money Lords . . . are diligently preparing to put their usurpations in practise in America, the same as they have long been doing in England and Ireland, where they have interfered with the rights of the people to life, liberty, and the pursuit of happiness," he wrote in 1882. "First usurping all the land, and hiring bands of armed men, to compel the laboring to pay all the tribute they choose to exact from them, or starve to death, which they prefer." For him, the United States Constitution, with its protections of property rights, was still "a Covenant with Death," an instrument of "cruel, heartless despotism."[73]

In 1883 Valentine went back to Warren County to make his home with Jane's brother-in-law, Henry T. Butterworth. The kindly Butterworth family welcomed him, but within two years the relationship had become strained. "It is just the same old story," wrote one of the family, "a constant correspondence and visiting female mediums to investigate etc. and mother has had from one to a half doz at a time to wait on and cook for from a day to weeks." Henry T. Butterworth was equally frank in his assessment. "He has worked here incessantly over two years and it amounts to worse than nothing, only to make himself vexed and mad because the Dr. June and other prophecys [*sic*] are proving to be lies." Butterworth concluded sorrowfully that "he is an insane man." For a few more years Valentine continued his wandering. Finally, about 1890, he settled in Indianapolis with his family.[74]

For the next decade Valentine lived quietly in Indianapolis. He made his peace with religion, attending a variety of churches, but most often the Orthodox Friends meeting not too far from his home. In politics he continued his nonconformist ways. "We are all very much mortified that he is going to vote for Bryan—the wildest ticket in the field," a disgusted Libbie wrote just before the presidential election of 1896.[75]

In 1900 Valentine and Jane observed their seventieth anniversary, doubtless an occasion for mixed feelings for the whole family. He died March 23, 1904, almost 95. Jane survived him by two years, dying in 1906 at the age of 100. Valentine's obituary presented his life in the most respectable way imaginable. He was a "noted abolitionist," a reformer of the school of Brook Farm, a friend

Valentine Nicholson in 1900. Original in possession of Theodore L. Steele.

of Edwin M. Stanton and Lucretia Mott. Nothing was said of spiritualism, or socialism, or of Universal Inquiry and Reform.[76]

The lives of the Universal Reformers after 1846 thus went further on many of the paths they had embarked on earlier. Some continued to embrace communitarianism. All remained committed to radical reforms. Many experimented with radical politics, especially those that challenged the capitalist system. They also continued their religious searches, with most finding a home in spiritualism. On the other hand, their commitment to nonresistance faded, as they reentered politics and made their peace with coercive government.

Most striking is the ongoing commitment of the Universal Reformers to challenging competitive capitalism. They were not, of course, agreed on how best to do that. For John O. Wattles, it meant participation in communitarianism in Ohio, Illinois, and Indiana. Both Valentine Nicholson and Orson S. Murray tried to revive Prairie Home, or a semblance thereof, in Warren County, Ohio; and it was only the opposition of Jane Nicholson that kept Valentine

Jane Nicholson in 1900.
Original in possession of
Theodore L. Steele.

from investigating still other communitarian ventures in the 1850s. In the 1870s he did again participate in one, this time among the Shakers. It was some time after Universal Reform collapsed before Abraham Brooke would compromise with competitive capitalism in any way. Collins, while apparently eschewing communitarianism, was committed to cooperative economics in the 1870s and 1880s.

The Universal Reformers also remained committed abolitionists. The Brookes and Nicholsons aided both free blacks and fugitive slaves. Murray still made "the slave power" and its minions prime targets of the struggling *Regenerator*. Wattles went to "Bleeding Kansas" in the 1850s to fight for freedom. Only Collins appears to have turned his back completely on the antislavery cause.

It was not surprising that Universal Reformers found themselves drawn into new radical reforms after 1850. Woman's rights was probably the most notable example. The first woman's rights conventions in both Ohio and Indiana featured Universal Reformers in prominent roles. John O. Wattles was one of the most important figures in the movement in Kansas in its first stirrings. Valentine Nicholson was still working for the cause in the 1880s. Two of the nation's first female physicians, Mary F. Thomas and Marenda B. Randall, were former residents of, respectively, Marlborough and Skaneateles.

It is also not surprising to find that few of the Universal Reformers appear to have returned to the verities of "sectism" and "priestcraft." The Collinses appear to have been almost unique, and John A. Collins's return to the "bosom of the orthodox pro-slavery church" was, of course, only temporary. Of the other Universal Reformers of whose subsequent careers we have knowledge, only Mary F. Thomas became a member of an evangelical church, in her case the Methodist. For many, especially the Hicksites, the logical progression was to the Progressive or Congregational Friends, quite possibly the most radical religious persuasion that could be found in antebellum America, repudiating all denominational discipline and organization and every semblance of creedalism, committed to virtually every reform cause, no matter how ultraist.

Particularly striking, of course, is the attraction that spiritualism held for Universal Reformers. Of the six leaders, only the atheist Murray was not a convert. Wattles, Mendenhall, Nicholson, and Brooke were all early and enthusiastic investigators of spiritualist phenomena, and all remained supporters, at least in some degree, until they died. It is unclear when Collins became a spiritualist, but he died a convinced one.

The Universal Reformers were, of course, hardly unique in feeling the attraction of spiritualism. It held particular appeal for Progressive Friends—by the 1870s virtually all had become involved in the spiritualist movement. And numerous antebellum reformers were caught up in it.

Historians have advanced various explanations for the appeal of spiritualism. Some have seen it as satisfying one of the oldest of all human urges—to have contact once again with loved ones "gone before." Some have linked it to the emerging woman's rights movement. Some have seen it as the ultimate flowering of the Romantic repudiation of a cold, mechanical world order.

For the Universal Reformers, however, another attraction would be crucial. They had striven mightily for nothing less than a remaking of the world, according to what they were convinced was nothing less than God's plan for it. They had actually commenced the work of ushering in the Government of God, only to see it fail. Thus it was only natural that they would look for new leadings, new light. And how better to do it than through the guidance of angels and good spirits?

Even as they moved toward spiritualism, however, the Universal Reformers were leaving behind nonresistance. With the exception of Collins, none ever explicitly repudiated it. Instead, nonresistance slipped from them without much apparent notice or reflection. There is nothing to indicate that any of the Universal Reformers actively bore arms during the Civil War (all would have been rather old for that), but there is also nothing to show that they had any qualms about it. Certainly, by the 1850s, all had made their peace with politics.

When Esther Wattles died in 1908, her obituary described her as one of the last of a noble band, the abolitionists who had fearlessly crusaded against slavery and brought about emancipation. Her husband's life was also duly noted—a missionary who had found his calling as a reformer at home rather than abroad. But of nonresistance and communities and Universal Inquiry and Reform there was not a word. With Esther Wattles's death the last adult memories passed away. Her obituary might well have been that of Universal Inquiry and Reform. As part of the abolitionist movement, it was remembered as idealistic and heroic. In its advocacy of woman's rights, it may well have laid some of the foundations for that movement in at least three states. But its legacies of communitarianism and nonresistance, like the legacies of the larger communitarian and nonresistant movements, were uncertain.[77]

APPENDIX

THE CONSTITUTION OF THE FRATERNAL BROTHERHOOD

Preamble

To the Constitution of the Fraternal Brotherhood

Whereas in the course of human progression, new and higher conditions of life become developed, which necessarily call for a new and more perfect system of government in human affairs; and whereas, the present systems of government religion and commerce, have filled their measure of good, and can no longer supply the high demands of liberty and justice as now being called for by the higher unfoldings of humanity; and whereas, it is one of the divine economies of wisdom to cease using any and all means, when because formerly, except to assess, and seek those that are better adapted to the accomplishing of the great and divine objects of life, it therefore becomes the duty of all persons who feel themselves developed upon the higher planes of practical humanity to use their individual and united efforts to advance and promote these high and holy ends.

Constitution

One for this purpose, a new order of human society is hereby organized upon the principles of Liberty, Justice, and Equality to be called the Fraternal Brotherhood.

Objects

Our object is

1st To unfold and unite all affections of mankind, and to harmonize isolated interests in the mutual and general good.

2nd To establish local Fraternities throughout the earth, and to unite with them in all peaceable and honorable means to promote their general happiness.

3rd To institute a perfect system of equitable commerce by making cost the limit of price, between all such Fraternities where ever they may exist.

4th To secure to each member of the Fraternity, a comfortable home, by means of honest industry, without overtaxing the system with labor, so as to conflict with the laws of life and health.

5th To render labor honorable and attractive, by securing to each member, such occupations as harmonize with their organic inclinations.

6th To educate all in the arts and sciences, and to give them a thorough knowledge of the laws of life and health and their adaptation to the physical world.

7th To give all a true and philosophical conception of their spiritual nature, and the relation they sustain to the angelic world.

Rights and Occupations

Man being septenary in his nature, his natural rights or wants on earth may be reduced to seven general kinds, viz.

1st Soil, on which to labor, 2nd A Habitation in which to dwell, 3rd Raiment wherewith to be clad, 4th Food to sustain life, 5th Implements where with to produce, 6th A knowledge of his physical being and its surroundings, 7th A knowledge of his spiritual nature and the being by which it is governed.

All of which may be obtained by dividing each fraternity into seven divisions or groups, and each group following one of the natural employments of life, which consist in the following occupations, viz.

1st Aggriculture [sic], 2nd Domestic, 3rd Mechanical, 4th Manufactury, 5th Commercial, 6th Education of the physical, 7th Education of the spiritual

Plan of Operation

1st Of buildings. These to be built on the Circular and Septenary principle, i.e., they are to be built in circular teers [sic], and seven teers to constitute the habitation of one Fraternity. An Educational edifice to occupy the center of the domain. The extension circle to contain the dwellings and to be intermediately occupied by those for a mechanical and Commercial purpose.

2nd Individuality of families. Each family to own a separate apartment for dwelling house and gardening purposes.

3rd Cooperation of labor. All members following the same occupation, to work in groups, and to hold equal shares in the Firm to which they belong

4th Equitable distribution of profits. Each member to be compensated according to time and value of labor and to be entitled to all the resources of life and comfort, at cost, making their interests mutual.

5th Of Guaranties. Each member to hold a certificate from the clerk, for the amount of capitol [sic] they invest.

6th Of Superintendents. These to consist of one Instructor to each group of the Fraternity, to be chosen by the group to which he or she belong, and one Clerk to be chosen by the Fraternity, whose duty it is to keep a just and correct minute of all the commercial proceedings, and the general progress of the confederacy, and to receive compensation equal with other members.

7th Of Obituary and withdrawal. Any member personally withdrawing, or when any member dies, leaving heirs with out the Fraternity, such member or the heirs their of shall not be entitled to a final settlement, or return of the property invested, or the value thereof, in any time less than from 2 to 5 years, to be paid in five equal payments at the end of one and two 3 4 and 5 years from the date of said death or withdrawal.

Agreement

We whose names are here annexed do agree to be governed by the principles set forth in this constitution, so long as they seem to effect the objects herein contained, but will change and adopt any new and better system of government, when made tangible to our understanding.

Source: Valentine Nicholson Papers, Indiana Historical Society

NOTES

Introduction

1. Valentine Nicholson, "Autobiography," July 4, 1881, typescript, Valentine Nicholson Papers (Indiana Historical Society, Indianapolis); Henry T. Butterworth to Elizabeth Nicholson, Feb. 27, 1885, ibid.

2. David Brion Davis, "The Emergence of Immediatism in British and American Antislavery Thought," *Mississippi Valley Historical Review*, 49 (Sept. 1962), 215. For the evolution of antislavery thought, see David Brion Davis, *The Problem of Slavery in Western Culture* (Ithaca: Cornell University Press, 1966); and David Brion Davis, *The Problem of Slavery in the Age of Revolution, 1770–1823* (Ithaca: Cornell University Press, 1975).

3. Davis, "Emergence of Immediatism," 228.

4. James Brewer Stewart, *Holy Warriors: The Abolitionists and American Slavery* (New York: Hill and Wang, 1976), 38–49.

5. Gilbert Hobbs Barnes, *The Antislavery Impulse, 1830–1844* (New York: Harcourt Brace, 1964), 3–28; Bertram Wyatt-Brown, "Conscience and Career: Young Abolitionists and Missionaries," in *Antislavery, Religion, and Reform: Essays in Memory of Roger Anstey*, ed. Christine Bolt and Seymour Drescher (Hamden, Conn.: Archon, 1980), 183–203.

6. Stewart, *Holy Warriors*, 35. The literature on Charles G. Finney and his impact on antebellum reform is considerable. See, for example, Whitney R. Cross, *The Burned-over District: The Social and Intellectual History of Enthusiastic Religion in Western New York, 1800–1850* (Ithaca: Cornell University Press, 1950), 151–69; Robert H. Abzug, *Passionate Liberator: Theodore Dwight Weld and the Dilemma of Reform* (New York: Oxford University Press, 1980), 39–51; Nancy A. Hewitt, *Women's Activism and Social Change: Rochester, New York, 1822–1872* (Ithaca: Cornell University Press, 1984), 28–29; and Paul E. Johnson, *A Shopkeeper's Millennium: Society and Revivals in Rochester, New York, 1815–1837* (New York: Hill and Wang, 1978).

7. There is a vast literature in answer to the question: "Who were the abolitionists?" The starting point is David H. Donald, "Toward a Reconsideration of the Abolitionists," in *Lincoln Reconsidered* (New York: Vintage, 1956), 19–36. David H. Donald's argument that abolitionists were the products of "status anxiety" provoked a number of examinations. Among the most influential are Larry Gara, "Who Was an Abolitionist?" in *The Antislavery Vanguard: New Essays on the Abolitionists*, ed. Martin Duberman (Princeton: Princeton University Press, 1965), 32–51; Lawrence J. Friedman, *Gregarious Saints: Self and Community in American Abolitionism, 1830–1870* (New York: Cambridge University Press, 1982), 11–40; Edward Magdol, *The Antislavery Rank and File: A Social*

Profile of the Abolitionists' Constituency (Westport: Greenwood, 1986); and Wyatt-Brown, "Conscience and Career."

8. For millennialism, see Ernest Lee Tuveson, *Redeemer Nation: The Idea of America's Millennial Role* (Chicago: University of Chicago Press, 1968). For its connections with reform, see Ronald G. Walters, *American Reformers, 1815–1860* (New York: Hill and Wang, 1978), 21–37; and Michael Barkun, *Crucible of the Millennium: The Burned-Over District of New York in the 1840s* (Syracuse: Syracuse University Press, 1986).

9. Davis, "Emergence of Immediatism."

10. John L. Thomas, *The Liberator: William Lloyd Garrison: A Biography* (Boston: Little Brown, 1963), 114–28; Stewart, *Holy Warriors,* 50–53.

11. Stewart, *Holy Warriors,* 50–73; Thomas, *Liberator,* 188–208.

12. Stewart, *Holy Warriors,* 89.

13. Aileen S. Kraditor, *Means and Ends in American Abolitionism: Garrison and His Critics on Strategy and Tactics, 1834–1850* (Chicago: Ivan R. Dee, 1989), 78–117; John R. McKivigan, *The War on Proslavery Religion: Abolitionism and the Northern Churches, 1830–1865* (Ithaca: Cornell University Press, 1984), 56–73, 93–110.

14. Blanche Glassman Hersh, *The Slavery of Sex: Feminist Abolitionists in America* (Urbana: University of Illinois Press, 1978), 6–38; Gerda Lerner, *The Grimke Sisters from South Carolina: Pioneers for Woman's Rights and Abolition* (New York: Schocken, 1971), 165–204.

15. Lewis Perry, *Radical Abolitionism: Anarchy and the Government of God in Antislavery Thought* (Ithaca: Cornell University Press, 1973), 58; Valarie H. Ziegler, *The Advocates of Peace in Antebellum America* (Bloomington: Indiana University Press, 1992), 48–87.

16. Perry, *Radical Abolitionism,* 18–91.

17. Ibid., 92–128.

18. Stewart, *Holy Warriors,* 74–96.

19. There is no comprehensive work on Quaker benevolence and philanthropy. For a suggestive treatment of its origins, see Sydney V. James, *A People among Peoples: Quaker Benevolence in Eighteenth-Century America* (Cambridge: Harvard University Press, 1963); but cf. Jack D. Marietta, *The Reformation of American Quakerism, 1748–1783* (Philadelphia: University of Pennsylvania Press, 1984). A good brief account is Hugh Barbour and J. William Frost, *The Quakers* (Westport: Greenwood, 1988), 153–67.

20. On the Hicksite separation, see Robert W. Doherty, *The Hicksite Separation: A Sociological Analysis of Religious Schism in Early Nineteenth-Century America* (New Brunswick: Rutgers University Press, 1967); and H. Larry Ingle, *Quakers in Conflict: The Hicksite Reformation* (Knoxville: University of Tennessee Press, 1986). For a view of the Orthodox somewhat different from that of Robert W. Doherty and H. Larry Ingle, see Thomas D. Hamm, *The Transformation of American Quakerism: Orthodox Friends, 1800–1907* (Bloomington: Indiana University Press, 1988), 12–35.

21. Ingle, *Quakers in Conflict,* 3–15, 38–61.

22. Rufus M. Jones, *The Later Periods of Quakerism* (2 vols., London: Macmillan, 1921), I, 470–72, 477, 480–81. Before the twentieth century, American Quakers had no

national decision-making bodies. Yearly meetings, made up of Friends in a particular geographical area, possessed ultimate authority. Yearly meetings were made up of quarterly meetings, which met four times a year to pass on matters of business. Quarterly meetings, in turn, were made up of two or more monthly meetings, the basic business unit among Friends. Monthly meetings had the power to receive and disown (the Quaker term for excommunicate) members, solemnize marriages, and hold property. See Hamm, *Transformation,* xvi-xvii.

23. I examine this in my paper, "The Limits of the Peace Testimony: Hicksite Friends and the Nonresistance Movement," paper read at Swarthmore College Conference on Nineteenth-Century Feminist Strategies for Peace, March 21, 1993.

24. See, generally, Ingle, *Quakers in Conflict;* and Doherty, *Hicksite Separation.*

25. For a ferocious attack on Quakers, especially Hicksite Quakers, by a leading Presbyterian abolitionist, see Samuel Hanson Cox, *Quakerism Not Christianity: or, Reasons for Renouncing the Doctrine of Friends* (New York: D. Fanshaw, 1833).

26. Catherine L. Albanese, *Nature Religion in America: From the Algonkian Indians to the New Age* (Chicago: University of Chicago Press, 1990), 1-15, 117-52.

27. There is a sizable literature on antebellum American communitarianism. Incisive interpretative works include Rosabeth Moss Kanter, *Commitment and Community: Communes and Utopias in Sociological Perspective* (Cambridge: Harvard University Press, 1972); Michael Fellman, *The Unbounded Frame: Freedom and Community in Nineteenth-Century American Utopianism* (Westport: Greenwood, 1973); Edward K. Spann, *Brotherly Tomorrows: Movements for the Cooperative Society in America, 1820–1920* (New York: Columbia University Press, 1988); and Arthur Eugene Bestor Jr., *Backwoods Utopias: The Sectarian and Owenite Phases of Communitarian Socialism in America, 1663–1829* (Philadelphia: University of Pennsylvania Press, 1950). For specific movements, see John F. C. Harrison, *Quest for the New Moral World: Robert Owen and the Owenites in Britain and America* (New York: Charles Scribner's Sons, 1969); Carl J. Guarneri, *The Utopian Alternative: Fourierism in Nineteenth-Century America* (Ithaca: Cornell University Press, 1991); and Stephen J. Stein, *The Shaker Experience in America: A History of the United Society of Believers* (New Haven: Yale University Press, 1992). For gender considerations, see Louis J. Kern, *An Ordered Love: Sex Roles and Sexuality in Victorian Utopias—The Shakers, the Mormons, and the Oneida Community* (Chapel Hill: University of North Carolina Press, 1981); Carol A. Kolmerten, *Women in Utopia: The Ideology of Gender in the American Owenite Communities* (Bloomington: Indiana University Press, 1990); and Wendy Chmielewski, Louis J. Kern, and Marilyn Klee Hartzell, eds., *Women in Spiritual and Communitarian Societies in the United States* (Syracuse: Syracuse University Press, 1993). The only work looking at Quakers and communitarian movements is T. D. Seymour Bassett, "The Quakers and Communitarianism," *Bulletin of Friends Historical Association,* 43 (Autumn 1954), 84-99.

28. For Hopedale, see Perry, *Radical Abolitionism,* 129-57. For Skaneateles, see John L. Thomas, "Antislavery and Utopia," in *The Antislavery Vanguard,* ed. Duberman, 240-69; and Lester Grosvenor Wells, *The Skaneateles Communal Experiment, 1843–1846* (Syracuse: Onondaga Historical Association, 1953). Carleton Mabee, in his discussion of

communities that grew out of the nonresistant movement, mentions only Skaneateles. See Carleton Mabee, *Black Freedom: The Nonviolent Abolitionists from 1830 through the Civil War* (New York: Macmillan, 1970), 79–80.

29. See note 27.

30. Perry, *Radical Abolitionism*, xi.

1. The Evangelical Roots of Universal Reform

1. John R. Totten, "Thacher-Thatcher Genealogy," *New York Genealogical and Biographical Record*, 43 (July 1912), 256, 265; Timothy Hopkins, *Kelloggs in the New World* (N.p., n.d.), 373; Dwight H. Bruce, *Onondaga's Centennial* (2 vols., Boston: Historical Publishing Company, 1896), I, 779; *The History of Edwards County, Illinois, including Edwards and Wabash Counties* (Philadelphia: J. L. McDonough, 1883), 66; Willard C. Heiss, comp., Howland-Otis-Wattles Genealogy, Willard C. Heiss Collection (Friends Collection, Lilly Library, Earlham College, Richmond, Ind.); W. M. Beauchamp, *Revolutionary Soldiers Resident or Dying in Onondaga County, New York* (Syracuse: Onondaga Historical Association, 1913), 277.

2. Theano Wattles Case genealogical chart, ca. 1950, John O. Wattles Papers (Western Reserve Historical Society, Cleveland); Peleg Thomas, "A Hymn for the Young Convert" [1830], ibid.; Richard L. Bushman, *From Puritan to Yankee: Character and the Social Order in Connecticut, 1690–1765* (New York: Norton, 1967), 183–95; D. Hamilton Hurd, *History of New London County, Connecticut, with Biographical Sketches of Many of Its Pioneers and Prominent Men* (Philadelphia: J. W. Lewis, 1882), 524.

3. Case genealogical chart; Theano Wattles Case to Mrs. Sprentall, Nov. 14, 1924, Wattles Papers; Valentine Nicholson, Autobiography, July 1, 1881, typescript, p. 57 (Valentine Nicholson Papers, Indiana Historical Society, Indianapolis); Mrs. O. E. Morse, "Sketch of the Life and Work of Augustus Wattles," *Collections of the Kansas State Historical Society*, 17 (1928), 290.

4. John O. Wattles to Daughters, July [1853], Wattles Papers.

5. Erastus and John O. Wattles family record, n.d., Wattles Papers; Peleg Thomas, Poem on death of Eliza Wattles, Jan. 5, 1833, ibid.; Eliza Wattles scrapbook, ibid.; Morse, "Sketch," 290–99; John L. Myers, "Antislavery Activities of Five Lane Seminary Boys in 1835–36," *Bulletin of the Historical and Philosophical Society of Ohio*, 21 (April 1963), 110–11.

6. Wattles family record; Bertram Wyatt-Brown, "Conscience and Career: Young Abolitionists and Missionaries," in *Anti-Slavery, Religion, and Reform: Essays in Memory of Roger Anstey*, ed. Christine Bolt and Seymour Drescher (Hamden, Conn.: Archon, 1980), 199; Wattles to Daughters, July [1853], Nov. 18, 1854, Wattles Papers.

7. Wattles to Daughters, July [1853]; Esther Whinery Wattles, Reminiscences, n.d., Wattles Papers; "Trigonometry and Surveying" Notebook, Dec. 24, 1824, ibid.; School subscription list, March 20, 1833, ibid.; Esther Wattles, "Miscellaneous Writings," n.d., ibid.; Stewart Holbrook, *The Yankee Exodus: An Account of Migration from New England* (Seattle: University of Washington Press, 1968), 18–19.

8. Wattles to Daughters, July [1853]. This letter describes a visit to Goshen and is valuable for its reminiscences of John O. Wattles's early life, the only ones known to have survived. For the centrality of the conversion experience in the lives of evangelical reformers, see Wyatt-Brown, "Conscience and Career," 192–93; James Brewer Stewart, *Holy Warriors: The Abolitionists and American Slavery* (New York: Hill and Wang, 1976), 13–14; and Ronald G. Walters, *American Reformers, 1815–1860* (New York: Hill and Wang, 1978), 21–37.

9. Wyatt-Brown, "Conscience and Career"; Esther Wattles, "Reminiscences."

10. Milton C. Sernett, *Abolition's Axe: Beriah Green, Oneida Institute, and the Black Freedom Struggle* (Syracuse: Syracuse University Press, 1986), 32–37; "Oneida Institute. Order of Exercises at the Anniversary, Wednesday, August 31, 1831," Wattles Papers.

11. John O. Wattles Diary, June 23, 1833, Wattles Papers; John O. Wattles to "Dear Brother," Dec. 25, 1835, box 2, Treasurer's Office Papers (Oberlin College Archives, Mudd Library, Oberlin, Ohio).

12. John O. Wattles, "Holy Living," notes on back of "Oneida Institute. Order of Exercises," Wattles Papers; Untitled Notebook [ca. 1833], ibid.

13. Wattles Diary, June 25, June 29, July 20, 1833; John O. Wattles to "Dear Brother."

14. Wattles Diary, July 20, July 27, Aug. 1, Aug. 10, Aug. 11, 1833.

15. Wattles to "Dear Brother"; Morse, "Sketch," 290–91; Myers, "Antislavery Activities," 110–11; Lawrence Thomas Lesick, *The Lane Rebels: Evangelicalism and Antislavery in Antebellum America* (Metuchen, N.J.: Scarecrow, 1980); Celestia Wattles, Memorandum on Augustus Wattles [ca. 1900], Wattles Papers; Oliver Johnson, *William Lloyd Garrison and His Times* (Boston: Houghton Mifflin, 1881), 170.

16. "From Augustus Wattles," *Philanthropist*, Nov. 7, 1837; James B. Shotwell, *A History of the Schools of Cincinnati* (Cincinnati: School Publishing Company, 1902), 447–61; Wendell Phillips Dabney, *Cincinnati's Colored Citizens: Historical, Sociological, and Biographical* (Cincinnati: Dabney Publishing Co., 1926), 101–102.

17. Edward Nicholas Clopper, *An American Family: Its Ups and Downs through Eight Generations in New Amsterdam, New York, Pennsylvania, Maryland, Ohio, and Texas, from 1650 to 1880* (Huntington, W. V.: Standard Printing & Publishing Co., 1950), 279–81, 284, 419; Stanley Harrold, *Gamaliel Bailey and Antislavery Union* (Kent: Kent State University Press, 1986), 16–17.

18. Clopper, *American Family*, 279–80; Advertisement, *Philanthropist*, Dec. 18, 1838.

19. School attendance record, 1838, Wattles Papers; Catherine Ludlow et al. agreement [1838], ibid.; John O. Wattles, Essay on the Millennium, Oct. 12, 1838, ibid.

20. Sarah Stephens to John O. Wattles, Oct. 25, 1840, Wattles Papers; Elizabeth L. Dyer to John O. Wattles, July 30, 1840, ibid.; Douglas Andrew Gamble, "Moral Suasion in the West: Garrisonian Abolitionism, 1831–1861" (Ph.D. diss., Ohio State University, 1973), 191–218.

21. Gamble, "Moral Suasion," 207; "Church, Ministry, and Sabbath Conference," *Non-Resistant*, Oct. 28, 1840; "Letter from John O. Wattles," ibid., Jan. 25, 1841; ibid., Feb. 10, 1841; ibid., June 24, 1840; ibid., April 28, 1841; "Henry C. Wright—Non-Resistance Agencies," ibid., Oct. 18, 1840; "From Vermont," *Pennsylvania Freeman*, 3rd Mo. 17, 1841; "Interesting Letter from J. O. Wattles," *Vermont Telegraph*, April 7, 1841.

22. John A. Collins has no adequate biography. The best available account is in Robert S. Fogarty, *Dictionary of American Communal and Utopian History* (Westport: Greenwood, 1980), 24–25. Considerable detail on his early life appears in John A. Collins, "A Papal Bull," *Communitist*, Jan. 29, 1845. For Collins's education, see *Catalogue of the Trustees, Instructors, & Students of Burr Seminary, Manchester, June 1835* (Windsor, Vt.: Chronicle, 1835); and *General Catalogue of the Theological Seminary, Andover, Massachusetts, 1808–1908* (Boston: Thomas Todd [1909]), 177.

23. Collins, "Papal Bull"; "Communication from M. W. Jenkins," *Regenerator*, Dec. 13, 1847; "John A. Collins," *Anti-Slavery Bugle*, Aug. 28, 1846; Deborah Weston to Anne Warren Weston, May 3, 1839, vol. 11, p. 95, Weston Family Papers (Rare Books Department, Boston Public Library, Boston); American Antiquarian Society, comp., *Index of Marriages in Massachusetts Centinel and Columbian Centinel, 1784 to 1840* (4 vols., Boston: G. K. Hall, 1961), I, 806.

24. *General Catalogue*, 177; Sydney E. Ahlstrom, *A Religious History of the American People* (New Haven: Yale University Press, 1972), 394.

25. *General Catalogue*, 177; J. Earl Thompson Jr., "Abolitionism and Theological Education at Andover," *New England Quarterly*, 47 (June 1974), 237–61.

26. For accounts of this controversy, see John L. Thomas, *The Liberator: William Lloyd Garrison: A Biography* (Boston: Little Brown, 1963), 236–64; and John R. McKivigan, *The War against Proslavery Religion: Abolitionism and the Northern Clergy, 1830–1865* (Ithaca: Cornell University Press, 1984), 61–62. For the larger questions of women in the abolitionist movement, see Aileen S. Kraditor, *Means and Ends in American Abolitionism: Garrison and His Critics on Strategy and Tactics, 1834–1850* (Chicago: Ivan R. Dee, 1989), 37–77; and Blanche Glassman Hersh, *The Slavery of Sex: Feminist-Abolitionists in America* (Urbana: University of Illinois Press, 1978), 18–24.

27. Thomas, *Liberator*, 264–72. For Collins's own account, see John A. Collins, *Right and Wrong among the Abolitionists of the United States; or the Object, Principles, and Measures of the Original American Anti-Slavery Society Unchanged: Being a Defence against the Assaults of the Recently Formed Massachusetts Abolition, and the American and Foreign Anti-Slavery Societies: Embodying a Statement of Facts, from Official and Other Documents, with Respect to the Origin and Progress of the Division among the Abolitionists of the United States* (Glasgow: Geo. Gallis, 1841), 67.

28. Lawrence J. Friedman, *Gregarious Saints: Self and Community in American Abolitionism, 1830–1870* (New York: Cambridge University Press, 1982), 45–46; Kraditor, *Means and Ends*, 51; *Eleventh Annual Report, Presented to the Massachusetts Anti-Slavery Society, By Its Board of Managers, January 25, 1843* (Boston [1843]), 44, 87; *Ninth Annual Report of the Board of Managers of the Massachusetts Anti-Slavery Society. Presented January 27, 1841* (Boston [1841]), 32; Johnson, *William Lloyd Garrison*, 300; Collins, *Right and Wrong*, 64; Lucia Weston to Deborah Weston, July 1839, vol. 11, p. 128, Weston Papers; Carleton Mabee, *Black Freedom: The Nonviolent Abolitionists from 1830 through the Civil War* (New York: Macmillan, 1970), 76.

29. *Ninth Annual Report*, 32–33; *Eleventh Annual Report*, 40–41; Thomas, *Liberator*, 289–90.

30. Thomas, *Liberator*, 290–91.

31. Ibid., 291–92.

32. Collins, *Right and Wrong,* 64; Deborah Weston to Lucia Weston, June 16, 1840, vol. 13, p. 86, Weston Papers.

33. John A. Collins to Gerrit Smith, Sept. 14, 1840, box 7, Gerrit Smith Papers (Arents Research Library, Syracuse University, Syracuse, N.Y.); Collins to William Lloyd Garrison, Sept. 1, 1840, in [Francis Jackson Garrison and Wendell Phillips Garrison], *William Lloyd Garrison, 1805–1879: The Story of His Life Told by His Children* (4 vols., New York: Century, 1885–89), II, 414–15; Thomas, *Liberator,* 301–304.

34. C. Duncan Rice, *The Scots Abolitionists, 1833–1861* (Baton Rouge: Louisiana State University Press, 1981), 99–101.

35. C. C. Burleigh to J. S. Gibbons, Sept. 26, 1840, vol. 10, p. 2, Anti-Slavery Collection (Boston Public Library); John A. Collins credentials, Sept. 25, 1840, ibid., vol. 10, p. 1; Collins, *Right and Wrong,* 49, 64; Garrison to Collins, Oct. 16, 1840, in *The Letters of William Lloyd Garrison,* ed. Walter M. Merrill and Louis Ruchames (6 vols., Cambridge: Belknap, 1971–81), II, 717–20; Garrison to Elizabeth Pease, Dec. 1, 1840, ibid., II, 729.

36. Collins, *Right and Wrong,* 45–46, 60–62.

37. Ibid., 45–46, 56–59, 70–71; Rice, *Scots Abolitionists,* 102–105; Collins to Charles Stuart, Nov. 4, 1840, vol. 10, p. 33, Anti-Slavery Collection; Collins to Pease, Dec. 8, 1840, vol. 10, p. 81, ibid.

38. Rice, *Scots Abolitionists,* 102–103.

39. Charles Lenox Remond to Richard Allen, Jan. 7, 1841, in *The Black Abolitionist Papers,* ed. C. Peter Ripley et al. (5 vols., Chapel Hill: University of North Carolina Press, 1983–85), I, 85–87; Collins to Pease, Dec. 8, 1840; Collins to H. G. Chapman, Jan. 2, 1841, vol. 15, p. 6, Weston Papers.

40. Rice, *Scots Abolitionists,* 107–13.

41. Ibid., 113.

42. Ibid., 101, 111; Betty Fladeland, *Abolitionists and Working-Class Problems in the Age of Industrialization* (Baton Rouge: Louisiana State University Press, 1984), 118–19; Gregory Claeys, *Machinery, Money, and the Millennium: From Moral Economy to Socialism, 1815–1860* (Princeton: Princeton University Press, 1987), 34–66.

43. Collins to Pease, Aug. 15, 1841, vol. 12. 1, p. 103, Anti-Slavery Collection; J. A. Collins letter, *Pennsylvania Freeman,* June 2, 1841.

44. Collins to Pease, Aug. 15, 1841; Collins to Pease, July 4, 1841, Anti-Slavery Collection.

45. [Garrison and Garrison], *William Lloyd Garrison,* III, 17–18; Garrison and Ellis Gray Loring to Collins, April 1, 1841, in *Letters,* ed. Merrill and Ruchames, III, 20–21; Garrison to Pease, June 1, 1841, ibid., III, 24.

46. [Garrison and Garrison], *William Lloyd Garrison,* III, 17–18; "Letter from the General Agent of the Massachusetts Anti-Slavery Society," *Liberator,* Jan. 21, 1842; Garrison to Pease, Sept. 16, 1841, in *Letters,* ed. Merrill and Ruchames, III, 30; William S. McFeely, *Frederick Douglass* (New York: Norton, 1991), 87–89; Mabee, *Black Freedom,* 112–26.

47. Caroline Weston to Deborah Weston, June 24, 1842, vol. 17, p. 75, Weston Papers; Garrison to Helen E. Garrison, Nov. 21, 1842, in *Letters,* ed. Merrill and Ruchames, III, 108–109; John A. Collins, "American A. S. Society—Prospect of the Cause," *Liberator,*

May 20, 1842; John A. Collins, *The Anti-Slavery Picknick: A Collection of Speeches, Poems, Dialogues, and Songs, Intended for Use in Schools and Anti-Slavery Society Meetings* (Boston: H. W. Williams, 1842); Don Gleason Hill, ed., *The Record of Births, Marriages, and Deaths, and Intentions of Marriage, in the Town of Dedham* (2 vols., Dedham, Mass.: Dedham Transcript, 1886), II, 194.

48. David M. Ludlum, *Social Ferment in Vermont, 1791–1850* (New York: Columbia University Press, 1939), 57.

49. William B. Murray, *Descendants of Jonathan Murray, of East Guilford, Connecticut* (Peoria, 1958), 74; *Some of the Work of Charles B. Murray, Editor of the Cincinnati Price Current for Forty One Years, in Special Commercial and Statistical Journalism* (Cincinnati, 1914), 7. Charles B. Murray was the son of Orson S. Murray.

50. *Biographical Encyclopedia of Ohio* (Philadelphia: Galaxy Publishing Co., 1876), 232.

51. Ibid; Jonathan Murray obituary, *Regenerator*, May 8, 1846; [Charles B. Murray], "Death of Orson S. Murray," clipping [1885], Orson S. Murray Scrapbook, Nicholson Papers.

52. *Some of the Work*, 7.

53. [Murray], "Death of Orson S. Murray"; Russel B. Nye, *William Lloyd Garrison and the Humanitarian Reformers* (Boston: Little Brown, 1955), 5–35.

54. [Murray], "Death of Orson S. Murray." On colonization, see P. J. Staudenraus, *The African Colonization Movement, 1816–1865* (New York: Columbia University Press, 1961).

55. Thomas, *Liberator*, 147–54.

56. Orson S. Murray to Amos A. Phelps, Oct. 11, 1833, vol. 3, p. 49, Anti-Slavery Collection; John L. Myers, "The Beginning of Antislavery Agencies in Vermont, 1832–1836," *Vermont History*, 36 (Summer 1968), 131.

57. Myers, "Beginning," 131–32.

58. Stewart, *Holy Warriors*, 51; [Murray], "Death of Orson S. Murray."

59. Henry Crocker, *History of the Baptists in Vermont* (Bellows Falls, Vt.: P. H. Gobie Press, 1913), 124–25; Murray to Garrison, March 15, 1835, vol. 3, p. 22, Anti-Slavery Collection; Myers, "Beginning," 133; [Murray], "Death of Orson S. Murray"; John G. Whittier, "The Antislavery Convention of 1833," *Atlantic Monthly*, 33 (Feb. 1874), 168.

60. [Murray], "Death of Orson S. Murray"; Myers, "Beginning," 135; Murray to William Goodell, *Liberator*, March 8, 1834; O. S. Murray, "Mobocracy in Vermont," ibid., Feb. 28, 1835; Murray to editor of *Vermont State Journal*, ibid., Oct. 18, 1834; Murray letter, ibid., March 21, 1835.

61. "The Last Vermont Telegraph," *Vermont Telegraph*, Oct. 6, 1843; Ludlum, *Social Ferment*, 58–59. It is unclear how Murray raised the money to purchase the controlling interest.

62. "Last Vermont Telegraph"; Editorial, *Vermont Telegraph*, Oct. 1, 1835; ibid., June 2, 1836.

63. See, for example, "Temperance," *Vermont Telegraph*, Oct. 12, 1836; or the issue of September 28, 1836, with its columns on education, moral reform, abolition, and peace. For nonresistance generally, see Lewis Perry, *Radical Abolitionism: Anarchy and the Government of God in Antislavery Thought* (Ithaca: Cornell University Press, 1973); and

Valarie H. Ziegler, *The Advocates of Peace in Antebellum America* (Bloomington: Indiana University Press, 1992), 48–87.

64. Ludlum, *Social Ferment*, 169–75; Editorial, *Vermont Telegraph*, July 5, 1837; Garrison to Murray, Aug. 11, 1837, in *Letters*, ed. Merrill and Ruchames, II, 276–80.

65. Ludlum, *Social Ferment*, 169–71; "State Peace Convention," *Vermont Telegraph*, Aug. 28, 1837.

66. "State Peace Convention"; Ludlum, *Social Ferment*, 169–71.

67. Vermont Peace Society Constitution, *Vermont Telegraph*, Oct. 3, 1838; "On Earth Peace—Good Will Towards Men," ibid.; Perry, *Radical Abolitionism*, 55–91.

68. "On Earth Peace"; Murray letter, *Liberator*, Oct. 12, 1838.

69. Peter Brock, *Pacifism in the United States from the Colonial Era to the First World War* (Princeton: Princeton University Press, 1968), 550; "The Telegraph," *Vermont Telegraph*, Sept. 23, 1840.

70. "The Telegraph"; Ludlum, *Social Ferment*, 60; Editorial, *Vermont Telegraph*, Sept. 7, 1842; "To Postmasters & Subscribers," ibid., Dec. 28, 1842; "Sectarianism," ibid., Nov. 28, 1842; "My Pecuniary Affairs," ibid., March 29, 1843. Such objections appeared as early as 1837; typical was a subscriber in Cambridge, Vermont, who wrote to Murray that "we are all Anty [slavery] here but want a religeous [*sic*] paper when we sign for it." See "A Curiosity," *Liberator*, April 14, 1837.

71. "Last Vermont Telegraph"; Myers, "Beginning," 135; Ludlum, *Social Ferment*, 164–65; Crocker, *History*, 463; Editorial, *Vermont Telegraph*, Oct. 23, 1839; ibid., Oct. 6, 1841; " 'Vermont Observer'—Imposition Added to Fraud," ibid., Nov. 23, 1842; "My Suspension from the Orwell Church," ibid., Nov. 9, 1842. Eventually Murray condemned all "sectarian" antislavery societies. See "Sectarian Antislavery Societies," ibid., Oct. 12, 1842.

72. "Prospectus of Volume XV," *Vermont Telegraph*, Sept. 21, 1842.

73. Ibid.: "Editorial Correspondence," ibid., Feb. 15, 1843; Editorial, ibid., Dec. 7, 1842; [Murray], "Death of Orson S. Murray."

74. "Editorial Correspondence"; "Sectarian Anti-Slavery Societies," *Vermont Telegraph*, Feb. 15, 1843; "He Throws Away the Bible," ibid., April 19, 1843; Ahlstrom, *Religious History*, 503.

75. "My Late Tour," ibid., Sept. 28, 1842; "He Throws Away the Bible."

76. Editorial, ibid., Sept. 21, 1842.

77. "Social Reform and Human Progress," ibid., Feb. 8, 1843; "Lectures," ibid., Jan. 11, 1843; "Editorial Correspondence," ibid., Jan. 25, 1843; Oliver Johnson, "Annual Meeting of the Vermont Anti-Slavery Society," *Liberator*, March 1, 1839; "The Vermont Telegraph," *Non-Resistant*, April 22, 1840; H. C. Wright, "Non-Resistance Convention," ibid., Jan. 16, 1842.

2. The Hicksite Quaker Roots of Universal Reform

1. O. S. Murray, "Quaker Quiet—Refinement of Violence," *Regenerator*, June 1, 1844.

2. Valentine Nicholson obituary, *Indianapolis News*, March 24, 1904, clipping, Valentine Nicholson Papers (Indiana Historical Society, Indianapolis); Elizabeth Nich-

olson, "Valentine Nicholson," n.d., ibid.; John Pegg to Valentine Nicholson, 1st Mo. 9, 1878, ibid.; Valentine Nicholson, Autobiography, July 4, 1881, typescript, p. 1, ibid.; William Wade Hinshaw, ed., *Encyclopedia of American Quaker Genealogy* (6 vols., Ann Arbor: Edwards Brothers, 1936–50), I, 833, V, 105, 195; Kenneth Lee Carroll, *Joseph Nichols and the Nicholites: A Look at the "New Quakers" of Maryland, Delaware, North and South Carolina* (Easton, Md.: Easton Publishing Company, 1962), 33–45, 47, 49; David E. Pegg to Judith Mendenhall, 2nd Mo. 13, 1896, box 2, Hobbs-Mendenhall Papers (Southern Historical Collection, University of North Carolina, Chapel Hill).

3. Nicholson, Autobiography, 1–3. On Richard McNemar and the Union Village Shakers, see Stephen J. Stein, *The Shaker Experience in America: A History of the United Society of Believers* (New Haven: Yale University Press, 1992), 58–62.

4. Nicholson, Autobiography, 1–2.

5. Valentine Nicholson, Antislavery Reminiscences, ca. 1895, Nicholson Papers; Hinshaw, ed., *Encyclopedia*, V, 105, 195, 573. For John Pegg, see Willard C. Heiss, ed., *Abstracts of the Records of the Society of Friends in Indiana* (7 vols., Indianapolis: Indiana Historical Society, 1962–77), II, 194. For Lydia Cook, see ibid., VI, 320; and Lydia P. Cook to Margaret White, 3rd Mo. 4, 1832, box 3, Furnas Family Papers (Friends Historical Library, Swarthmore College, Swarthmore, Pa.). Mary (Pegg) Mendenhall's son Nereus Mendenhall was for many years the leading Quaker educator in North Carolina and an influential Friend. See Errol T. Elliott, *Quaker Profiles from the American West* (Richmond, Ind.: Friends United Press, 1972), 1–22.

6. Hinshaw, ed., *Encyclopedia*, V, 105, 136; Jane F. Nicholson, "Memories of Long Ago," 1885, typescript, Nicholson Papers; Wales-Irwin genealogical notes, ibid. References to Jane Nicholson's relatives are scattered throughout Valentine Nicholson's autobiography.

7. Elizabeth Nicholson account of LaPorte County life, 1921, typescript, Nicholson Papers; Valentine Nicholson letter, *Herald of Freedom*, Dec. 8, 1843. Valentine Nicholson did not leave a clear chronology of these years; his daughter Elizabeth wrote that the family was in LaPorte County from 1835 until 1837. Apparently the Nicholsons rented land or squatted until 1836, when Valentine and a brother-in-law purchased forty acres. Valentine Nicholson continued to buy land in LaPorte County even after returning to Ohio. See LaPorte County Deeds, Book C, p. 261; Book F, p. 360; Book I, pp. 299–300 (LaPorte County Recorder's Office, LaPorte, Ind.). When he bought eighty acres on September 1, 1837, he gave his residence as Warren County, Ohio. Ibid., Book F, p. 360. When he sold his father's old farm March 19, 1838, he was still living in Warren County. See Clinton County Deeds, Book L, p. 540 (Clinton County Recorder's Office, Wilmington, Ohio). By August 8, 1839, the Nicholsons gave Greene County, Ohio, as their residence. See LaPorte County Deeds, Book I, pp. 123, 135.

8. Nicholson, Autobiography, 6.

9. Ibid., 6–7. For the influence of Thomas Paine on other radical reformers of the period, see Nancy A. Hewitt, *Women's Activism and Social Change: Rochester, New York, 1822–1872* (Ithaca: Cornell University Press, 1984), 257.

10. Nicholson, Autobiography, 9–11. I place this event in the winter of 1842–43, since Nicholson dated it "several weeks" before an abolitionist meeting in Lebanon, Ohio, at

which Salmon P. Chase spoke. Such a meeting took place March 24–25, 1843. See ibid., 18–19; and "Convention at Harveysburg," *Philanthropist*, March 14, 1843. In 1845 Nicholson sent a brief account of the encounter to Orson S. Murray's *Regenerator*, placing it in "the winter of '42." See Valentine Nicholson, "Licentiousness," *Regenerator*, July 7, 1845.

11. Nicholson, Autobiography, 11–14.

12. Ibid., 15–16.

13. Ibid., 16.

14. Ibid., 17–19.

15. Ibid., 19. For Jane Nicholson's differences with her husband, see Valentine Nicholson to Isaac and Amy Post, 12th Mo. 16, 1849, box 3, Isaac and Amy Kirby Post Papers (Department of Rare Books and Manuscripts, Rush Rhees Library, University of Rochester, Rochester, N.Y.). For mesmerism, see Robert C. Fuller, *Mesmerism and the American Cure of Souls* (Philadelphia: University of Pennsylvania Press, 1982), 16–68.

16. Valentine Nicholson to Post and Post, 12th Mo. 16, 1849; Nicholson, Autobiography, 4–5; Valentine Nicholson to Wilbur H. Siebert, Sept. 10, 1892, box 77, Wilbur H. Siebert Collection (Ohio Historical Society, Columbus); Valentine Nicholson letter, *Herald of Freedom*, Dec. 8, 1843.

17. Valentine Nicholson letter, *Herald of Freedom*, Dec. 8, 1843; Nicholson, Antislavery Reminiscences. There is a considerable literature on the Quaker ambivalence about the antislavery movement. For its roots, see Jean R. Soderlund, *Quakers and Slavery: A Divided Spirit* (Princeton: Princeton University Press, 1985). The best account of the divisions between 1830 and 1850 is still Thomas E. Drake, *Quakers and Slavery in America* (New Haven: Yale University Press, 1950), 133–66. Much remains to be done on Quaker women and the nineteenth-century woman's rights movement. Useful treatments include Margaret Hope Bacon, *Mothers of Feminism: The Story of Quaker Women in America* (San Francisco: Harper and Row, 1986), 101–19; Nancy A. Hewitt, "The Fragmentation of Friends: The Consequences for Quaker Women in Antebellum America," in *Witnesses for Change: Quaker Women over Three Centuries*, ed. Elisabeth Potts Brown and Susan Mosher Stuard (New Brunswick: Rutgers University Press, 1989), 93–108; and Hewitt, *Women's Activism*, passim. The only scholar to give attention to Quakers and nonresistance is Peter Brock. See his *The Quaker Peace Testimony, 1660 to 1914* (York, Eng.: Sessions, 1990), 161–64.

18. Douglas Andrew Gamble, "Moral Suasion in the West: Garrisonian Abolition, 1831–1861" (Ph.D. diss., Ohio State University, 1973), 97.

19. *History of Stark County, Ohio* (Chicago: Baskin and Battey, 1881), 719, 921. I calculated Abraham Brooke's birth date from his tombstone in the Marlborough Cemetery in Stark County, Ohio.

20. *History of Stark County*, 921; Bliss Forbush, *A History of Baltimore Yearly Meeting of Friends: Three Hundred Years of Quakerism in Maryland, Virginia, the District of Columbia, and Central Pennsylvania* (Baltimore: Baltimore Yearly Meeting, 1972), 52; *History of Clinton County, Ohio* (Chicago: W. H. Beers, 1882), 409; Hinshaw, ed., *Encyclopedia*, IV, 891; Sandy Spring (Hicksite) Monthly Meeting (Md.) Marriage Records (Friends Historical Library, Swarthmore College, Swarthmore, Pa.).

21. Thomas D. Hamm, *The Transformation of American Quakerism: Orthodox Friends, 1800–1907* (Bloomington: Indiana University Press, 1988), 26–27; Robert Kelly, *The Cultural Pattern in American Politics: The First Century* (New York: Knopf, 1979), 167; Sereno W. Streeter to Theodore Weld, March 15, 1836, in *Letters of Theodore Dwight Weld, Angelina Grimke Weld, and Sarah Grimke, 1822–1844*, ed. Gilbert H. Barnes and Dwight L. Dumond (2 vols., Gloucester, Mass.: Peter Smith, 1965), I, 279; "Extract of a Letter from A. Brooke," *National Anti-Slavery Standard*, Oct. 8, 1840.

22. Robert Samuel Fletcher, *A History of Oberlin College from Its Foundation through the Civil War* (2 vols., Oberlin: Oberlin College, 1943), I, 53, 55, 162, 183; *Letters of Theodore Weld*, I, 36, 278–79.

23. Streeter to Weld, March 15, 1836, in *Letters of Theodore Weld*, I, 278–79; Abraham Brooke to Asa Mahan, 5th Mo. 9, 1836, Treasurer's Papers (Oberlin College Archives, Mudd Library, Oberlin, Ohio); Gamble, "Moral Suasion," 97.

24. Hinshaw, ed., *Encyclopedia*, IV, 891; Gamble, "Moral Suasion," 239–41.

25. Hinshaw, ed., *Encyclopedia*, IV, 891, V, 478; Clinton County Deeds, Book L, pp. 347, 398.

26. Clinton County Deeds, Book L, pp. 347, 398.

27. Gamble, "Moral Suasion," 162–71, 175; Charles C. Burleigh to J. Miller McKim, Aug.-Sept. 1839, J. Miller McKim Papers (Manuscripts Department, Olin Graduate Library, Cornell University, Ithaca, N.Y.); Notice, *Philanthropist*, Oct. 29, 1839; "Lytles Creek A. S. Society," ibid., May 26, 1840; "Clinton County Anti-Slavery Society," ibid., Sept. 17, 1842.

28. "Slave Labor," *Philanthropist*, Sept. 4, 1838; Abraham Brooke letter, *Free Labor Advocate*, 2nd Mo. 7, 1842. For the Free Produce movement generally among Friends, see Ruth Ketring Neurmberger, *The Free Produce Movement: A Quaker Protest against Slavery* (Durham: Duke University Press, 1942).

29. A. Brooke, "Slave Case in Warren—Mob Violence," *Philanthropist*, Oct. 28, 1840.

30. Ibid.

31. Ibid. For the legal issues involved in such cases, see Paul Finkelman, *An Imperfect Union: Slavery, Federalism, and Comity* (Chapel Hill: University of North Carolina Press, 1981), 155–80.

32. Brooke, "Slave Case in Warren."

33. Ibid.

34. A. Brooke, "Slave Case—Imprisonment of Abolitionists," *Philanthropist*, April 28, 1841; "First Imprisonment of Abolitionists," *Protectionist*, 5th Mo. 16, 1841.

35. Brooke, "Slave Case—Imprisonment."

36. Ibid.; "First Imprisonment."

37. *History of Clinton County*, 381; Wilbur H. Siebert, *The Underground Railroad from Slavery to Freedom* (New York: Macmillan, 1898), 419, 429; E. B. Dakin to W. H. Siebert, Oct. 12, 1898, box 103, Siebert Collection; Geo. M. Dakin to Siebert, Aug. 24, 1898, ibid.; Joel P. Davis to Siebert, Sept. 10, 1892, ibid.

38. There is a voluminous literature on the 1840 split. See Gilbert Hobbs Barnes, *The Antislavery Impulse, 1830–1844* (New York: Harcourt Brace, 1964), 161–70; John L. Thomas, *The Liberator: William Lloyd Garrison: A Biography* (Boston: Little Brown, 1963), 281–304; Aileen S. Kraditor, *Means and Ends in American Abolitionism: Garrison*

and His Critics on Strategy and Tactics, 1834–1850 (Chicago: Ivan R. Dee, 1989), passim; Bertram Wyatt-Brown, *Lewis Tappan and the Evangelical War on Slavery* (Cleveland: Case Western Reserve University Press, 1969), 185–200; and Hugh Davis, *Joshua Leavitt: Evangelical Abolitionist* (Baton Rouge: Louisiana State University Press, 1990), 134–63. For Gamaliel Bailey's views, see Editorial, *Philanthropist,* April 18, 1840; and Stanley Harrold, *Gamaliel Bailey and Antislavery Union* (Kent: Kent State University Press, 1986), 21–22.

39. Gamble, "Moral Suasion," 194–200; Gamaliel Bailey to James G. Birney, April 18, 1840, in *Letters of James Gillespie Birney, 1831–1857,* ed. Dwight L. Dumond (2 vols., Gloucester, Mass.: Peter Smith, 1965), I, 557.

40. Gamble, "Moral Suasion," 203; A. Brooke, "Once More," *Philanthropist,* July 21, 1840; Kraditor, *Means and Ends,* passim.

41. See the account of the Massillon meeting in *Philanthropist,* June 9, 1840.

42. For the Liberty party and its role in the antislavery movement, see Louis S. Gerteis, *Morality and Utility in American Antislavery Reform* (Chapel Hill: University of North Carolina Press, 1987), 44–46; Betty Fladeland, *James Gillespie Birney: Slaveholder to Abolitionist* (Ithaca: Cornell University Press, 1955), 175–89; Thomas, *Liberator,* 324–26; Richard H. Sewall, *Ballots for Freedom: Antislavery Politics in the United States, 1837–1860* (New York: Oxford University Press, 1976), 43–106; and Ronald G. Walters, *The Antislavery Appeal: American Abolitionism after 1830* (Baltimore: Johns Hopkins University Press, 1978), 13–18. For the Liberty party in Ohio, see Vernon L. Volpe, *Forlorn Hope of Freedom: The Liberty Party in the Old Northwest, 1838–1848* (Kent: Kent State University Press, 1990).

43. Harrold, *Gamaliel Bailey,* 25–40; Gamble, "Moral Suasion," 204–206; Abraham Brooke letter, *Philanthropist,* July 28, 1840.

44. A. Brooke, "Petitions," *Philanthropist,* Nov. 10, 1840; A. Brooke, "Extract of a Letter from Ohio," *National Anti-Slavery Standard,* July 7, 1842.

45. Hinshaw, ed., *Encyclopedia,* V, 516, 585; Henry Hart Beeson, *The Mendenhalls: A Genealogy* (Houston, 1969), 71; Ebenezer C. Tucker, *History of Randolph County, Indiana* (Chicago: A. E. Kingman, 1882), 338; Hiram and Martha Mendenhall Family Bible records, photostat, Willard C. Heiss Collection (Friends Collection, Lilly Library, Earlham College, Richmond, Ind.); *History of Clinton County, Ohio,* 658.

46. Tucker, *History of Randolph County,* 388; Hiram Mendenhall Estate Papers, 1851–1856, Heiss Collection; Hiram Mendenhall to Joseph H. Mendenhall, Dec. 24, 1851, transcript, ibid.; Hiram Mendenhall to Nathan Mendenhall, March 8, 1851, transcript, ibid.; Clipping, *Indianapolis Star,* Sept. 13, 1921, ibid.; J. H. Mendenhall, "In Memory of Hiram and Martha Mendenhall," *Winchester* (Ind.) *Journal,* Aug. 11, 1880.

47. Mendenhall, "In Memory"; Warren County Deeds, Book 13, p. 111, Book 16, p. 539, Book 29, p. 451 (Warren County Recorder's Office, Lebanon, Ohio).

48. Hinshaw, ed., *Encyclopedia,* V, 570, 585; Mendenhall, "In Memory"; Census of Orthodox and Hicksite Friends, 1833, in Minutes of the Meeting for Sufferings, Indiana Yearly Meeting of Friends (Orthodox), 10th Mo. 3, 1834 (Indiana Yearly Meeting Archives, Friends Collection, Earlham); *The Quaker, Being a Series of Sermons by Members of the Society of Friends* (4 vols., Philadelphia: Marcus T. C. Gould, 1827–28). It is possible that the Mendenhalls had seen *Discourses, Delivered in the Several Meetings of the Society*

of Friends, in Philadelphia, Germantown, Abington, Byberry, Newtown, Falls, and Trenton, by Elias Hicks (Philadelphia: Joseph & Edward Parker, 1825).

49. Mendenhall Family Bible record; Hinshaw, ed., *Encyclopedia*, V, 585; Mendenhall, "In Memory"; Willard C. Heiss, "Hiram Mendenhall and the Union Home Community," *Bulletin of Friends Historical Association*, 44 (Spring 1955), 43; Willard C. Heiss, "An Early Quaker Family of Randolph County: The Ancestry and Some of the Descendants of Nathan Mendenhall and Ann, His Wife," typescript, n.d., Heiss Collection.

50. Warren County Deeds, Book 13, p. 211, Book 16, p. 529, Book 25, p. 451; Heiss, "Hiram Mendenhall," 43–44; Tucker, *History of Randolph County*, 338, 393. Hiram Mendenhall's land dealings between 1835 and 1840 are in the Randolph County deed books in the Randolph County Recorder's Office in Winchester, Indiana.

51. Randolph County Commissioners Book T, pp. 123, 138, 194 (Randolph County Commissioners Office, Winchester, Ind.); Heiss, "Hiram Mendenhall," 44; Tucker, *History of Randolph County*, 61.

52. *Richmond* (Ind.) *Palladium*, Aug. 23, 1838, Feb. 1, 1840; W. L. Smith, *Indiana Methodism: Sketches and Incidents* (Valparaiso, Ind., 1892), 69; Mrs. Herbert E. Brown, "The Reverend William Hunt Family," *Indiana Magazine of History*, 34 (June 1938), 139; Tucker, *History of Randolph County*, 194–95, 391; Lewis Hicklin, "Cause in Indiana," *Philanthropist*, Feb. 25, 1840; Dorothy Riker and Gayle Thornbrough, eds., *Indiana Election Returns, 1816–1851* (Indianapolis: Indiana Historical Bureau, 1960), 243.

53. *Richmond* (Ind.) *Palladium*, Aug. 23, 1838; Emma Lou Thornbrough, *The Negro in Indiana: A Study of a Minority* (Indianapolis: Indiana Historical Bureau, 1957), 68.

54. Mendenhall, "In Memory"; Marion C. Miller, "The Antislavery Movement in Indiana" (Ph.D. diss., University of Michigan, 1938), 65; Bailey to Gerrit Smith, July 23, 1838, box 2, Gerrit Smith Papers (Arents Research Library, Syracuse University, Syracuse, N.Y.); J. H. Mendenhall, "Sketch of the Origin, Use & Method of Operating the Old Underground Railroad," Jan. 1, 1896, box 77, Siebert Collection; Gamble, "Moral Suasion," 129; *Proceedings of the Indiana Convention Assembled to Organize a State Anti-Slavery Society Held in Milton, Wayne County, September 12, 1838* (Cincinnati: Samuel A. Alley, 1838).

55. Thomas D. Hamm et al., "Moral Choices: Two Indiana Quaker Communities and the Abolitionist Movement," *Indiana Magazine of History*, 87 (June 1991), 119–20; Miller, "Antislavery Movement," 65; *Reminiscences of Levi Coffin, the Reputed President of the Underground Railroad* (Cincinnati: Robert Clarke, 1880), 225–28; Bailey to Birney, Jan. 23, 1840, *Letters of James Gillespie Birney*, ed. Dumond, I, 522. The only known file of the *Protectionist* is in the Indiana Division, Indiana State Library, Indianapolis.

56. Arnold Buffum to Lewis Tappan, 1st Mo. 12, 1841, vol. 11, p. 23, Anti-Slavery Collection (Rare Books Department, Boston Public Library, Boston); Lillie Buffum Chace Wyman and Arthur Crawford Wyman, *Elizabeth Buffum Chace 1806–1899: Her Life and Its Environment* (2 vols., Boston: W. B. Clarke, 1914), I, 4–21, 30, 44; Birney to Buffum, Nov. 8, 1839, *Letters of James Gillespie Birney*, ed. Dumond, I, 502–505; Editorial, *Protectionist*, 8th Mo. 21, 1841, pp. 148–51; Elizabeth Buffum Chace, *Anti-Slavery Reminiscences* (Central Falls, R.I.: E. L. Freeman and Son, 1891), 8, 10, 20; Drake, *Quakers and Slavery*, 136–37; Louis Filler, *The Crusade against Slavery, 1830–1860* (New York: Harper and Row, 1960), 60; Buffum to Smith, 12th Mo. 7, 1835, box 5, Smith Papers.

57. Editorial, *Protectionist*, 1st Mo. 1, 1841; ibid., 3rd Mo. 1, 1841; Miller, "Antislavery Movement," 79; Theodore Clarke Smith, *The Liberty and Free Soil Parties in the Old Northwest* (New York: Longmans, Green, & Co., 1987), 43–44; Andrew W. Young, *History of Wayne County, Indiana* (Cincinnati: Robert Clarke & Co., 1872), 268; Gamble, "Moral Suasion," 210–11.

58. For the hostility of Orthodox Friends toward Buffum, see Editorial, *Protectionist*, 8th Mo. 20, 1841; and Wyman and Wyman, *Elizabeth Buffum Chace*, I, 80–81.

59. Robert V. Remini, *Henry Clay: Statesman for the Union* (New York: W. W. Norton, 1991), 613; *Richmond Palladium*, Aug. 20, 1842; Centerville, Ind., *Wayne County Record*, Sept. 7, 1842.

60. Editorial, *Free Labor Advocate*, 9th Mo. 24, 1842; Bernhard Knollenberg, *Pioneer Sketches of the Upper Whitewater Valley: Quaker Stronghold of the West* (Indianapolis: Indiana Historical Society, 1945), 75; Charles W. Osborn, "Henry Clay at Richmond," *Indiana Magazine of History*, 4 (Dec. 1908), 120; Remini, *Henry Clay*, 613–19.

61. Editorial, *Free Labor Advocate*, 10th Mo. 15, 1842; *Wayne County Record*, Sept. 21, 1842, Oct. 5, 1842; Philip C. Kabel interview with Amos Mendenhall, Oct. 1, 1900, Philip C. Kabel Papers (Indiana Historical Society, Indianapolis).

62. Editorial, *Free Labor Advocate*, 10th Mo. 15, 1842; *Wayne County Record*, Oct. 5, 1842; Kabel interview with Mendenhall.

63. Daniel Worth to Benjamin Stanton, Oct. 13, 1842, *Free Labor Advocate*, 10th Mo. 29, 1842; *Richmond Palladium*, Oct. 8, 1842; Knollenberg, *Pioneer Sketches*, 79.

64. *Wayne County Record*, Oct. 5, 1842; *Richmond Palladium*, Oct. 8, 1842; Remini, *Henry Clay*, 617–19; Worth to Stanton.

65. Charles F. Coffin and William H. Coffin, "Henry Clay at Richmond," *Indiana Magazine of History*, 4 (Dec. 1908), 128; *Wayne County Record*, Oct. 5, 1842; Editorial, *Free Labor Advocate*, 12th Mo. 10, 1842; Remini, *Henry Clay*, 619.

66. Remini, *Henry Clay*, 619–20; Knollenberg, *Pioneer Sketches*, 81–82; Oswego County Liberty Party Central Committee to Hiram Mendenhall, n.d., *Free Labor Advocate*, 3rd Mo. 25, 1843; *Eleventh Annual Report, Presented to the Massachusetts Anti-Slavery Society, By Its Board of Managers, January 25, 1843* (Boston, 1843), 31.

67. *Wayne County Record*, Oct. 5, 1842; Randolph County Circuit Court Complete Record, roll 17, spring term 1850 (Randolph County Clerk of Courts Office, Winchester, Ind.). By 1841, Hiram Mendenhall owned 668 acres in Randolph County. By 1844 he had sold about 540 acres of this, without any purchases. See notes from the now-lost 1841 Randolph County Tax Duplicate in Heiss Collection; and Randolph County Deeds, Book I, 54, 223, 224, 226, 379, 380, 395, Book J, p. 9, Book K, p. 190.

3. The Society for Universal Inquiry and Reform Begins

1. John L. Thomas, *The Liberator: William Lloyd Garrison: A Biography* (Boston: Little Brown, 1963), 302–303.

2. Ibid., 301–304; Ralph Waldo Emerson, "The Chardon Street Convention," in *The Complete Works of Ralph Waldo Emerson* (12 vols., New York: Sully and Kleinteich, 1883), X, 351–54.

3. Samuel Myers to E. Quincy, 11th Mo. 1, 1840, *Liberator,* Nov. 27, 1840; Thomas E. Longshore to Quincy, Nov. 2, 1840, ibid.; "Roll of Members of the Convention," ibid.

4. "Communities," ibid., Dec. 25, 1840. The article was the work of someone connected with Adin Ballou and the Hopedale Community. See Lewis Perry, *Radical Abolitionism: Anarchy and the Government of God in Antislavery Thought* (Ithaca: Cornell University Press, 1973), 142.

5. "Communities," *Liberator,* March 6, 1841.

6. "Reform in Human Society," ibid., May 7, 1841; Esther Whinery Wattles Autobiography, n.d., John O. Wattles Papers (Western Reserve Historical Society, Cleveland); Abraham Allen biography, ca. 1892, box 103, Wilbur H. Siebert Collection (Ohio Historical Society, Columbus); E. B. Dakin to Wilbur H. Siebert, Oct. 12, 1898, ibid.; Valentine Nicholson, "Law, Gospel, Creeds, Constitutions, Infidels, Christians, Communities, 'Fourierites,' Grahamites, Etc.," *Regenerator,* May 8, 1844; Abraham Allen, "Man Hunting in Ohio," *Pennsylvania Freeman,* 11th Mo. 29, 1838.

7. "Reform in Human Society."

8. Ibid.

9. Ibid.

10. Douglas Andrew Gamble, "Moral Suasion in the West: Garrisonian Abolition, 1831–1861" (Ph.D. diss., Ohio State University, 1973), 238–79; Oliver Johnson to Isaac T. Hopper, Oct. 25, 1841, Miscellaneous Manuscripts Collection (Ohio Historical Society).

11. A. Brooke, "The Other Side," *National Anti-Slavery Standard,* Sept. 2, 1841.

12. A. Brooke, "An Appeal," *Philanthropist,* Nov. 17, 1841.

13. Gamble, "Moral Suasion," 228–34; Stanley Harrold, *Gamaliel Bailey and Antislavery Union* (Kent: Kent State University Press, 1986), 58–59; Edward Brooke letter, *Philanthropist,* March 16, 1842; J. A. Dugdale letter, ibid., April 13, 1842.

14. John A. Collins letter, *Liberator,* May 7, 1842; J. A. Collins, "American A. S. Society—Prospect of the Cause," ibid., May 20, 1842; J. A. Collins, "Good News from Ohio," ibid., June 24, 1842; John R. McKivigan, *The War against Proslavery Religion: Abolitionism and the Northern Churches, 1830–1865* (Ithaca: Cornell University Press, 1984), 208–209.

15. Gamble, "Moral Suasion," 248–50.

16. William Birney to James G. Birney, June 9, 1842, in *Letters of James Gillespie Birney, 1831–1857,* ed. Dwight L. Dumond (2 vols., Gloucester, Mass.: Peter Smith, 1965), II, 697–98.

17. A. Brooke, "Matters and Things in the East," *National Anti-Slavery Standard,* Oct. 6, 1842; John A. Collins letter, *Liberator,* June 17, 1842.

18. Gamble, "Moral Suasion," 248–50; "Clinton County Anti-Slavery Society," *Philanthropist,* Sept. 17, 1842; A. Kelley to Gerrit Smith, July 29, 1843, box 18, Gerrit Smith Papers (Arents Research Library, Syracuse University, Syracuse, N.Y.). As late as December 1842, Samuel Brooke and John O. Wattles were delegates to a Liberty party convention. See Gamble, "Moral Suasion," 267.

19. Gamble, "Moral Suasion," 252–60. For Abby Kelley, see Dorothy Sterling, *Ahead of Her Time: Abby Kelley and the Politics of Antislavery* (New York: Norton, 1991).

20. A. Brooke letter, *Philanthropist,* Oct. 6, 1842.

21. Seth E. Furnas Sr., *A History of Indiana Yearly Meeting* (N.p.: Indiana Yearly Meeting Religious Society of Friends General Conference, 1968), 37–38, 41–42; James H. Norton, "Quakers West of the Alleghenies and in Ohio to 1861" (Ph.D. diss., Case Western Reserve University, 1965), 321, 330, 336; William Wade Hinshaw, ed., *Encyclopedia of American Quaker Genealogy* (6 vols., Ann Arbor: Edwards Brothers, 1936–50), V, 471, 478, 540–41.

22. Johnson to Hopper; Joseph A. Dugdale, "The Friends—Anti-Slavery," *Philanthropist*, April 7, 1837; Joseph A. Dugdale letter, *Liberator*, May 21, 1836; Indiana Yearly Meeting Epistle to New York Yearly Meeting, 1833, box 2, Evans Family Papers (Ohio Historical Society). For Elias Hicks's views of slavery, see Bliss Forbush, *Elias Hicks: Quaker Liberal* (New York: Columbia University Press, 1956), 144–48.

23. Genesee Yearly Meeting Epistle to Indiana Yearly Meeting, 1837, box 2, Evans Papers; Hopper to N. P. Rogers, 2nd Mo. 14, 1842, box 1, Nathaniel P. Rogers Papers (Quaker Collection, Haverford College, Haverford, Pa.); Thomas E. Drake, *Quakers and Slavery in America* (New Haven: Yale University Press, 1950), 133–66.

24. *Memorials concerning Deceased Friends, Published by Direction of the Yearly Meeting of New York* (New York: James Egbert, 1859), 162–65; Drake, *Quakers and Slavery*, 161.

25. Drake, *Quakers and Slavery*, 162; Oliver Johnson letter, *Liberator*, March 12, 1841; *Correspondence between Oliver Johnson and George F. White, a Minister of the Society of Friends* (New York: Oliver Johnson, 1841); "Rare Specimen of a Quaker Preacher," *National Anti-Slavery Standard*, March 25, 1841.

26. Isaac T. Hopper, *Narrative of the Proceedings of the Monthly Meeting of New York, and Their Subsequent Confirmation by the Quarterly and Yearly Meetings, in the Case of Isaac T. Hopper* (New York, 1843); Hopper to Joseph A. Dugdale, 9th Mo. 3, 1843, Joseph A. Dugdale Papers (Friends Historical Library, Swarthmore College, Swarthmore, Pa.).

27. "The Friends," *Philanthropist*, July 14, 1841.

28. Indiana Yearly Meeting (Hicksite) Men's Minutes, 9th Mo. 28, 1840 (Ohio Valley Yearly Meeting Archives, Wilmington College, Wilmington, Ohio); Green Plain Monthly Meeting (Hicksite) Men's Minutes, 1835–1845 (ibid.); Sarah B. Dugdale obituary, 1880, Dugdale Papers; Joseph A. Dugdale obituary, 1896, ibid.; Valentine Nicholson, Autobiography, July 4, 1881, typescript, p. 27, Valentine Nicholson Papers (Indiana Historical Society, Indianapolis).

29. Indiana Yearly Meeting (Hicksite) Men's Minutes, 9th Mo. 28, 1840, 9th Mo. 27, 1841.

30. Ibid., 9th Mo. 27, 1841.

31. Johnson to Hopper; James Mott to Dugdale, 9th Mo. 11, 1841, Dugdale Papers.

32. Johnson to Hopper.

33. Indiana Yearly Meeting (Hicksite) Men's Minutes, 9th Mo. 26, 1842; James Canning Fuller to Elizabeth Pease, 9th Mo. 19, 1842, vol. 12.2, p. 90, Anti-Slavery Collection (Rare Books Department, Boston Public Library, Boston); Joseph A. Dugdale, "A Letter from Ohio," *National Anti-Slavery Standard*, July 6, 1843.

34. Indiana Yearly Meeting (Hicksite) Men's Minutes, 9th Mo. 26, 1842; Fuller to Pease; Joseph A. Dugdale, "Reform among the Quakers," Centerville *Indiana True Democrat*, March 27, 1850.

35. Fuller to Pease; Indiana Yearly Meeting (Hicksite) Men's Minutes, 9th Mo. 26, 1842.

36. A. Brooke, "Letter from Ohio," *National Anti-Slavery Standard*, Nov. 24, 1842; Dugdale, "Letter from Ohio." For the separation among the Orthodox Friends, and its impact on Abraham Brooke's neighborhood, see Ruth Anna Ketring, *Charles Osborn in the Anti-Slavery Movement* (Columbus: Ohio State Archaeological and Historical Society, 1937), 50–70; and *Journal of the Life, Travels, and Gospel Labors of Thomas Arnett* (Chicago: Publishing Association of Friends, 1884), 143–47.

37. "Ohio Convention," *Herald of Freedom*, Nov. 18, 1842; "Great Convention at Oakland," *Free Labor Advocate*, 11th Mo. 19, 1842; "Convention at Oakland," ibid., 11th Mo. 26, 1842; "Letter from John O. Wattles," *National Anti-Slavery Standard*, Oct. 20, 1842; Francis Jackson to N. P. Rogers, July 28, 1842, box 1, Rogers Papers.

38. "Great Convention at Oakland"; "Convention at Oakland."

39. "Great Convention at Oakland"; "Convention at Oakland."

40. Nicholson, Autobiography, 20.

41. Ibid., 19–20; "Social Reform and Human Progress," *Vermont Telegraph*, Feb. 8, 1843.

42. A brief account of the proceedings of this meeting can be found in J. A. Collins, "Social Reform and Human Progress," *Liberator*, Feb. 17, 1843. More complete is "Social Reform and Human Progress" in the *Vermont Telegraph*, on which this is based. Nicholson's account is in his autobiography, 19–20. For Aaron L. Benedict, see Wilbur H. Siebert, *The Underground Railroad from Slavery to Freedom* (New York: Macmillan, 1898), 76–77; and Hinshaw, ed., *Encyclopedia*, IV, 1146. For the Gilberts, see Marius R. Robinson to Emily Robinson, Feb. 13, 1837, Marius R. Robinson Papers (Western Reserve Historical Society, Cleveland).

43. *History of Stark County, Ohio* (Chicago: Baskin and Battey, 1881), 719.

44. Henry Tutwiler to James G. Birney, Nov. 7, 1832, in *Letters of James Gillespie Birney*, ed. Dumond, I, 38; Gilbert Hobbs Barnes, *The Antislavery Impulse, 1830–1844* (New York: Harcourt Brace, 1964), 68; Russel B. Nye, "Marius Robinson: A Forgotten Abolitionist," *Ohio State Archeological and Historical Quarterly*, 55 (April-June 1946), 138–54; Emily Robinson to Marius R. Robinson, Jan. 13, 1837, Robinson Papers.

45. Nye, "Marius Robinson," 138–54; Dwight Lowell Dumond, *Antislavery: The Crusade for Freedom in America* (Ann Arbor: University of Michigan Press, 1961), 220.

46. R. C. Smedley, *History of the Underground Railroad in Chester and the Neighboring Counties of Pennsylvania* (Lancaster, Pa.: Journal, 1883), 182, 186; Edwin Neal Fussell, *Genealogy of the Fussell Family: Comprising a Complete Record to 1890 of the Descendants of Bartholomew Fussell, born 9-28-1754, died 10-17-1838* (New York, 1891), 6–9; Edwin Fussell to Esther Lewis, Aug. 3, Aug. 19, 1836, box 3, Graceanna Lewis Papers (Friends Historical Library); Rebecca Lewis Fussell Diary, June 10, 1838, box 9, ibid.; Willard C. Heiss, ed., *Abstracts of the Records of the Society of Friends in Indiana* (7 vols., Indianapolis: Indiana Historical Society, 1962–77), IV, 108a. For an incisive description of Rebecca Lewis Fussell's background, see Joan M. Jensen, *Loosening the Bonds: Mid-Atlantic Farm Women, 1750–1850* (New Haven: Yale University Press, 1986), 129–41.

47. Edwin Fussell to William Fussell, Nov. 29, 1836, box 3, Lewis Papers; Edwin Fussell to Graceanna Lewis, Jan. 19, Aug. 21, 1837, ibid.; Edwin Fussell to Fall Creek Monthly Meeting, 2nd Mo. 7, 1842, typescript, ibid.; Edwin Fussell to Esther Lewis, Dec. 13, 1841, ibid.; Joshua L. Fussell to William Howland, 8th Mo. 2, 1840, Talcott-Howland Papers (Department of Rare Books and Manuscripts, Rush Rhees Library, University of Rochester, Rochester, N.Y.); Edwin Fussell, "A Voice from Indiana," *Liberator,* Oct. 4, 1839.

48. The constitution was reprinted with the accounts of the meeting in both the *Liberator* and the *Vermont Telegraph.*

49. For Maria Weston Chapman, see Walter M. Merrill and Louis Ruchames, eds., *The Letters of William Lloyd Garrison* (6 vols., Cambridge: Belknap, 1971–81), II, xxiv. For Richard Davis Webb, see Douglas C. Riach, "Richard Davis Webb and Antislavery in Ireland," in *Antislavery Reconsidered: New Perspectives on the Abolitionists,* ed. Lewis Perry and Michael Fellman (Baton Rouge: Louisiana State University Press, 1979), 149–67. For Nathaniel P. Rogers, see Perry, *Radical Abolitionism,* 117–28; and Robert Adams, "Nathaniel Peabody Rogers, 1794–1846," *New England Quarterly,* 20 (Sept. 1947), 365–76. For Orson S. Fowler, see Ronald G. Walters, *American Reformers, 1815–1860* (New York: Hill and Wang, 1978), 160–61. For Henry C. Wright, see Lewis Perry, *Childhood, Marriage, and Reform: Henry Clarke Wright, 1797–1870* (Chicago: University of Chicago Press, 1980). For Amos Bronson Alcott, see Perry, *Radical Abolitionism,* 81–87; and Odell Shepard, *Pedlar's Progress: The Life of Bronson Alcott* (Boston: Little Brown, 1937). For Parker Pillsbury, see his *Acts of the Anti-Slavery Apostles* (Concord, N. H., 1883). For Albert Brisbane, see Carl J. Guarneri, *The Utopian Alternative: Fourierism in Nineteenth-Century America* (Ithaca: Cornell University Press, 1991), 25–34. For Harriet Martineau, see R. K. Webb, *Harriet Martineau: A Radical Victorian* (New York: Columbia University Press, 1960).

50. Editorial, *Vermont Telegraph,* Feb. 8, 1843.

51. Ibid.

52. "Property Meetings at Lynn," *Liberator,* Feb. 17, 1843. For Oliver Johnson, George Bradburn, Sydney H. Gay, and James Boyle, see Merrill and Ruchames, eds., *Letters,* II, xxvi-xxvii, 346, 588, IV, 269. For James N. Buffum and railroad segregation, see J. A. Collins, "Eastern Railroad—Colorphobia—Lynch Law—Robbery—Quakerism," *National Anti-Slavery Standard,* Oct. 28, 1841. For Mary S. Gove, see Edward T. James et al., eds., *Notable American Women, 1607–1950: A Biographical Dictionary* (3 vols., Cambridge: Belknap, 1971), II, 627–29; and Bertha-Monica Stearns, "Two Forgotten New England Reformers," *New England Quarterly,* 6 (March 1933), 59–84.

53. The following discussion is based on "Property Meetings at Lynn." For the competing communitarian visions among abolitionists, see John L. Thomas, "Antislavery and Utopia," in *The Antislavery Vanguard: New Essays on the Abolitionists,* ed. Martin Duberman (Princeton: Princeton University Press, 1965), 240–69; and Perry, *Radical Abolitionism,* 129–57.

54. "Property Meetings at Lynn."

55. Ibid.

56. Ibid.

57. "Reform and Human Society," *Liberator*, Feb. 17, 1843. For this decision and a copy of John A. Collins's letter with the questions, see Nicholson, Autobiography, 21–27.

58. *Eleventh Annual Report, presented to the Massachusetts Anti-Slavery Society, By Its Board of Managers, January 25, 1843* (Boston, 1843), 85, 94; *Twelfth Annual Report, Presented to the Massachusetts Anti-Slavery Society, By its Board of Managers, January 24, 1844* (Boston, 1844), 34; "Property Convention in Worcester, Mass.," *Herald of Freedom*, March 17, 1843.

59. Nicholson, Autobiography, 27–28; Edwin Fussell to Rebecca L. Fussell, April 12, 1843, box 3, Lewis Papers; "C. C. Burleigh's Narrative," *Pennsylvania Freeman*, 10th Mo. 6, 1841.

60. Edwin Fussell to Rebecca L. Fussell, May 3, 1843, box 3, Lewis Papers; Nicholson, Autobiography, 27–28.

61. Nicholson, ibid.

62. Ibid., 28–29; Thomas, *Liberator*, 331–32; "Editorial Correspondence," *Vermont Telegraph*, May 24, 1843.

63. Nicholson, Autobiography, 28–29. For the Hutchinson family, see Carol Brink, *Harps in the Wind: The Story of the Singing Hutchinsons* (New York: Macmillan, 1947).

64. "Universal Inquiry and Reform," *Vermont Telegraph*, May 24, 1843; Guarneri, *Utopian Alternative*, 35–59; James, ed., *Notable American Women*, II, 647; Johnson to Gerrit Smith, Jan. 31, 1842, box 23, Gerrit Smith Papers (Arents Research Library, Syracuse University, Syracuse, N.Y.); Louis Filler, *The Crusade against Slavery, 1830–1860* (New York: Harper and Row, 1960), 152; Yuri Suhl, *Eloquent Crusader: Ernestine Rose* (New York: Messner, 1970); Sterling, *Ahead of Her Time*, 124–49.

65. Nicholson, Autobiography, 29–30. Orson S. Murray had condemned organizations six months earlier. See "Editorial Correspondence," *Vermont Telegraph*, Nov. 2, 1842. "No-organization" was advocated by some other extreme nonresistants, especially Nathaniel P. Rogers. See Perry, *Radical Abolitionism*, 117–28.

66. Ibid.; "Universal Inquiry and Reform."

67. Editorial, *Vermont Telegraph*, May 24, 1843; Edwin Fussell to Rebecca Fussell, June 17, 1843, box 3, Lewis Papers; Nicholson, Autobiography, 30.

68. Nicholson, Autobiography, 30; Valentine Nicholson letter, *Herald of Freedom*, Dec. 8, 1843. On LaRoy Sunderland, see John D. Davies, *Phrenology, Fad and Science: A Nineteenth-Century American Crusade* (Hamden, Conn.: Archon, 1971), 130.

69. Nicholson, Autobiography, 30–31.

70. Ibid., 31–33. John was John Hopper, Isaac T. Hopper's son, and a favorite of Lydia Maria Child. See Milton Meltzer and Patricia G. Holland, eds., *Lydia Maria Child: Selected Letters, 1817–1880* (Amherst: University of Massachusetts Press, 1982), 140.

71. Nicholson, Autobiography, 33.

72. Ibid., 33, 35; Edwin Fussell to Rebecca Fussell, June [July] 2, 1843, box 3, Lewis Papers.

73. Nicholson, Autobiography, 33–34.

74. Ibid., 34; Syracuse, N.Y., *Onondaga Standard*, May 24, 1843.

75. Nicholson, *Autobiography*, 36–37; "First Annual Meeting," *Vermont Telegraph*, April 26, 1843.

76. Nicholson, *Autobiography*, 35–36; Dugdale, "Letter from Ohio"; "Dr. Brooke's Letter," *Herald of Freedom*, Aug. 4, 1843.

77. Joshua V. H. Clark, *Onondaga; or Reminiscences of Earlier and Later Times* (2 vols., Syracuse: Stoddard and Babcock, 1849), II, 312.

4. The Hundred Conventions

1. "Notice," *National Anti-Slavery Standard*, March 2, 1843; *The Life and Times of Frederick Douglass* (New York: Pathway, 1941), 252.

2. J. A. Collins, "Grand Anti-Slavery Movement," *National Anti-Slavery Standard*, June 22, 1843; Editorial, *Liberator*, June 16, 1843.

3. "Notice," *Liberator*, June 16, 1843.

4. James Monroe to Maria Weston Chapman, July 10, 1843, vol. 18, p. 78, Weston Family Papers (Rare Books Department, Boston Public Library, Boston); "Letter from John Orvis," *Vermont Telegraph*, Aug. 9, 1843; "Mobbing Revived in Vermont," ibid., July 19, 1843; "Universal Inquiry and Reform," ibid., July 12, 1843; *Life and Times of Frederick Douglass*, 252–53; John O. Wattles, "Slavery Debates: Middlebury," John O. Wattles Papers (Western Reserve Historical Society, Cleveland); W. A. White, "Intelligence from Western Conventions," *Liberator*, July 20, 1843.

5. *Life and Times of Frederick Douglass*, 253–54.

6. Frederick Douglass to Chapman, Sept. 10, 1843, vol. 19, p. 35, Weston Papers; Abby Kelley to Chapman, Aug. 2, 1843, ibid., p. 9; Wattles, "Slavery Debates."

7. *Life and Times of Frederick Douglass*, 254–55; Douglass to Chapman, Sept. 10, 1843; Kelley to Chapman, Aug. 2, 1843.

8. Kelley to Chapman, Aug. 2, 1843.

9. Kelley to Monroe, Oct. 2, 1843, box 1, James Monroe Papers (Oberlin College Archives, Mudd Library, Oberlin, Ohio); Kelley to Gerrit Smith, July 19, July 28, 1843, box 18, Gerrit Smith Papers (Arents Research Library, Syracuse University, Syracuse, N.Y.); George Bradburn to J. Miller McKim, Dec. 21, 1843, J. Miller McKim Papers (Manuscripts Department, Olin Graduate Library, Cornell University, Ithaca, N.Y.); William Lloyd Garrison to Henry Clarke Wright, Oct. 1, 1844, in *The Letters of William Lloyd Garrison*, ed. Walter M. Merrill and Louis Ruchames (6 vols., Cambridge: Belknap, 1971–81), III, 266. For a somewhat different view of Abby Kelley and the Hundred Conventions, see Dorothy Sterling, *Ahead of Her Time: Abby Kelley and the Politics of Antislavery* (New York: Norton, 1991), 178–79.

10. John A. Collins to Chapman, July 14, 1843, vol. 18, p. 82, Weston Papers; Collins to Chapman, Aug. 23, 1843, vol. 19, p. 20, ibid.; Anne Warren Weston to Lucia Weston and Deborah Weston, Sept. 28, 1843, ibid., p. 40; Eunice M. Collins to Chapman, Aug. 15, 1843, ibid., p. 19; William S. McFeely, *Frederick Douglass* (New York: W. W. Norton, 1991), 107–108.

11. "Letter from John Orvis"; "The Hundred Conventions," *Herald of Freedom,* Sept. 8, 1843; *Life and Times of Frederick Douglass,* 255; Benjamin Quarles, *Frederick Douglass* (New York: Atheneum, 1970), 31; Sydney Howard Gay, "The Conventions," *Liberator,* Sept. 1, 1843.

12. A. Brooke, "Social Reform," *Philanthropist,* Aug. 16, 1843; "Notice," *Vermont Telegraph,* Aug. 16, 1843; "Notice," *Free Labor Advocate,* 8th Mo. 8, 1843; Monroe to Chapman, Sept. 1, 1843, vol. 19, p. 32, Weston Papers.

13. Monroe to Chapman, Sept. 1, 1843; Andrew Hanna to Monroe, May 19, 1843, box 1, Monroe Papers; O. K. Hawley to Monroe, Aug. 1843, ibid.

14. S. H. Gay to Garrison, *Liberator,* Sept. 8, 1843; "Letter from William A. White," ibid., Sept. 22, 1843.

15. "Letter from William A. White."

16. Abraham Brooke to Chapman, Oct. 5, 1843, vol. 19, p. 46, Weston Papers; "The One Hundred Conventions," *Liberator,* Sept. 22, 1843; Douglas Andrew Gamble, "Moral Suasion in the West: Garrisonian Abolition, 1831–1861" (Ph.D. diss., Ohio State University, 1973), 276–78.

17. Marion C. Miller, "The Antislavery Movement in Indiana" (Ph.D. diss., University of Michigan, 1938), 2; Emma Lou Thornbrough, *Indiana in the Civil War Era, 1850–1880* (Indianapolis: Indiana Historical Society and Indiana Historical Bureau, 1965), 14–16, 19; Joseph G. Rayback, *Free Soil: The Election of 1848* (Lexington: University Press of Kentucky, 1970), 185; E. Smith to Luther Lee, Sept. 19, 1851, *True Wesleyan,* Oct. 18, 1851.

18. "Notice," *Free Labor Advocate;* Charles L. Remond to Amy K. Post, Sept. 27, 1843, box 1, Isaac and Amy Kirby Post Papers (Department of Rare Books and Manuscripts, Rush Rhees Library, University of Rochester, Rochester, N.Y.).

19. Sydney Howard Gay, "Letter from Indiana," *National Anti-Slavery Standard,* Oct. 19, 1843. For Daniel Puckett, see *Indiana Yearly Meeting of Anti-Slavery Friends, Minutes, 1846,* appendix.

20. Douglass to Chapman, Sept. 10, 1843; Remond to Post. No account has survived of the activities of John O. Wattles, Edwin Fussell, and Valentine Nicholson.

21. Dorothy Riker and Gayle Thornbrough, comps., *Indiana Election Returns, 1816–1851* (Indianapolis: Indiana Historical Bureau, 1960), 40, 45; Editorial, *Protectionist,* 11th Mo. 16, 1841, p. 347; "Letters from Edwin Fussell," *National Anti-Slavery Standard,* Nov. 3, 1843.

22. "Letters from Edwin Fussell"; "Letter from George Bradburn," *National Anti-Slavery Standard,* Oct. 19, 1843.

23. "Letter from William A. White"; "Letter from George Bradburn."

24. "Letter from William A. White"; "Letter from George Bradburn."

25. "Letter from William A. White"; "Letter from George Bradburn"; John L. Forkner and Byron H. Dyson, *Historical Sketches and Reminiscences of Madison County, Indiana* (Anderson, Ind., 1897), 750–52; R. C. Smedley, *History of the Underground Railroad in Chester and the Neighboring Counties of Pennsylvania* (Lancaster: Journal, 1883), 187–88.

26. "Letter from George Bradburn"; "Letter from Edwin Fussell," *National Anti-Slavery Standard,* Feb. 15, 1844; Smedley, *History,* 188.

27. Smedley, *History*, 187–88; McFeely, *Frederick Douglass*, 110; Gamble, "Moral Suasion," 283. Some of the rioters were arrested, but charges against them were eventually dismissed on a technicality after threats of another mobbing. See "Letter from Edwin Fussell"; "Extract from Letter from Dr. Fussell," *National Anti-Slavery Standard*, Oct. 3, 1844.

28. "Letter from George Bradburn"; Thomas D. Hamm, "Daniel Worth: Persistent Abolitionist" (Senior Honors thesis, Butler University, 1979), 38; Sydney Howard Gay, "The Hundred Conventions," *Liberator*, Oct. 20, 1843; S. H. Gay, "The Hundred Conventions," ibid., Jan. 26, 1844.

29. Brooke to Chapman, Oct. 5, 1843; Brooke to Chapman, Oct. 10, 1843, vol. 19, p. 51, Weston Papers; Remond to Post, Sept. 27, 1843.

30. Remond to Post, Sept. 27, 1843; "Notice," *Free Labor Advocate*, 10th Mo. 6, 1843.

31. Brooke to Chapman, Oct. 10, 1843.

32. George Bradburn to John A. Collins, Nov. 21, 1843, vol. 13, p. 18, Anti-Slavery Collection (Rare Books Department, Boston Public Library, Boston); Gamble, "Moral Suasion," 282–83.

33. Gamble, "Moral Suasion," 281; Kelley to Monroe, Oct. 2, 1843, box 1, Monroe Papers.

34. Brooke to Chapman, Oct. 5, 1843.

5. The Communities

1. John O. Wattles letter, *Regenerator*, Jan. 29, 1844.

2. John Humphrey Noyes, *History of American Socialisms* (New York: Hillary House, 1961), 309.

3. Ibid., 310; John O. Wattles, "History of Communities," *Communitist*, June 18, 1845. There is disagreement about the date of founding. John Humphrey Noyes and John O. Wattles put it in 1841. Thomas Michener, in an article dated January 20, 1845, wrote that the community "began rising of two years ago." Nathan C. Meeker wrote that it began early in 1842. See Noyes, *History*, 310; Wattles, "History"; Thomas Michener, "The Marlborough Community," *Communitist*, March 12, 1845; Nathan C. Meeker, "Marlborough Association," *People's Rights and Working Man's Advocate*, July 27, 1844.

4. Noyes, *History*, 311; "Obituary," *Philanthropist*, Feb. 14, 1844; Valentine Nicholson, Autobiography, July 4, 1881, typescript, pp. 36–37, Valentine Nicholson Papers (Indiana Historical Society, Indianapolis); "Annual Report of the Stark County Anti-Slavery Society," *Philanthropist*, Oct. 22, 1842; Jacob Ferris, "Letter from Brother Ferris—the Property System," *Regenerator*, April 25, 1844; Amos Gilbert, "Theology and Ethics," ibid., May 1, 1844; Esther Wattles, Autobiography, n.d., John O. Wattles Papers (Western Reserve Historical Society, Cleveland); Marius Robinson to Emily Robinson, 2nd Mo. 13, 1837, Marius R. Robinson Papers (Western Reserve Historical Society, Cleveland); William Wade Hinshaw, ed., *Encyclopedia of American Quaker Genealogy* (6 vols., Ann Arbor: Edwards Brothers, 1936–50), IV, 777, 846; Owen Thomas obituary, Hartford, Mich., *Daysprings*, June 27, 1894. For Mary F. Thomas, see Edward T. James et al., eds.,

Notable American Women, 1607–1950: A Biographical Dictionary (3 vols., Cambridge: Belknap, 1971), III, 450–51. Emily Rakestraw Robinson had lived at New Garden as a girl. See Emily Robinson interview, box 103, Wilbur H. Siebert Collection (Ohio Historical Society, Columbus).

5. Amos Gilbert, "Marlborough Community," *Regenerator,* May 11, 1844; Michener, "Marlborough Community."

6. Noyes, *History,* 311; Meeker, "Marlborough Association"; A. J. MacDonald, "Marlborough Community," pp. 309–10, A. J. MacDonald Mss. (Beinecke Rare Book and Manuscript Library, Yale University, New Haven, Conn.); A. Brooke, "Universal Inquiry and Reform," *Vermont Telegraph,* Sept. 6, 1843.

7. MacDonald, "Marlborough Community," 309–10; Gilbert, "Marlborough Community."

8. MacDonald, "Marlborough Community," 310.

9. Ibid.; Noyes, *History,* 311.

10. Noyes, *History,* 310–13; Stark County Deeds, Book 32, pp. 207–208 (Stark County Recorder's Office, Canton, Ohio); Ibid., Book 35, pp. 513–14.

11. Noyes, *History,* 313–15; Abraham Brooke to Maria Weston Chapman, Oct. 10, 1843, vol. 19, p. 51, Weston Family Papers (Rare Books Department, Boston Public Library, Boston).

12. Noyes, *History,* 314–15.

13. Ibid., 313–14.

14. Ibid., 313–14. After the community broke up, in January 1846 Jonathan Thomas, Edward Brooke, Lewis Morgan, and Marius Robinson as trustees sold the community land to Edward and William Brooke and Marius and Emily Robinson. See Stark County Deeds, Book 35, pp. 514–20.

15. Nicholson, Autobiography, 49–55; "Notice," *Free Labor Advocate,* 1st Mo. 26, 1844; Valentine Nicholson letter, ibid., 12th Mo. 29, 1843.

16. Nicholson, Autobiography, 55–56; Rachel Pim, *Ancestry and Descendants of Nathan Pim, 1641–1904* (Damascus, Ohio, 1904).

17. Nicholson, Autobiography, 50–51; John O. Wattles, "Report from Brother Wattles," *Regenerator,* April 4, 1844.

18. "Report from Brother Wattles."

19. Ibid.; John O. Wattles, "Humanity's Home in the West," *Regenerator,* March 28, 1844.

20. "Report from Brother Wattles."

21. Nicholson, Autobiography, 55–56.

22. Ibid., 56.

23. "Prairie Home," n.d., Nicholson Papers; Benjamin B. Davis to Hugh Hilles, 8th Mo. 22, 1841, ibid.; List of Prairie Home Residents, n.d., Wattles Papers; Hinshaw, ed., *Encyclopedia,* IV, 810, 812–13, 826, 852–53; Joel P. Davis to Wilbur H. Siebert, Sept. 10, 1892, box 103, Siebert Collection; Willard C. Heiss, "Hiram Mendenhall and the Union Home Community," *Bulletin of Friends Historical Association,* 44 (Spring 1955), 50.

24. Joel P. Davis to Siebert, Sept. 10, 1892; Benjamin B. Davis to Hilles, 8th Mo. 22,

1841; "Anti-Slavery Convention, Jay County, Indiana," *Philanthropist,* April 28, 1840; John Carroll Whinery interview with Siebert, Aug. 21, 1892, box 103, Siebert Collection.

25. "Prairie Home"; Willard C. Heiss, ed., *Abstracts of the Records of the Society of Friends in Indiana* (7 vols., Indianapolis: Indiana Historical Society, 1962–77), II, 414, IV, 316; Thomas D. Hamm et al., "Moral Choices: Two Indiana Quaker Communities and the Abolitionist Movement," *Indiana Magazine of History,* 87 (June 1991), 117–54; A. J. MacDonald, "Prairie Home Community Near West Liberty, Logan Co. O 1844," pp. 273, 283, 285, A. J. MacDonald Mss. (Beinecke Rare Book and Manuscript Library); Mary Clark to Mary P. Rogers, Feb. 10, 1840, box 1, Nathaniel Peabody Rogers Papers (Quaker Collection, Haverford College, Haverford, Pa.); Walter M. Merrill and Louis Ruchames, eds., *The Letters of William Lloyd Garrison* (6 vols., Cambridge: Belknap, 1971–81), II, 693–94; "Drag Out at Manchester," *Herald of Freedom,* March 2, 1843; John B. Chandler letter, ibid., Oct. 21, 1843; W. D. Schooley to Siebert, Nov. 18, 1893, box 81, Siebert Collection; Parker Pillsbury, *Acts of the Anti-Slavery Apostles* (Concord, N. H., 1883), 158. For Harlow Hard, see above, 137. It is possible that Nicholson intended to refer to *Edwin* Gardner and sisters Emily and Irena, Orthodox Friends from Union County, Indiana, with strong reform interests.

26. Nicholson, Autobiography, 64–65; O. S. Murray, "Storm on Lake Erie," *Subterranean and Working Man's Advocate,* Nov. 2, 1844.

27. Murray, "Storm on Lake Erie." See also, "The Infidel in a Gale," *Regenerator,* April 28, 1845.

28. Murray, "Storm on Lake Erie"; Nicholson, Autobiography, 66.

29. Nicholson, Autobiography, 60–64.

30. Ibid., 60.

31. Ibid., 57–58.

32. Amos Gilbert, "Talk about Communities," *Regenerator,* May 4, 1844. See also B.C. Gilbert, "Communities in the West," ibid., May 11, 1844.

33. Nicholson, Autobiography, 57.

34. Noyes, *History,* 321–23; John O. Wattles, "Prairie Home Community," *Communitist,* Nov. 13, 1844.

35. Wattles, "Prairie Home"; Wattles, "History of Communities."

36. Noyes, *History,* 324–26; Maria Mendenhall Michener Reminiscence, 1915, Willard C. Heiss Collection (Friends Collection, Lilly Library, Earlham College, Richmond, Ind.).

37. Nicholson, Autobiography, 57–58; MacDonald, "Prairie Home," 273.

38. John O. Wattles memorandum on Prairie Home, 1844, Wattles Papers.

39. Nicholson, Autobiography, 60; Samuel Larned letter, *Regenerator,* June 8, 1844. At this time recipients of letters paid the postage.

40. Samuel Larned letter, *Regenerator,* June 15, 1844.

41. MacDonald, "Prairie Home," 271–72.

42. Ibid., 272–74.

43. Noyes, *History,* 318, 320–21.

44. MacDonald, "Prairie Home," 279–80.

45. Noyes, *History,* 279–80.

46. Ibid., 322–23.

47. Wattles, "Prairie Home"; MacDonald, "Prairie Home," 281.

48. Wattles, "Prairie Home"; MacDonald, "Prairie Home," 287–88.

49. MacDonald, "Prairie Home," 289; Nicholson, Autobiography, 58, 60.

50. Nicholson, Autobiography, 64.

51. Ibid., 67.

52. Ibid., 68–70; Noyes, History, 326–27. For one of Valentine Nicholson's letters, see "Prairie Home Community—Letter from Valentine Nicholson," Working Man's Advocate, Nov. 30, 1844. This account agrees in every particular with Nicholson's autobiography.

53. Nicholson, Autobiography, 67–68.

54. Ibid., 71, 75.

55. Merrill and Ruchames, eds., Letters, II, 693–94; MacDonald, "Prairie Home," 425.

56. "Prairie Home," Regenerator, June 5, 1845; Valentine Nicholson, "Prairie Home," ibid., May 12, 1845; O. S. Murray, "Prairie Home," ibid.

57. "Prairie Home," Regenerator, June 5, 1845.

58. "Prairie Home Community—Letter from Valentine Nicholson."

59. MacDonald, "Prairie Home," 274–75; Nicholson, Autobiography, 53–55. A. J. MacDonald's account of Highland Home is a section of his description of his experiences visiting Prairie Home.

60. Oswald K. Reames, The Story of a Place Called Goshen: The People and Early Meetings Associated with It (n.p., 1961); History of Logan County and Ohio (Chicago: Baskin & Co., 1880), 420–21.

61. Nicholson, Autobiography, 53–54.

62. History of Logan County, 400–401; Anna E. Shaddinger, comp., The Micheners in America (Rutland, Vt.: Charles E. Tuttle, 1958), 172, 186; Hinshaw, ed., Encyclopedia, IV, 838, 1290.

63. Nicholson, Autobiography, 54; Goshen Monthly Meeting (Hicksite) Men's Minutes, 2nd Mo. 20, 1841 (Ohio Valley Yearly Meeting Archives, Wilmington College, Wilmington, Ohio); Indiana Yearly Meeting (Hicksite) Men's Minutes, 9th Mo. 26, 1843 (ibid.); Ibid., 9th Mo. 25, 1837; "A Disclaimer," Philanthropist, July 14, 1841; "An Epistle from a Conference of Friends, Held at Green Plain, Ohio," Free Labor Advocate, 12th Mo. 6, 1843.

64. Nicholson, Autobiography, 54–55.

65. George Taylor, "Letter from Brother Taylor," Regenerator, April 29, 1844.

66. Edwin Michener, "Deity, Accountability, God's Laws, Materialism, Etc.," Regenerator, May 25, 1844; O. K. Reames to Willard Heiss, Nov. 30, 1952, Heiss Collection; MacDonald, "Prairie Home," 276; John Dugdale to William R. Dugdale, March 4, 1844, Dugdale-Hilles Papers, Heiss Collection.

67. MacDonald, "Prairie Home," 275–76.

68. Ibid., 276; Michener, "Deity."

69. MacDonald, "Prairie Home," 274–77.

70. Wattles, "Prairie Home."

71. "Anti-Slavery Convention, Jay Co."; J. H. Mendenhall, "Sketch of the Origin, Use & Method of Operating the Old Underground Railroad," Jan. 1, 1896, box 77, Siebert Collection.

72. "Agreement for Settlement of Property by William R. Dugdale, George Williams et al.," June 21, 1845, Dugdale-Hilles Papers; Hinshaw, ed., *Encyclopedia*, IV, 238–39, 812, 823, 826, 830, 833; Heiss, ed., *Abstracts*, I, 217, 220, 223, 224, II, 428–31; Dwight L. Smith, "Burials in West Grove Cemetery, Penn Township, Jay County, Indiana," 1982 (Friends Collection).

73. "Constitution of the Fraternal Brotherhood," attached to Joseph H. Mendenhall to Nicholson, Dec. 19, 1844, Nicholson Papers.

74. Ibid.

75. Dwight L. Smith interview with Nathan M. Scott, Sept. 6, 1939, Dugdale-Hilles Papers.

76. Matilda Hilles to Rebecca Irey, April 6, 1845, ibid.

77. William H. Hilles to Hugh Hilles, Oct. 12, 1845, Dugdale-Hilles Papers; "Agreement for Settlement."

78. Heiss, "Hiram Mendenhall."

79. John O. Wattles to Esther Whinery [1843], Wattles Papers.

80. "Community," *Free Labor Advocate*, 11th Mo. 1, 1843.

81. *Richmond* (Ind.) *Palladium*, Oct. 7, 1847; "Female Anti-Slavery Meeting," *Free Labor Advocate*, 12th Mo. 24, 1841; Heiss, ed., *Abstracts*, I, 216; Errol T. Elliott, *Quakers on the American Frontier: A History of the Westward Migrations, Settlements, and Developments of Friends on the American Continent* (Richmond, Ind.: Friends United Press, 1969), 397; Israel French to Halliday Jackson, 1st Mo. 18, 10th Mo. 10, 1828, 7th Mo. 5, 9th Mo. 18, 1829, Halliday Jackson Papers (Friends Historical Library, Swarthmore College, Swarthmore, Pa.); Hinshaw, ed., *Encyclopedia*, V, 472, 520; Lillie Buffum Chace Wyman and Arthur Crawford Wyman, *Elizabeth Buffum Chace 1806–1899: Her Life and Its Environment* (2 vols., Boston: W. B. Clarke, 1914), I, 89.

82. Heiss. ed., *Abstracts*, III, 125; Hinshaw, ed., *Encyclopedia*, V, 787; *Autobiography of Allen Jay, Born 1831, Died 1910* (Philadelphia: John C. Winston, 1910), 45; John W. Miller, *Indiana Newspaper Bibliography* (Indianapolis: Indiana Historical Society, 1982), 132.

83. Heiss, ed., *Abstracts*, IV, 223, VI, 312–13; Henry County Wills, Book D, pp. 455–57 (Henry County Clerk of Courts Office, New Castle, Ind.); Hamilton County, Indiana, Probate Orders, Book B, pp. 375–77 (Hamilton County Clerk of Courts Office, Noblesville, Ind.); *History of Hamilton County, Indiana, with Illustrations and Biographical Sketches of Some of Its Prominent Men and Pioneers* (Chicago: Kingman, 1880), 61, 134, 136–37; Leanna K.Roberts et al., *A History of Westfield and Washington Township* (Noblesville, Ind.: Image Builders, 1984), 12–18.

84. Heiss, ed., *Abstracts*, IV, 316.

85. John O. Wattles, "Reply to Benjamin Warden's Inquiries in Regard to Communities in the West," *Regenerator*, May 25, 1844.

86. Ibid.

87. George Taylor, "A Voice from Indiana," *Regenerator*, June 22, 1844; J. Rufus Hin-

shaw, "Slavery," typescript, 1911 (Henry County Historical Society, New Castle, Ind.); Elwood Pleas, *Henry County: Past and Present: A Brief History of the County, 1821 to 1871* (New Castle, Ind.: Pleas Brothers, 1871), 73; *Life and Travels of Addison Coffin* (Cleveland: William G. Hubbard, 1897), 63–64.

88. Taylor, "Voice from Indiana."

89. Ibid.

90. Heiss, ed., *Abstracts*, I, 241, 246, 256, IV, 170; Pleas, *Henry County*, 110–11; "Letter from Rebecca Edgerton," *Free Labor Advocate*, 9th Mo. 13, 1845; Thomas D. Hamm, *The Antislavery Movement in Henry County, Indiana* (New Castle, Ind.: Henry County Historical Society, 1987), 66; Hamm et al., "Moral Choices," 127, 153; *New Castle* (Ind.) *Courier*, Aug. 27, 1875.

91. Emily [Gardner] to Esther Wattles and Joel P. Davis [June 1844], Wattles Papers.

92. "Notice," *Free Labor Advocate*, 7th Mo. 19, 1844.

93. Kersey Grave letter, *Communitist*, Nov. 13, 1844.

94. *History of Wayne County, Indiana* (2 vols., Chicago: Interstate, 1884), I, 639; "The Cause Abroad," *Pennsylvania Freeman*, 10th Mo. 17, 1839; Kersey Grave letter, *Free Labor Advocate*, 8th Mo. 31, 1844; Heiss, ed., *Abstracts*, I, 108; *Biographical History of Eminent and Self-Made Men of the State of Indiana* (2 vols., Cincinnati: Western Biographical Publishers, 1880), 6th District, 31–32.

95. Kersey Grave letter, *Communitist*, Nov. 13, 1844.

96. Randolph County Deeds, Book K, p. 252 (Randolph County Recorder's Office, Winchester, Ind.); Heiss, ed., *Abstracts*, IV, 279; D. Winston Jones letter, *Herald of Progression*, June 1845. According to his tombstone, Asa Bales died Sept. 10, 1845. Huldah Wickersham died June 2, 1845. See "Letter from Rebecca Edgerton."

97. Heiss, "Hiram Mendenhall," 48–50; Heiss, ed., *Abstracts*, I, 224, 251, II, 359, 415; Hinshaw, ed., *Encyclopedia*, IV, 359, V, 789–90.

98. Heiss, "Hiram Mendenhall," 50; Hinshaw, ed., *Encyclopedia*, IV, 319, 560, 812–13; 1850 U.S. Census, Population Schedules, Henry County, Indiana, p. 297.

99. Hiram Mendenhall letter, *Herald of Progression*, June 1845; Pusey Grave deposition, Feb. 21, 1850, Hiram Mendenhall lawsuit file, Heiss Collection.

100. Pusey Grave deposition; Mendenhall letter; Thurston Conant, Pusey Grave, and Mark Patty deposition, Aug. 30, 1848, Mendenhall file; Randolph Circuit Court Complete Record Civil, spring 1850 term, roll 40 (Randolph County Clerk of Courts Office, Winchester, Ind.).

101. Mendenhall letter; "Letter from W. Rufus Merine," *Herald of Progression*, July 1845.

102. Mendenhall letter; Pusey Grave deposition.

103. Hiram Mendenhall deposition, Aug. 1847, Mendenhall file; Conant, Grave, and Patty deposition.

104. Mendenhall deposition; Pusey Grave deposition.

105. Mendenhall deposition; Conant, Grave, and Patty deposition. See also the files of claims, 1851–1855, in the Hiram Mendenhall estate file, Heiss Collection.

106. "Union Home," *Herald of Progression*, March 1846.

107. Randolph Circuit Court Complete Record, roll 40.

108. *History of Medina County and Ohio* (Chicago: Baskin & Battey, 1881), 255–56, 419–21, 448; State of Vermont, General Index to Vital Records, microfilm, s.v. Harlow Hard; Genealogical Society of Utah, *International Genealogical Index: Ohio* (Salt Lake City, 1988), s.v. Harlow Hard; 1850 U.S. Census, Population Schedules, Marshall County, Indiana, p. 933.

109. 1850 Marshall County census, p. 933; 1840 U.S. Census, Population Schedules, Delaware County, Ohio, p. 256; *History of Medina County*, 255–56; Daniel McDonald, *History of Marshall County, Indiana, 1836 to 1880* (Chicago: Kingman, 1881), 101, 104.

110. Harlow Hard to Stephen S. Harding, Feb. 22, 1843, *Free Labor Advocate*, 3rd Mo. 25, 1843; H. Hard letter, ibid., 4th Mo. 20, 1844.

111. Charles Mowland letter, *Regenerator*, Aug. 4, 1844; Marshall County Deeds, Book F, pp. 193–94 (Marshall County Recorder's Office, Plymouth, Ind.); ibid., Book J, pp. 15–16. For the water-cure movement, see Susan E. Cayleff, *Wash and Be Healed: The Water-Cure Movement and Women's Health* (Philadelphia: Temple University Press, 1987), 17–48.

112. Harlow Hard letter, *Regenerator*, June 19, 1845; "Extract of a Letter," *Herald of Progression*, June 1845.

113. "Extract."

114. Ibid.; Harlow Hard letter.

115. "Extract."

116. Editorial, *Herald of Progression*, Oct. 1845; Harlow Hard to Libanus Allen, Nov. 19, 1845, *Regenerator*, Dec. 11, 1845.

117. "Communication from Harlow Hard," *Regenerator*, April 6, 1846; Harlow Hard, "Worship—War," ibid., July 21, 1846; "Communication from Harlow Hard," ibid., June 23, 1847; Harlow Hard Estate file, box 249, case 1, Marshall County Probates (Marshall County Clerk of Courts Office, Plymouth, Ind.).

118. Arthur Eugene Bestor Jr., *Backwoods Utopias: The Sectarian and Owenite Phases of Communitarian Socialism in America, 1663–1829* (Philadelphia: University of Pennsylvania Press, 1950), 207–208; H. W. Beckwith, *History of Fountain County, Together with Historic Notes on the Wabash Valley* (Chicago: H. H. Hill and N. Iddings, 1881), 399–400; Fountain County Deeds, Book 1, p. 121 (Fountain County Recorder's Office, Covington, Ind.); Rebecca Hardin, *My Father's People* (Mooresville, Ind.: Dickinson Printing Co., 1982), 47–49, 55, 71.

119. Beckwith, *History of Fountain County*, 399–400; Bestor, *Backwoods Utopias*, 208–209; J. Wesley Whicker to Demarchus C. Brown, May 8, 1915, Coal Creek Community Church of God Collection (Indiana Division, Indiana Historical Society); William Ludlow v. Jonathan Crane et al., Feb. 4, 1832, ibid.

120. Ruth Crane letter, *Regenerator*, April 1, 1844; Ruth Crane, "A Voice from Indiana," ibid., May 18, 1844; Hardin, *My Father's People*, 83; Taylor, "Voice from Indiana."

121. Ruth Crane letter; Crane, "Voice from Indiana"; Abraham R. Crane letter, *Herald of Progression*, May 1845.

122. Thomas Evans letter, *Herald of Progression*, June 1845.

123. "Grand Prairie Home Community," *Regenerator*, Aug. 4, 1845.

124. T. Evans, "Grand Prairie Home Community," *Regenerator*, Oct. 20, 1845; "Letter from Brother Johnson," *Herald of Progression*, Feb. 1846.

125. "Letter from Gilbert F. Bailey," *Herald of Progression*, April 1846; Evans, "Grand Prairie."

126. "Letter from Gilbert F. Bailey"; "Letter from Brother Johnson"; "Grand Prairie Home Community"; Crane, "Voice from Indiana."

127. "Letter from Gilbert F. Bailey"; Editorial, *Herald of Progression*, April 1846.

128. Gilbert F. Bailey, "Grand Prairie Community," *Regenerator*, Sept. 7, 1846; Beckwith, *History of Fountain County*, 354.

129. Lester Grosvenor Wells, *The Skaneateles Communal Experiment, 1843–1846* (Syracuse, N.Y.: Onondaga Historical Association, 1953), 2–3.

130. Syracuse, N.Y., *Onondaga Standard*, April 12, May 3, 1843.

131. See above, pp. 85–86.

132. *Onondaga Standard*, Aug. 23, 1843.

133. Q. A. Johnson to Nicholson, Aug. 23, 1843, Nicholson Papers.

134. Nicholson, Autobiography, 37–38. This section of Valentine Nicholson's autobiography is a transcription of a long letter from Quincy A. Johnson dated Dec. 8, 1843. The original apparently has not survived.

135. Ibid., 38; "A Short Sermon," *Communitist*, April 23, 1845.

136. "Community Convention at Skaneateles," *Herald of Freedom*, Oct. 27, 1843.

137. Ibid.

138. Onondaga County Deeds, Book 84, pp. 378–79, 407 (Onondaga County Clerk's Office, Syracuse, N.Y.); Nicholson, Autobiography, 39; Peter S. Jennison, *The History of Woodstock, Vermont, 1890–1983* (Woodstock: Countryman Press, 1985), 64–65.

139. Noyes, *History*, 139; Quincy A. Johnson obituary, *Onondaga Standard*, Dec. 5, 1856, Quincy A. Johnson file (Onondaga Historical Association, Syracuse, N.Y.). For evaluations of Johnson's role, see Noyes, *History*, 168; H. Roger Grant, ed., "The Skaneateles Community: A New York Utopia," *Niagara Frontier*, 22 (1975), 70; John L. Thomas, "Antislavery and Utopia," in *The Antislavery Vanguard: New Essays on the Abolitionists*, ed. Martin Duberman (Princeton: Princeton University Press, 1965), 257–58; Mark Holloway, *Heavens on Earth: Utopian Communities in America, 1680–1880* (London: Turnstile Press, 1951), 125; William Alfred Hinds, *American Communities* (Chicago: Charles H. Kerr, 1902), 255; and Robert S. Fogarty, *Dictionary of American Communal and Utopian History* (Westport: Greenwood, 1980), 165.

140. The only account we have of this series of confrontations is in Johnson's letter in Nicholson autobiography, 38–39.

141. Ibid., 40–41.

142. Ibid., 41.

143. Ibid.

144. Ibid., 41–44.

145. Noyes, *History*, 163–68. Johnson's letter to Nicholson includes the propositions. See Nicholson, Autobiography, 42–44.

146. Nicholson, Autobiography, 45; Noyes, *History*, 166–67.

147. Nicholson, Autobiography, 45–46.
148. Ibid.
149. Ibid., 46–48.
150. Ibid., 39; "Community Herald," Regenerator, April 1, 1844; Lyndsay Swift, Brook Farm: Its Members, Scholars, and Visitors (New York: Corinth, 1961), 175. For John Orvis and Marianne Dwight, and their experiences at Brook Farm, see Marianne Dwight, Letters from Brook Farm, ed. Amy L. Reed (Poughkeepsie: Vassar College, 1928).
151. Noyes, History, 168–69; Nicholson, Autobiography, 46; Onondaga County Deeds, Book 84, pp. 278, 407.
152. Wells, Skaneateles Communal Experiment, 6–7; R. S. Orvis, "Our Condition," Herald of Freedom, April 26, 1844.
153. "Social Reorganization—Convention at Boston," Regenerator, Jan. 4, 1843 [sic— should be 1844]; Samuel Sellers Jr. letter, Herald of Freedom, Jan. 12, 1844; "Decennial Meeting of the American Anti-Slavery Society," ibid., Dec. 29, 1843.
154. "Social Reorganization."
155. "Preamble and Constitution of the New England Social Reform Society," Jan. 31, 1844, broadside, vol. 20, p. 21, Weston Papers; William White letter, Regenerator, April 1, 1844; "A Convention," Herald of Freedom, Jan. 26, 1844; "Meetings at Milford," ibid.; "Lowell Convention," ibid., March 9, 1844.
156. E. Gould Buffum, "Creeds and Communities," Regenerator, Feb. 26, 1844. This article includes editorial commentary by Orson S. Murray.
157. Marenda B. Randall, "Report from Skaneateles," Regenerator, April 1, 1844; "The Skaneateles Community," Working Man's Advocate, July 20, 1844.
158. Wells, Skaneateles Communal Experiment, 13; "Skaneateles Community." The latter apparently was reprinted from the Onondaga Standard.
159. Nicholson, Autobiography, 38–39; John A. Collins, A Bird's Eye View of Society as it Is, and as It Should Be (Boston: J. P. Mendum, 1844), 30–31; Wells, Skaneateles Communal Experiment, 9; Orvis, "Our Condition."
160. John Finch's account is reprinted in Grant, "Skaneateles Community," 68–72.
161. Ibid., 71.
162. Ibid., 70; Noyes, History, 168; Nicholson, Autobiography, 38–39; The Social Pioneer and Herald of Progress (Boston: J. P. Mendum [1844]), 10; Samuel Sellers, "Skaneateles Community—John A. Collins," Liberator, Feb. 28, 1845.
163. "Skaneateles Community."
164. Grant, ed., "Skaneateles Community," 70; "How to Succeed," Communitist, Oct. 30, 1844.
165. "Our Experience, Prospects, and Wants." Communitist, Sept. 18, 1845.
166. Ibid.
167. The deed establishing the community mentions the following as "actual residents": George Pryor, William O. Duvall, Solomon Johnson, John Parkley, Samuel Simpson, Maria Loomis, William D. Rector, Milo Cook, Robert Tuttle, John Orvis, William Herrington, William C. Russom, James Smith, Leonard Sayer, Horace Schenck, R. S. Orvis, and Joseph A. Whitemarsh. It names as "at work upon, & to improve the premises" Hiram Orvis, James Jackson, Martin W. Combs, Ezra C. Smith, Stephen

Abbott, Jacob Rayley, H. R. Park, Silas Bliss, William L. Turley, Nathaniel Whitney [Whiting?], Jacob Orvis, John Tobias, S. C. Rowley, Joseph B. Cowell, William Canada, Benjamin Barney, William Snooks, John Barron, and Edward Chapman. See Onondaga County Deeds, Book 84, pp. 378–79.

168. Edmund Norman Leslie, *Skaneateles: History of the Earliest Settlement and Reminiscences of Later Times* (New York: Andrew H. Kellogg, 1902), 177; Wells, *Skaneateles Communal Experiment*, 11. On Samuel Sellers, see his letter in the *Vermont Telegraph*, Sept. 27, 1843; and Anthony F. C. Wallace, *Rockdale: The Growth of an American Village in the Early Industrial Revolution* (New York: W. W. Norton, 1972), 220–25. On Joseph Savage, see obituary, 1878, Joseph Savage file, (Onondaga Historical Association). On Maria Loomis, see Elisha S. Loomis, *Descendants of Joseph Loomis in America and His Antecedents in the Old World* (N.p., 1908), 275. On William C. Benson, see Merrill and Ruchames, eds., *Letters*, II, 272. On Darius R. Stone, see his letter in the *Herald of Freedom*, May 5, 1843. For Ezra C. Smith, see "Communication from M. W. Jenkins," *Regenerator*, Dec. 13, 1847.

169. Editorial, *Herald of Progression*, June 25, 1846; Joseph A. Whitemarsh, "Declaration of Sentiments," *Liberator*, March 1, 1839; Joseph A. Whitemarsh letter, ibid., Jan. 12, 1838; "Light and Liberty," *Non-Resistant*, Sept. 9, 1840.

170. Randall, "Report"; M. L., "Diet," *Communitist*, April 9, 1845; A. J. MacDonald, "Skaneateles Community, Community Place, Mottville, Onondaga Co., N.Y., 1843–1846," n.d., p. 100, MacDonald Mss.

171. Noyes, *History*, 175–79.

172. John A. Collins, "One Year's Experience," *Communitist*, Sept. 18, 1844; Maria Loomis, "Explanation," ibid., March 12, 1845; "Celebration of the First of January, 1846," ibid., Jan. 8, 1846.

173. Collins, "One Year's Experience"; Loomis, "Explanation."

174. Darius R. Stone letter, *Herald of Freedom*, Jan. 23, 1846; "Skaneatelas [*sic*] Community—Letter from Marenda B. Randall," *Working Man's Advocate*, Nov. 30, 1844.

175. Barbara Bendall Spain and Karen Richards Anklin, *Skaneateles . . . Glimpses of the Past* (Moravia, N.Y.: Village Printer, 1987), 70; Sellers, "Skaneateles Community"; R. S. Orvis, "The Use and Abuse of General Terms in Their Application to Theoretical and Practical Morality," *Communitist*, Oct. 30, 1844; John A. Collins, "Our First Year," ibid., Sept. 18, 1844; "The New Year," ibid., Jan. 15, 1845; "Celebration."

176. "The Communitist," *Communitist*, June 18, 1845; "To Our Readers," ibid., Sept. 25, 1845; "New Arrangement," ibid., Sept. 12, 1845; "The Communitist," *Herald of Freedom*, Jan. 26, 1844.

177. "Our Position," ibid., Feb. 19, 1846.

178. Wells, *Skaneateles Communal Experiment*, 14; "That Charter," *Communitist*, Nov. 27, 1845; "Correspondence," ibid., March 5, 1846.

179. Wells, *Skaneateles Communal Experiment*, 11, 14.

180. Ibid., 14–15.

181. Noyes, *History*, 173; "John A. Collins," *Anti-Slavery Bugle*, Aug. 28, 1846; Wells, *Skaneateles Communal Experiment*, 15.

182. Wells, *Skaneateles Communal Experiment*, 15; Editorial, *Communitist*, Oct. 23, 1845; *Onondaga Standard*, Sept. 18, 1847, clipping, Skaneateles Community file; ibid., April 24, 1851, ibid.

183. Edward K. Spann, *Brotherly Tomorrows: Movements for a Cooperative Society in America, 1820–1920* (New York: Columbia University Press, 1989), xiv.

184. Rosabeth Moss Kanter, *Commitment and Community: Communes and Utopias in Sociological Perspective* (Cambridge: Harvard University Press, 1972), 75–125.

6. The Ideology of Universal Reform

1. Maria Loomis, "A Short Sermon," *Communitist*, April 21, 1845.

2. James H. Norton, "Quakers West of the Alleghenies and in Ohio to 1861" (Ph.D. diss., Case Western Reserve University, 1965), 26, 33, 72, 91, 124–26, 336; Willard Heiss, *A List of All the Friends Meetings That Exist or Ever Have Existed in Indiana* (Indianapolis: John Woolman Press, 1961), 65–68; John Williams to Micajah T. Williams, 12th Mo. 18, 1835, Micajah Terrell Williams Papers (Ohio Historical Society, Columbus); Willard C. Heiss, "Hiram Mendenhall and the Union Home Community," *Bulletin of Friends Historical Association*, 44 (Spring 1955), 44–50.

3. Valentine Nicholson, Autobiography, July 4, 1881, typescript, pp. 6–7, 57, Valentine Nicholson Papers (Indiana Historical Society, Indianapolis); William Wade Hinshaw, ed., *Encyclopedia of American Quaker Genealogy* (6 vols., Ann Arbor: Edwards Brothers, 1936–50), V, 147, 214; Edwin Fussell to Esther Lewis, Aug. 3, Aug. 19, 1836, box 3, Graceanna Lewis Papers (Friends Historical Library, Swarthmore College, Swarthmore, Pa.); Edwin Fussell to Esther Lewis, William Fussell, and George Miller, 7th Mo. 19, 1838, ibid.; Israel French to Halliday Jackson, 1st Mo. 14, 1833, Halliday Jackson Papers (Friends Historical Library); Willard C. Heiss, ed., *Abstracts of the Records of the Society of Friends in Indiana* (7 vols., Indianapolis: Indiana Historical Society, 1962–77), I, 208; Lillie Buffum Chace Wyman and Arthur Crawford Wyman, *Elizabeth Buffum Chace, 1806–1899: Her Life and Its Environment* (2 vols., Boston: W. B. Clarke, 1914), I, 88–89; Joseph Allen letter, *Communitist*, Feb. 26, 1845.

4. See above, pp. 112, 129, 131–32.

5. For John O. Wattles, see above, pp. 4–8. For the Robinsons, see Russel B. Nye, "Marius Robinson: A Forgotten Abolitionist Leader," *Ohio State Archeological and Historical Quarterly*, 55 (April-June 1946), 138–54; and Marius Robinson to Emily Robinson, Jan. 13, Jan. 23, 2nd Mo. 13, 1837, Marius R. Robinson Papers (Western Reserve Historical Society, Cleveland). For John A. Collins, see Lawrence S. Friedman, *Gregarious Saints: Self and Community in American Abolition, 1830–1870* (New York: Cambridge University Press, 1982), 45–46.

6. John O. Wattles, untitled essay [ca. 1844], John O. Wattles Papers (Western Reserve Historical Society, Cleveland); John O. Wattles Miscellaneous Manuscripts Transcribed by Esther Wattles, n.d., ibid.; "Randolph, Vermont: Series of Community Meetings," [1843], ibid. Editorial, *Herald of Progression*, Oct. 1845; ibid., April 1846.

7. Rebecca L. Fussell to Esther Lewis, Jan. 1, 1843, box 3, Lewis Papers; Emily [Gardner] to Esther Wattles and Joel P. Davis [1844], Wattles Papers; Wattles Transcripts.

8. Nicholson, Autobiography, 57; "Our Position," *Communitist*, Feb. 19, 1846.

9. [Gardner] to Esther Wattles and Davis; John O. Wattles letter, *Regenerator*, Jan. 29, 1844.

10. Editorial, *Communitist*, Nov. 13, 1844.

11. A. Brooke, "The Liberty Party and the Ohio American Anti-Slavery Society," *Philanthropist*, Jan. 4, 1843. For abolitionist constitutionalism, see Staughton Lynd, "The Abolitionist Critique of the United States Constitution," in *The Antislavery Vanguard: New Essays on the Abolitionists*, ed. Martin Duberman (Princeton: Princeton University Press, 1965), 209–39.

12. Benjamin B. Davis letter, *Herald of Progression*, Nov. 1845; "Submissiveness," ibid., April 1846; John O. Wattles, untitled essay on human nature, n.d., Wattles Papers; "Pleasing Intelligence from New York," *Communitist*, Sept. 18, 1844.

13. "Community," *Herald of Progression*, Nov. 1846; "Submissiveness."

14. "Progression," *Herald of Progression*, Nov. 1846; Maria Loomis, "The Use and Abuse of General Terms," *Communitist*, Sept. 18, 1844; Maria Loomis, "The Scylla and Charybdis," ibid., May 7, 1845.

15. "Submissiveness."

16. John O. Wattles, "Humanity's Home in the West," *Regenerator*, March 23, 1844; Catherine L. Albanese, *Nature Religion in America from the Algonkian Indians to the New Age* (Chicago: University of Chicago Press, 1990), 8–11, 80–152.

17. "Social Reform," *Communitist*, July 10, 1844; "Community," *Herald of Progression*, March 1846; "Randolph, Vermont."

18. "Randolph, Vermont"; [Gardner] to Esther Wattles and Davis; "Letter from John Orvis, of Vermont," *Vermont Telegraph*, Aug. 9, 1843; Emily Robinson to Marius Robinson, Jan. 13, 1837, Robinson Papers.

19. "The Community System," *New York Tribune*, clipping, Dec. 6, 1843, Skaneateles Community file (Onondaga Historical Association, Syracuse, N.Y.); Wattles, untitled essay on human nature; "Randolph, Vermont." For the Inner Light, see Thomas D. Hamm, "The Problem of the Inner Light in Nineteenth-Century Quakerism," in *The Lamb's War: Quaker Essays to Honor Hugh Barbour*, ed. Michael L. Birkel and John W. Newman (Richmond, Ind.: Earlham College Press, 1992), 101–107.

20. "Show Us the Light," *Herald of Progression*, April 15, 1845; "Submissiveness"; "Randolph, Vermont"; R. S. Orvis, "The Use and Abuse of General Terms in Their Application to Theoretical and Practical Morality," *Communitist*, Oct. 30, 1844. At least one communitarian feared that this would lead to absolute moral relativism. See E. W. Capron, "An Inquiry," *Vermont Telegraph*, Aug. 23, 1843.

21. Editorial, *Herald of Progression*, May 1845; John O. Wattles, "Community," *Regenerator*, Jan. 29, 1844; "Social Re-Organization," *Vermont Telegraph*, Sept. 13, 1843.

22. For the "market revolution" and its implications, see Charles G. Sellers Jr., *The Market Revolution: Jacksonian America, 1815–1846* (New York: Oxford University Press, 1991); Harry L. Watson, *Liberty and Power: The Politics of Jacksonian America* (New York:

Noonday, 1990), 17–41; and Sean Wilentz, "Society, Politics, and the Market Revolution, 1815–1848," in *The New American History*, ed. Eric Foner (Philadelphia: Temple University Press, 1990), 51–68.

23. Jonathan A. Glickstein, " 'Poverty Is Not Slavery': American Abolitionists and the Competitive Labor Market," in *Antislavery Reconsidered: New Perspectives on the Abolitionists*, ed. Lewis Perry and Michael Fellman (Baton Rouge: Louisiana State University Press, 1979), 199. See also Ronald G. Walters, *The Antislavery Appeal: American Abolitionism after 1830* (Baltimore: Johns Hopkins University Press, 1978), 111–28.

24. "Wealth—Its Production and Distribution," *Communitist*, Sept. 25, 1845; E. W. Capron letter, ibid., May 7, 1845; "The Future," *Herald of Progression*, April 15, 1845. Wattles quoted Gamaliel Bailey.

25. E. W. Capron letter; "Visit to the Country," *Herald of Progression*, May 22, 1846; John A. Collins, *Bird's Eye View of Society As It Is, and As It Should Be* (Boston: J. P. Mendum, 1844), 13.

26. "Randolph, Vermont"; Samuel Sellers, "Views of Man and Society," *Communitist*, June 18, 1845; "Chattel Slavery vs. Poverty Slavery," ibid., Feb. 26, 1845.

27. John O. Wattles, "Acquisitiveness," *Herald of Progression*, Feb. 1846; Collins, *Bird's Eye View*, 12; John A. Collins letter, *Communitist*, Oct. 30, 1844; "Letter from Dr. Brooke, of Ohio," *Liberator*, March 24, 1843; Glickstein, " 'Poverty Is Not Slavery.' "

28. Valentine Nicholson letter, *Regenerator*, Feb. 1, 1844; A. Brooke letter, ibid., March 4, 1844; Collins, *Bird's Eye View*, 14; J. H. Mendenhall to Valentine Nicholson, Dec. 19, 1844, with attachment, Nicholson Papers; "Randolph, Vermont"; J. M. B., "Wealth and Crime," *Communitist*, Feb. 26, 1844; John A. Collins letter, *Herald of Freedom*, Jan. 21, 1843.

29. J. M. B., "Wealth and Crime"; J. M. Beckett, "Workings of the Banking System," *Communitist*, June 4, 1845; "Letter from Brother Brooke," *Regenerator*, April 18, 1844; Sellers, *Market Revolution*, 355–59; Joseph A. Whitemarsh, "Declaration of Sentiments," *Liberator*, March 1, 1839.

30. Valentine Nicholson, "Socialism," *National Anti-Slavery Standard*, Sept. 14, 1843; W. H. Whinery, "Examine Yourselves," *Young America*, Feb. 28, 1846; "Letter from Dr. Brooke"; A. Brooke, "Social Reform," *Philanthropist*, Aug. 15, 1843; Abraham Brooke letter, *Herald of Freedom*, Aug. 11, 1843; "The Working Man," *Communitist*, Sept. 18, 1844; "Mike Walsh," ibid., Jan. 29, 1845; "Letter from Milo A. Townsend," *Herald of Progression*, Dec. 1845; "Voice of Industry," ibid., March 1846; "A Voice from a Cotton Mill," *Regenerator*, April 8, 1844. For an analysis of these issues, see Marcus Cunliffe, *Chattel Slavery and Wage Slavery: The Anglo-American Context, 1830–1860* (Athens: University of Georgia Press, 1979).

31. John O. Wattles, "A Community Character," *Herald of Progression*, May 1845; Editorial, ibid.

32. Collins, *Bird's Eye View*, 14; W. H. Whinery, "Present Relations," *Regenerator*, Feb. 22, 1847; "Wealth—Its Production and Distribution," ibid., Sept. 25, 1845.

33. "Letter from A. Brooke," *Vermont Telegraph*, Aug. 23, 1843; "Randolph, Vermont."

34. A. Brooke, "Universal Inquiry and Reform," *Vermont Telegraph*, Aug. 23, 1843;

"Letter from Dr. Brooke"; Darius R. Swezey letter, *Communitist*, Jan. 15, 1846; "Randolph, Vermont"; Editorial, *Herald of Progression;* Jacob Ferris, "Letter from Brother Ferris—The Property System," *Regenerator,* April 29, 1844.

35. W. H. Whinery, "Prospectus—A Horticultural Association," *Regenerator,* June 23, 1845; William H. Whinery, "Community," ibid., Jan. 25, 1847; "Communication from Valentine Nicholson," ibid., Feb. 1, 1844; A. Brooke, "Universal Inquiry and Reform," *Vermont Telegraph,* Sept. 6, 1843.

36. "Letter from A. Brooke"; "Letter from Brother Nicholson," *Regenerator,* May 4, 1844; John O. Wattles, "Letter from Augustus Wattles," *Herald of Progression,* Jan. 1846. For the deeds for the Skaneateles and Union Home communities, see Onondaga County Deeds, Book 84, pp. 378–79 (Onondaga County Recorder's Office, Syracuse, N.Y.); and Randolph County Deeds, Book K, p. 252 (Randolph County Recorder's Office, Winchester, Ind.). The only deeds relating to Marlborough are those selling community lands after the community's dissolution, doubtless recorded at the insistence of the purchasers. See Stark County Deeds, Book 32, pp. 513–20 (Stark County Recorder's Office, Canton, Ohio). Searches of deeds in Logan and Champaign counties in Ohio and in Jay, Marshall, and Warren counties in Indiana showed no deeds recorded for communities there.

37. Valarie H. Ziegler, *The Advocates of Peace in Antebellum America* (Bloomington: Indiana University Press, 1992), 13; "Constitution of the Grand Prairie Harmonial Institute," 1853, Wattles Papers; "Manual Labor School," *Herald of Progression,* Jan. 1846.

38. John O. Wattles, untitled essay on natural law, transcribed by Esther Wattles, Wattles Papers; "Randolph, Vermont"; Valentine Nicholson, "Socialism," *National Anti-Slavery Standard,* Sept. 14, 1843, George Taylor letter, *Regenerator,* April 29, 1844; Marenda B. Randall letter, ibid., April 1, 1844.

39. Collins, *Bird's Eye View,* 13, 27; "Prospectus of Volume XV," *Vermont Telegraph,* Sept. 21, 1843. For producerism, see Marvin Meyers, *The Jacksonian Persuasion* (Palo Alto: Stanford University Press, 1958).

40. "Our Cause in New York," *Communitist,* Sept. 4, 1844; "Letter from A. Brooke"; "Letter from Brother Nicholson"; Morton and Lucia White, *The Intellectual versus the City: From Thomas Jefferson to Frank Lloyd Wright* (New York: Mentor, 1964), 32–62.

41. "Chattel Slavery."

42. "Acquisitiveness"; Editorial, *Herald of Progression,* May 1845; Whinery, "Prospectus."

43. Collins, *Bird's Eye View,* 25–26; "Letter from Walter Scott," *Herald of Progression,* Aug. 1, 1846; Whinery, "Examine Yourselves"; Nicholson, "Socialism."

44. Collins, *Bird's Eye View,* 30–32.

45. Ronald G. Walters, *American Reformers, 1815–1860* (New York: Hill and Wang, 1978), 146–47; Paul Starr, *The Social Transformation of American Medicine* (New York: Basic, 1983), 30–59; Jack Larkin, *The Reshaping of Everyday Life, 1790–1840* (New York: Harper and Row, 1988), 72–73, 86–91.

46. Walters, *American Reformers,* 147–49; Stephen Nissenbaum, *Sex, Diet, and Debility in Jacksonian America: Sylvester Graham and Health Reform* (Westport: Greenwood, 1980).

47. Esther Wattles to Theano Wattles, June 1877, Wattles Papers; Sarah Stephens to John O. Wattles, Oct. 25, 1840, ibid.; Esther Wattles, Reminiscences, n.d., ibid.; Valentine Nicholson, "Law, Gospel, Creeds, Constitutions, Infidels, Christians, Communities, 'Fourierites,' Grahamites, Etc.," *Regenerator*, May 8, 1844; "Temper and Diet," *Vermont Telegraph*, May 3, 1843.

48. Wattles, "Humanity's Home"; John O. Wattles, "Reform and Reformers," *Regenerator*, Feb. 8, 1844; John O. Wattles, untitled essay on health, n.d., Wattles Papers.

49. "Diet," *Communitist*, March 26, 1845; G. W. Rollins, "Health," ibid., July 16, 1845; [Gardner] to Esther Wattles and Davis; Marenda B. Randall letter, *Regenerator*, April 1, 1844.

50. "Letter from Harlow Hard," *Herald of Progression*, April 1846; W. H. Whinery letter, *Regenerator*, May 25, 1846.

51. Nicholson, "Law, Gospel, Creeds"; [Gardner] to Esther Wattles and Davis.

52. John O. Wattles, "Dietetics," *Herald of Progression*, Oct. 1845; S. Larned letter, *Regenerator*, June 15, 1844; William H. Whinery, "Milk," ibid.

53. John Humphrey Noyes, *History of American Socialisms* (New York: Hillary House, 1961), 176–79, 318; Marenda B. Randall letter, *Regenerator*, April 1, 1844; Whinery, "Prospectus."

54. "Letter from Brother Johnson," *Herald of Progression*, Feb. 1846; Wattles, "Humanity's Home"; Kersey Grave letter, *Communitist*, Oct. 13, 1844.

55. R. Chafee letter, *Communitist*, June 18, 1845; Collins, *Bird's Eye View*, 13; Mark D. Stoneman letter, *Herald of Progression*, March 1846; Wattles, untitled essay on health.

56. Larned letter.

57. Blanche Glassman Hersh, *The Slavery of Sex: Feminist-Abolitionists in America* (Urbana: University of Illinois Press, 1978), 131–32; Margaret Hope Bacon, *Mothers of Feminism: The Story of Quaker Women in America* (San Francisco: Harper and Row, 1986), 101–19; Nancy A. Hewitt, "The Fragmentation of Friends: The Consequences for Quaker Women in Antebellum America," in *Witnesses for Change: Quaker Women over Three Centuries*, ed. Elisabeth Potts Brown and Susan Stuard Mosher (New Brunswick: Rutgers University Press, 1989), 104–105.

58. "The New Year," *Communitist*, Jan. 15, 1846.

59. M. B. R., "Female Slavery," ibid., July 10, 1844; "Social Reorganization," ibid., Oct. 2, 1844; Maria French, "Drag Out at Manchester," *Herald of Freedom*, March 2, 1843. For Ernestine L. Rose, see Yuri Suhl, *Eloquent Crusader: Ernestine Rose* (New York: Messner, 1970).

60. Maria Loomis, "A Dialogue on Dress," *Communitist*, Oct. 30, 1844; Emily [Gardner] to Esther Wattles, March 10 [1846], Wattles Papers; "Manual Labor School," *Herald of Progression*, Jan. 1846; Collins, *Bird's Eye View*, 26–27.

61. Collins, *Bird's Eye View*, 27; Orvis, "Use and Abuse"; Wattles, "Humanity's Home."

62. William Leach, *True Love and Perfect Union: The Feminist Reform of Sex and Society* (New York: Basic, 1980), passim; Randall, "Female Slavery."

63. John O. Wattles, untitled essay on marriage, n.d., Wattles Papers; "Women's Department," *Herald of Progression*, Nov. 1846; Marenda B. Randall letter, *Herald of Free-*

dom, Feb. 16, 1844. For women as guardians, see Mary P. Ryan, *Cradle of the Middle Class: The Family in Oneida County, New York, 1790–1865* (New York: Cambridge University Press, 1981), 116–27; and Christine Stansell, *City of Women: Sex and Class in New York, 1789–1860* (New York: Knopf, 1986), xii-xiii, 68–75.

64. On Skaneateles, see above, p. 146. For a differing view, see Carol A. Kolmerten, *Women in Utopia: The Ideology of Gender in the American Owenite Communities* (Bloomington: Indiana University Press, 1990), 159. For women's roles in utopian communities, see Wendy Chmielewski, Louis J. Kern, and Marilyn Klee Hartzell, eds., *Women in Spiritual and Communitarian Societies in the United States* (Syracuse: Syracuse University Press, 1993).

65. On Catherine Murray, see "Women's Department," *Herald of Progression,* Nov. 1846.

66. Maria Michener Mendenhall, Reminiscence, 1915, typescript, Willard C. Heiss Collection (Friends Collection, Lilly Library, Earlham College, Richmond, Ind.); Valentine Nicholson to Isaac Post and Amy Post, 12th Mo. 16, 1849, box 3, Isaac and Amy Kirby Post Papers (Department of Rare Books and Manuscripts, Rush Rhees Library, University of Rochester, Rochester, N.Y.); Esther Wattles to John O. Wattles, July 4 [1848], Wattles Papers; "Reply of Elizabeth Nicholson to the U.G.R.R. Circular," n.d., box 111, Wilbur H. Siebert Collection (Ohio Historical Society, Columbus).

67. Hersh, *Slavery of Sex,* 37–79.

68. Lester Grosvenor Wells, *The Skaneateles Communal Experiment, 1843–1846* (Syracuse: Onondaga Historical Association, 1953), 8; "Letter from Brother Brooke," *Regenerator,* April 18, 1844; Valentine Nicholson letter, *Free Labor Advocate,* 4th Mo. 20, 1844. For the question of Free Love in nineteenth-century communities, see John C. Spurlock, *Free Love: Marriage and Middle-Class Radicalism in America, 1825–1860* (New York: New York University Press, 1988), 23–106, 139–63.

69. "Views of Frances Wright Darusmont on Marriage," *Communitist,* April 9, 1845; *The Social Pioneer and Herald of Progress* (Boston: J. P. Mendum [1844]), 26; Philip Gleason, "From Free-Love to Catholicism: Dr. and Mrs. Thomas L. Nichols at Yellow Springs," *Ohio Historical Quarterly,* 70 (Oct. 1961), 283–307. For Harlow Hard, see above, p. 139.

70. Wattles, "Reform and Reformers"; John O. Wattles, "Present State of the Human Family," n.d., Wattles Papers; Wattles, untitled essay on marriage; "Where Is the Right?" *Herald of Progression,* June 1845.

71. "Where Is the Right?" Harlow Hard to Libanus Allen, Nov. 19, 1845, *Regenerator,* Dec. 11, 1845; John B. Chandler, "Universal Reform," ibid., May 11, 1844; Randall letter.

72. "Evils of Individual Interests," *Communitist,* Jan. 1, 1846.

73. "Letter from Brother Brooke"; Wattles, untitled essay on marriage; [John O. Wattles], *Few Thoughts on Marriage* (Salem, Ohio: S. H. Painter, 1844), 17–18.

74. [Wattles], *Few Thoughts,* 18–22.

75. M. Loomis, "Marriage," *Communitist,* July 10, 1844; Samuel Sellers, "Marriage," ibid., July 2, 1845; "Extract from a Letter," ibid.; Wattles, untitled essay on marriage.

76. [Wattles], *Few Thoughts* 3–4. John C. Spurlock sees Wattles as a forerunner of the Free Love philosophy of the 1850s. Wattles may have anticipated certain Free

Love ideas, but there is nothing to indicate that he embraced them. See Spurlock, *Free Love*, 88.

77. Ibid., 10–12.

78. Ibid., 14, 27–28; Wells, *Skaneateles*, 7–8; Orvis, "Use and Abuse"; "Married," *Communitist*, Jan. 29, 1846; "Celebration of the First of January, 1846," ibid., Jan. 8, 1846. Lester G. Wells argues that the Skaneateles community's indifference to formalizing marriages by state or clergy is evidence that "free love was advocated." See Wells, *Skaneateles*, 7. Given the statements by residents at Skaneateles and the other communities, however, that is doubtful. For the marriages of Abby Kelley with Stephen S. Foster and Theodore Weld with Angelina Grimke, see Dorothy Sterling, *Ahead of Her Time: Abby Kelley and the Politics of Antislavery* (New York: W. W. Norton, 1991), 220–21; and Robert H. Abzug, *Passionate Liberator: Theodore Dwight Weld and the Dilemma of Reform* (New York: Oxford University Press, 1980), 197–200. Samuel Brooke was a witness at the Kelley-Foster wedding.

79. Editorial, *Herald of Progression*, Jan. 1846; Wattles, "Reform and Reformers."

80. Elbert Russell, *The History of Quakerism* (New York: Macmillan, 1942), 400; Stewart Holbrook, *The Yankee Exodus: An Account of Migration from New England* (Seattle: University of Washington Press, 1968), 297–312.

81. Collins, *Bird's Eye View*, 27–28; Emily Gardner letter, *Herald of Progression*, March 1846; John O. Wattles, untitled essay on education [1838], Wattles Papers.

82. "Randolph, Vermont"; Lawrence A. Cremin, *American Education: The National Experience, 1783–1876* (New York: Harper and Row, 1980), 83–91, 288–97. There were some contacts between the Universal Reformers and the Transcendentalists. Wattles was at least acquainted with Amos Bronson Alcott. See Odell Shepard, *Pedlar's Progress: The Life of Bronson Alcott* (Boston: Little Brown, 1937), 299. Correspondence from Charles Lane, Alcott's associate, often appeared in the *Vermont Telegraph* in 1842 and 1843.

83. Wattles, untitled essay on education; Whinery letter; "Social Reform," *Communitist*, July 10, 1844.

84. "Success of Community," *Communitist*, May 21, 1845; Letter from Clinton County, Ohio, ibid., July 30, 1845; Maria Loomis, "Reformers," ibid., Nov. 13, 1845; Collins, *Bird's Eye View*, 21; "Randolph, Vermont."

85. "Randolph, Vermont"; "Letter from Augustus Wattles," *Herald of Progression*, Jan. 1846. The quotations are editorial comments by John O. Wattles.

86. Wattles, untitled essay on education; Collins, *Bird's Eye View*, 28.

87. "Correspondence," *Communitist*, June 18, 1845; Collins, *Bird's Eye View*, 28; Collins, "One Year's Experience"; John O. Wattles, "Mental Culture for the Formation of Community," n.d., Wattles Papers.

88. Editorial, *Herald of Progression*, Feb. 1846; Collins, *Bird's Eye View*, 24; Elizabeth L. Dyer to John O. Wattles, July 30, 1840, Wattles Papers.

89. "Social Reorganization," *Communitist*, Sept. 4, 1844; Albanese, *Nature Religion*, 8–11.

90. E. W. Capron, "The Hicksite 'Quaker's' Creed," *Regenerator*, March 8, 1847; Lindsay Swift, *Brook Farm: Its Members, Scholars, and Visitors* (New York: Corinth,

278
❖ Notes to pages 196–200 ❖

1961), 175; Joseph Savage obituary, clipping, 1878, Savage file (Onondaga Historical Association); Quincy A. Johnson obituary, clipping, 1856, Quincy A. Johnson file, ibid.; Maria Loomis, "Presbyterian Meeting," *Communitist*, July 30, 1845.

91. Brooke, "Universal Inquiry"; "Letter from John Orvis," *Vermont Telegraph*, Nov. 16, 1842; "Randolph, Vermont."

92. For come-outer movements, see John R. McKivigan, *The War on Proslavery Religion: Abolitionism and the Northern Churches, 1830–1865* (Ithaca: Cornell University Press, 1984); and Lewis Perry, *Radical Abolitionism: Anarchy and the Government of God in Antislavery Thought* (ibid., 1973). For a contemporary evaluation by Abraham Brooke's brother, see *Slavery and the Slaveholder's Religion, as Opposed to Christianity* (Cincinnati, 1846), 50–52. For Patten Davis, see his letter in *Herald of Freedom*, Jan. 28, 1841. For Marius Robinson, see Homer C. Boyle, "An Appreciation of Marius Robinson," 1927, Robinson Papers.

93. Hinshaw, ed., *Encyclopedia*, V, 471; "An Epistle," *National Anti-Slavery Standard*, Nov. 21, 1843; Joseph A. Dugdale, "Letter from Ohio," ibid., July 6, 1843; Indiana Yearly Meeting (Hicksite) Men's Minutes, 9th Mo. 23, 1843 (Ohio Valley Yearly Archives, Wilmington College, Wilmington, Ohio).

94. Hinshaw, ed., *Encyclopedia*, V. 471, 478; Miami Monthly Meeting (Hicksite) Men's Minutes, 6th Mo. 26, 1844 (Ohio Valley Yearly Meeting Archives); Samuel M. Janney to Elizabeth M. Janney, 3rd Mo. 12, 1844, box 2, Samuel M. Janney Papers (Friends Historical Library); Esther Whinery, "The Friends and Slavery," *National Anti-Slavery Standard*, July 13, 1843. Esther Whinery's letter was reprinted from the *Philanthropist*. For a resignation letter from a Friend in the East, see James Sellers Jr. "To Darby Monthly Meeting of Friends," *Regenerator*, May 25, 1844.

95. E. W. Capron letter, *Communitist*, Dec. 11, 1844; "Social Re-Organization," ibid., Oct. 1, 1844; Brooke, "Universal Inquiry"; John B. Chandler letter, *Herald of Freedom*, Oct. 21, 1843.

96. M. B. Randall, "Sunday," *Communitist*, July 10, 1844; Loomis, "Social Reform"; Collins, *Bird's Eye View*, 14; "Randolph, Vermont."

97. Nicholson, "Law, Gospel, Creeds"; "Letter from Harlow Hard," *Herald of Progression*, April 1846.

98. John O. Wattles, "Let There Be No Strife," n.d., Wattles Papers; "The American Board of Commissioners for Foreign Missions"; *Communitist*, Oct. 9, 1845; "The Regenerator—Where Shall It Be Located?" *Vermont Telegraph*, July 19, 1843.

99. Wattles, "Let There Be No Strife"; E. W. Capron, "Ignorance vs. Knowledge," *Communitist*, Mach 12, 1845; "Letter from Phil B. Holmes," ibid., Aug. 21, 1845; Loomis, "Social Reform"; D. Winston Jones letter, *Herald of Progression*, June 1845; Rebecca Lewis Fussell Diary, June 24, 1838, box 9, Graceanna Lewis Papers (Friends Historical Library); Edwin Michener, "Deity, Accountability, God's Laws, Materialism, Skepticism, Etc.," *Regenerator*, May 25, 1844; "Randolph, Vermont"; Abraham Brooke letter, *Herald of Freedom*, Aug. 11, 1843; "Infidelity—Old and New," *Vermont Telegraph*, April 12, 1843.

100. M. B. Randall, "Sunday"; "Magnetism," *Communitist*, April 23, 1845. For a fe-

rocious blast at an Episcopal Christmas service, see Marenda B. Randall letter, *Herald of Freedom*, Jan. 12, 1844.

101. Wattles, "Community"; S. F. letter, *Communitist*, Feb. 26, 1845.

102. John Mitchell, "The Signs of the Times," *Communitist*, July 16, 1845; Jno. Robb Jr. letter, *Herald of Progression*, April 1846; Jones letter; Collins, *Bird's Eye View*, 6.

103. Stephens to John O. Wattles, Oct. 25, 1840; Editorial, *Herald of Progression*, Dec. 1845; M. L., "Quaker Meeting—Lake Scenery, Etc.," *Communitist*, June 18, 1845; O. S. Murray, "Quaker Quiet—Refinement of Violence," *Regenerator*, June 1, 1844.

104. Bacon, *Mothers of Feminism*, 113–14; *Minutes and Proceedings of Green Plain Yearly Meeting of Friends, Who Have Adopted the Congregational Order* (Columbus: Scott & Bascom, 1849), 5–6.

105. Joseph A. Dugdale, "Reform among the Quakers," Centerville *Indiana True Democrat*, March 27, 1850. The article was a reprint of an 1846 exchange in the Lebanon, Ohio, *Western Star*. David Evans and Joseph A. Dugdale were debating a statement by Congregational Friends in New York that the Green Plain Friends endorsed.

106. "Correspondents," *Herald of Progression*, Sept. 1845; "Letter from Brother Brooke"; "Letter from Brother Nicholson"; Nicholson, "Law, Gospel, Creeds"; *The Social Pioneer and Herald of Progress* (Boston: J. P. Mendum [1844], 59.

107. Loomis, "Reformers"; Collins, "One Year's Experience"; *Social Pioneer*, 64; "Obituary," *Communitist*, Feb. 11, 1845; "Thomas Paine," ibid., Feb. 26, 1846.

108. H. Hard, "Gods—Prayers to Them—Worship of Them—Manufacture of Them," *Regenerator*, Aug. 4, 1845; "The Harbinger," *Communitist*, Dec. 4, 1845; "Christianity," ibid., Jan. 18, 1845; "John A. Collins," *Anti-Slavery Bugle*, Aug. 28, 1846; Michener, "Deity, Accountability"; Joseph Allen letter; "Randolph, Vermont."

109. Q. A. Johnson, "Religion, Innate," *Communitist*, Aug. 21, 1844; Michener, "Deity, Accountability"; "Acquisitiveness"; John O. Wattles, untitled essay on mind, Miscellaneous Manuscripts Transcribed by Esther Wattles; Brooke, "Universal Inquiry."

110. "Letter from Milo A. Townsend," *Herald of Progression*, Dec. 1845; "The Nonconformist," ibid., July 1845; "Letter from Rebecca T. Pool," ibid., Jan. 1846; Randall, "Sunday"; Nicholson, "Law, Gospel, Creeds"; Albanese, *Nature Religion*, 8–11, 80–152.

111. Ernest Lee Tuveson, *Redeemer Nation: The Idea of America's Millennial Role* (Chicago: University of Chicago Press, 1968); Michael Barkun, *Crucible of the Millennium: The Burned-Over District of New York in the 1840s* (Syracuse: Syracuse University Press, 1986), 31–62; Sydney E. Ahlstrom, *A Religious History of the American People* (New Haven: Yale University Press, 1972), 979–80.

112. "Randolph, Vermont"; John O. Wattles, untitled essay on the millennium, ca. 1836, Wattles Papers; D. R. Stone, "The Inquisition: Western New York," *Herald of Freedom*, March 31, 1843. Orson S. Murray was especially critical of Millerism. See, for example, "Editorial Correspondence," *Vermont Telegraph*, Nov. 2, 1842; and "Second Advent," ibid., May 10, 1843.

113. John O. Wattles letter, *Regenerator*, Feb. 8, 1844; Whinery letter, ibid., May 25, 1844; [Gardner] to Esther Wattles and Davis; Rees E. Price letter, *Herald of Progression*, Oct. 1845; "Letter from Joshua W. Engle," ibid., May 22, 1846.

114. N. H. Whiting used the Shakers as proof that community was feasible. See "Randolph, Vermont."

115. For Fourierism, see Walters, *American Reformers*, 68, 169–70; and Carl J. Guarneri, *The Utopian Alternative: Fourierism in Nineteenth Century America* (Ithaca: Cornell University Press, 1991).

116. "Harbinger"; Lorenzo Mabbett, "The Treadwheel of Association Better than the Sofa of Isolation," *Communitist*, Jan. 22, 1846; "Social Reform," *Herald of Progression*, Aug. 1, 1846.

117. Nicholson, "Law, Gospel, Creeds"; "Communication from Valentine Nicholson," *Regenerator*, Feb. 1, 1844; Maria Loomis, "Explanation," *Communitist*, March 12, 1845; A. Brooke, "Social Reform," *Philanthropist*, Aug. 15, 1843; Swift, *Brook Farm*, 175–76. See also E. W. Capron, "Universal Inquiry and Reform," *Vermont Telegraph*, Sept. 20, 1843.

118. On Adin Ballou, see Perry, *Radical Abolitionism*, 129–58; John L. Thomas, "Antislavery and Utopia," in *The Antislavery Vanguard*, ed. Duberman (Princeton: Princeton University Press, 1965), 249–54; William S. Heywood, ed., *Autobiography of Adin Ballou* (Lowell: Vox-Populi Press & Thompson & Hill, 1896); and Noyes, *History*, 119–32. For John Humphrey Noyes, see Robert Allerton Parker, *A Yankee Saint: John Humphrey Noyes and the Oneida Community* (New York: G. P. Putnam's Sons, 1935); and Robert David Thomas, *The Man Who Would Be Perfect: John Humphrey Noyes and the Utopian Impulse* (Philadelphia: University of Pennsylvania Press, 1977).

119. Raymond Lee Murray, *Sex and Marriage in Utopian Communities: 19th Century America* (Bloomington: Indiana University Press, 1973), 93–97; Louis J. Kern, *An Ordered Love: Sex Roles and Sexuality in Victorian Utopias—The Shakers, the Mormons, and the Oneida Community* (Chapel Hill: University of North Carolina Press, 1981), 207–209.

120. Thomas D. Hamm, *The Transformation of American Quakerism: Orthodox Friends, 1800–1907* (Bloomington: Indiana University Press, 1988), 1–12; Thomas, "Antislavery and Utopia," 256; Noyes, *History*, 175–80; "Semi-Infidelity among Reformers," *Vermont Telegraph*, July 12, 1843.

121. William Lloyd Garrison to Henry Clarke Wright, Dec. 16, 1843, *The Letters of William Lloyd Garrison*, ed. Walter M. Merrill and Louis Ruchames (6 vols., Cambridge: Belknap, 1971–81), III, 240–41; Perry, *Radical Abolitionism*, 63–69; Thomas, "Antislavery and Utopia," 249–54.

122. Kolmerten, *Women in Utopia*, 159.

123. M. L., "The Infidel Convention," *Communitist*, April 9, 1845; "Robert Owen," ibid., Sept. 4, 1844; "Robert Owen's Visit," ibid., May 21, 1845; "Evils of Individual Interests"; Suhl, *Eloquent Crusader*, 25–28, 50–51.

124. Noyes, *History*, 318; Willard C. Heiss, "Hiram Mendenhall and the Union Home Community," *Bulletin of Friends Historical Association*, 44 (Spring 1955), 49. I found no reference to Robert Owen or Owenism in the writings of Abraham Brooke, Valentine Nicholson, or John O. Wattles.

125. Noyes, *History*, 81–92; Walters, *American Reformers*, 63–64; John F. C. Harrison,

Quest for the New Moral World: Robert Owen and the Owenites in Britain and America (New York: Charles Scribner's Sons, 1969).
126. Walters, *American Reformers*, 63–64.

7. The Fates of Reformers

1. Esther Whinery Wattles, Miscellaneous Writings, n.d., John O. Wattles Papers (Western Reserve Historical Society, Cleveland).
2. Editorial, *Regenerator*, Dec. 1, 1848.
3. S. Sellers to Maria Weston Chapman, April 13, 1846, vol. 22, p. 38, Weston Family Papers (Rare Books Department, Boston Public Library, Boston); "John A. Collins— The Daytonian," *Regenerator*, Sept. 7, 1846.
4. "John A. Collins"; *Harbinger* clipping, n.d., Skaneateles Community file (Onondaga Historical Association, Syracuse, N.Y.).
5. "John A. Collins"; *New York Tribune* clipping, 1847, Skaneateles Community file; Anne Warren Weston to Chapman, June 5, 1849, vol. 25, p. 76, Weston Papers.
6. "Punishments," *Regenerator*, Jan. 1, 1849; John A. Collins to Frederick Douglass, June 4, 1881, reel 3, microfilm, Frederick Douglass Papers (Manuscripts Division, Library of Congress, Washington, D.C.); *New York Tribune*, March 9, April 8, Nov. 11, 1852, Nov. 29, 1855, clippings, Skaneateles Community file; Samuel May Jr. to Richard D. Webb, July 12, 1864, vol. 16, p. 8, Anti-Slavery Collection (Rare Books Department).
7. *New York Tribune* clipping, Oct. 10, 1853, Skaneateles Community file; Collins to William Lloyd Garrison, May 1, 1879, vol. 40, p. 117, William Lloyd Garrison Papers (Rare Books Department); Robert S. Fogarty, *Dictionary of American Communal and Utopian History* (Westport: Greenwood, 1980), 24–25.
8. Collins to Garrison; Collins to Douglass.
9. Carl J. Guarneri, *The Utopian Alternative: Fourierism in Nineteenth-Century America* (Ithaca: Cornell University Press, 1991), 393–94.
10. Willard C. Heiss, "Hiram Mendenhall and the Union Home Community," *Bulletin of Friends Historical Association*, 44 (Spring 1955), 48–49; J. H. Mendenhall, "In Memory of Hiram and Martha Mendenhall," *Winchester* (Ind.) *Journal*, Aug. 11, 1880.
11. Ebenezer C. Tucker, *History of Randolph County, Indiana* (Chicago: Kingman, 1882), 338; Hiram Mendenhall to Nathan Mendenhall, March 9, 1851, typescript, Willard C. Heiss Collection (Friends Collection, Lilly Library, Earlham College, Richmond, Ind.).
12. Hiram Mendenhall to Nathan Mendenhall.
13. Hiram Mendenhall to Joseph H. Mendenhall, Dec. 24, 1851, typescript, Heiss Collection.
14. Tucker, *History of Randolph County*, 338.
15. Joseph Gregory, "Fruit Hills," *Regenerator*, Aug. 18, 1845; John White, "Fruit Hills," ibid., Sept. 7, 1846; A. J. MacDonald, "Orson S. Murray," p. 425, A. J. MacDonald Mss. (Beinecke Library, Yale University, New Haven, Conn.).

16. MacDonald, "Orson S. Murray," 426.

17. Albert Post, *Popular Free Thought in America, 1825–1850* (New York: Columbia University Press, 1943), 66–68. For Orson S. Murray's course generally, see the *Regenerator* for these years.

18. MacDonald, "Orson S. Murray," 426; Carlos O. Murray, "Fruit Hills—The Regenerator," *Regenerator*, Dec. 4, 1846.

19. MacDonald, "Orson S. Murray," 426–27; "Death of Orson S. Murray," 1885, clipping, Orson S. Murray scrapbook, Valentine Nicholson Papers (Indiana Historical Society, Indianapolis); *Some of the Work of Charles B. Murray, Editor of the Cincinnati Price Current for Forty-One Years, in Special and Statistical Journalism* (Cincinnati, 1914).

20. "Death of Orson S. Murray."

21. Ibid.

22. "Letter from Brother Brooke," *Regenerator*, April 18, 1844; A. Brooke letter, ibid., June 9, 1845; A. J. MacDonald, "Dr. Brooke's Experiment," MacDonald Mss., 395–99.

23. A. Brooke to Garrison, Jan. 28, 1847, vol. 17, p. 6, Garrison papers; ibid., April 14, 1848, vol. 18, p. 21.

24. Brooke to Garrison, April 24, 1848.

25. Albert John Wahl, "The Congregational or Progressive Friends in the Pre-Civil-War Reform Movement" (Ph.D. diss., Temple University, 1951), 23–42; *Memoirs of Samuel M. Janney, Late of Lincoln, Loudoun County, Va., a Minister in the Religious Society of Friends* (Philadelphia: Friends Book Association, 1881), 58–66; William Wade Hinshaw, ed., *Encyclopedia of American Quaker Genealogy* (6 vols., Ann Arbor: Edwards Brothers, 1936–50), V, 478.

26. *Minutes and Proceedings of the Annual Meeting of Friends, Composed of Parts of Ohio and Indiana, Held at Green Plain, Clark County, Ohio, Who Have Adopted the Congregational Order* (Springfield, Ohio: Halsey & Emerson, 1848); *Minutes and Proceedings of Green Plain Yearly Meeting of Friends, Who Have Adopted the Congregational Order of Church Government* (Columbus: Scott & Bascom, 1849); ibid. (Wilmington, Ohio: D. & T. McKibbin, 1850).

27. *Minutes . . . of Green Plain Yearly Meeting, 1850*, pp. 4–9.

28. Wahl, "Congregational or Progressive Friends," 176–87; Robert W. Audretch, comp., *The Salem, Ohio 1850 Women's Rights Convention Proceedings* (Salem, Ohio, 1976), 18–22.

29. Edward T. James et al., eds., *Notable American Women, 1607–1950: A Biographical Dictionary* (3 vols., Cambridge: Belknap, 1971), III, 450–51; "Mary F. Thomas," typescript, n.d., Mary F. Thomas File (Wayne County Historical Museum, Richmond, Ind.); Emma Lou Thornbrough, *Indiana in the Civil War Era, 1850–1880* (Indianapolis: Indiana Historical Society and Indiana Historical Bureau, 1965), 35–36; Elizabeth Cady Stanton et al., eds., *History of Woman Suffrage* (6 vols., Rochester, 1889–1922), I, 64–65, 389; Peter S. Jennison, *The History of Woodstock, Vermont, 1890–1983* (Woodstock: Countryman Press, 1985), 64–65; Centerville, *Indiana True Democrat*, Oct. 23, 1851; Louise R. Noun, *Strong-Minded Women: The Emergence of the Woman-Suffrage Movement in Iowa* (Ames: Iowa State University Press, 1969), 134–35.

30. Abraham Brooke to Jane Nicholson, June 22, 1855, Nicholson Papers; Elizabeth Brooke to Jane Nicholson and Valentine Nicholson, March 13, 1855, ibid.

31. Douglas Andrew Gamble, "Moral Suasion in the West: Garrisonian Abolition, 1830–1861" (Ph.D. diss., Ohio State University, 1973), 402, 428, 441–42, 449–50, 458; Abraham Brooke to Valentine Nicholson, Sept. 23, 1859, Nicholson Papers; Hannah Brantingham to Wilbur H. Siebert, Jan. 4, 1893, box 110, Wilbur H. Siebert Collection (Ohio Historical Society, Columbus); Siebert interview with Reuben Erwin, Aug. 13, 1895, ibid.

32. Gamble, "Moral Suasion," 464–67. I took Abraham Brooke's death from his tombstone in the Marlborough Cemetery.

33. John O. Wattles letter, *Regenerator* May 18, 1844; Esther Whinery Wattles Reminiscences, n.d., John O. Wattles Papers.

34. For the Wattleses' move to Cincinnati and Esther Wattles's teaching, see Wattles Reminiscences. For John O. Wattles's work with black schools, see *History of the Schools of Cincinnati* (Cincinnati, 1900), 185. A complete run of the *Herald of Progression* is in the Wattles Papers.

35. *History of the Schools of Cincinnati*, 183–84; William Coyle, ed., *Ohio Authors and Their Books: Biographical Data and Selective Bibliographies for Ohio Authors, Native and Resident, 1796–1850* (Cleveland: World Publishing, 1962), 300; *A Law Case Exhibiting the Most Extraordinary Developments Peculiar to Modern Times, Arising from an Implicit Obedience to the Dictates of Mesmeric Clairvoyance, as Related by a Mormon Prophet* (Cincinnati: Daily Atlas, 1848), 13; "The Cincinnati Brotherhood, 1845-6-7," MacDonald Mss.; John C. Spurlock, *Free Love: Marriage and Middle-Class Radicalism in America, 1825–1860* (New York: New York University Press, 1988), 89–90.

36. Wattles Reminiscences; *Liberty Hall and Cincinnati Gazette,* Dec. 23, 1847.

37. Wattles Reminiscences.

38. Esther Wattles to John O. Wattles, July 4 [1848], Wattles Papers.

39. Ibid.

40. Ibid. Theano Wattles Case related her parents' sexual history to her cousin Deborah Smith, to whom she also left their papers. Smith some time in the 1950s related it to Willard Heiss.

41. John O. Wattles to Esther Wattles [July 1848], Wattles Papers; John J. Halsey, *A History of Lake County, Illinois* (N.p., Roy S. Bates, 1912), 428. Seth Paine later returned to Chicago to found a bank based on ultraist principles and to publish the *Christian Banker,* which mixed moral reform with Paine's economic speculations and spiritualist communications. A. T. Andreas, *History of Cook County, Illinois* (Chicago, 1884), 316–20.

42. Wattles Reminiscences.

43. Ibid.

44. "Declaration of the Sentiments of the Grand Prairie Harmonial Association," Sept. 20, 1853, Wattles Papers.

45. Levi A. McKnight, *Progress of Education in Benton County* (N.p., 1906), 36; Harry Evans, "Grand Prairie Harmonical [*sic*] Institute," *Indiana Magazine of History* 12 (Dec. 1916), 351–52; Ruth Baldwin Stembel, *The Baldwin Heritage* (n.p., n.d.), 86. In

1872 an Indiana newspaper dredged up a copy of Grand Prairie's constitution and used it to argue that Horace Greeley, now the Democratic presidential candidate, was an advocate of Free Love who had sent cargoes of prostitutes to the community. See *Winchester* (Ind.) *Journal,* Oct. 23, 1872.

46. For the births of the children, see the family Bible record in the Wattles Papers. For John O. Wattles's journeys in 1853 and 1854, see his letters in ibid. For Esther Wattles's choice of children's names, see Deborah Smith to Willard C. Heiss, June 22, 1950, Willard C. Heiss Collection. For the 1854 woman's rights convention, see Stanton et al., eds., *History,* I, 376.

47. Spurlock, *Free Love,* 89; William T. Coggeshall, *The Signs of the Times, Comprising a History of the Spirit Rappings in Cincinnati* (Cincinnati, 1851), 123. Theano Wattles Case believed to the end of her life that her father heard voices. See Smith to Heiss, Feb. 24, 1951, Heiss Collection.

48. Emma Hardinge, *Modern American Spiritualism: A Twenty Years Record of the Communion between Earth and the World of Spirits* (New Hyde Park, N.Y.: University Books, 1970), 27–42; Ronald G. Walters, *American Reformers, 1815–1860* (New York: Hill and Wang, 1978), 163–71.

49. Walters, *American Reformers,* 163–71; Ann Braude, *Radical Spirits: Spiritualism and Women's Rights in Nineteenth-Century America* (Boston: Beacon, 1989), 2, 17, 73, 76; R. Laurence Moore, *In Search of White Crows: Spiritualism, Parapsychology, and American Culture* (New York: Oxford University Press, 1977), 70–101.

50. Robert H. Abzug, *Passionate Liberator: Theodore Dwight Weld and the Dilemma of Reform* (New York: Oxford University Press, 1980), 252; John O. Wattles letter, *Spiritual Telegraph,* July 23, 1859; John O. Wattles to Esther Wattles, Nov. 1854, Wattles Papers; John O. Wattles to Isaac and Amy Post, Dec. 1855, box 3, Isaac and Amy Kirby Post Papers (Rare Books and Manuscripts Department, Rush Rhees Library, University of Rochester, Rochester, N.Y.).

51. Wattles Reminiscences; Mrs. E. O. Morse, "Sketch of the Life and Work of Augustus Wattles," *Kansas State Historical Society Collections,* 17 (1928), 294–97. For "Bleeding Kansas" generally, see David M. Potter, *The Impending Crisis, 1848–1861* (New York: Harper and Row, 1976), 145–76, 199–224.

52. Wattles Reminiscences; Morse, "Sketch," 297–98.

53. Wattles Reminiscences; J. H. Stearns, "Some Lost Towns of Kansas," *Kansas State Historical Society Collections,* 12 (1911–12), 429; John O. Wattles to Gerrit Smith, Jan. 4, Feb. 16, 1859, box 38, Gerrit Smith Papers (Arents Research Library, Syracuse University, Syracuse, N.Y.); Lawrence *Kansas Republican,* Sept. 23, 1858, clipping, Nicholson Papers; Potter, *Impending Crisis,* 216. Letters from John O. Wattles to his family from Washington in 1859 are in the Wattles Papers.

54. William Ansel Mitchell, *Linn County, Kansas: A History* (N.p., 1928), 336–37.

55. Joseph G. Gambone, ed., "The Forgotten Feminist of Kansas: The Papers of Clarina I. H. Nichols, 1854–1885," *Kansas Historical Quarterly* 40 (Autumn 1974), 437–38; Wattles Reminiscences; John O. Wattles Obituary, clipping, 1859, Wattles Papers. The obituary is probably from the Lawrence *Herald of Freedom.*

56. Wattles Reminiscences; Esther Wattles obituary, 1908, Wattles Papers.

57. Valentine Nicholson, Autobiography, July 4, 1881, typescript, 75–76, Nichol-
son Papers; Elizabeth Nicholson memorandum, 1877, ibid.; Josiah Warren to Valentine
Nicholson, Aug. 13, 1849, ibid.; William H. Hilles to Hugh Hilles, Oct. 12, 1845, Dugdale-
Hilles Papers, Heiss Collection; Spurlock, *Free Love*, 109–15.

58. Valentine Nicholson letter, *Anti-Slavery Bugle*, Dec. 18, 1846; ibid., Oct. 31, 1845;
"Subscription to Sustain the Anti-Slavery Movement," ibid., June 4, 1847; Valentine
Nicholson to Chapman [1845], vol. 24, p. 121, Weston Papers; Valentine Nicholson to
Garrison, July 16, 1847, vol. 17, p. 59, Garrison Papers; Oliver W. Nixon to Jane Nicholson,
Jan. 25, 1895, Nicholson Papers; Valentine Nicholson to Siebert, Sept. 10, 1892, box 77,
Siebert Collection.

59. Gamble, "Moral Suasion," 351; Valentine Nicholson letter, *Anti-Slavery Bugle*,
Sept. 18, 1846. For the establishment of the *North Star*, see William S. McFeely, *Frederick
Douglass* (New York: Norton, 1991), 146–53.

60. "The Signs of the Times No. 1: The Harveysburg Academy Etc.," Ledger A,
Nicholson Papers; "The Signs of the Times No. 2: The Harveysburg Academy & the
People," ibid.; *History of Henry County, Indiana* (Chicago: Interstate, 1884), 884–85;
Walter Edgerton, *The History of the Separation in Indiana Yearly Meeting of Friends*
(Cincinnati: Achilles Pugh, 1856), 239–41.

61. "Signs of the Times No. 1"; "Signs of the Times No. 2"; *History of Henry County*,
884.

62. Valentine Nicholson, "Comeouterism," *Anti-Slavery Bugle*, May 15, 1846; *Minutes of Green Plain Yearly Meeting, 1849*, p. 5. Valentine Nicholson never rejoined the
Hicksite Friends. Jane Nicholson and her daughters remained members until their
deaths. See Hinshaw, ed., *Encyclopedia*, V, 105.

63. Family record, Nicholson Papers; Valentine Nicholson to *Spirit World*, May 18,
1851, Ledger A, ibid.

64. Valentine Nicholson to Isaac and Amy Post, 12th Mo. 16, 1849, box 3, Post Papers.

65. Ibid.

66. Valentine Nicholson to *Spirit World*; Andrew Jackson Davis, *The Magic Staff:
An Autobiography* (New York: A. J. Davis & Co., 1876), 545.

67. Valentine Nicholson to Isaac and Amy Post.

68. Spurlock, *Free Love*, 185–91.

69. Ibid., 125–31; Philip Gleason, "From Free-Love to Catholicism: Dr. and Mrs.
Thomas L. Nichols at Yellow Springs," *Ohio Historical Quarterly*, 70 (Oct. 1961), 284–87.

70. "Correspondence: Letter from One of Our Publishers," *Nichols' Monthly*, 3 (Nov.
1856), 248–50; Gleason, "From Free-Love to Catholicism," 198–307; Bertha-Monica
Stearns, "Memnonia: The Launching of a Utopia," *New England Quarterly*, 15 (June
1942), 280–95. In 1875 an old associate wrote to Valentine Nicholson: "But you are among
the Shakers, and perhaps have had your hunger sated. You have traveled far. From free
love to absolute continence, however, is not so far for you, maybe, as it would be for
me." See ⸻ Coates to Valentine Nicholson, May 27, 1875, Nicholson Papers. There
were other communities tied to spiritualism. See, for example, Bret E. Carroll, "Spiritualism and Community in Antebellum America: The Mountain Cove Episode," *Communal Studies*, 12 (1992), 20–39.

71. Jane Nicholson to Elizabeth Nicholson [ca 1872], Dec. 21, 1870, Nicholson Papers; Jane Nicholson to Mary E. and Elizabeth Nicholson, Jan. 16, Jan. 23, 1870, ibid.; Valentine Nicholson to Martha McKay, Jan. 10, 1869, ibid.; Grace Julian Clarke, "Elizabeth Nicholson: In Memoriam," 1926, ibid; Mary E. Nicholson obituary, 1928, ibid.; Warren County Power of Attorney Record, Book 1, p. 31 (Warren County Recorder's Office, Lebanon, Ohio). I am grateful to Martha Nicholson McKay's grandson, Theodore L. Steele of Indianapolis, for sharing his memories of his grandparents and great-aunts.

72. See the correspondence in note 71 and Valentine Nicholson to Jane Nicholson and Martha McKay, Apr. 22, 1871, Nicholson Papers; Valentine Nicholson to McKay, Jan. 29, 1872, July 7, 1873, ibid. A number of Valentine Nicholson's diaries from the 1870s are in the Nicholson Papers.

73. Valentine Nicholson letter, *Rights of Man*, April 29, 1882, clipping, Nicholson Papers; clipping, Oct. 19, 1882, ibid; Matilda Gage Joslyn to Valentine Nicholson, March 12, 1880, ibid.

74. Emma Danforth to Mary E. Nicholson, Feb. 27, 1885, Nicholson Papers; Henry T. Butterworth to Mary E. Nicholson, Feb. 24, 1885, ibid.

75. Jane Nicholson to T. M. Wales, July 12, 1896, Nicholson Papers; Elizabeth Nicholson to Wales [Nov. 1, 1896], ibid.

76. See the obituaries and anniversary notice clippings in the Nicholson Papers.

77. Esther Wattles obituary.

BIBLIOGRAPHY

Manuscripts

Rare Books Department, Boston Public Library

Anti-Slavery Collection
William Lloyd Garrison Papers
Weston Family Papers

Manuscripts Department, Olin Graduate Library, Cornell University, Ithaca, N.Y.

J. Miller McKim Papers

Friends Collection, Lilly Library, Earlham College, Richmond, Ind.

Dugdale-Hilles Papers
Economy Anti-Slavery Society Records
Willard C. Heiss Collection
Indiana Yearly Meeting of Friends (Orthodox) Meeting for Sufferings Minutes
Smith, Dwight, "Burials in West Grove Cemetery, Penn Township, Jay County, Indiana," 1982

Quaker Collection, Haverford College, Haverford, Pa.

Nathaniel Peabody Rogers Papers

Henry County Historical Society, New Castle, Ind.

Hinshaw, J. Rufus, "Slavery," typescript, 1911

Indiana Division, Indiana State Library, Indianapolis

Coal Creek Church of God Collection

Indiana Historical Society, Indianapolis

Philip C. Kabel Papers
Valentine Nicholson Papers

Library of Congress, Washington, D.C.

Frederick Douglass Papers

Southern Historical Collection, University of North Carolina, Chapel Hill

Hobbs-Mendenhall Papers

Oberlin College Archives, Mudd Library, Oberlin, Ohio

James Monroe Papers
Treasurer's Office Papers

Ohio Historical Society, Columbus

Evans Family Papers
Miscellaneous Manuscripts Collection
Wilbur H. Siebert Collection
Micajah Terrell Williams Papers

Onondaga Historical Association, Syracuse, N.Y.

Family Files
Skaneateles Community File

Department of Rare Books and Manuscripts, Rush Rhees Library, University of Rochester, Rochester, N.Y.

Isaac and Amy Kirby Post Papers
Talcott-Howland Papers

Friends Historical Library, Swarthmore College, Swarthmore, Pa.

Joseph A. Dugdale Papers
Furnas Family Papers
Halliday Jackson Papers
Samuel M. Janney Papers
Graceanna Lewis Papers
Lucretia Mott Papers
Sarah Hopper Palmer Papers
Sandy Spring (Hicksite) Monthly Meeting (Md.) Marriage Records

Arents Research Library, Syracuse University, Syracuse, N.Y.

Albert H. Brisbane Papers
Gerrit Smith Papers

Wayne County Historical Museum, Richmond, Ind.

Mary F. Thomas File

Western Reserve Historical Society, Cleveland

Marius R. Robinson Papers
John O. Wattles Papers

Ohio Valley Yearly Meeting Archives, Wilmington College, Wilmington, Ohio

Goshen Monthly Meeting (Hicksite) Men's Minutes
Green Plain Monthly Meeting (Hicksite) Men's Minutes
Indiana Yearly Meeting (Hicksite) Men's Minutes
Miami Monthly Meeting (Hicksite) Men's Minutes

Beinecke Rare Book and Manuscript Library, Yale University, New Haven, Conn.

A. J. MacDonald Mss.

Courthouse Records

Champaign County, Ohio, Urbana

Common Pleas Court Minutes
Deed Books

Clinton County, Ohio, Wilmington

Deed Books
Wills

Fountain County, Indiana, Covington

Circuit Court Records
Deed Books

Hamilton County, Indiana, Noblesville

Probate Records

Henry County, Indiana, New Castle

Wills

LaPorte County, Indiana, LaPorte

Deed Books

Marshall County, Indiana, Plymouth

Deed Books
Estates

Onondaga County, New York, Syracuse

Deed Books

Randolph County, Indiana, Winchester

Circuit Court Complete Records
Commissioners Records
Deed Books
Probate Records

Stark County, Ohio, Canton

Deed Books

Warren County, Ohio, Lebanon

Deed Books
Power of Attorney Record

Periodicals

Anti-Slavery Bugle, Salem, Ohio, 1845–1861
Communitist, Skaneateles, N.Y., 1844–1846
Free Labor Advocate and Anti-Slavery Chronicle, New Garden, Ind., 1842–1849
Friends' Intelligencer, Philadelphia, 1838–1839, 1844–1850
Harbinger, New York, 1845–1849

Herald of Freedom, Concord, N. H., 1838–1846
Herald of Progression, Cincinnati, 1845–1846
Indiana True Democrat, Centerville, Ind., 1848–1852
Liberator, Boston, 1831–1865
National Anti-Slavery Standard, New York, 1840–1850
Nichols' Monthly, Cincinnati, 1855–1857
Non-Resistant, Boston, 1839–1841
Onondaga Standard, Syracuse, N.Y., 1843–1846
Palladium, Richmond, Ind., 1831–1861
Pennsylvania Freeman, Philadelphia, 1838–1844
Philanthropist, Cincinnati, 1836–1844
Practical Christian, Milford, Mass., 1843–1850
Protectionist, New Garden, Ind., 1840–1841
Regenerator, New York and Fruit Hills, Ohio, 1844–1852
Vermont Telegraph, Brandon, Vt., 1835–1843
Wayne County Record, Centerville, Ind., 1842
Working Man's Advocate, New York, 1844–1846
Young America, New York, 1844

Published Primary Sources

American Anti-Slavery Society. *Minutes,* 1834–1840.
American Antiquarian Society, comp., *Index of Marriages in Massachusetts Centinel and Columbian Centinel, 1784 to 1840.* 4 vols., Boston: G. K. Hall, 1961.
Arnett, Thomas. *Journal of the Life, Travels, and Gospel Labors of Thomas Arnett.* Chicago: Publishing Association of Friends, 1884.
Audretch, Robert W., comp. *The Salem, Ohio 1850 Women's Rights Convention Proceedings.* Salem, Ohio, 1976.
Barnes, Gilbert H., and Dwight L. Dumond, eds. *Letters of Theodore Dwight Weld, Angelina Grimke Weld, and Sarah Grimke, 1822–1844.* 2 vols. Gloucester, Mass.: Peter Smith, 1965.
Brooke, Samuel. *Slavery and the Slaveholder's Religion, as Opposed to Christianity.* Cincinnati, 1846.
Catalogue of the Trustees, Instructors, & Students of Burr Seminary, June 1835. Windsor, Vt.: Chronicle, 1835.
Chace, Elizabeth Buffum. *Anti-Slavery Reminiscences.* Central Falls, R. I.: E. L. Freeman and Son, 1891.
Clark, Joshua V. H. *Onondaga or Reminiscences of Earlier and Later Times.* 2 vols. Syracuse: Stoddard and Babcock, 1849.
Coffin, Addison. *Life and Travels of Addison Coffin.* Cleveland: William G. Hubbard, 1897.
Coffin, Charles F., and William H. Coffin, "Henry Clay at Richmond." *Indiana Magazine of History.* 4 (Dec. 1908), 123–28.

Coffin, Levi. *Reminiscences of Levi Coffin, the Reputed President of the Underground Railroad.* Cincinnati: Robert Clarke, 1880.

Coggeshall, William T. *The Signs of the Times, Comprising a History of the Spirit Rappings in Cincinnati.* Cincinnati, 1851.

Collins, John A. *The Anti-Slavery Picknick: A Collection of Speeches, Poems, Dialogues, and Songs, Intended for Use in Schools and Anti-Slavery Meetings.* Boston: H. W. Williams, 1842.

————. *Bird's Eye View of Society As It Is, and As It Should Be.* Boston: J. P. Mendum, 1844.

————. *Right and Wrong among the Abolitionists of the United States: or the Object, Principles, and Measures of the Original American Anti-Slavery Society Unchanged: Being a Defence against the Assaults of the Recently Formed Massachusetts Abolition and the American and Foreign Anti-Slavery Societies: Embodying a Statement of Facts, from Official and Other Documents, with Respect to the Origin and Progress of the Division among the Abolitionists of the United States.* Glasgow: Geo. Gallis, 1841.

Cox, Samuel Hanson. *Quakerism Not Christianity: or, Reasons for Renouncing the Doctrine of Friends.* New York: D. Fanshaw, 1833.

Davis, Andrew Jackson. *The Magic Staff: An Autobiography.* New York: A. J. Davis & Co., 1876.

Douglass, Frederick. *Life and Times of Frederick Douglass.* New York: Pathway, 1941.

Dumond, Dwight L., ed. *Letters of James Gillespie Birney, 1831–1857.* 2 vols. Gloucester, Mass.: Peter Smith, 1965.

Dwight, Marianne. *Letters from Brook Farm.* Ed. Amy L. Reed. Poughkeepsie: Vassar College, 1928.

Edgerton, Walter. *A History of the Separation in Indiana Yearly Meeting of Friends.* Cincinnati: Achilles Pugh, 1856.

Emerson, Ralph Waldo. *The Complete Works of Ralph Waldo Emerson.* 12 vols. New York: Sully and Kleinteich, 1883.

Gambone, Joseph G., ed. "The Forgotten Feminist of Kansas: The Papers of Clarina I. H. Nichols, 1854–1885." *Kansas Historical Quarterly.* 40 (Autumn 1974), 410–59.

Genealogical Society of Utah. *International Genealogical Index: Ohio.* Salt Lake City, 1988.

General Catalogue of the Theological Seminary, Andover, Massachusetts, 1808–1908. Boston: Thomas Todd, [1909].

Green Plain Yearly Meeting of Congregational Friends. *Minutes and Proceedings of the Annual Meeting of Friends, Composed of Parts of Ohio and Indiana, Held at Green Plain, Clark County, Ohio, Who Have Adopted the Congregational Order.* Springfield, Ohio: Halsey & Emerson, 1848.

————. *Minutes and Proceedings of Green Plain Yearly Meeting of Friends, Who Have Adopted the Congregational Order.* Columbus: Scott & Bascom, 1849. Ibid., Wilmington, Ohio: D. & T. McKibbin, 1850.

Heiss, Willard C., ed. *Abstracts of the Records of the Society of Friends in Indiana.* 7 vols.: Indianapolis: Indiana Historical Society, 1962–1977.

Heywood, William S., ed. *Autobiography of Adin Ballou*. Lowell: Vox-Populi Press & Thompson & Hill, 1896.

Hicks, Elias. *Discourses, Delivered in the Several Meetings of the Society of Friends, in Philadelphia, Germantown, Abington, Byberry, Newtown, Falls, and Trenton*. Philadelphia: Joseph & Edward Parker, 1825.

Hill, Don Gleason. *The Record of Births, Marriages, and Deaths, and Intentions of Marriage, in the Town of Dedham*. 2 vols. Dedham, Mass.: Dedham Transcript, 1886.

Hinshaw, William Wade, ed. *Encyclopedia of American Quaker Genealogy*. 6 vols. Ann Arbor: Edwards Brothers, 1936–1950.

Hopper, Isaac T. *Narrative of the Proceedings of the Monthly Meeting of New-York, and Their Subsequent Confirmation by the Quarterly and Yearly Meetings, in the Case of Isaac T. Hopper*. New York, 1843.

Indiana Yearly Meeting of Anti-Slavery Friends. *Minutes, 1846*.

Janney, Samuel M. *Memoirs of Samuel M. Janney, Late of Lincoln, Loudoun County, Va., a Minister in the Religious Society of Friends*. Philadelphia: Friends Book Association, 1881.

Jay, Allen. *Autobiography of Allen Jay, Born 1831, Died 1910*. Philadelphia: John C. Winston, 1910.

Johnson, Oliver. *Correspondence between Oliver Johnson and George F. White, a Minister of the Society of Friends*. New York: Oliver Johnson, 1841.

———. *William Lloyd Garrison and His Times*. Boston: Houghton-Mifflin, 1881.

A Law Case Exhibiting the Most Extraordinary Developments Peculiar to Modern Times, Arising from an Implicit Obedience to the Dictates of Mesmeric Clairvoyance, as Related by a Mormon Prophet. Cincinnati: Daily Atlas, 1848.

Massachusetts Anti-Slavery Society. *Annual Reports*. 1838–1845.

Meltzer, Milton, et al., eds. *Lydia Maria Child: Selected Letters, 1817–1880*. Amherst: University of Massachusetts Press, 1982.

Merrill, Walter M., and Louis Ruchames, eds. *The Letters of William Lloyd Garrison*. 6 vols. Cambridge: Belknap, 1971–1981.

New York Yearly Meeting (Hicksite). *Memorials concerning Deceased Friends, Published by Direction of the Yearly Meeting of New York*. New York: James Egbert, 1859.

Noyes, John Humphrey. *History of American Socialisms*. New York: Hillary House, 1961.

Osborn, Charles W. "Henry Clay at Richmond." *Indiana Magazine of History*. 4 (Dec. 1908), 117–23.

Pillsbury, Parker. *Acts of the Anti-Slavery Apostles*. Concord, N.H.: 1883.

Proceedings of the Indiana Convention Assembled to Organize a State Anti-Slavery Society Held in Milton, Wayne County, September 12, 1838. Cincinnati: Samuel A. Alley, 1838.

The Quaker, Being a Series of Sermons by Members of the Society of Friends. 4 vols. Philadelphia: Marcus T. C. Gould, 1827–28.

Riker, Dorothy, and Gayle Thornbrough, eds. *Indiana Election Returns, 1816–1851*. Indianapolis: Indiana Historical Bureau, 1960.

Ripley, C. Peter, et al. *The Black Abolitionist Papers*. 5 vols. Chapel Hill: University of North Carolina Press, 1985–1992.

Smedley, R. C. *History of the Underground Railroad in Chester and the Neighboring Counties of Pennsylvania*. Lancaster, Pa.: Journal, 1883.

Smith, W. L. *Indiana Methodism: Sketches and Incidents*. Valparaiso, Ind., 1892.

Social Pioneer and Herald of Progress. Boston: J. P. Menden, [1844].

Stanton, Elizabeth Cady, et al., eds. *History of Woman Suffrage*. 6 vols., Rochester, 1889–1922.

United States Census Office. *Population Schedules of the Sixth Census of the United States, 1840: Ohio*. Washington, D.C.: National Archives and Records Service, 1967.

———. *Population Schedules of the Seventh Census of the United States, 1850: Indiana*. Washington, D.C.: National Archives and Records Service, 1963.

Vermont, State of. *General Index to Vital Records*. N.p., n.d.

[Wattles, John O.] *Few Thoughts on Marriage*. Salem, Ohio: S. H. Painter, 1844.

Whittier, John G. "The Antislavery Convention of 1833." *Atlantic Monthly*. 33 (Feb. 1874), 166–72.

Secondary Sources

Abzug, Robert H. *Passionate Liberator: Theodore Dwight Weld and the Dilemma of Reform*. New York: Oxford University Press, 1980.

Adams, Robert. "Nathaniel Peabody Rogers, 1794–1846." *New England Quarterly*. 20 (Sept. 1947), 365–76.

Ahlstrom, Sydney E. *A Religious History of the American People*. New Haven: Yale University Press, 1972.

Albanese, Catherine L. *Nature Religion in America: From the Algonkian Indians to the New Age*. Chicago: University of Chicago Press, 1990.

Andreas, A. T. *History of Cook County, Illinois*. Chicago, 1884.

Bacon, Margaret Hope. *Mothers of Feminism: The Story of Quaker Women in America*. San Francisco: Harper and Row, 1986.

Barbour, Hugh, and J. William Frost. *The Quakers*. Westport: Greenwood, 1988.

Barkun, Michael. *Crucible of the Millennium: The Burned-Over District of New York in the 1840s*. Syracuse: Syracuse University Press, 1986.

Barnes, Gilbert Hobbs. *The Antislavery Impulse, 1830–1844*. New York: Harcourt Brace, 1964.

Bassett, T. D. Seymour. "The Quakers and Communitarianism." *Bulletin of Friends Historical Association*. 43 (Autumn 1954), 84–99.

Beauchamp, W. M. *Revolutionary Soldiers Resident or Dying in Onondaga County, New York*. Syracuse: Onondaga Historical Association, 1913.

Beckwith, H. W. *History of Fountain County, Indiana, Together with Historic Notes on the Wabash Valley*. Chicago: H. H. Hill and N. Iddings, 1881.

Beeson, Henry Hart. *The Mendenhalls: A Genealogy*. Houston, 1969.

Bestor, Arthur Eugene, Jr. *Backwoods Utopias: The Sectarian and Owenite Phases of Communitarian Socialism in America: 1663–1829*. Philadelphia: University of Pennsylvania Press, 1950.

Biographical Encyclopedia of Ohio. Philadelphia: Galaxy Publishing Co., 1876.

Biographical History of Eminent and Self-Made Men of the State of Indiana. 2 vols. Cincinnati: Western Biographical Publishing Co., 1880.

Birkel, Michael L., and John W. Newman, eds. *The Lamb's War: Quaker Essays to Honor Hugh Barbour.* Richmond, Ind.: Earlham College Press, 1992.

Bolt, Christine, and Seymour Drescher, eds. *Antislavery, Religion, and Reform: Essays in Memory of Roger Anstey.* Hamden, Conn.: Archon, 1980.

Braude, Ann. *Radical Spirits: Spiritualism and Women's Rights in Nineteenth-Century America.* Boston: Beacon, 1989.

Brink, Carol. *Harps in the Wind: The Story of the Singing Hutchinsons.* New York: Macmillan, 1947.

Brock, Peter. *Pacifism in the United States from the Colonial Era to the First World War.* Princeton: Princeton University Press, 1968.

———. *The Quaker Peace Testimony, 1660 to 1914.* York, Eng.: Sessions, 1990.

Brown, Elisabeth Potts, and Susan Mosher Stuard. *Witnesses for Change: Quaker Women over Three Centuries.* New Brunswick: Rutgers University Press, 1989.

Brown, Mrs. Herbert E. "The Reverend William Hunt Family." *Indiana Magazine of History.* 34 (June 1938), 139.

Bruce, Dwight H. *Onondaga's Centennial.* 2 vols. Boston: Historical Publishing Co., 1896.

Bushman, Richard L. *From Puritan to Yankee: Character and the Social Order in Connecticut, 1690–1765.* New York: Norton, 1967.

Carroll, Bret E. "Spiritualism and Community in Antebellum America: The Mountain Cove Episode." *Communal Studies.* 12 (1992), 20–39.

Carroll, Kenneth Lee. *Joseph Nichols and the Nicholites: A Look at the "New Quakers" of Maryland, Delaware, North and South Carolina.* Easton, Md.: Easton Publishing Co., 1962.

Cayleff, Susan E. *Wash and Be Healed: The Water-Cure Movement and Women's Health.* Philadelphia: Temple University Press, 1987.

Chmielewski, Wendy, Louis J. Kern, and Marilyn Klee Hartzell, eds. *Women in Spiritual and Communitarian Societies in the United States.* Syracuse: Syracuse University Press, 1993.

Claeys, Gregory. *Machinery, Money, and the Millennium: From Moral Economy to Socialism, 1815–1860.* Princeton: Princeton University Press, 1987.

Clopper, Edward Nicholas. *An American Family: Its Ups and Downs through Eight Generations in New Amsterdam, New York, Pennsylvania, Maryland, Ohio, and Texas, from 1650 to 1880.* Huntington, W. V.: Standard Printing & Publishing Co., 1950.

Coyle, William, ed. *Ohio Authors and Their Books: Biographical and Selective Bibliographies for Ohio Authors, Native and Resident, 1796–1850.* Cleveland: World Publishing, 1962.

Cremin, Lawrence A. *American Education: The National Experience, 1783–1876.* New York: Harper and Row, 1980.

Crocker, Henry. *History of the Baptists in Vermont.* Bellows Falls, Vt.: P. H. Gobie Press, 1913.

Cross, Whitney R. *The Burned-over District: The Social and Intellectual History of Enthusiastic Religion in Western New York, 1800–1850.* Ithaca: Cornell University Press, 1950.

Cunliffe, Marcus. *Chattel Slavery and Wage Slavery: The Anglo-American Context, 1830–1860.* Athens: University of Georgia Press, 1979.

Dabney, Wendell Phillips. *Cincinnati's Colored Citizens: Historical, Sociological, and Biographical.* Cincinnati: Dabney Publishing Co., 1926.

Davies, John D. *Phrenology, Fad and Science: A Nineteenth-Century American Crusade.* Hamden, Conn.: Archon, 1971.

Davis, David Brion. "The Emergence of Immediatism in British and American Antislavery Thought." *Mississippi Valley Historical Review.* 49 (Sept. 1962), 209–30.

———. *The Problem of Slavery in the Age of Revolution, 1770–1823.* Ithaca: Cornell University Press, 1975.

———. *The Problem of Slavery in Western Culture.* Ithaca: Cornell University Press, 1966.

Davis, Hugh. *Joshua Leavitt: Evangelical Abolitionist.* Baton Rouge: Louisiana State University Press, 1990.

Doherty, Robert W. *The Hicksite Separation: A Sociological Analysis of Religious Schism in Early Nineteenth-Century America.* New Brunswick: Rutgers University Press, 1967.

Donald, David H. *Lincoln Reconsidered.* New York: Vintage, 1956.

Drake, Thomas E. *Quakers and Slavery in America.* New Haven: Yale University Press, 1950.

Duberman, Martin, ed. *The Antislavery Vanguard: New Essays on the Abolitionists.* Princeton: Princeton University Press, 1965.

Dumond, Dwight Lowell. *Antislavery: The Crusade for Freedom in America.* Ann Arbor: University of Michigan Press, 1961.

Elliott, Errol T. *Quaker Profiles from the American West.* Richmond, Ind.: Friends United Press, 1972.

———. *Quakers on the American Frontier: A History of the Westward Migrations, Settlements, and Developments of Friends on the American Continent.* Richmond, Ind.: Friends United Press, 1969.

Evans, Harry. "Grand Prairie Harmonical [*sic*] Institute." *Indiana Magazine of History.* 12 (Dec. 1916), 351–52.

Fellman, Michael. *The Unbounded Frame: Freedom and Community in Nineteenth Century American Utopianism.* Westport: Greenwood, 1973.

Filler, Louis. *The Crusade against Slavery, 1830–1860.* New York: Harper and Row, 1960.

Finkelman, Paul. *An Imperfect Union: Slavery, Federalism, and Comity.* Chapel Hill: University of North Carolina Press, 1981.

Fladeland, Betty. *Abolitionists and Working-Class Problems in the Age of Industrialization.* Baton Rouge: Louisiana State University Press, 1984.

———. *James Gillespie Birney: Slaveholder to Abolitionist.* Ithaca: Cornell University Press, 1955.

Fletcher, Robert Samuel. *A History of Oberlin College from Its Foundation through the Civil War.* 2 vols. Oberlin: Oberlin College, 1943.

Fogarty, Robert S. *Dictionary of American Communal and Utopian History.* Westport: Greenwood, 1980.

Foner, Eric, ed. *The New American History.* Philadelphia: Temple University Press, 1990.

Forbush, Bliss. *Elias Hicks: Quaker Liberal.* New York: Columbia University Press, 1956.

———. *A History of Baltimore Yearly Meeting of Friends: Three Hundred Years of Quakerism in Maryland, Virginia, the District of Columbia, and Central Pennsylvania.* Baltimore: Baltimore Yearly Meeting, 1972.

Forkner, John L., and Byron H. Dyson. *Historical Sketches and Reminiscences of Madison County, Indiana.* Anderson, Ind., 1897.

Friedman, Lawrence J. *Gregarious Saints: Self and Community in American Abolitionism, 1830–1870.* New York: Cambridge University Press, 1982.

Fuller, Robert C. *Mesmerism and the American Cure of Souls.* Philadelphia: University of Pennsylvania Press, 1982.

Furnas, Seth E., Sr. *A History of Indiana Yearly Meeting.* N.p.: Indiana Yearly Meeting Religious Society of Friends General Conference, 1968.

Fussell, Edwin Neal. *Genealogy of the Fussell Family: Comprising a Complete Record to 1890 of the Descendants of Bartholomew Fussell, born 9-28-1754, died 10-17-1838.* New York, 1891.

Gamble, Douglas Andrew. "Moral Suasion in the West: Garrisonian Abolitionism, 1831–1861." Ph.D. diss., Ohio State University, 1973.

[Garrison, Francis Jackson, and Wendell Phillips Garrison]. *William Lloyd Garrison, 1805–1879: The Story of His Life Told by His Children.* 4 vols. New York: Century, 1885–1889.

Gerteis, Louis S. *Morality and Utility in American Antislavery Reform.* Chapel Hill: University of North Carolina Press, 1987.

Gleason, Philip. "From Free Love to Catholicism: Dr. and Mrs. Thomas L. Nichols at Yellow Springs." *Ohio Historical Quarterly.* 70 (Oct. 1961), 283–307.

Grant, H. Roger, ed. "The Skaneateles Community: A New York Utopia." *Niagara Frontier.* 22 (1975), 68–72.

Guarneri, Carl J. *The Utopian Alternative: Fourierism in Nineteenth-Century America.* Ithaca: Cornell University Press, 1991.

Halsey, John J. *A History of Lake County, Illinois.* N.p.: Roy S. Bates, 1912.

Hamm, Thomas D. *The Antislavery Movement in Henry County, Indiana.* New Castle, Ind.: Henry County Historical Society, 1987.

———. "Daniel Worth: Persistent Abolitionist." Senior Honors Thesis, Butler University, 1979.

———. "The Limits of the Peace Testimony: Hicksite Friends and the Nonresistance Movement." Paper read at Swarthmore College Conference on Nineteenth-Century Feminist Strategies for Peace, March 21, 1993.

———. *The Transformation of American Quakerism: Orthodox Friends, 1800–1907.* Bloomington: Indiana University Press, 1988.

———, et al. "Moral Choices: Two Indiana Quaker Communities and the Abolitionist Movement." *Indiana Magazine of History.* 87 (June 1991), 117–54.

Hardin, Rebecca. *My Father's People.* Mooresville, Ind.: Dickinson Printing Co., 1982.

Hardinge, Emma. *Modern American Spiritualism: A Twenty Years Record of the Communion between Earth and the World of Spirits.* New Hyde Park, N.Y.: University Books, 1970.

Harrison, John F. C. *Quest for the New Moral World: Robert Owen and the Owenites in Britain and America.* New York: Charles Scribner's Sons, 1969.

Harrold, Stanley. *Gamaliel Bailey and Antislavery Union.* Kent: Kent State University Press, 1986.

Heiss, Willard C. "Hiram Mendenhall and the Union Home Community." *Bulletin of Friends Historical Association.* 44 (Spring 1955), 43–50.

———. *A List of All the Friends Meetings That Exist or Ever Have Existed in Indiana.* Indianapolis: John Woolman Press, 1961.

Hersh, Blanche Glassman. *The Slavery of Sex: Feminist Abolitionists in America.* Urbana: University of Illinois Press, 1978.

Hewitt, Nancy A. *Women's Activism and Social Change: Rochester, New York, 1822–1872.* Ithaca: Cornell University Press, 1984.

Hinds, William Alfred. *American Communities.* Chicago: Charles H. Kerr, 1902.

History of Clinton County, Ohio. Chicago: W. H. Beers, 1882.

History of Edwards County, Illinois, including Edwards and Wabash Counties. Philadelphia: J. L. McDonough, 1883.

History of Hamilton County, Indiana, with Illustrations and Biographical Sketches of Some of Its Prominent Men and Pioneers. Chicago: Kingman, 1880.

History of Henry County, Indiana. Chicago: Interstate, 1884.

History of Logan County, Ohio. Chicago: Baskin & Co., 1881.

History of Medina County, Ohio. Chicago: Baskin & Battey, 1881.

History of Stark County, Ohio. Chicago: Baskin & Battey, 1881.

History of the Schools of Cincinnati. Cincinnati, 1902.

History of Wayne County, Indiana. 2 vols. Chicago: Interstate, 1884.

Holbrook, Stewart. *The Yankee Exodus: An Account of Migration from New England.* Seattle: University of Washington Press, 1968.

Holloway, Mark. *Heavens on Earth: Utopian Communities in America, 1680–1880.* London: Turnstile Press, 1951.

Hopkins, Timothy. *Kelloggs in the New World.* N.p., n.d.

Hurd, D. Hamilton. *History of New London County, Connecticut, with Biographical Sketches of Many of Its Pioneers and Prominent Men.* Philadelphia: J. W. Lewis, 1882.

Ingle, H. Larry. *Quakers in Conflict: The Hicksite Reformation.* Knoxville: University of Tennessee Press, 1986.

James, Edward T., et al., eds. *Notable American Women, 1607–1950: A Biographical Dictionary.* 3 vols.: Cambridge: Belknap, 1971.

James, Sydney V. *A People among Peoples: Quaker Benevolence in Eighteenth-Century America.* Cambridge: Harvard University Press, 1963.

Jennison, Peter S. *The History of Woodstock, Vermont, 1890–1983.* Woodstock: Country-man Press, 1985.

Jensen, Joan M. *Loosening the Bonds: Mid-Atlantic Farm Women, 1750–1850.* New Haven: Yale University Press, 1986.

Johnson, Paul E. *A Shopkeeper's Millennium: Society and Revivals in Rochester, New York, 1815–1837.* New York: Hill and Wang, 1978.

Jones, Rufus M. *The Later Periods of Quakerism.* 2 vols. London: Macmillan, 1921.

Kanter, Rosabeth Moss. *Commitment and Community: Communes and Utopias in Sociological Perspective.* Cambridge: Harvard University Press, 1972.

Kelly, Robert. *The Cultural Pattern in American Politics: The First Century* (New York: Knopf), 1979.

Kern, Louis J. *An Ordered Love: Sex Roles and Sexuality in Victorian Utopias—the Shakers, the Mormons, and the Oneida Community.* Chapel Hill: University of North Carolina Press, 1981.

Ketring, Ruth Anna. *Charles Osborn in the Anti-Slavery Movement.* Columbus: Ohio State Archaeological and Historical Society, 1937.

Knollenberg, Bernhard. *Pioneer Sketches of the Upper Whitewater Valley: Quaker Stronghold of the West.* Indianapolis: Indiana Historical Society, 1945.

Kolmerten, Carol A. *Women in Utopia: The Ideology of Gender in American Owenite Communities.* Bloomington: Indiana University Press, 1990.

Kraditor, Aileen S. *Means and Ends in American Abolitionism: Garrison and His Critics on Strategy and Tactics, 1834–1850.* Chicago: Ivan R. Dee, 1989.

Larkin, Jack. *The Reshaping of Everyday Life, 1790–1840.* New York: Harper and Row, 1988.

Leach, William. *True Love and Perfect Union: The Feminist Reform of Sex and Society.* New York: Basic, 1980.

Lerner, Gerda. *The Grimke Sisters from South Carolina: Pioneers for Woman's Rights and Abolition.* New York: Schocken, 1971.

Lesick, Lawrence Thomas. *The Lane Rebels: Evangelicalism and Anti-slavery in Antebellum America.* Metuchen, N.J.: Scarecrow, 1980.

Leslie, Edmund Norman. *Skaneateles: History of the Earliest Settlement and Reminiscences of Later Times.* New York: Andrew H. Kellogg, 1902.

Loomis, Elisha S. *Descendants of Joseph Loomis in America and His Antecedents in the Old World.* N.p., 1908.

Ludlum, David M. *Social Ferment in Vermont, 1791–1850.* New York: Columbia University Press, 1939.

Mabee, Carleton. *Black Freedom: The Nonviolent Abolitionists from 1830 through the Civil War.* New York: Macmillan, 1970.

McDonald, Daniel. *History of Marshall County, Indiana, 1836 to 1880.* Chicago: Kingman, 1881.

McFeely, William S. *Frederick Douglass.* New York: Norton, 1991.

McKivigan, John R. *The War on Proslavery Religion: Abolitionism and the Northern Churches, 1830–1865.* Ithaca: Cornell University Press, 1984.

McKnight, Levi A. *Progress of Education in Benton County, Indiana.* N.p., 1906.

Magdol, Edward. *The Antislavery Rank and File: A Social Profile of the Abolitionists' Constituency.* Westport: Greenwood, 1986.

Marietta, Jack D. *The Reformation of American Quakerism, 1748–1783.* Philadelphia: University of Pennsylvania Press, 1984.

Meyers, Marvin. *The Jacksonian Persuasion.* Palo Alto: Stanford University Press, 1958.

Miller, John W. *Indiana Newspaper Bibliography.* Indianapolis: Indiana Historical Society, 1982.

Miller, Marion C. "The Antislavery Movement in Indiana." Ph.D. diss., University of Michigan, 1938.

Mitchell, William Ansell. *Linn County, Kansas: A History.* N.p., 1928.

Moore, R. Laurence. *In Search of White Crows: Spiritualism, Parapsychology, and American Culture.* New York: Oxford University Press, 1977.

Morse, Mrs. O. E. "Sketch of the Life and Work of Augustus Wattles." *Collections of the Kansas State Historical Society.* 17 (1928), 290–99.

Murray, Raymond Lee. *Sex and Marriage in Utopian Communities: 19th Century America.* Bloomington: Indiana University Press, 1973.

Murray, William B. *Some of the Descendants of Jonathan Murray, of East Guilford, Connecticut.* Peoria, 1958.

Myers, John L. "The Antislavery Activities of Five Lane Seminary Boys in 1835–36." *Bulletin of the Historical and Philosophical Society of Ohio.* 21 (April 1963), 95–111.

———. "The Beginning of Antislavery Agencies in Vermont, 1832–1836." *Vermont History.* 36 (Summer 1968), 126–41.

Neurmberger, Ruth Ketring. *The Free Produce Movement: A Quaker Protest against Slavery.* Durham: Duke University Press, 1942.

Nissenbaum, Stephen. *Sex, Diet, and Debility in Jacksonian America: Sylvester Graham and Health Reform.* Westport: Greenwood, 1980.

Norton, James H. "Quakers West of the Alleghenies and in Ohio to 1861." Ph.D. diss., Case Western Reserve University, 1965.

Noun, Louise R. *Strong-Minded Women: The Emergence of the Woman-Suffrage Movement in Iowa.* Ames: Iowa State University Press, 1969.

Nye, Russel B. "Marius Robinson: A Forgotten Abolitionist." *Ohio State Archeological and Historical Quarterly.* 55 (April June 1946), 138–54.

———. *William Lloyd Garrison and the Humanitarian Reformers.* Boston: Little Brown, 1955.

Parker, Robert Allerton. *A Yankee Saint: John Humphrey Noyes and Oneida Community.* New York: G. P. Putnam's Sons, 1935.

Perry, Lewis. *Childhood, Marriage, and Reform: Henry Clarke Wright, 1797–1870.* Chicago: University of Chicago Press, 1980.

———. *Radical Abolitionism: Anarchy and the Government of God in Antislavery Thought.* Ithaca: Cornell University Press, 1973.

———, and Michael Fellman, eds. *Antislavery Reconsidered: New Perspectives on the Abolitionists.* Baton Rouge: Louisiana State University Press, 1979.

Pim, Rachel. *Ancestry and Descendants of Nathan Pim, 1641–1904.* Damascus, Ohio, 1904.

Pleas, Elwood. *Henry County; Past and Present: A Brief History of the County, from 1821 to 1871.* New Castle, Ind.: Pleas Brothers, 1871.

Post, Albert. *Popular Free Thought in America, 1825–1850.* New York: Columbia University Press, 1943.

Potter, David M. *The Impending Crisis, 1848–1861.* New York: Harper and Row, 1976.

Quarles, Benjamin. *Frederick Douglass.* New York: Atheneum, 1970.

Rayback, Joseph G. *Free Soil: The Election of 1848.* Lexington: University Press of Kentucky, 1970.

Reames, Oswald K. *The Story of a Place Called Goshen: The People and Early Meetings Associated with It.* N.p., 1961.

Remini, Robert V. *Henry Clay: Statesman for the Union.* New York: Norton, 1991.

Rice, C. Duncan. *The Scots Abolitionists, 1833–1861.* Baton Rouge: Louisiana State University Press, 1981.

Roberts, Leanna K., et al. *A History of Westfield and Washington Township.* Noblesville, Ind.: Image Builders, 1984.

Russell, Elbert. *The History of Quakerism.* New York: Macmillan, 1942.

Ryan, Mary. *Cradle of the Middle Class: The Family in Oneida County, New York, 1790–1865.* New York: Cambridge University Press, 1981.

Sellers, Charles G., Jr. *The Market Revolution: Jacksonian America, 1815–1848.* New York: Oxford University Press, 1991.

Sernett, Milton C. *Abolition's Axe: Beriah Green, Oneida Institute, and the Black Freedom Struggle.* Syracuse: Syracuse University Press, 1986.

Sewall, Richard H. *Ballots for Freedom: Antislavery Politics in the United States, 1837–1860.* New York: Oxford University Press, 1976.

Shaddinger, Anna F., comp. *The Micheners in America.* Rutland, Vt.: Charles E. Tuttle, 1958.

Shepard, Odell. *Pedlar's Progress: The Life of Bronson Alcott.* Boston: Little Brown, 1937.

Shotwell, James B. *A History of the Schools of Cincinnati.* Cincinnati: School Publishing Company, 1902.

Siebert, Wilbur H. *The Underground Railroad from Slavery to Freedom.* New York: Macmillan, 1898.

Smith, Theodore Clarke. *The Liberty and Free Soil Parties in the Old Northwest.* New York: Longmans, Green & Co., 1897.

Soderlund, Jean R. *Quakers and Slavery: A Divided Spirit.* Princeton: Princeton University Press, 1985.

Some of the Work of Charles B. Murray, Editor of the Cincinnati Price Current for Forty One Years, in Special Commercial and Statistical Journalism. Cincinnati, 1914.

Spain, Barbara Bendall, and Karen Richards Anklin. *Skaneateles . . . Glimpses of the Past.* Moravia, N.Y.: Village Printer, 1987.

Spann, Edward K. *Brotherly Tomorrows: Movements for a Cooperative Society in America, 1820–1920.* New York: Columbia University Press, 1989.

Spurlock, John C. *Free Love: Marriage and Middle-Class Radicalism in America, 1825–1860*. New York: New York University Press, 1988.

Stansell, Christine. *City of Women: Sex and Class in New York, 1789–1860*. New York: Knopf, 1986.

Starr, Paul. *The Social Transformation of American Medicine*. New York: Basic, 1983.

Staudenraus, P. J. *The African Colonization Movement, 1816–1865*. New York: Columbia University Press, 1961.

Stearns, Bertha-Monica. "Memnonia: The Launching of a Utopia." *New England Quarterly*. 15 (June 1942), 280–95.

——. "Two Forgotten New England Reformers." *New England Quarterly*. 6 (March 1933), 59–84.

Stearns, J. H. "Some Lost Towns of Kansas." *Kansas State Historical Society Collections*. 12 (1911–1912), 429.

Stein, Stephen J. *The Shaker Experience in America: A History of the United Society of Believers*. New Haven: Yale University Press, 1992.

Stembel, Ruth Baldwin. *The Baldwin Heritage*. N.p., n.d.

Sterling, Dorothy. *Ahead of Her Time: Abby Kelley and the Politics of Antislavery*. New York: Norton, 1991.

Stewart, James Brewer. *Holy Warriors: The Abolitionists and American Slavery*. New York: Hill and Wang, 1976.

Suhl, Yuri. *Eloquent Crusader: Ernestine Rose*. New York: Messner, 1970.

Swift, Lyndsay. *Brook Farm: Its Members, Scholars, and Visitors*. New York: Corinth, 1961.

Thomas, John L. *The Liberator: William Lloyd Garrison: A Biography*. Boston: Little Brown, 1963.

Thompson, J. Earl, Jr. "Abolitionism and Theological Education at Andover." *New England Quarterly*. 47 (June 1974), 237–61.

Thornbrough, Emma Lou. *Indiana in the Civil War Era, 1850–1880*. Indianapolis: Indiana Historical Society and Indiana Historical Bureau, 1965.

——. *The Negro in Indiana: A Study of a Minority*. Indianapolis: Indiana Historical Bureau, 1957.

Totten, John R. "Thacher-Thatcher Genealogy." *New York Genealogical and Biographical Record*. 43 (July 1912), 249–72.

Tucker, Ebenezer C. *History of Randolph County, Indiana*. Chicago: A. E. Kingman, 1882.

Tuveson, Ernest Lee. *Redeemer Nation: The Idea of America's Millennial Role*. Chicago: University of Chicago Press, 1968.

Volpe, Vernon L. *Forlorn Hope of Freedom: The Liberty Party in the Old Northwest, 1838–1848*. Kent: Kent State University Press, 1990.

Wahl, Albert John. "The Congregational or Progressive Friends in the Pre-Civil-War Reform Movement." Ph.D. diss., Temple University, 1951.

Wallace, Anthony F. C. *Rockdale: The Growth of an American Village in the Early Industrial Revolution*. New York: Norton, 1972.

Walters, Ronald G. *American Reformers, 1815–1860*. New York: Hill and Wang, 1978.

——. *The Antislavery Appeal: American Abolitionism after 1830*. Baltimore: Johns Hopkins University Press, 1978.

Watson, Harry L. *Liberty and Power: The Politics of Jacksonian America.* New York: Noonday, 1990.

Wells, Lester Grosvenor. *The Skaneateles Communal Experiment, 1843–1846.* Syracuse: Syracuse University Press, 1953.

White, Morton, and Lucia White. *The Intellectual versus the City: From Thomas Jefferson to Frank Lloyd Wright.* New York: Mentor, 1964.

Wyatt-Brown, Bertram. *Lewis Tappan and the Evangelical War against Slavery.* Cleveland: Case Western Reserve University Press, 1969.

Wyman, Lillie Buffum Chace, and Arthur Crawford Wyman. *Elizabeth Buffum Chace 1806–1899: Her Life and Its Environment.* 2 vols. Boston: W. B. Clarke, 1914.

Young, Andrew W. *History of Wayne County, Indiana.* Cincinnati: Robert Clarke & Co., 1872.

Ziegler, Valarie H. *The Advocates of Peace in Antebellum America.* Bloomington: Indiana University Press, 1992.

INDEX

202–203, 216; disowned by Quakers, 197; later life, 216–18

Brooke, Edward: 42, 59, 62, 76, 104, 106, 107

Brooke, Elizabeth (Lukens): 41, 104, 187, 216, 217, 218

Brooke, Hannah: 59, 64

Brooke, James: 41, 59, 63

Brooke, Margaret: 42

Brooke, Mary (Matthews): 41

Brooke, Mary: 42

Brooke, Samuel Jr.: 73, 76, 277

Brooke, Samuel Sr.: 40, 42

Brooke, Sarah (Gerrigues): 40, 42

Brooke, William: 41, 42, 59

Brown, Aaron: 122

Brown, Ann (Stanton): 122

Brown, Horton: 109, 120, 123, 124, 197

Brown, William Wells: 94

Brownson, Orestes A.: 150

Buffum, Arnold: 39, 52, 53, 54, 129, 145, 151

Buffum, E. Gould: 151

Buffum, James N.: 78

Burleigh, Charles C.: 14, 43, 61

Butterworth, Henry T.: 34, 113, 230

Butterworth, Nancy (Wales): 34

Cadwallader, Priscilla Hunt: 34

Campbell, Margaret: 226

Capron, Eliab W.: 172, 196, 198, 199

Center Monthly Meeting: 33–34, 59, 65, 66, 69, 129

Chandler, John B.: 112, 120, 145, 190, 198

Chandler, Judith: 112

Chandler, Mariah (Church): 112

Channing, William H.: 82, 150

Chapman, Henry G.: 15

Chapman, Maria Weston: 76, 94

Chardon Street Convention: 13–14, 57–58, 59

Chartists: 16

Chester Township Anti-Slavery Society: 42

Child, Lydia Maria: xvi, 84, 85, 87

Childs, A. L.: 221

Childs, Cornelia: 221

Cities, fear of: 178–79

Clay, Henry: 31, 54–56, 214

Cleaver, Deborah (Dutton): 111, 134

Cleaver, Eli: 111

Clinton County Anti-Slavery Society: 43, 60, 64

Coffin, William H.: 56

Collins, Adaline (Burgess): 10, 13

Collins, Eunice (Messenger): 18, 188, 212

Collins, John Anderson: xvi, xxiv, 13, 17, 29, 30, 32, 40, 57, 58, 103, 161, 164, 188; birth, 8; education, 10; marriages, 10, 18; and abolition, 11–16, 17–18, 63–64; in Great Britain, 13–17; accusations against, 14; and Society for Universal Inquiry and Reform, 71–73, 76–79, 82–83, 85–87; and Hundred Conventions, 80, 88–94, 102; and Skaneateles Community, 143–58; views on government, 166, 167; views on human nature, 169, 170; views on economics, 172–73, 180; views on labor, 175, 178; views on property, 176; views on woman's rights, 185–87; views on marriage, 189; views on education, 193–95; views on religion, 195–98, 200–204, 208, 211–13; later life, 232–33

Colonization: xvii, 20

Colver, Nathaniel: 10, 11, 14

Come-Outerism: 2, 159, 196–97, 226. *See also* Congregational Friends

Communitarianism: 58–59, 158–60, 205–10; roots of xxiv–xxv; Ohio supporters, 59–61; and John O. Wattles, 219–21, 231; and Valentine Nicholson, 227–28. *See also* Society for Universal Inquiry and Reform; *specific communities*

Communitist: 157

Conant, Jerusha: 134

Conant, Thurston: 134, 135, 136

Congregational Friends: 201–202, 216–17, 226, 230

Cook, Lydia (Pegg): 34

Cooper, John D.: 130

Cornell, Moses: 219

Crane, Abraham R.: 14

Crane, Jonathan: 140

Crane, Ruth (Romine): 141, 142

Crowell, Sarah H.: 185

Dana, Charles A.: 150

Davis, Benjamin B.: 59, 111, 112, 138, 167

Davis, Eli: 111, 138

Davis, Joel P.: 111, 138, 165, 218

Davis, Mary B. (Ingram): 111

Davis, Patten: 168, 196, 197

Dean, Matthias: 140

Diet reform: 105, 116, 124, 142, 155, 159, 161, 180–84, 215

Dorsey, James M.: 140

Douglass, Frederick: xvi, 8, 17, 144, 150, 196, 225; and Hundred Conventions, 81, 82, 89–94, 97–101